Building Applications
with Microsoft® Outlook™ 98

Microsoft Press

PUBLISHED BY
Microsoft Press
A Division of Microsoft Corporation
One Microsoft Way
Redmond, Washington 98052-6399

Library of Congress Cataloging-in-Publication Data
Building Applications with Microsoft Outlook 98 / Microsoft
    Corporation.
        p.   cm.
    Includes index.
    ISBN 1-57231-718-3
    ISBN 1-57231-929-1 (International Edition)
    1. Microsoft Outlook.   2. Time management--Computer programs.
3. Business forms--Computer programs.   4. Application software-
-Development.   I. Microsoft Corporation.
    HD69.T54B85 1998
    005.369--dc21   98-2769
                                                                      CIP

Printed and bound in the United States of America.

    2 3 4 5 6 7 8 9   QMQM   3 2 1 0 9 8

Distributed in Canada by ITP Nelson, a division of Thomson Canada Limited.

A CIP catalogue record for this book is available from the British Library.

Microsoft Press books are available through booksellers and distributors worldwide. For further information about international editions, contact your local Microsoft Corporation office. Or contact Microsoft Press International directly at fax (425) 936-7329. Visit our Web site at mspress.microsoft.com.

Acquisitions Editor: David Clark
Project Editor: Maureen Williams Zimmerman

Acknowledgments

Because the process of producing a book is a group effort, I'd like to thank all those people who helped make this possible. Thanks go to Casey Doyle, Gwen Lowery, Laura Brenner, Donalee Edwards, Lori Fields, Kristin Lynn Bergsma, Stephanie McKinney, Darlene Rudd, Cheryl Channing, Peter Ashmore, Jeff Gilbert, Robin Lyle, Bart McKeirnan, Frank Lee, David Goodhand, Darrique Barton, Bill Metters, Warren Halcott, and Jay Abbott.

And special thanks to my wife Gloria for her constant kindness, love, and support.

Peter J. Krebs
1997

Peter originally wrote this book in 1997 to introduce Outlook 97 as a platform for developing great groupware applications. It has been my privilege to oversee its update for Outlook 98. Because Peter had done such a great job the first time around, this task was particularly easy and required little in substantive change in the book. Even so, there was enough work to keep a number of people busy for several months, as we made sure that procedures, art, and other details were appropriate for the new version.

Deserving special recognition are Jaye Colorado and Carola Klass, the principal writer and editor for the project. Their quick intelligence, unflagging energy, and ability to focus on the minutest of details were critical to the completion of this project. Others deserving acknowledgment are: Charlie Armstrong, who prepared the art for publication; Brad Matter, who prepared the manuscript for publishing; Maureen Zimmerman, our liaison at Microsoft Press; and Randy Byrne, Drew Carlson, David Carson, Stephanie Conroy, Bill Jacob, James Reynolds, Randy Stuckless, and Mike Swinford, who provided technical review and assistance.

Jim Groves
1998

Contents

Introduction vii

Part 1 Introducing Microsoft Outlook 98 1

Chapter 1 Applications You Can Create with Outlook 3

Chapter 2 Outlook Design Tools 15

Part 2 Quick Guide to Building Applications 27

Chapter 3 Customize Built-in Modules 29

Chapter 4 Design a Custom Application 61

Part 3 Building Blocks of Applications 95

Chapter 5 Forms 97

Chapter 6 Controls, Fields, and Properties 139

Chapter 7 Actions 183

Chapter 8 Folders 221

Part 4 Beyond the Basics 265

Chapter 9 Use Visual Basic Scripting Edition with Outlook 267

Chapter 10 The Business Card Request Application 341

Chapter 11 The Help Desk Application 389

Chapter 12 The Document Tracking Application 429

Chapter 13 Distribute and Maintain Applications 477

Index 495

Introduction

In This Chapter

Who Should Use This Book   viii
How This Book Is Organized   ix
Use the Companion CD-ROM   x

With the versatility of Outlook 98, many of your workgroup's applications have become easier to build and integrate:

- Use instant workgroup solutions that ship with Outlook and can be modified to your specifications.

- Develop applications quickly using built-in forms and customizing standard forms.

- Scale applications with Microsoft® Visual Basic® Scripting Edition (VBScript) to meet growing demands on popular applications.

- Integrate Microsoft Office documents, spreadsheets and databases into items that can be e-mailed or posted in a newsgroup or discussion folder.

- Centralize security and management of your customized invoicing, informational, personnel, inventory, and decision making applications.

Instant workgroup solutions   With Outlook, creating groupware applications has never been faster or easier. That's because Outlook ships with full-featured Calendar, Tasks, and Contacts modules that can be created and customized in Public Folders. This offers instant groupware capabilities, so users can share calendars, schedules, task lists, and customer contact information among their workgroup or across the organization.

Fast application development With Outlook application design tools, you can get information-sharing applications up and running quickly—often without programming. And you can easily modify solutions on the fly because Outlook Forms are interpreted, not compiled. When building an application, you always start with either a built-in module, a sample application, or a standard form, so most of the functionality is already there. In fact, you can often build high-quality applications in a matter of days.

Scalable application development Many groupware applications grow in popularity and require additional functionality as their use becomes more widespread. Outlook provides for this by supporting a scalable set of development tools. For example, you can create procedures to control forms and folders using VBScript supplied with Outlook. If your application requires additional functionality, you can use the full power of Automation and Microsoft® Visual Basic® or Microsoft® Visual Basic® for Applications to create and program Outlook objects and meet your organization's communication needs.

Office integration Outlook is tightly integrated with the other Microsoft Office 97 applications, so you can create solutions applications that bring the best features of each application under one umbrella. For example, you can create an Outlook Form that serves as a mail-enabled front-end to a Microsoft Access 97 database. Or you can use Microsoft Visual Basic for Applications to create a macro in Microsoft Excel that automatically mails a sales report to a distribution list when a command button is clicked in a Microsoft Excel worksheet.

Centralized management and security Because Outlook runs on Microsoft Exchange Server, Outlook applications can take full advantage of the central administration, replication, and security features of Microsoft Exchange Server. For example, you can develop an application on your computer, and then turn it over to an administrator who installs it on Microsoft Exchange Server. Once on the server, the administrator can set access permissions and replication properties for the folder, so the folder is both secure and replicated across the organization.

Who Should Use This Book

Both programmers and non-programmers can pick up this book and find the information they need to develop groupware applications. In Part 2, "Quick Guide to Building Applications," I show how just about anyone can quickly create a completely usable groupware application without programming. You don't need to be a hard-core developer to build Outlook applications, although programming experience is certainly a plus. Regardless of your experience level, this book gives you an inside view of the components that make up a groupware application. It also offers helpful hints from the Outlook development team to get you around some rough spots in the product. In Part 4, "Beyond the Basics," I provide plenty of VBScript examples, along with several sample applications that show how you can streamline processes in your office with Outlook applications.

How This Book Is Organized

This book consists of the following four parts.

Part 1   Introducing Outlook

Chapter 1, "Applications You Can Create with Outlook," discusses the processes and problems best suited for Outlook solutions and shows you the kind of Request, Discussion, Tracking, and Reference applications you can build to streamline communications in your organization. Chapter 2, "Outlook Design Tools," showcases the tools available for creating Outlook applications.

Part 2   Quick Guide to Building Applications

Chapter 3, "Customize Built-in Modules," shows you how to create instant groupware applications by modifying the built-in Contacts application, customizing it for tracking customer correspondence related to a beta program, and then copying it to Public Folders on Microsoft Exchange Server. Chapter 4, "Design a Custom Application," shows you how to build a Discussion application called Products Ideas that makes it possible for users to submit, read, and respond to new products ideas.

Part 3   Building Blocks of Applications

Chapter 5, "Forms," introduces the form design process, and covers fundamental form design tasks such as adding controls and fields, creating new actions, setting form properties, and publishing forms. Chapter 6, "Controls, Fields, and Properties," covers the fundamental skills and information you need to effectively use controls, fields, and properties on a form. It also explains the unique features of each commonly used control, and then offers some strategies for implementing these controls and fields in an application. Chapter 7, "Actions," discusses the easiest way to create responses for Message forms, explains how to create custom Reply actions for Message forms, and then shows how to create custom Reply to Folder actions for Post forms. Chapter 8, "Folders," takes an in-depth look at the folder design process, discusses how to manage forms, and explains how to create custom views. It also covers setting folder permissions and building rules.

Part 4   Beyond the Basics

Chapter 9, "Use Visual Basic Scripting Edition with Outlook," introduces VBScript and provides a wide variety of code examples for the most commonly performed tasks using VBScript in Outlook. Chapter 10, "The Business Card Request Application," takes you step-by-step through the process of building an application that automates a request process. Chapter 11, "The Help Desk Application," showcases a variety of design techniques, including how multiple folder and form types can be used in an application. Chapter 12, "The Document Tracking Application," is a good example of an application that provides a user-friendly and mail-enabled front-end to a Microsoft Access 97 database. Chapter 13, "Distribute and Maintain Applications," shows you how to distribute forms in folders and provides some techniques for maintaining applications. It also covers how mobile users can use off-line folders, increasing the effectiveness of using applications in collecting and recording information while in the field.

Use the Companion CD-ROM

The companion CD-ROM contains complete Outlook 98 files, including: program and Help files, converters, Development Tools, Office Assistants, Script Debugger, and other add-ins. It also includes a sample personal folder, which contains most of the applications covered in this book.

You might want to make a copy of the applications and dissect the ones you're most interested in to see how they're developed. You can also customize these applications and put them to work in your organization.

First, install Outlook 98 program files and Development Tools. Then, install the companion applications in a personal folder (.pst) file on your hard disk. Finally, you will add the .pst file to your Outlook environment.

Note The examples on the CD-ROM and in this book require a Microsoft Exchange system to use Public Folders. The applications may need modification for use in an Internet Only environment.

▶ To install Outlook 98 program files

1 Insert the CD-ROM into your CD-ROM drive.

2 Double-click **My Computer**, and then double-click your CD-ROM drive.

3 Double-click the **Outlook** folder.

4 Double-click **Setup.exe**.

5 Follow the prompts to select the desired components.

▶ To install Outlook 98 development tools

1 When the system restarts, on the Windows task bar click **Start**, click **Settings**, and then click **Control Panel**.

2 In the **Control Panel** folder, double-click **Add/Remove Programs**.

3 In the **Add/Remove Programs Properties** dialog box, double-click **Microsoft Outlook 98**.

4 In the **Outlook 98 Active Setup** dialog box, click on **Add New Components**.

5 Click **Install from CD**.

6 On the **Outlook 98 Components** page in Microsoft Internet Explorer, select **Development Tools**, and then click **Next**.

7 Click **Install Now**.

8 When Setup finishes, click **Yes** to restart.

The Development Tools component includes Microsoft Outlook 98 Customization and Forms and Visual Basic Reference Help files, as well as a Script Debugger.

The Sample Personal Folder includes applications that may be used as foundations for similar applications in your company, such as Help Desk, Vacation Requests, Product Ideas, Training Management, While You Were Out, and Document Tracking applications.

▶ **To install the Sample Personal Folder**

1 Double-click **My Computer**.

2 Double-click the hard drive volume where you want to install the sample personal folder.

3 Create a new folder for the sample personal folder. For example, C:\Building Applications with Outlook.

4 Return to the top level of **My Computer**, and then double-click the CD-ROM.

5 Select **Building Microsoft Outlook 98 Applications.pst**, and then select **Copy** from the File menu.

6 Return to the top level of **My Computer**, and then navigate to your newly created folder.

7 On the **File** menu, click **Paste**.

8 Select **Building Microsoft Outlook 98 Applications.pst**, and then select **Properties** from the **File** menu.

9 Clear the **Read Only** check box.

10 Click **OK** and then close **My Computer**.

Next, you will add this .pst file to your Outlook environment, so the applications can be seen and used.

Add the Personal Folder (.pst) File to Outlook

The Building Microsoft Outlook 98 Applications file is actually a personal folder (.pst) file that contains sample forms and files, information on where to access Help files, shortcuts to Web sites, and a sample database.

▶ **To add the Building Microsoft Outlook 98 Applications (.pst) file**

1 Open Outlook.

2 On the **File** menu, point to **Open**, and then click **Personal Folders File (.pst)**.

3 Locate the Building Microsoft Outlook 98 Applications file you installed from the companion CD-ROM, and then click the file—for example, C:\Building Applications with Outlook\Building Microsoft Outlook 98 Applications.pst. Click OK.

The file is now added as the Building Microsoft Outlook 98 Applications personal folder on your local hard disk drive and appears when you select **Folder List** on the **View** menu.

If you wish to remove this personal folder, you must remove the service from Outlook and delete the files from the hard disk drive.

▶ **To remove the Building Microsoft Outlook 98 Applications (.pst) file**

1 Select **Services** on the Outlook **Tools** menu, and then click **Building Microsoft Outlook 98 Applications** on the **Services** page.

2 Click **Remove**, and then click **Yes** in the message box. Click **OK**.

3 Open **Windows Explorer** and select the .pst file.

4 Click the **Delete** icon.

Technical Support for the Companion CD-ROM

Every effort has been made to ensure the accuracy of this book and the contents of the companion CD-ROM. Microsoft Press® provides corrections for books through the World Wide Web at the following address:

http://mspress.microsoft.com/support/sup_er.htm

If you have comments, questions, or ideas regarding this book or the companion CD-ROM, please mail or e-mail them to Microsoft Press at the following addresses:

Postal Mail

Microsoft Press

Attn: Building Microsoft Outlook 98 Editor

One Microsoft Way

Redmond, WA 98052-6399

E-mail

mspinput@microsoft.com

Please note that product support is not offered through the above mail addresses. For support information on Outlook, see the documentation for the appropriate product support phone number.

What's on the Companion CD-ROM

The companion CD-ROM, which is arranged much like the book, is divided into five parts.

Help and Web Sites Folder

The Help and Web Sites folder provides supplemental information to help you design Outlook applications. As such, it provides two folders, the Help folder and the Web Sites folder.

Help folder   This folder includes a Readme file that gives you information on where you can find Outlook Customization and Forms Help, and Outlook Visual Basic Reference Help.

Web Sites folder   As shown in Figure I-1, the Web Sites folder contains shortcut items that you can double-click to open the Microsoft Outlook Web site or the Microsoft Visual Basic Scripting Edition Web site.

Figure I-1   The Web Sites folder

Quick Guide Folder

The Quick Guide folder contains two folders that showcase how you can quickly build Microsoft Outlook applications.

Beta Contacts As shown in Figure I-2, the Beta Contacts folder demonstrates how you can easily customize built-in Outlook modules, such as Contacts, to build instant groupware.

Figure I-2 The Beta Contacts folder

Product Ideas Provides a Discussion application that makes it possible for users to submit, read, and respond to new product ideas.

Building Blocks Folder

The Building Blocks folder contains several folders and forms that serve as good examples for implementing controls, fields, properties, and actions. In addition, the Classified Ads and Training Management folders provide excellent examples of how custom views can be designed.

Classified Ads Enables users to post, view, and make purchase offers on items in the Classified Ads folder, as shown in Figure I-3. This application provides a good example of building views in a folder.

Figure I-3 The Classified Ads folder

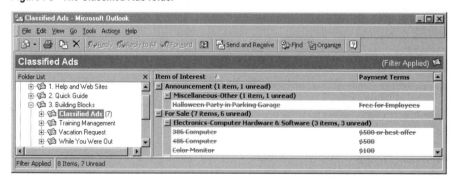

Training Management Enables course administrators to create an online catalog and potential students to register for and evaluate classes. Provides a good example of building views and creating response actions.

Vacation Request Automates the vacation request and approval process with several forms and custom actions that enable the supervisor to automatically approve or deny a vacation. In this book, this application is used to demonstrate how actions work and how controls, properties, and fields can be implemented on a form.

While You Were Out Contains a While You Were Out form that provides a good example of how Message forms can be customized to standardize communication in your organization.

Beyond the Basics Folder

The Beyond the Basics folder contains applications that demonstrate how Microsoft VBScript can be used to program Outlook applications.

Business Card Requests Shows how a Message form and a public folder can be used to automate a Request process in your organization. This also provides a good example of how properties and controls are implemented on a form.

Document Tracking This application shows how forms, folders, documents, and a database can be integrated to streamline request and tracking processes. As shown in Figure I-4, the Document Tracking folder shows the status of a document as well as the tasks that have been performed on the document. When a document is saved in this folder, a record is created for the item in a Microsoft Access 97 database.

Figure I-4 The Document Tracking folder

Help Desk Application Automates the process of submitting, assigning, and tracking Help Desk Requests. Provides a good example of a multiple-folder application and how to use Entry IDs to identify and locate items in a folder.

VBScript   Contains the Library Orders folder and the VBScript Samples folder. The Library Orders folder provides a sample application that shows how you can use VBScript to automate the process of ordering library materials. The VBScript Samples folder provides a variety of items that contain command buttons that trigger sample VBScript procedures.

Miscellaneous Applications Folder

This folder contains an application that demonstrates how Automation calls can be used to access information in the Address Book. It also provides a utility for restoring the default forms in your forms cache.

Get MAPI Info   Contains a form that demonstrates how Collaboration Data Objects (CDO) can be used to return user information from the Address Book.

PART 1

Introducing Microsoft Outlook 98

Contents

Chapter 1   Applications You Can Create with Outlook   3

Chapter 2   Outlook Design Tools   15

Applications You Can Create with Outlook

In This Chapter

Types of Applications You Can Create   5

Folder Applications   11

For More Form and Folder Ideas   14

As I was nearing the end of this project, a production manager at Microsoft came to my office and asked me how long it would take to build a form that would enable her to track the progress of marketing documents from the time they are submitted to the time they are printed or posted on the network. Before I answered, I asked her to describe the process she wanted to use the form for. She said writers in Marketing or User Assistance submit documents to a production manager who is responsible for arranging a variety of tasks, including editing, copyediting, legal approval, part number assignment, virus checking, and printing or posting the document on the network. Like most processes, producing marketing materials is a group effort, requiring a variety of people from different departments to perform a disparate set of tasks to complete a job.

When I asked her how the processes are currently handled, she told me that after writers hand off a document, they are required to enter the document information into a database. Task assignment and tracking, she said, is handled on an informal basis. She also explained that the writers don't like using the database, because they find it hard to use. After listening to her describe the process, I agreed to develop the application, with the understanding that she would provide me with a flowchart of the process and a document describing the fields she wanted on the form. In the end, it took three days to build the application, which you'll find in Chapter 12, "The Document Tracking Application." Perhaps most important, it proved to me how valuable Outlook can be in an organization.

The Document Tracking application brings out the best in Outlook for several reasons. First, it automates and streamlines a real-world process. Now writers can submit documents and document information using a form in electronic mail. The submitted items are stored in a public folder so production managers can track the status of the document's progress. In addition, task assignment is automated, so production managers can click a button to send a part number or legal approval request via electronic mail. Perhaps equally important, each participant in the process collaborates on the same item in the Document Tracking folder, so the production process is never held up because a piece of paper is sitting on someone's desk. In addition, after a person completes a task such as copyediting, he can update the Document Tracking form and save it in the Document Tracking folder. When this happens, the item is not only updated in the Document Tracking folder, but is also written to a Microsoft Access database, so production managers can run queries and end-of-the-month performance reports.

As demonstrated in this example, you can create Outlook applications to accomplish a wide variety of tasks. Here are just a few of the things you can accomplish with Outlook applications.

Share information   You can build applications that make it possible for users to share all types of information, including schedules, tasks, contacts, documents, product ideas, and customer feedback.

Structure information   You can build forms and folders to structure information so it's not only easy to read but easy to find. For example, you can create a Preferred Vendors public folder so managers can quickly find qualified vendors that have been referred by other managers in the organization. Or you can use the Product Ideas application supplied with this book to make it possible for users to submit, organize, and view new product ideas in a public folder.

Distribute information   You can create forms that make it possible for users to send announcements, sales reports, documents, and request-for-services items. For example, you can create a Bulk Mailer form so you can automatically notify all users in a particular contact list when a product update is available.

Collect information   You can create forms and folders for collecting information. For example, you can create a User Feedback form and public folder for collecting information about a product under development. Or you can use the Classified Ads application supplied with this book to make it possible for users to submit and respond to classified ads.

Collaborate on information   One of the benefits of Outlook is that it makes it possible for each user to collaborate on the same item. For example, with the Product Ideas application, a variety of users from different locations can all participate in an online discussion about a particular product feature. With the Document Tracking application, users can collaborate on a task in the Document Tracking public folder.

Streamline processes   You can create applications that are modeled on paper-based processes in your organization. For example, you can create forms and folders that make it possible for users to electronically submit vacation requests, travel plans, copier requests, purchase orders, status reports, classified ads, and training class registration.

Work offline   One of the advantages of Outlook over a pure Web mail interface is its ability for mobile users to work offline and consolidate their work later. For example, you can create front ends to databases, allowing workers in the field to collect data, and then synchronize this information when they return to the office. For more information about offline folder (.oft) files, see Chapter 13, "Distribute and Maintain Applications."

Types of Applications You Can Create

The two main building blocks of Outlook applications are forms and folders. With the Outlook design tools described in Chapter 2, you can create the following types of applications:

- **Applications that consist entirely of forms**   These are forms that are not associated with a specific folder, such as the While You Were Out form.

- **Applications that consist of a custom folder and standard forms**   Often when you create a folder, you create custom views for the folder but use the standard Outlook forms. For example, you might create a Contacts folder in a public folder and create custom views for the folder, but not change the standard forms supplied with the folder.

- **Applications that consist of a custom folder and custom forms**   In many cases, you customize both the folder and the form to build an application. For example, the Training Management, Classified Ads, and Document Tracking applications all consist of customized forms and folders.

Forms You Can Create

With the Outlook form in Design mode, you can create a wide spectrum of forms to perform a variety of tasks. When you create forms with Outlook, you never start from scratch. Instead, you base the forms you create on a standard form of a specific type supplied with Outlook. Standard form types include Message, Post, Office Document, and built-in modules, such as Contacts or Appointment. Because most of the functionality is already available in these forms, you can often create custom forms by adding additional fields and controls to the standard forms, or removing any controls you do not need.

In this section, we look at the different types of forms you can create or customize in Outlook. For more information, see "Outlook Form Design Mode" in Chapters 2 and 5.

Message Forms

Message forms are forms that are based on the Outlook Mail Message form. As such, Message forms make it possible for users to send information to other users or to a public folder. Message forms are often used to streamline a request process or approval process. Here are some examples of Message forms.

Vacation Request The Vacation Request application, covered in Part 3, "Building Blocks of Applications," contains a Vacation Request form, as shown in Figure 1.1. The Vacation Request form makes it possible for a user to send a vacation request to a manager. The Vacation Request application also contains a Vacation Approved form and a Vacation Denied form so a manager can respond to a request.

Figure 1.1   The Vacation Request form

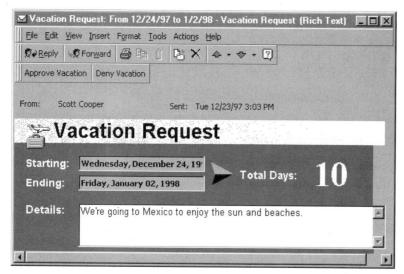

Business Card Request This form makes it possible for users to automatically fill in and send a Business Card Request to the Business Card Requests public folder. For more information, see Chapter 10, "The Business Card Request Application."

Status Report You can also create a form making it possible for users to send weekly or monthly status reports to their manager. Submitted status reports can be stored in a personal folder or public folder and used for reference at review time.

Mileage Report You can also create a form making it possible for users to submit their monthly mileage reports to their manager for approval. When approved, the information in the Mileage Report item can be written to a database.

Post Forms for Posting Items in a Folder

Post forms are used to post items in a folder and to post responses to items in a folder. Post forms are used in applications that enable users to conduct online discussions, such as the Product Ideas folder covered in Chapter 4, "Design a Custom Application." As such, Post forms serve as the foundation for creating threaded conversations in views. Post forms are also used for applications that require users to respond to a particular item, such as the Training Management application, in which the Evaluation form is used to post a response to a Course Offering item.

Here are a few ideas for Post forms using Outlook in Design mode.

Product Ideas   The Product Ideas application consists of a Product Idea form for posting product ideas in the Product Ideas folder and a Product Idea Response form for posting responses to product ideas in the folder. Innovative, new ideas are readily shared and recorded in a public folder for all to access.

See Also   For more information, see Chapter 4, "Design a Custom Application."

Figure 1.2   The Product Ideas folder with the Product Idea form in the background

Job Posting You could also create a Job Posting form that structures information and makes it possible for Human Resources to post a job opening in the Job Postings folder.

Job Candidate You could also create a Job Candidates application, which consists of a Job Candidate form and a Response form. A manager or human resource administrator can submit a Job Candidate item to the Job Candidates public folder.

After each user interviews the candidate, they use the Response form to submit their hiring recommendations to the Job Candidates folder, where the summary of opinions can be reviewed by the manager.

Office Document Forms

With Office Document forms, you can create forms using Office 97 applications such as Microsoft Excel, Microsoft Word, or Microsoft PowerPoint®. For example, you might want to streamline a scheduling process by creating a Weekly Schedule form for managers, so they can fill out a Microsoft Excel Weekly Schedule worksheet that's embedded in the form. In this way, managers can distribute a schedule to their workgroup.

Here are a few more examples of the kinds of Office Document forms you can create.

Computer and Software Inventory As shown in Figure 1.3, you can create a Computer and Software Inventory form based on a Microsoft Word document. To record computer configuration, the user opens the Computer and Software Inventory form in the Computer Inventory folder, fills in the worksheet, and then clicks the **Post** button on the form. An administrator can open the Computer and Software Inventory item in the folder and view the updated information.

Figure 1.3 The Computer and Software Inventory form

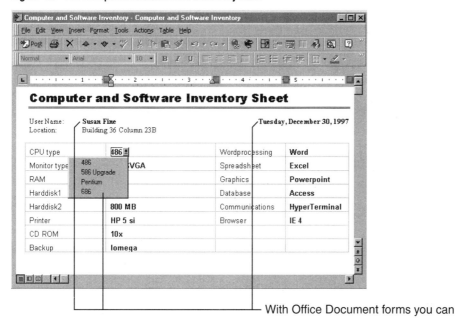

With Office Document forms you can use Office 97 (or later) features, such as the drop-down list, or UserName and DateTime fields.

Sales Report You can create a Sales Report form based on a Microsoft Excel chart for mailing weekly sales reports to a distribution list.

Invoice You can create an Invoice form based on a Microsoft Excel worksheet for mailing invoices or for posting them in a folder.

Service Contract You can create forms based on Microsoft Word documents for service contract agreements, exit interview forms, or for a variety of other purposes that require semi-structured information in a form.

See Also For more information on integrating Office Documents into Outlook, see Chapter 5, "Forms."

Built-in Modules Forms

You can customize forms based on the forms in the built-in modules—Appointment, Task, Contacts, and Journal—to take advantage of the specific functionality of the module.

Here are a few ideas for the types of forms you can create based on the forms in the Outlook built-in modules.

Assigned Help Task form   You can create forms such as the Assigned Help Task form, as shown in Figure 1.4, that make it possible to update and track the progress of a task. As shown below, the standard **Task** page is hidden, and a custom page is added to the form. The standard Status and % Complete fields are added to the custom page.

Figure 1.4   The Assigned Help Task form with the Assigned Help Tasks folder in the background

Document Tracking form   The Document Tracking application, covered in Chapter 12, contains a Document Tracking form based on the standard Task form. For this application, the Document Tracking form is used by different people involved in the document production process to update the Document Tracking item after a task is completed.

Folder Applications

Folders in Outlook are generally used for the following purposes:

- To facilitate online discussions about a particular topic, as demonstrated with the Product Ideas folder.

- To store, organize, and share information, as demonstrated with the Classified Ads, Training Management, and Web Sites folders.

- To record and track information that is constantly updated, as demonstrated with the Assigned Help Tasks folder and the Document Tracking folder.

Folders Based on Built-in Modules

With the built-in modules such as Appointment, Tasks, and Contacts, you can create an instant workgroup solution by creating a folder in Public Folders. You can then modify the folder for the specific purpose of your workgroup or organization. Here are a few ideas for the types of applications you can build based on built-in module folders.

Beta Contacts folder   With the Beta Contacts folder, managers can post contacts for a beta testing program. The Beta Contacts folder, as shown in Figure 1.5, is based on the built-in Contacts module.

Figure 1.5   The Beta Contacts folder based on the built-in Contacts folder

Shared Calendar application   You can create a Calendar folder in Public Folders, so events relating to a particular group can be easily recorded and shared. For example, you might want to create a shared Calendar that contains events related to the product development cycle, so that product announcements, press releases, trade shows, and shipping dates are accessible to the entire workgroup.

Discussion Folders

Most often, Discussion folders serve as a central location for users to submit, share, and respond to ideas and information. Discussion folders feature views with *threaded conversations*, so users can view the history of responses to a particular item.

Product Ideas folder   The Product Ideas folder makes it possible for users to post and respond to new product ideas in the Product Ideas folder. In addition, users can post responses to product idea responses. Responses to a particular item are located underneath and indented from the original item, creating the threaded conversation view.

Training Management folder   With the Training Management folder, training personnel can post Course Catalog items in the folder, as shown in Figure 1.6. After a Course Catalog item is posted, personnel can post a Course Offering item as a response to the Course Catalog item. After a user completes a course, she can post an Evaluation item as a response to the Course Offering item.

Figure 1.6   The Training Management folder

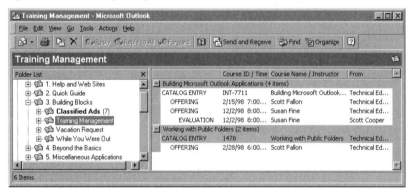

Tracking Folders

Tracking folders make it possible for users to record and review information that is constantly updated.

Document Tracking folder   This folder contains Document Tracking items that are constantly updated by participants in the production process, such as the people who edit, copyedit, and post the document on the server.

Assigned Help Tasks folder   This folder, as shown in Figure 1.7, makes it possible for a Help Desk technician or manager to view the status of a Help Desk Request. When a technician changes the status of a task or completes a task, the status is updated in the By Status view in the Assigned Help Tasks folder.

Figure 1.7   The Assigned Help Tasks folder

Reference Applications

You can store just about any kind of information in a folder, including product specifications, feature proposals, sales reports, software prototypes, employee status reports, Web site addresses, and training materials.

Specification Library   As a development team works on a project, they can store product specifications in a public folder so other members of the development team, as well as sales and marketing personnel, have access to the documents.

Status Reports   Managers as well as employees may want to store weekly status reports in a public folder for reference at review time.

Web Sites   These folders are great for storing Web addresses. Web Site folders can be personal folders for private use or public folders that the entire workgroup can contribute to.

VBScript Samples   These folders provide a good medium for collecting communal sample scripts. As shown in Figure 1.8, the Microsoft Visual Basic Scripting Edition (VBScript) Samples folder contains sample procedures for a variety of commonly performed tasks that can be accomplished using VBScript.

Figure 1.8   The VBScript Samples folder

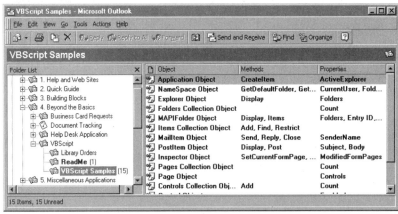

For More Form and Folder Ideas

For additional information about the types of applications you can create, visit the Microsoft Outlook Web site at:

http://www.microsoft.com/outlook

CHAPTER 2

Outlook Design Tools

In This Chapter

Help and Web Sites   15
Outlook Form Design Mode   17

Microsoft Outlook offers great design tools for creating custom forms and folders. For example, in Design mode, Outlook provides an AutoLayout feature that automatically positions controls as you add them to a form. In addition, a Script Editor window is provided in Design mode, so you can use Microsoft Visual Basic Scripting Edition (VBScript) in your forms to control folders, forms, fields, and controls. And when working with Outlook folders, you can create custom views directly in the folder by dragging fields to or from the column heading row. In many cases, you don't even need to open a dialog box to create a view.

In this chapter, you'll get a quick introduction to the tools that you use to design Outlook applications. Along the way, you'll see some of the features that you can use to make designing applications quicker and easier.

Help and Web Sites

In the Building Microsoft Outlook 98 Applications folder supplied with this book, you'll find a Help and Web Sites folder, as shown in Figure 2.1. In this folder, you'll find Readme files with information on how you can install the Outlook Customization and Forms Help and Outlook Visual Basic Reference Help, in case you didn't install these while installing Outlook. If you have Microsoft Internet Explorer 3.0 or higher installed, you can also click an item in the Web Sites folder to go directly to the Microsoft VBScript Web site or the Microsoft Outlook Web site.

Important   If you have not added the Building Microsoft Outlook 98 Applications folder, see the Introduction of this book for instructions.

▶ **To open the Help and Web Sites folder**

- Click **Folder List** on the **View** menu. Select the Building Microsoft Outlook 98 Applications folder, and then open the 1. Help and Web Sites folder, as shown in Figure 2.1.

Figure 2.1   The contents of the Help and Web Sites folder in the Building Microsoft Outlook 98 Applications folder

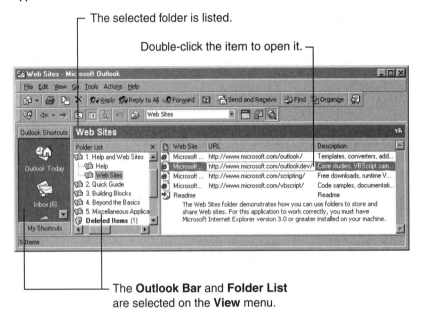

The selected folder is listed.

Double-click the item to open it.

The **Outlook Bar** and **Folder List**
are selected on the **View** menu.

Here is a quick summary of the contents of the Help and Web Sites folder.

Help folder   This folder contains information about Outlook Customization and Forms help and Outlook Visual Basic Reference help. Outlook Customization and Forms help provides comprehensive information about supported properties and methods for Outlook controls. It also provides valuable tips and techniques supplied by the Outlook development team. Outlook Visual Basic Reference help includes the Outlook object model and descriptions of supported Outlook objects, methods, properties, and events.

Web Sites folder   This folder contains shortcuts you can click (if you have the Microsoft Internet Explorer 3.0 or higher) to go to the following sites:

- **http://www.microsoft.com/vbscript/**   The VBScript Web site contains comprehensive VBScript, code samples, frequently asked questions, documentation and tutorials, hot links, scripting engine information, and training and newsgroup information.

- **http://www.microsoft.com/scripting/** The Scripting Technologies Web site contains information on hosting scripting with Microsoft Visual Basic Scripting Edition, script control for VBScript, runtime VBScript objects, free downloads, and a script debugger.

- **http://www.microsoft.com/outlookdev/** The Outlook Developer Forum Web site contains case studies, VBScript samples, form samples, free downloads, training information, and valuable tips and techniques for creating Outlook applications.

- **http://www.microsoft.com/outlook/** The Microsoft Office Outlook web site contains templates, converters, add-ins, troubleshooting tips, product and pricing information, a feature matrix, and configuration guides.

▶ **To visit a Web site**

1   In the Folder List, open the Web Sites folder.

2   Double-click an item in the folder to go to the Web site you want.

Outlook Form Design Mode

The ability to customize and create forms is built directly into Outlook, so opening a form in Design mode is as easy as opening a new form, choosing **Forms** on the **Tools** menu, and then clicking **Design This Form**. When the form is in Design mode, the **Form Design** toolbar and the **Field Chooser** appear. As shown in Figure 2.2, you can add fields and controls to the form by dragging the fields from the **Field Chooser** to the form. When you add a field to a form using the **Field Chooser**, Outlook automatically creates a control and a label for the field and binds the control to the field. With the Outlook AutoLayout feature, the controls are automatically aligned with existing controls on the form. To enter Run mode, you click **Run this Form** on the **Form** menu. In this way, you can easily switch back and forth between Design and Run mode to check the layout of a form at run time.

▶ **To view an Outlook form in Design mode**

1   On the Outlook **Actions** menu, click **New Mail Message**, or click the **New Mail Message** icon on the **Standard** toolbar. You may also select a form, such as Appointment, which most closely resembles your end application.

2   On the form **Tools** menu, choose **Forms** and then click **Design This Form**.

Note   Message and Discussion/Post forms are fully customizable. While Office Document forms can't be directly modified, you can add VBScript to the form and modify the Office document. You can customize Task, Appointment, and Journal forms by adding additional pages to the forms, but the existing pages cannot be modified. This also applies to the Contact form, but you can modify the first page of a Contact form. See Chapter 5, "Forms," for more information.

Figure 2.2 Outlook Design mode tools

When the form is in Design mode, the
Outlook **Form Design** toolbar appears.

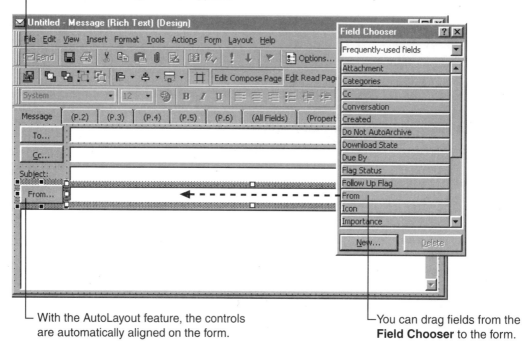

With the AutoLayout feature, the controls
are automatically aligned on the form.

You can drag fields from the
Field Chooser to the form.

Here are just a few advantages of developing forms using Outlook design capabilities.

Outlook forms are fully 32-bit forms so they're fast, and perhaps equally important,
they're small, averaging about 10K.

Outlook forms are interpreted so they're easy for designers to keep track of and
update. With Outlook forms, designers don't need to worry about searching through
folders or directories to find uncompiled source files to make changes to a form.

In Design mode, an Outlook form provides a grid and a variety of alignment tools,
including AutoLayout, to make sure your forms have a professional appearance.

Properties Dialog Box

To set properties for controls and fields that you add to forms, you use the **Properties** dialog box, which is accessible while Outlook is in Design mode, as shown in Figure 2.3.

▶ **To view the Properties dialog box**

- With the form in Design mode, right-click an existing control on the form. For this example, you can right-click the Subject control, and then click **Properties** on the shortcut menu.

Figure 2.3   The Properties dialog box available in Design mode

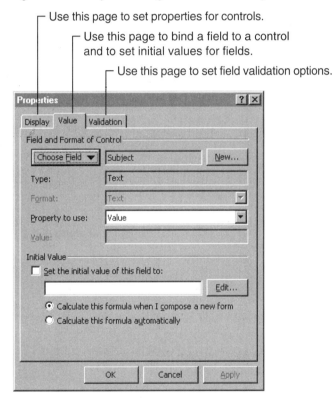

┌ Use this page to set properties for controls.

   ┌ Use this page to bind a field to a control
    and to set initial values for fields.

      ┌ Use this page to set field validation options.

Advanced Properties Dialog Box

With the **Advanced Properties** dialog box, you can set properties for controls. As shown in Figure 2.4, the **Advanced Properties** dialog box is used to set the **ControlTipText** property for a control.

▶ **To view the Advanced Properties dialog box**

• With the form in Design mode, right-click an existing control (the Subject control in this example), and then click **Advanced Properties** on the shortcut menu.

Figure 2.4   The Advanced Properties dialog box available in Design mode

You can specify the control tip that appears when the pointer is positioned over the control.

See Also   For more information about using the **Properties** dialog box or the **Advanced Properties** dialog box, see Chapter 6, "Controls, Fields, and Properties."

The Visual Basic Expression Service

Using the Visual Basic Expression Service provided in Outlook, you can create validation criteria for fields, you can create formulas to calculate field values, and you can create formulas that combine text strings in a field.

To explore this capability using the Business Card Request form, open the form in Design mode.

▶ **To open the Business Card Request form in Design mode**

1   On the Folder List, select the Business Card Request folder.

2   On the **Actions** menu, select **New Business Card Request**.

3   To get into Design mode, select **Forms** on the **Tools** menu, and then click **Design This Form**.

▶ **To open the Visual Basic Expression Service**

1   With the form in the Design mode, right-click an existing control (in this example, the **CardAddress** control), and then click **Properties** on the shortcut menu.

2   Click the **Value** tab, and then click **Edit**.

As shown in Figure 2.5, the Visual Basic Expression Service is used to create a formula for a field in the Business Card Request form.

Figure 2.5.   With the Visual Basic Expression Service, you can create formulas for fields.

The Visual Basic Expression Service
is used to create a formula for a field.

With the Visual Basic Expression Service, you can:

- **Validate fields**   You can create validation formulas to ensure that a specific value or a value range is entered in a field, or to ensure that a field value is not exceeded.

- **Create formulas for calculating values in fields**   For example, you can create a formula for a Total field that multiplies hours by hourly rate.

- **Create Combination fields**   You can create formulas that combine field values and text fragments together or you can create Combination fields that show the value of the first non-empty field in the item.

See Also   For more information about the Visual Basic Expression Service, see Chapter 6, "Controls, Fields, and Properties."

Script Editor and VBScript

With the Script Editor, available in Design mode, you can program Outlook forms using VBScript. VBScript is a subset of the Visual Basic language and is designed to be a small, lightweight interpreted language. Using VBScript, the Outlook 98 Object Model, and the Forms 2.0 Object Library, you can accomplish a wide variety of programming tasks. For example, you can set the current form page when the form opens in Compose mode. Or you can create a procedure that automatically sends a notification message to a distribution list when a new item is posted in a folder.

▶ To view the Script Editor

- With the form in Design mode, click **View Code** on the **Form** menu.

The Script Editor has templates for all the item events. To add an event template to your script in the Script Editor, click **Event Handler** on the **Script** menu, click an event name in the list, and then click **Add**. The appropriate **Sub...End Sub** or **Function...End Function** statement is inserted. As shown in Figure 2.6, the **Item_Open** function is added to the Script Editor window for the Business Card Request form, and code is added to the event to hide the **Status** page of the form when the form is in Compose mode.

Figure 2.6 The Script Editor window shows the Item_Open function.

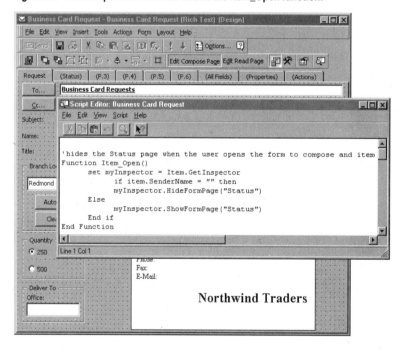

See Also For more information about using VBScript, see Chapter 9, "Use Visual Basic Scripting Edition with Outlook."

Folder View Design Tools

With Outlook, you can create custom views by adding, removing, and rearranging fields in the **Column Heading** row of the folder. For example, you can create a column by dragging a field from the **Field Chooser** to the **Column Heading** row.

▶ To add or remove a column using the Field Chooser

1   Select a folder on the Folder List. Click **Toolbars** on the **View** menu, and then click **Advanced**.

2   Select **Field Chooser** from the **Advanced** toolbar.

3   Drag the field you want to add as the new column to the **Column Heading** row, as shown in Figure 2.7. Use the double-arrow marker to position the new column heading in the **Column Heading** row.

4   To remove the column heading, drag the column heading you added away from the **Column Heading** row until an X appears, and then release the mouse button.

As shown in Figure 2.7, the **Comments or Issues** column is created by dragging the Comments or Issues field from the **Field Chooser** to the **Column Heading** row.

Figure 2.7   The Beta Contacts folder and the Field Chooser

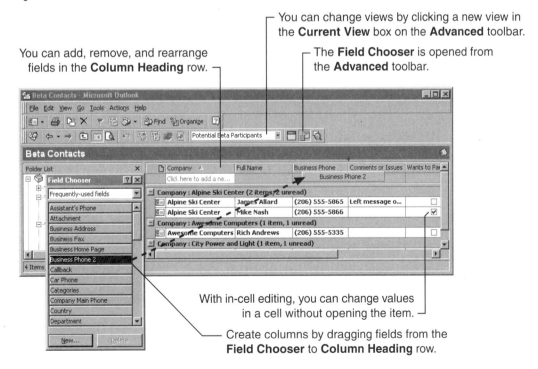

You can change views by clicking a new view in the **Current View** box on the **Advanced** toolbar.

You can add, remove, and rearrange fields in the **Column Heading** row.

The **Field Chooser** is opened from the **Advanced** toolbar.

With in-cell editing, you can change values in a cell without opening the item.

Create columns by dragging fields from the **Field Chooser** to **Column Heading** row.

Drag and Drop Grouping You can group items in a folder by a particular field simply by dragging the field you want to group by above the **Column Heading** row. On the **Advanced** toolbar, click the **Group By** icon. Click and drag a field from the **Field Chooser** to the area above the **Column Heading** row. You cannot group or sort by combination or formula fields.

Format Columns The ability to format columns gives you great flexibility in designing views. For example, in many cases, you want the column label to be different than the name of the field the column is based on. To format a column, right-click the column heading, and then click **Format Columns** on the shortcut menu. You can then choose the options you want.

In-Cell editing When the in-cell editing option is turned on for a folder, users can edit and enter information in cells within the folder without opening a form. For example, in the Beta Contacts folder, as shown earlier in Figure 2.7, users can click in a **Wants to Participate** cell on the far right, to add or remove a check box icon in the cell. To activate in-cell editing, select **Current View** on the **View** menu, and then click **Customize Current View**. Click **Other Settings,** and then choose the **Allow in-cell editing** check box in the **Rows** box.

Best Fit feature This feature automatically arranges the column size to fit the text in the column heading label. To choose the **Best Fit** option for a column, right-click the column heading, and then click **Best Fit** on the shortcut menu.

Show Only Custom Views Quite often, users are confused by the large number of views available in a folder. To alleviate this problem, Outlook makes it possible to show only the custom views created for the folder. To select this option, select **Current View** on the **View** menu, and then click **Define Views**. Then select the **Only show views created for this folder** check box.

Folder Properties Dialog Box

With the folder **Properties** dialog box, as shown in Figure 2.8, you define folder attributes and behavior. For example, you can define who can access the folder and the functions they can perform, and you can create rules that automatically process items as they arrive in a folder.

▶ **To view the folder Properties dialog box**

• Right-click the folder, and then click **Properties** on the shortcut menu.

Note To view all available **Properties** dialog box pages for a folder, the folder must be located in the Mailbox or Public folders. Also note that the **Outlook Address Book** page is only available for Contact type folders.

Figure 2.8   The folder Properties dialog box

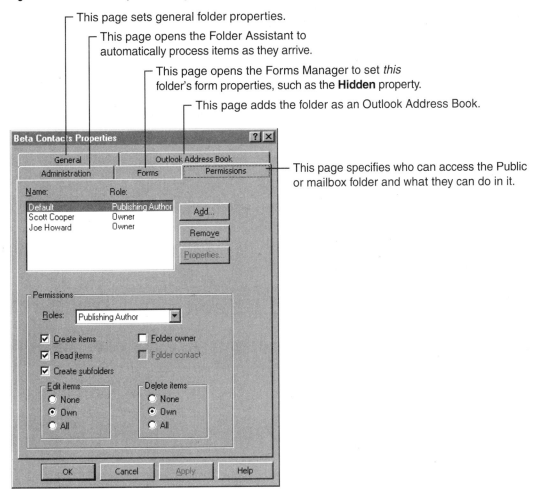

┌ This page sets general folder properties.

┌ This page opens the Folder Assistant to
automatically process items as they arrive.

┌ This page opens the Forms Manager to set *this*
folder's form properties, such as the **Hidden** property.

┌ This page adds the folder as an Outlook Address Book.

┌ This page specifies who can access the Public
or mailbox folder and what they can do in it.

See Also   For more information about designing folders or designing folder views, see Chapter 8, "Folders."

Quick Guide to Building Applications

Contents

Chapter 3   Customize Built-in Modules   29

Chapter 4   Design a Custom Application   61

Customize Built-in Modules

In This Chapter

Overview of the Folder You Create   31

Create New Folders   34

Create Custom Views   35

Create Items for the Beta Contacts Folder   42

Enter Dates in the Beta Participants View   45

Customize the Contacts Form   46

Test the Form at Design Time   55

Publish the Form   55

Specify the Default Form for the Folder   56

Test the Application   57

Delete the Items You Created   57

Copy the Folder to Public Folders   57

Set Permissions   58

Release the Application   59

What's Next   60

As a desktop information manager, Outlook provides built-in personal management tools such as Calendar, Tasks, Contacts, and Journal that can significantly increase user productivity. While these modules work great for individual use, their value is dramatically increased when they're located in a public folder because they allow users to share calendars, schedules, task lists, and customer information among workgroups or across the organization. In fact, with the built-in modules in Outlook, creating groupware is as simple as creating a module in Public Folders.

Note   The examples in this book, and in the companion CD-ROM, require Microsoft Exchange to create and access public folders.

This chapter is designed to show how you can easily customize built-in Outlook modules to suit the needs of your workgroup or organization. In this chapter, you transform the Contacts module into a groupware application that enables users to record, share, and track the history of customer correspondence. When you're finished with this chapter, you should have a better understanding of both the limits and possibilities of customizing built-in modules. Perhaps equally important, you should have a whole new set of ideas about the kinds of applications you can create using these modules as a starting point. Here are a few ideas.

 Calendar   can be created in Public Folders and used to post, share, and update schedules for activities such as training classes, sporting events, and company functions. For a product launch, you might want to post milestone events such as trade shows, press tours, and the product ship date in the Calendar folder.

 Tasks   can be created in Public Folders and used to post and track the tasks completed by each member of a project team. In addition, the Tasks folder can be used to delegate responsibilities to a staff of temporary workers or to track workgroup members' hours, billing information, and mileage.

 Contacts   can be created in Public Folders and used to post contact names, phone numbers, addresses, and company information, so it can be shared by a workgroup. With Contacts, users can post and track correspondence with sales contacts, potential customers, vendors, contractors, and co-workers.

 Journal   can be created in Public Folders and used to log and track information such as the amount of time an individual or workgroup spends on a particular task, on a project, or with a specific customer.

Note   For the Notes module, you can add custom views to the folder, but you cannot modify the built-in form.

Overview of the Folder You Create

The Contacts module is designed primarily for individuals to keep track of their personal contacts. As such, it offers a built-in Contact form and a variety of views, including an Address Cards view, a Phone List view, and a By Company view, as shown in Figure 3.1. In this chapter, you transform the Contacts module into the Beta Contacts application.

Figure 3.1   The Beta Contacts folder you create

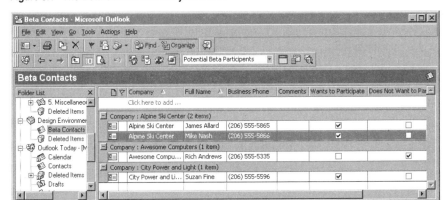

In this chapter, you also transform the Contacts module into a groupware application that is used to track correspondence with participants in a beta software program. For those of you not involved in the software industry, most software companies send early copies of their software to their preferred customers for early testing and feedback. This process, also known as beta testing, usually involves close communication between the people running the beta program and the beta participants.

To build the Beta Contacts application based on the Contacts module, you first create a new Contacts folder in Public Folders. You then rename the folder and add custom views to it. Next, you modify the built-in Contacts form. Finally, you set permissions on the folder so only those individuals involved in the beta program can access it.

The Beta Contacts folder   This folder is based on the built-in Contacts module. The Beta Contacts folder is created in Public Folders so that the information in the folder can be shared among members of a workgroup. In this chapter, you first create the Design Environment folder so you have a place for creating and testing applications, as shown in Figure 3.2.

Figure 3.2   The Beta Contacts folder is created in the Design Environment personal folder (.pst) file.

The Beta Contacts folder is created in the
Design Environment personal folder.

The Potential Beta Participants view   As part of the customization process, you create a Potential Beta Participants view. This view groups contacts by company and enables users of the Beta Contacts application to select a check box in a column to specify that the contact wants to participate in the beta program. The Potential Beta Participants view is shown in Figure 3.3.

Figure 3.3   The Beta Contacts folder with the Potential Beta Participants view selected

The Potential Beta Participants
view is applied to the folder.

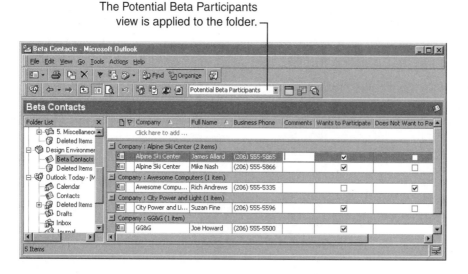

The Beta Participants view You also add a view to the Beta Contacts folder that uses a filter to show only the contacts that have agreed to participate in the beta program. In addition, you add fields to the Beta Participants view that enable users of the Beta Contacts folder to update and track the status of correspondence either sent to or returned by customers, as shown in Figure 3.4.

Figure 3.4   The Beta Contacts folder with the Beta Participants view selected

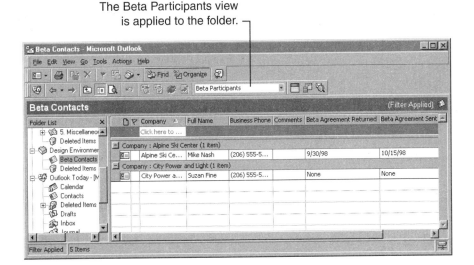

The Beta Contacts form Finally, you customize the form that comes with the Contacts module by adding a page to the form. You then add controls to the page, and bind the controls to custom fields that you add to the Beta Contacts folder. Figure 3.5 shows the additional page you design for the Beta Contacts form.

Figure 3.5 The Beta Contacts form with the Company Profile page selected

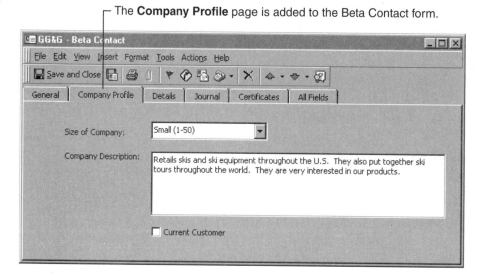

Create New Folders

To start, you create a new personal folder (.pst) file called Design Environment. This is the folder you use throughout this book for creating and testing folders. We recommend you start building your Outlook applications by creating forms and views in a personal folder (.pst) file. After you've tested the forms and views, you can then copy the folder to a public folder, if necessary.

Create the Design Environment Personal Folder (.pst) File

The Design Environment personal folder (.pst) file you create is a private folder, meaning that only you can view its contents. This secure environment is ideal for building applications.

▶ **To create the Design Environment folder**

1 On the **File** menu, click **New,** and then select **Personal Folders File (.pst)**.

2 In the list box, select a folder location. This is the location of the .pst file in which the contents of the folder are stored.

3 In the **File Name** text box, type **Design Environment**, and then click **Create.** This is the name of the .pst file on the local file system.

4   The **Create Microsoft Personal Folders** dialog box opens. In the **Name** text box, type **Design Environment**, and then click **OK**. This is the name of the personal folder, as it appears on the Folder List in Outlook.

Create the Beta Contacts Folder

Now you create the Beta Contacts folder as a subfolder of the Design Environment folder. When you create the Beta Contacts folder, you specify that the folder contains Contact items, so the folder automatically inherits the properties and functionality of the built-in Contacts module.

▶ **To create the Beta Contacts folder**

1   In the Folder List, right-click the **Design Environment** folder.

2   Click **New Folder**.

3   In the **Name** text box, type **Beta Contacts**.

4   In the **Folder contains** drop-down list box, select **Contact Items**.

   When you click **Contact Items**, the folder automatically takes on the characteristics of the Contacts module.

5   Click **OK**.

6   If a prompt appears, select your choice in the **Add shortcut to Outlook Bar** dialog box.

7   Right-click on the **Beta Contacts** folder, and then click on **Properties**.

8   In the **Description** text box, type the following:

   This folder contains beta program contacts. It also contains beta program status that shows whether the company is a beta customer, and whether they have returned their beta material.

Create Custom Views

With Outlook, you can create custom views to organize and show information in the folder so the information users want is easy to find. For the Beta Contacts folder, you create two views:

The Potential Beta Participants view   lets users keep track of those people who agree over the telephone to participate in the beta program.

The Beta Participants view   lets users view only those contacts who have agreed to participate in the beta program.

Create the Potential Beta Participants View

Let's assume you and a few others in your workgroup are responsible for contacting a list of companies to see if they want to participate in the beta program. To keep track of who agrees to participate, you can create the Potential Beta Participants view. To create this view, you add user-defined fields to the Beta Contacts folder. Once you create these fields, you build a view with columns based on these fields.

▶ **To create the Potential Beta Participants view**

1 In the Folder List, click the **Beta Contacts** folder in the Design Environment folder.

2 On the **View** menu, select **Current View**, and then click **Define Views**.

3 In the **Define Views for "Beta Contacts"** list box, click **By Company**, and then click **Copy**.

   In this case, you save time by basing the new view on the existing By Company view.

4 In the **Name of new view** text box, type **Potential Beta Participants**.

5 Click **This folder, visible to everyone**, and then click **OK**.

6 In the **View Summary** box, click **OK**.

7 In the **Define Views for "Beta Contacts"** list box, click **Apply View**.

Remove Fields

Many of the fields in the By Company view aren't necessary for the Potential Beta Participants view, so you can remove them by dragging them from the **Column Heading** row.

▶ **To remove fields**

- Drag the following column headings away from the **Column Heading** row until an **X** appears through the column heading, and then release the mouse button.

  - Attachment (shown as a paper clip in the column heading)
  - Job Title
  - File As
  - Department
  - Business Fax
  - Home Phone
  - Mobile Phone
  - Categories

Add New Fields

Next you add the Wants to Participate, Does Not Want to Participate, and Primary Contact fields to the view.

▶ **To add new fields**

1 Right-click anywhere in the **Column Heading** row, click **Field Chooser**, and then click **New**.

2 In the **Name** text box, type **Wants to Participate**.

3 In the **Type** drop-down list box, click **Yes/No**, and then click **OK**.

4 Click **New**.

5 In the **Name** text box, type **Does Not Want to Participate**.

6 In the **Type** drop-down list box, click **Yes/No**, and then click **OK**.

7 Repeat steps 4, 5, and 6, but in step 5, type **Primary Contact** in the **Name** text box. Make sure you choose a Yes/No type field.

Change the Order of the Company and Full Name Columns

With Outlook, you can change the order of column headings by dragging them to new locations.

▶ **To drag the Company column heading**

• Drag the **Company** column heading until a double-arrow marker appears over the border where you want to place the column, as shown in Figure 3.6.

Figure 3.6   The Company column is placed in front of the Full Name column.

The **Company** column heading is dragged to a new location in the **Column Heading** row.

Add the Column Headings to the Column Heading Row

To add column headings, you drag the fields you created earlier from the **Field Chooser** to the **Column Heading** row.

▶ **To drag the fields to the Column Heading row**

1   From the **Field Set** drop-down list on the **Field Chooser**, select **All Document Fields**.

2   Drag the Comments field from the **Field Chooser** to the **Column Heading** row and position it to the right of the **Business Phone** column heading. The double-arrow marker shows you where the new column heading will be inserted in the **Column Heading** row.

3   From the **Field Set** drop-down list, select **User-defined fields in folder**.

4   Drag the Wants to Participate field from the **Field Chooser** to the **Column Heading** row and position it to the right of the **Comments** column heading.

5   Drag the Does Not Want to Participate field from the **Field Chooser** to **the Column Heading** row and position it to the right of the **Wants to Participate** column heading.

6   Drag the Primary Contact field from the **Field Chooser** to the **Column Heading** row and position it to the right of the **Does Not Want to Participate** column heading.

Adjust the Column Widths to Best Fit

To resize columns, you can right-click the column heading, and then click **Best Fit**.

▶ **To adjust the column widths**

1 Right-click the **Comments** column heading, and then click **Best Fit**.

2 Repeat for the **Wants to Participate**, **Does Not Want to Participate**, **and Primary Contact** column headings.

The view should now look similar to the view as shown in Figure 3.7.

Figure 3.7   The column widths are adjusted for Best Fit in the Potential Beta Participants view.

The **Current View** box is available
on the **Advanced** toolbar.

Create the Beta Participants View

Next, you create a view that shows only the people who are primary contacts and who have agreed to participate in the beta program. This view enables folder users to track what has been sent by beta coordinators and returned by the beta participants. For example, once a contact agrees to participate in the beta program, you send them a Beta Agreement to read and sign. Then, once the Beta Agreement has been returned, you send out the Beta Package, complete with the product and the necessary feedback forms.

▶ **To create the Beta Participants view**

1   In the Folder List, click the **Beta Contacts** folder.

2   On the **View** menu, choose **Current View**, and then click **Define Views**.

3   In the **Views for Folder "Beta Contacts"** list box, click **Potential Beta Participants**, and then click **Copy**.

4   In the **Name of new view** text box, type **Beta Participants**.

5   Click **This Folder, Visible to Everyone**, click **OK twice**, and then click **Apply View**.

Remove Fields

Many of the fields in the Potential Beta Participants view aren't necessary for the Beta Participants view, so you can remove them.

▶ **To remove fields from the view**

● Drag the following column headings away from the **Column Heading** row until an **X** appears through the column heading, and then release the mouse button.

  ● Comments

  ● Wants to Participate

  ● Does Not Want to Participate

  ● Primary Contact

Add New Fields

Next, you add the Beta Agreement Sent, Beta Agreement Returned, and Beta Package Sent fields to the view. The user can directly enter information in these fields without opening the form.

▶ **To add new fields**

1   On the **Outlook Advanced** toolbar, click the **Field Chooser** icon.

2   Click **New** on the **Field Chooser**.

3   In the **Name** text box, type **Beta Agreement Sent**.

4   In the **Type** drop-down list box, click **Date/Time**.

5   In the **Format** field, click the m/dd/yy format, and then click **OK**.

6   Repeat steps 2-5 for both the Beta Agreement Returned and Beta Package Sent fields.

7   Click **OK**.

Add the Column Headings to the Column Heading Row

Now you add the new fields to the **Column Heading** row.

▶ **To drag the fields to the Column Heading row**

1   Drag the Beta Agreement Sent field from the **Field Chooser** to the **Column Heading** row and position it to the right of the **Business Phone** column heading. The double-arrow marker shows you where the new column heading will be inserted in the **Column Heading** row.

2   Drag the Beta Agreement Returned field from the **Field Chooser** to the **Column Heading** row and position it to the right of the Beta Agreement Sent field.

3   Drag the Beta Package Sent field from the **Field Chooser** to the **Column Heading** row and position it to the right of the Beta Agreement Sent field.

Adjust the Column Widths to Best Fit

Next, you adjust the column widths for the **Beta Agreement Sent**, **Beta Agreement Returned**, and **Beta Package Sent** column headings.

▶ **To adjust the column widths**

1   Right-click the **Beta Agreement Sent** column heading, and then click **Best Fit**.

2   Repeat for the **Beta Agreement Returned** and **Beta Package Sent** column headings.

Your Beta Participants view should now look similar to the view shown in Figure 3.8.

Figure 3.8 The Beta Participants view

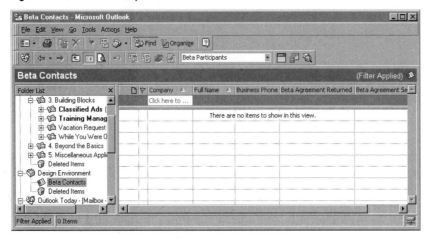

Create a Filter for the Beta Contacts View

With a filter, you can create a set of criteria that determines the items that are shown in a view. For the Beta Participants view, you create a filter that displays only items that have a check in the Wants to Participate and Primary Contact fields.

▶ **To create a filter**

1 On the **View** menu, select **Current View**, click **Customize Current View**, and then click **Filter**.

2 In the **Filter** dialog box, click **Advanced**.

3 Click **Field**, point to **User-defined fields in folder**, and then select **Wants to Participate**.

4 In the **Value** text box, type **Yes**, and then click **Add to List**.

5 Click **Field**, point to **User-defined fields in folder**, and then click **Primary Contact**.

6 In the **Value** text box, type **Yes**, and then click **Add to List**.

7 Click **OK** twice.

Create Items for the Beta Contacts Folder

Now let's assume you're ready to call potential beta participants and you want to keep track of those customers who either agree or do not agree to participate. You might also want to type the results of your calls, such as "Left message on answering machine," in the Comments field.

Before you create items, you switch to the Potential Beta Participants view. This is the view in which you enter new contacts.

▶ **To switch to the Potential Beta Participants view**

- On the Outlook **Advanced** toolbar, click **Potential Beta Participants** in the **Current View** drop-down list box.

▶ **To create a Beta Contacts item**

- In the folder view, click the **Click here to add...** cell in the **Company** column, and then fill in the cells, as shown in Figure 3.9. After you finish typing in an item, click outside the cell. The item is then added to the folder. The values for the cells are shown in the following table.

Figure 3.9   The top row in the view lets you create a new item for the view.

Cell column	Value
Company	Alpine Ski Center
Full Name	James Allard
Business Phone	(206) 555-5865
Comments	Left message on answering machine 7-10
Wants to Participate	
Does Not Want to Participate	
Primary Contact	

Now let's assume you talked to Mike Nash and he agreed to participate in the program and to be the primary contact for the beta program for Alpine Ski Center.

▶ **To create a second Beta Contacts item**

- In the folder view, click the **Click here to add...** cell in the **Company** column, and then fill in the cells with the options shown in the following table.

Cell column	Value
Company	Alpine Ski Center
Full Name	Mike Nash
Business Phone	(206) 555-5866
Comments	
Wants to Participate	X
Does Not Want to Participate	
Primary Contact	X

To keep things interesting, let's create another item.

▶ **To create a third Beta Contacts item**

- In the folder view, click the **Click here to add...** cell in the **Company** column, and then fill in the cells with the options shown in the following table.

Cell column	Value
Company	Awesome Computers
Full Name	Rich Andrews
Business Phone	(206) 555-5335
Comments	
Wants to Participate	
Does Not Want to Participate	X
Primary Contact	

- Here's one more to create.

Cell column	Value
Company	City Power and Light
Full Name	Suzan Fine
Business Phone	(206) 555-5596
Comments	
Wants to Participate	X
Does Not Want to Participate	
Primary Contact	X

Your view should now look like the view shown in Figure 3.10.

Figure 3.10 The Potential Beta Participants view with the Beta Contact items

Beta Contact items are added to the folder.

Enter Dates in the Beta Participants View

Now let's assume you send Beta Agreement contracts to those people who agree to participate in the program. To do this, you use the Beta Participants view to enter the date that the Beta Agreement contracts are sent.

▶ **To switch to the Beta Participants view**

- On the Outlook **Advanced** toolbar, click **Beta Participants** in the **Current View** drop-down list box.

▶ **To enter the Beta Agreement Sent date in the fields**

- Click the Beta Agreement Sent field for Mike Nash, and then type the date, as shown in Figure 3.11.

Figure 3.11   The Beta Participants view with dates entered directly in the Beta Agreement Sent fields

Dates can be entered directly into the cells.

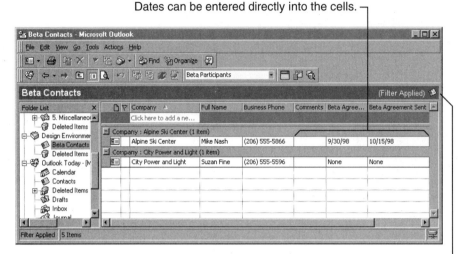

This filter is set to show records where Wants to Participate and Primary Contact fields' values are checked.

Customize the Contacts Form

Up to this point, we've focused on modifying the Beta Contacts application by adding custom views. Now we'll further customize the Beta Contacts application by modifying the built-in Contacts form.

In this example, you add a **Company Profile** page to the Contacts form, as shown in Figure 3.12.

Figure 3.12   The Company Profile page you add to the Contacts form

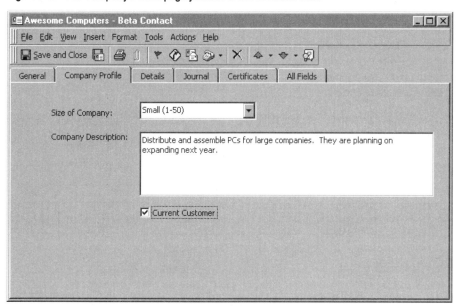

Open the Contacts Form

To customize a built-in form, first open it as you would to create an item. After the form is open, you switch between Design mode and Run mode.

▶ **To open the Contacts form in Design mode**

1   While in the Beta Contacts folder, click the **New Contact** icon on the Outlook **Standard** toolbar.

2   On the **Tools** menu of the **Untitled - Contact** window, select **Forms**, and then click **Design This Form**.

▶ **To switch from Design mode to Run mode**

1   On the **Form** menu, click **Run This Form**.

2   Close the Run mode window to return to Design mode.

Rename the New Page

The Contacts form provides several additional pages that you can add controls to. Notice that the additional pages are in parentheses. This indicates that the pages are hidden at run time. When you add controls to a page, the parentheses are automatically removed, so the page is visible at run time. For this example, you rename **(P.2)** to **Company Profile**.

▶ **To rename and show the page**

1   In Design mode on the Contacts form, click the **(P.2)** tab.

2   On the **Form** menu, click **Rename Page**.

3   In the **Page name** text box, type **Company Profile**, and then click **OK**.

4   On the **Form** menu, click **Display This Page**.

Add Controls to the Form

Now you use the **Control Toolbox** to add controls to the **Company Profile** page. After you add a control, you create a new field, and then bind the control to the field. In Outlook, a control is the physical component on the form in which the user enters, views, or clicks values. The field is the storage area in which the values from the controls are saved or loaded.

▶ **To show the Control Toolbox**

•   On the **Form Design** toolbar, click **Control Toolbox**.

Add a ComboBox Control

The ComboBox control you add to the **Company Profile** page enables users to select and view the size of a company, such as Small (1–50), Medium (51–500), and Large (501–1000+).

▶ **To add the ComboBox control**

•   From the **Control Toolbox**, drag a ComboBox control to the form. Then, drag the sizing handle on the right border of the control until the field is approximately the size of the field shown in Figure 3.13.

Figure 3.13   The ComboBox control is added to the Company Profile page.

The **Control Toolbox** from which you drag controls. ⌐

└ The ComboBox control is dragged to the form.

Set Properties for the ComboBox Control

When you set properties for the ComboBox control, you create a Size of Company field. When you create a new field for a control from the **Properties** dialog box, the field is automatically bound to the control. When a control is bound to a field, the values in the control are saved to the field when an item is composed. When an item is opened in a folder, the values from the fields are loaded into the controls.

▶ **To set properties for the ComboBox control**

1   Right-click the ComboBox control, click **Properties**, and then click the **Value** tab.

2   Click **New**.

3   In the **Name** text box, type **Size of Company**, and then click **OK**.

4   In the **List Type** drop-down list box, click **Droplist**.

With a Droplist ComboBox control, the user must select a value from the list. A drop-down-box, on the other hand, allows the user to type in the value, or choose from the list. If you intend to group fields, for example by Company size, based on values in a combo box, it's usually best to specify that the combo box is a drop-list, so that you can control the values upon which you group items in the folder.

5   In the **Possible Values** text box, type the following:

Small (1–50); Medium (51–500); Large (501–1000+)

6   Select the **Set the initial value of this field to** check box, type **"Small (1–50)"** in the text box below it, and then click **OK**.

Figure 3.14   Properties for the ComboBox control

Field to which the ComboBox control is bound.

Values that appear in the ComboBox list.

Value that appears in the ComboBox when the form first opens to create an item.

Add a Label for the ComboBox Control

Now you add a label for the ComboBox control to identify the control and to help the user understand the purpose of the control.

▶ **To add a label**

1   From the **Control Toolbox**, drag a Label control to the form.

2   In the label, select the word **Label1** and then type **Size of Company:**, as shown in Figure 3.15.

Figure 3.15   A label is added for the ComboBox control to identify its purpose.

— The Label control identifies the purpose of the ComboBox.

Add a TextBox Control

Now you add a TextBox control to the **Company Profile** page. This control enables users to enter and view a company description on the **Company Profile** page.

▶ **To add a TextBox control**

- From the **Control Toolbox**, drag a TextBox control to the form. Then, drag the sizing handle on the right border of the control until the field is approximately the size of the field shown in Figure 3.16.

Figure 3.16   A TextBox control is added to the Company Profile page.

A TextBox control is added to the form. ┑

Set Properties for the TextBox Control

Now you create a Company Description field that is automatically bound to the TextBox control. In addition, you select the **Multi-line** check box for the control so the user can enter multiple lines of text in it. You also select the **Resize with form** check box so the control size is adjusted to the size of the form.

▶ **To set properties for the TextBox control**

1 Right-click the TextBox control, click **Properties**, and then click the **Value** tab.

2 Click **New**.

3 In the **Name** text box, type **Company Description**, and then click **OK**.

4 Click the **Display** tab.

5 Select the **Resize with form** check box.

6 Select the **Multi-line** check box.

7 Click **OK**.

Add a Label for the TextBox Control

Now you add a label for the TextBox control so users know the purpose of the control.

▶ **To add a label**

1 From the **Control Toolbox**, drag a Label control to the form, and position it to the left of the TextBox control.

2 In the label, select the word **Label2**, and then type **Company Description:**.

3 To resize the label, drag the sizing handle on the right border of the label until all text in the label is visible.

Add a CheckBox Control

Finally, you add a CheckBox control to the form. This control enables users to specify if a company is a current customer.

▶ **To add a CheckBox control**

1 From the **Control Toolbox**, drag a CheckBox control to the form.

2 Click the CheckBox control, and then type **Current Customer**, as shown in Figure 3.17.

Figure 3.17   A CheckBox control is added to the Company Profile page.

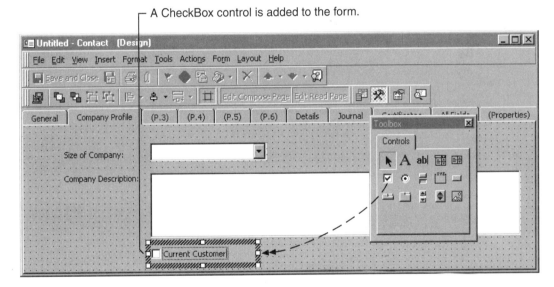

Set Properties for the CheckBox Control

Next, you create a Current Customer field to which the CheckBox control is bound.

▶ **To create the Current Customer field**

1 Right-click the CheckBox control, and then click **Properties**.

2 Click **New**.

3 In the **Name** text box, type **Current Customer**.

4 In the **Type** drop-down list box, click **Yes/No**.

5 In the **Format** drop-down list box, click **Icon**, and then click **OK** twice.

Set Form Properties

The Properties page of the form lets you name the form and specify a contact in case someone has suggestions for improvements or problems with the form.

▶ **To set form properties**

1 Click the **Properties** tab.

2 In the **Version** text box, type **1.0**.

3 In the **Form Number** text box, type **1.1**.

4 In the **Contact** text box, type your name, and in the **Description** text box type the following:

> **Use this form to post, view, and update Beta Contact items in the Beta Contacts folder**.

Figure 3.18   The Properties page of the Beta Contact form

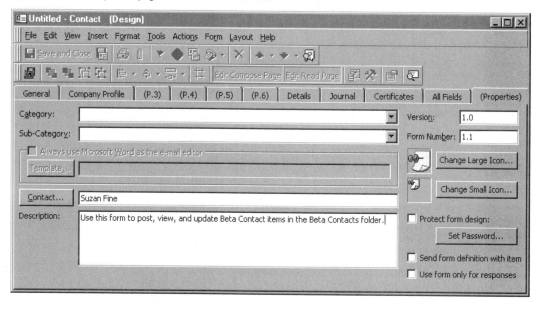

See Also   For more information about setting form properties, see Chapter 5, "Forms."

Test the Form at Design Time

Before you save a form or publish a form to a folder, it's a good idea to run the form to see how the form layout appears at run time. With Outlook, you can easily switch between Design mode and Run mode for the form.

▶ **To switch from Design mode to Run mode**

1 With the **Compose** page in Design mode, click **Run This Form** on the **Form** menu. View the **Compose** page of the form.

2 To test the **Read** page, send the form to your Inbox. Double-click on the item in your Inbox to view the **Read** page of the form.

3 To return to Design mode, close the Run mode window.

Publish the Form

After you run the form and you're satisfied with its layout, you can publish the form in the Beta Contacts folder. When you publish the form, the form is saved and registered in the Beta Contacts folder form library. Also, a menu item appears for the form on the **Actions** menu of the folder.

Forms with the same name, but different contents, may produce unpredictable results. For example, the Beta Contacts form in the Beta Contacts folder (Building Outlook 98 Applications) and the Beta Contacts form in the Beta Contacts folder (Design Environment) should be identical. If they are not, unique names should be used, or the forms should be updated using **Forms Manager**. For further information, see "The Forms Manager" in Chapter 13, "Distribute and Maintain Applications."

▶ **To publish the form to the Beta Contacts folder form library**

1 On the **Tools** menu, choose **Forms**, and then click **Publish Form As**.

2 In the **Display name** text box and the **Form name** text box, type **Beta Contact**.

   If for some reason the Beta Contacts folder is not selected (in the **Look In** box), click in the **Look In** drop-down list box and select the Beta Contacts folder.

3 Click **Publish**.

4 Close the form. When the message box appears, click **No** for **Do you want to save changes?** for most cases. Click **Yes** if you want to save a backup copy to the Beta Contacts folder.

5 Click the **Actions** menu, to verify that the form is published and available for use.

Figure 3.19   The Publish Form As dialog box is automatically filled in for you.

The display name is visible in the forms library of the current folder where it was published, and in the form title bar.

The form name is reflected in the full Message class designation.

Specify the Default Form for the Folder

Now that you've created a custom form, you no doubt want to run it to see if it works as expected. However, at this point, there are two possible forms that you can open. One form is the built-in Contacts form that's provided with Outlook. The other is the Beta Contact form you created. At this point, if you click the **New Contact** button on the **Standard** toolbar, the built-in Contacts form appears. To open the Beta Contact form you created, you must click New Beta Contact on the Outlook **Actions** menu. To avoid this step, you make the Beta Contact form the default form for the folder. Then, when the user clicks the New Contact button, the Beta Contact form appears.

▶ **To make the Beta Contact form the default form**

1   In the Folder List, right-click the **Beta Contacts** folder, and then click **Properties**.

2   Click the **General** tab.

3   In the **When posting to this folder, use** list box, click **Beta Contact**, and then click **OK**.

Test the Application

Let's test the Beta Contacts application and make sure the Beta Contact form opens when you click the **New Contact** button. First, however, let's switch to the Potential Beta Participants view.

▶ **To select the Potential Beta Participants view**

- In the **Current View** drop-down list box on the **Advanced** toolbar, click Potential Beta Participants.

▶ **To test the Beta Contact form**

1   While in the Beta Contacts folder, click the **New Contact** button on the **Standard** toolbar.

   You should see the Beta Contact form with the **Company Profile** tab.

2   Fill in the form, and then click **Save and Close**.

   The new item is posted in the Beta Contacts folder.

See Also   For more information about how forms and views work together, see Chapter 8, "Folders."

Delete the Items You Created

Before you make the form available to other users, you delete the items you created earlier in this chapter. You do this because the items you created earlier in the chapter without the Beta Contact form will show in the Contacts form when opened.

▶ **To delete the items in the Beta Contacts folder**

1   Hold down the SHIFT key, and then click the items in the Beta Contacts folder.

2   Press the DEL key.

3   Click **OK** in the message box.

Copy the Folder to Public Folders

Now that you've created forms and views for the Beta Contacts folder, and you've tested the folder to make sure it works as planned, you copy the folder from the Design Environment personal folder (.pst) file to Public Folders so the folder can be shared by a workgroup or across the entire organization. Before you copy the folder, you might want to see your administrator to find out the best location for the folder. In addition, you might need to see your administrator to get the appropriate permissions to copy the folder to its destination in Public Folders.

▶ **To copy the Beta Contacts folder**

1   In the Folder List, click the **Beta Contacts** folder.

2   On the **File** menu, point to **Folder**, and then click **Copy "Beta Contacts"**.

3   In the **Copy the selected folder to the folder** box, click the location you want the folder copied to, such as **Public Folders**, and then click **OK**.

See Also   For more information about distributing folders, see Chapter 13, "Distribute and Maintain Applications."

Set Permissions

With Permissions, you define who can open the folder and the functions they can perform in the folder. When you create a folder in Outlook, you are automatically given an Owner role for the folder. This means you have full permissions to create, edit, and delete items in the folder, and you have full permissions to change any folder properties. Also when you create a folder, a Publishing Author role is assigned to Default. This means that all users in the Microsoft Exchange Server system are automatically given permissions to create and open items in the folder, to delete and edit their own items, and to create subfolders.

For the Beta Contacts folder, you will limit access to the folder to only a few users by first setting the Default role to None. You then give a few of your co-workers a Publishing Author role so they can create, edit and delete items in the folder.

▶ **To set permissions for the Beta Contacts folder**

1   In the Folder List, right-click the **Beta Contacts** folder, and then click **Properties**.

2   Click the **Permissions** tab. This tab is only available if the folder is an Outlook Mailbox folder or a Public Folder.

3   In the **Name** list box, click **Default**, and then in the **Roles** drop-down list box, click **None**.

This prevents all users on the Microsoft Exchange Server system from opening the folder.

4   Click **Add**, select several of your co-workers' names from the list, click **Add**, and then **OK**.

5   In the **Name** list box, hold the Control key down and click each name you want to select. In the **Role** drop-down list box, click **Publishing Author.**

The **Permissions** page should now look similar to the illustration shown in Figure 3.20.

Figure 3.20   The Permissions page for the Beta Contacts folder in Public Folders

Release the Application

Before you release the application, you set the **Initial View on Folder** property to **Potential Beta Participants**. This will be the view users first see when they open the Beta Contacts folder.

▶ **To set administration properties**

1   In the Folder List, right-click the **Beta Contacts** folder, and then click **Properties**.

2   Click the **Administration** tab.

3   In the **Initial view on folder** drop-down list box, click **Potential Beta Participants**, and then click **OK**.

Now that the folder is ready for use, send a message to your co-workers to notify them that the application is available.

What's Next

In this chapter, we covered how to build a groupware application based on a built-in module. With built-in modules, most of the functionality is already defined, so generally all you need to do is make a few modifications to create an application with a specific purpose.

In the next chapter, we'll take a look at building a custom discussion application based on the Post to Folder form supplied with Outlook. Unlike the forms in built-in modules, the Post to Folder form can be completely customized, so you can use it for building a wide range of applications. To begin working with the Post to Folder form, you'll design a Product Ideas application that lets users post, read, and respond to new product ideas in a public folder.

CHAPTER 4

Design a Custom Application

In This Chapter

Overview of the Product Ideas Application 62

Create the Product Ideas Folder 65

Create the Product Idea Form 66

Create the Product Idea Response Form 78

Set the Actions 81

Create the Product Category View 87

Specify the Default Form for the Folder 90

Set the Hidden Property for the Product Idea Response Form 91

Test the Application 91

Copy the Folder to Public Folders 92

About Folder Permissions 93

Release the Application 93

What's Next 93

The Microsoft Outlook Post form can be used in conjunction with a public folder to build custom discussion applications that let users submit, share, and collaborate on ideas and information. Discussion applications provide a great way to facilitate communication in your organization because they enable users across the enterprise to conduct online conversations. Perhaps equally important, the history of correspondence is saved and organized in a public folder, so important ideas or critical conversations are always available for viewing at a later date. Discussion applications are especially useful for virtual corporations or flexible workgroups where members work together on a project, but work different hours or in different locations.

In this chapter, you'll build a Product Ideas application that lets users submit, read, and respond to new product ideas in a public folder. This application provides a good example of how a discussion application can be used in your organization to not only collect, store, and organize ideas, but also foster enterprise-wide dialog about subjects that are vital to your company's interest.

By the end of this chapter, you'll have the basic skills and concepts you need for building one of the most common types of groupware applications—the discussion application. As a result, you'll be able to build a wide variety of new applications to foster communication in your company. In addition, you'll also have a working discussion application that you can use as a basis for building other information-sharing applications.

Here are just a few suggestions for the types of discussion applications you can build:

Product Feedback   Lets users post feedback about existing products and features in a public folder. Other users, such as product developers, marketing, or sales personnel, can then respond to existing feedback items, thus creating an online discussion. Product Planners can review the folder on a periodic basis to get an overall idea of what users like and dislike about a particular product.

Technical Users Group   Serves as a forum for posting issues and problems, as well as solutions to problems. For example, if a person is having difficulty with a particular task, he can post his problem to the Technical Users Group public folder. In turn, another user can post a solution to the problem item, perhaps suggesting a workaround he discovered working on a similar task.

Vendor Services Application   Enables members of your organization to post, respond to, and read reviews of professional services provided by your company's vendors. For example, if a supervisor is looking for temporary word processing help, she can search the folder for a highly recommended vendor that's already been used in the company.

Restaurants and Accommodations Application   Lets users post, read, and respond to restaurant and hotel/motel reviews in a public folder. With this application, your company can quickly develop an online travel guide to help business travelers plan where to eat and stay when they're working away from the office.

Overview of the Product Ideas Application

The Product Ideas application consists of a Product Ideas folder and two forms: the Product Idea form and the Product Idea Response form. Here's how the Product Ideas application might by used by a sporting equipment manufacturer to help generate new ideas for products.

Let's assume Rich Andrews in Chicago opens the Product Ideas public folder, and then uses the Product Idea form to post an idea for a wooden kayak construction kit. Later in the, day Joe Howard in Boston reads the idea, and then uses the Product Idea Response form to post a response asking what kind of wood is best to use. A few minutes later, Suzan Fine reads the items posted by Rich Andrews and Joe Howard and uses the Product Idea Response form to post a response to Joe Howard's item. As shown in Figure 4.1, the resulting conversation is stored and organized in the folder.

Figure 4.1   The Product Ideas folder

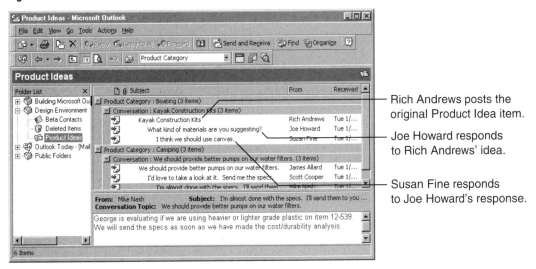

Rich Andrews posts the original Product Idea item.

Joe Howard responds to Rich Andrews' idea.

Susan Fine responds to Joe Howard's response.

The Product Category view   As part of the application design process, you add a custom view to the Product Ideas folder that groups items first by Product Category field, then by the Conversation field, as shown in Figure 4.2.

Figure 4.2   The Product Category view in the Product Ideas folder

Items are grouped by Product Category.

The custom Product Category view is selected in the **Current View** box, on the **Advanced** toolbar.

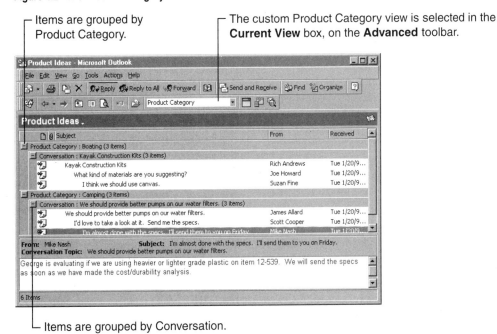

Items are grouped by Conversation.

The Product Idea form   The Product Idea form is a modified Post to Folder form. The New Product Idea form has both a **Compose** page and a **Read** page. With the **Compose** page, as shown in Figure 4.3, the user posts a new item in the Product Ideas folder. With the **Read** page, the user opens and views a posted item.

Figure 4.3   The Compose page of the Product Idea form

Users click the **Post** button to submit an idea to the Product Ideas folder.

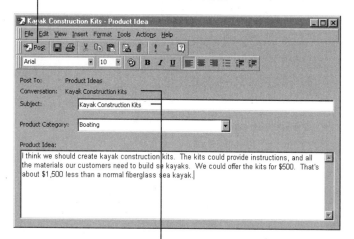

The value of the Conversation field is inherited from the Subject field.

The Product Idea Response form   The Product Idea Response form, as shown in Figure 4.4, serves two purposes. It lets users post a response to a product idea. In addition, it lets users post a response to the response. We'll take a look at how this is done later in this chapter.

Figure 4.4   The Compose page of the Product Idea Response form

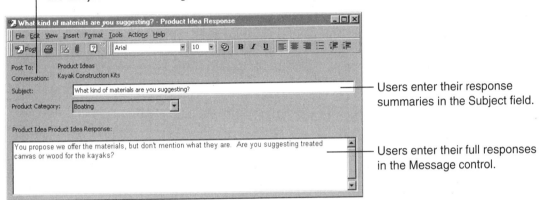

The Conversation field is inherited from the Subject field of the original item.

Users enter their response summaries in the Subject field.

Users enter their full responses in the Message control.

Create the Product Ideas Folder

To get started, you create the Product Ideas folder in the Design Environment personal folder, as shown in Figure 4.5.

If you haven't yet created the Design Environment folder, refer to "Create the Design Environment Personal Folder" in Chapter 3, "Customize Built-in Modules."

▶ **To create the Product Ideas folder**

1   In the Folder List, right-click the Design Environment folder, and then click **New Folder** on the shortcut menu.

2   In the **Name** text box of the **Create New Folder** dialog box, type **Product Ideas**.

3   In the **Folder contains** list box, click **Mail Items**.

4   Choose the **Design Environment** folder in the **Select where to place the folder** list box.

5   If a prompt appears, click your desired response in the **Add a shortcut to Outlook bar?** message box.

Figure 4.5 The Product Ideas folder is created in the Design Environment personal folder.

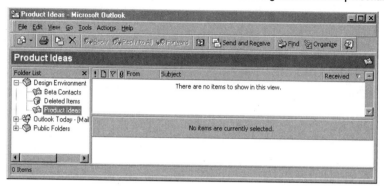

Create the Product Idea Form

The Product Idea form that you create will enable users to post new ideas to the Product Ideas folder. The Product Idea form is based on the standard Outlook Post form. The Outlook Post form supplies most of the functionality you need, so all you need to do to build the Product Idea form is add and remove a couple controls, and then set a few properties for the controls and the form. To design the Product Idea form, you'll modify the **Message** page of the Post form, as shown in Figure 4.6.

Figure 4.6 The finished version of the Compose page you create. The form is shown in Design mode.

— Subject control.

— Product Category control.

— Message control.

Open the Post to Folder Form

To build the Product Idea form, you open the Post form in the Product Ideas folder, and then switch to Design mode to modify the form.

▶ **To open the Post form in Design mode**

1   In the Folder List, click the Product Ideas folder.

2   On the **File** menu, select **New** and click **Post in This Folder**.

3   On the **Tools** menu of the form, select **Forms**, and then click **Design This Form**.

Edit the Compose Page

Most forms consist of two pages—a **Compose** page for submitting items and a **Read** page for opening and viewing items. In most cases, the **Compose** page is slightly different from the **Read** page. For example, the **Compose** page has a Post To control that shows where the item is posted, while the **Read** page has a From control to show who posted the item.

To edit the **Compose** page, you remove the Categories control, you resize the Message control, and you add a Product Category control. You also add or remove the associated labels for the controls.

Remove the Categories Control

For the form you're creating, the Categories control serves no purpose, so you delete it from the **Compose** page.

▶ **To remove the Categories control and its label**

1   Click the **CategoriesLabel** control, and then press DELETE.

2   Click the **Categories** control, and then press DELETE.

Adjust the Message Control

Now you move the Message control and resize it to make room for the Product Category control that you add to the form.

▶ **To adjust the Message control**

1   Drag the Message control bottom until it is near the bottom of the **Compose** page as shown in Figure 4.7.

2   Drag the Message control top border until it's approximately the size and location of the control in Figure 4.7.

▶ **To horizontally center the Message control**

• On the **Layout** menu, point to **Center in Form**, and then click **Horizontally**.

Figure 4.7   The Message control is adjusted to make room for the Product Category control.

The Product Category control will go here.

The Message control is moved to make room for the Product Category control.

Add the Product Category Control

The Product Category control is a ComboBox control that lets users select a product category, such as Boating or Fishing, or enter a new product category. Later in this chapter, you will build a view that groups items in the Product Ideas folder by product category. When product ideas are grouped in the folder by Product Category, it becomes much easier for the user to find ideas about a particular product.

▶ **To add the Product Category control**

1   On the **Form Design** toolbar, click the **Control Toolbox** button.

2   From the **Control Toolbox**, drag a ComboBox control to the form. Then place the pointer over a sizing handle on the right border of the control and drag the border until the field is approximately the size and position of the control shown in Figure 4.8.

Figure 4.8   The Product Category control is added to the Compose page.

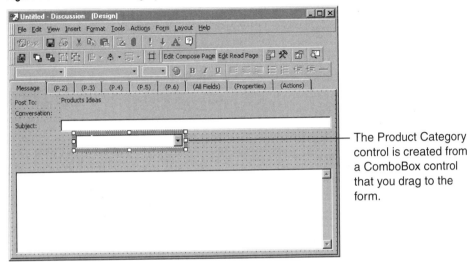

The Product Category control is created from a ComboBox control that you drag to the form.

Set the Properties for the Product Category Control

When you set properties for the Product Category control using the **Properties** dialog box, as shown in Figure 4.9, you name the control, and then you create a Product Category field for the control. When you create the field from the **Properties** dialog box, you automatically bind the field to the control. When a field is bound to the control, the value in the control at run time is saved to the field when the item is posted. The value is loaded into the control from the field when a posted item in a folder is opened.

▶ **To set the properties for the Product Category control**

1 Right-click the ComboBox control you added to the form, and then click **Properties** on the shortcut menu.

2 Click the **Display** tab.

3 In the **Name** text box, type **Product Category**.

4 Click the **Value** tab.

5 Click **New**.

6 In the **Name** text box, type **Product Category**, and then click **OK**.

The Product Category control is now bound to the Product Category field.

7 In the **Possible Values** text box, type:
Boating;Camping;Cycling;Fishing;Hiking;Running.

8 Select the **Set the initial value of this field to** check box, and then type **Boating** in the text box.

The initial value is the value that appears first in the control when the form first opens at run time.

9 Click **OK**.

Figure 4.9   The Properties dialog box for the Product Category control

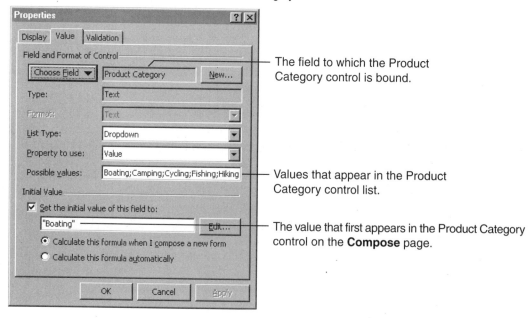

70 Building Applications with Microsoft Outlook 98

Add a Label for the Product Category Control

Now you add a label for the Product Category control so users know the purpose of the control.

▶ To add a Label control

1 From the **Control Toolbox**, drag a Label control to the **Compose** page, as shown in Figure 4.10.

2 Click the Label control, and then change its text to **Product Category:**.

Figure 4.10   The Product Category label is added to the form.

The label for the Product Category control is added to the form.

Align the Subject and Product Category Control

One way to make sure your forms have a professional look is to align the controls on the form. Outlook offers a variety of layout options, but in most cases you can align items simply by dragging the borders of controls until they are aligned the way you want. For example, on the **Compose** page, you can align the Subject and Product Category controls by dragging the left edge of the Subject control until it is aligned with the left edge of the Product Category control. Because the **Snap to Grid** option is on, the Subject control is automatically adjusted for you.

▶ To align the Subject and Product Category controls

- Click the Subject control, and then drag the left border of the Subject control until it is aligned with the left border of the Product Category control, as shown in Figure 4.11.

Figure 4.11   The Subject control is aligned with the Product Category control.

Add a Label for the Message Control

Now you add a label for the Message control to indicate to users the type of information they're supposed to type into the control. To make room for the label, you may need to make the Message control slightly smaller.

▶ **To add a Label control**

1   Drag a Label control from the **Control Toolbox** to the **Compose** page, as shown in Figure 4.12.

2   Click the Label control, and then type **Product Idea:**.

Figure 4.12   The Product Idea label is added to the Compose page.

Set the Tab Order for the Compose Page

The tab order defines the sequence in which the controls become active on the form when the user presses TAB. When you add controls to the form, the control name is added to the bottom of a list of controls in the **Tab Order** box. For the **Compose** page, you must move the Product Category control up the list so it follows directly after the Subject control.

▶ **To set the Tab Order for the Compose page**

1   On the **Layout** menu, click **Tab Order**.

2   In the **Tab Order** box, click **Product Category**, and then click **Move Up** until **Product Category** is above **Message**.

Note   Label controls, such as ConversationLabel and SubjectLabel, are listed in the **Tab Order** box, but are not included in the tab order.

Edit the Read Page

To edit the **Read** page, you copy the controls you added to the **Compose** page. Before you do this, however, you must switch to the **Read** page, adjust grid settings, delete the Categories control, and adjust the Message control to make room for new controls.

▶ **To switch to the Read page**

- On the **Form Design** toolbar, click **Edit Read Page**, as shown in Figure 4.13.

▶ **To delete the Categories control and its label**

1 Hold down the CTRL key, and then click the **Categories** control and its associated label.

2 Press DELETE.

▶ **To adjust the Message control**

1 Drag the Message control bottom border until is near the bottom of the **Read** page, as shown in Figure 4.13.

2 Drag the Message control top border until it's approximately the size and position of the control shown in Figure 4.13.

Tip   If necessary, you can automatically center the Message control on the form. To do this, click the Message control, point to **Center in Form** on the **Layout** menu, and then click **Horizontally**.

Figure 4.13   The Read page of the Product Idea form

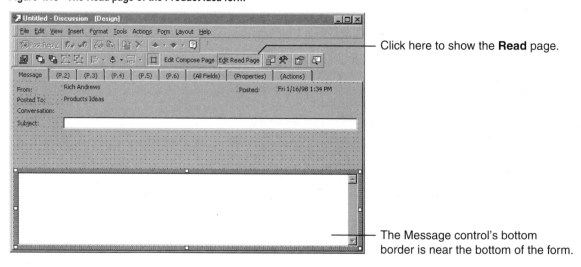

Click here to show the **Read** page.

The Message control's bottom border is near the bottom of the form.

Copy Controls from the Compose Page

Now you switch to the **Compose** page and copy the Product Category control, its label, and the Product Idea label. Then you switch back to the **Read** page where you paste the controls.

▶ **To copy the controls from the Compose page**

1   On the **Form Design** toolbar, click **Edit Compose Page**.

2   Hold down the CTRL key and click the Product Category control, the Product Category label, and the Product Idea label.

3   On the **Standard** toolbar, click **Copy**.

4   On the **Form Design** toolbar, click **Edit Read Page**.

5   When the **Read** page appears, click **Paste**, and then position the pasted controls on the page as shown in Figure 4.14.

6   Click the Subject control, and then drag the left border of the Subject control until it is approximately aligned with the left border of the Product Category control.

7   Hold down SHIFT and click the Product Category control.

8   In the **Layout** menu, point to **Align**, and then click **Left**.

Figure 4.14   The Read page of the Product Idea form

Controls are copied to the **Read** page.

Set the Tab Order for the Read Page

When designing forms, it's important to remember that when you change a design element on the **Compose** page, you most often need to make the same change on the **Read** page.

▶ **To set the tab order**

1 On the **Layout** menu, click **Tab Order**.

2 In the **Tab Order** box, click **Product Category**, and then click **Move Up**, until Product Category is below Subject.

Set Product Idea Form Properties

The Outlook **Properties** tab lets you define the overall attributes for the form, including the Caption property that appears in the title bar of the form window and the Contact property for specifying who to contact for upgrades or maintenance of the form. There are a variety of other properties you can set for the form, but for now, only set the properties listed below.

▶ **To set Product Idea form properties**

Click the **Properties** tab, and then fill in the values as shown below.

Property	Value
Contact	*Your name*
Description	Use this form to post and view product ideas in the Product Ideas folder.
Version	1.0
Form Number	1-1

See Also For more information about how to set form properties, see Chapter 5, "Forms."

Test the Form at Design Time

Before you save a form or publish it to a folder, it's a good idea to run the form to see how the form layout appears at run time. It's a good idea to test both the **Read** page and the **Compose** page of the form.

▶ **To switch between Design mode and Run mode when testing**

1 With the **Compose** page in Design mode, click **Run This Form** on the **Form** menu.

2 To test the **Read** page, send the form to yourself and view the received item in your Inbox.

3 To return to Design mode, close the Run mode window of the **Compose** page.

Make a Backup Copy of the Product Idea Form

While it's not absolutely necessary, it's usually a good idea to make a backup copy of the form before you publish it to a form library.

▶ **To save the Product Idea form**

1 With the form open, click **Save As** on the **File** menu.

2 In the **Save in** box, select the default Outlook template folder, such as C:\Program Files\Microsoft Office\Templates.

3 In the **File name** box, type a name for the form.

4 In the **Save as type** box, select **Outlook Template**.

5 Click **Save**.

▶ **To open your backup copy of a form**

1 Select **New** on the **File** menu, and then click **Choose Form**.

2 Click **Templates in File System** in the **Look In** drop-down list box, and then click on the form you'd like to open.

Publish the Product Idea Form

When you publish the Product Idea form to the Product Ideas folder, you register the form definition in the folder. As a result, a menu command appears on the **Actions** menu of Outlook when the user opens the Product Ideas folder. This is the menu command that enables users to open the Product Idea form and create a new Product Idea item

▶ **To publish the form to the Product Ideas folder**

1 Choose **Forms** on the **Tools** menu, and then click **Publish Form As**.

2 In the **Form name** text box and the **Display name** text box, type **Product Idea**.

3 If the text in the **Look In** drop-down list box is not Product Ideas, click the **Look In** drop-down list box, select the Product Ideas folder, and then click **OK**.

4 Click **Publish**.

5 In the **Send form definition with item** message box, choose **Yes** if this form will be sent to someone outside your forms library system. That way, they will have a self-contained form that can be viewed stand-alone. Select **No** if the recipient has the form published in Personal Forms Library, Organizational Forms Library or has access to the forms library of the folder. This keeps form size down and speeds form opening. For more information, see Chapter 13, "Distribute and Maintain Applications."

Tip   Click the Outlook **Actions** menu. You'll notice the **New Product Idea** command is added to the menu. Outlook automatically constructs the menu command by combining the word "New" with the Display name property "Product Idea."

Create the Product Idea Response Form

The Product Idea Response form, as shown in Figure 4.15, is very similar to the Product Idea form. Therefore, to create the Product Idea Response form, all you need to do is modify a few properties of the Product Idea form, change the form name, and then publish the form in the Product Ideas folder.

Figure 4.15   The Compose page of the Product Idea Response form

The Product Category control is read-only on the Product Idea Response form.

The label for the Message control is changed to indicate the form is used to respond to ideas.

Edit the Compose Page

To edit the **Compose** page, you change several properties for the Product Category control, and you change the label associated with the Message control. First, however, you must switch from the **Read** page to the **Compose** page.

▶ **To switch to the Compose page**

- On the **Form Design** toolbar, click **Edit Compose Page**.

Make the Product Category Control Read-Only

On the Product Idea Response form, you make the Product Category control a "read-only" control so the Product Category selected by the person who posted the New Idea cannot be changed by the person responding to the idea.

▶ **To make the Product Category control read-only**

1 On the **Compose** page, right-click the Product Category control, and then click **Properties**.

2 Click the **Display** tab, and then select the **Read only** check box.

3 Click **OK** to close.

Clear the Initial Value Property for the Product Category Field

Now you specify that the **Initial Value** property for the Product Category field is cleared. This ensures that the value from the Product Category field in the Product Idea item is copied to the Product Category field in the Product Idea Response item.

▶ **To clear the Initial Value property**

1 Right-click the Product Category control, and then click **Properties**.

2 Click the **Value** tab, clear the **Set the initial value of this field to** check box, and then click **OK**.

Change the Product Idea Label

Now you change the label above the Message control from "Product Idea:" to "Product Idea Response:". This helps to clarify the purpose of the Message control on the Product Idea Response form.

▶ **To change the label**

1 Click the Product Idea label (located above the Message control), and then click it again.

2 Change the text in the label to **Product Idea Response:**.

3 Resize the label.

Edit the Read Page

Now you switch to the **Read** page, set the Product Category control to read-only, and then change the Product Idea label to Product Idea Response.

▶ **To switch to the Read page**

• On the **Form Design** toolbar, click **Edit Read Page**.

▶ **To make the Product Category control read-only**

1 Right-click the Product Category control, and then click **Properties**.

2 Click the **Display** tab, select the **Read only** check box, and then click **OK**.

▶ **To change the Product Idea label**

1 Click the Product Idea label (above the Message control), and then click it again.

2 Change the label to **Product Idea Response:**.

3 Resize the label.

Set the Form Properties

Now you set the form properties for the Product Idea Response form.

▶ **To set the form properties**

Click the **Properties** tab, and then fill in the values as shown in the following table.

Property	Value
Contact	*Your name*
Description	Use this form to post or view a response to a product idea or to post or view a response to a product idea response.
Version	1.0
Form Number	1-1
Use Form Only For Responses	True (checked)

Make a Backup Copy of the Product Idea Response Form

Now you save the Product Idea Response form in the folder where you saved the Product Idea form.

▶ **To make a backup copy of the Product Idea Response form**

1 With the form open, click **Save As** on the **File** menu.

2 In the **Save in** list box, select the default Outlook template folder, such as C:\Program Files\Microsoft Office\Templates.

3 In the **File name** text box, type a name for the form.

4 In the **Save as type** drop-down list box, select **Outlook Template**.

5 Click **Save**.

▶ **To open your backup copy of a form**

1 Select **New** on the **File** menu, and then click **Choose Form**.

2 Click **Templates in File System** in the **Look In** drop-down list box, and then click on the form you'd like to open.

Publish the Product Idea Response Form

Before you publish the Product Idea Response form, you change the **Form Name** option in the **Publish Form As** dialog box to Product Idea Response. You then publish the Product Idea Response form to the Product Ideas Form Library.

▶ **To publish the Product Idea Response form**

1 On the **Tools** menu, select **Forms**, and then click **Publish Forms As**.

2 In the **Display name** text box and **Form name** text box, change the name to **Product Idea Response**.

   The **Message class** property automatically updates when you change the **Form** name.

   The Display name field reflects the form name on the **Actions** menu of the folder, and the caption on the title bar of the published form.

3 Click **Publish**.

4 Close the Product Idea Response form. In the **Save Changes?** message box, select **No** in most cases. Select **Yes** if you want a backup item in the current folder.

Set the Actions

Actions determine how a form handles responses. For example, the action that you create for the Product Idea form will enable users to respond to a Product Idea item with the Product Idea Response form. In addition, the action that you create for the Product Idea Response form will enable users to respond to a Product Idea Response item with the Product Idea Response form. In essence, the form will call itself for a response.

Set the Actions for the Product Idea Form

First, you open the Product Idea form in the Product Ideas folder. Then, you switch to Design mode for the form and set its actions.

▶ **To open the Product Idea form in Design mode**

1 Locate the Product Ideas folder in the Folder List and click once to open it.

2 On the Outlook **Actions** menu, hold down the SHIFT key and click **New Product Idea**.

   Holding down the SHIFT key when you open a form for design purposes is a good practice because it prevents any code in the form from executing when the form is opened. Note that the Product Ideas folder must be open for the **New Product Idea** command to appear on the **Actions** menu.

3 On the **Tools** menu of the Product Idea form, select **Forms**, and then click **Design This Form**.

Make the Reply to Folder Action Unavailable

When you create a new action for a Post form, you usually make the standard Post to Folder action unavailable. You do this for two reasons. First, you don't want standard Post items in the Product Ideas folder because they won't group correctly in custom views. Second, you want to avoid the confusion of presenting the user with two commands—**New Post in This Folder** and **New Product Idea**—that enable them to post an item in the folder.

▶ **To make the Reply to Folder action unavailable**

1 On the Product Idea form, click the **Actions** tab.

2 Double-click the **Reply to Folder** action.

3 Clear the **Enabled** check box, and then click **OK**.

The **Actions** page should now look like the **Actions** page shown in Figure 4.16.

Figure 4.16   The Reply to Folder action is made unavailable for the Product Idea form.

└ The Reply to Folder action is not
  enabled for the Product Idea form.

Create a New Action

Now you create a new action that specifies that a Product Idea Response button appears on the Product Idea form when the user opens a posted Product Idea. When the user clicks the **Product Idea Response** button, as shown in Figure 4.17, the Product Idea Response form appears. The user can then use this form to post a response in the folder.

Figure 4.17 The Product Idea Response button is added to the Product Idea form when a Product Idea item is opened in the folder.

The new action causes the **Product Idea Response** button to be placed on the **Read** page of the form.

▶ **To create a new action**

1 Click **New** on the **Actions** page of the Product Idea Response form.

2 In the **Action name** text box, as shown in Figure 4.18, type **Product Idea Response**.

"Product Idea Response" is the name of the command that appears on the Product Idea Response button on the Product Idea form when a posted item is opened. The **Product Idea Response** command also appears on the **Actions** menu of the folder when a Product Idea item is selected in the Product Ideas folder.

3 In the **Form name** drop-down list box, click **Product Idea Response**.

4 In the **Address form like a** drop-down list box, click **Reply to Folder**, and then click **OK**.

Figure 4.18   The Form Action Properties dialog box for the Product Idea form specifies the Product Idea Response form opens when the user clicks the Product Idea Response button.

The name that appears on the **Product Idea Response** button.

The form that appears when the **Product Idea Response** button is pressed.

The option indicating that the action opens the Product Idea Response form.

Make a Backup Copy of the Product Idea Form

Before you publish the form, it's a good idea to make a backup copy of the modified form.

▶ **To make a backup copy of the Product Idea form**

1   With the form open, click **Save As** on the **File** menu.

2   In the **Save in** list box, select the default Outlook template folder, such as C:\Program Files\Microsoft Office\Templates.

3   In the **File name** text box, type a name for the form.

4   In the **Save as type** drop-down list box, select **Outlook Template**.

5   Click **Save**.

▶ **To open your backup copy of a form**

1   Select **New** on the **File** menu, and then click **Choose Form**.

2   Click **Templates in File System** in the **Look In** drop-down list box, and then click on the form you'd like to open.

Publish the Product Idea Form

▶ **To publish the form**

1   On the **Tools** menu, select **Forms**, and then click **Publish Form As**.

2   In the window with the list of published forms, double-click **Product Idea**.

3   Close the Product Idea form. Click **No** to save changes. Click **Yes** if you want another backup draft saved to the current folder.

Set the Actions for the Product Idea Response Form

Now you open the Product Idea Response form and create a new Product Idea Response action so users can respond to a Product Idea Response item. In effect, users can create a "response to a response" by opening another instance of the Product Idea Response form. When you create the new action, the Product Idea Response button is added to the form when a posted Product Idea Response item is opened in the Product Ideas folder, as shown in Figure 4.19.

Figure 4.19   The Product Idea Response button appears on the form when the user opens a Product Idea Response item in the folder.

The **Product Idea Response** button that opens another instance of the Product Idea Response form.

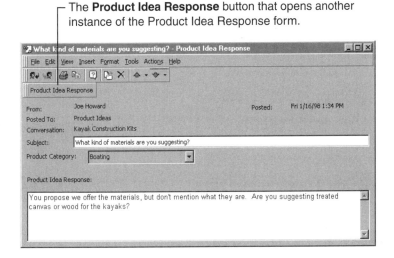

Open the Product Idea Response Form

To create a new action for the Product Idea Response form, you first open the form in Run mode, and then switch to Design mode so you can add the new actions to the form. Note that the Product Ideas folder must be open for the **New Product Idea Response** command to appear on the **Actions** menu.

▶ **To open the Product Idea Response form in Design mode**

1   On the Outlook **Actions** menu, hold down the SHIFT key and click **New Product Idea Response**.

2   On the **Tools** menu of the Product Idea form, select **Forms**, and then click **Design This Form**.

Make the Reply to Folder Action Unavailable

Just as you made the Reply to Folder action unavailable for the Product Idea form, you make it unavailable for the Product Idea Response form.

▶ **To make the Reply to Folder action unavailable**

1 On the Product Idea Response form, click the **Actions** tab.

2 Double-click the **Reply to Folder** action.

3 Clear the **Enabled** check box, and then click **OK**.

Create a New Action

Now you create a new action that causes the Product Idea Response button to appear on the Product Idea Response form when the user opens a posted Product Idea Response item.

▶ **To create a new action**

1 On the Product Idea Response form, click the **Actions** tab.

2 Click **New**.

3 In the **Action name** text box, type **Product Idea Response**.

4 In the **Form name** drop-down list box, click **Product Idea Response**.

5 In the **Address form like a** drop-down list box, click **Reply to Folder**, and then click **OK**.

Make a Backup Copy of the Product Idea Response Form

It's always a good idea to have a backup copy of the form.

▶ **To make a backup copy of the Product Idea Response form**

1 With the form open, click **Save As** on the **File** menu.

2 In the **Save in** drop-down list box, select the default Outlook template folder, such as C:\Program Files\Microsoft Office\Templates.

3 In the **File name** drop-down list box, double-click on **Product Idea Response**.

4 In the **Save as type** drop-down list box, select **Outlook Template**.

5 Click **Save**.

6 Select **Yes** to replace existing file.

Publish the Product Idea Response Form

▶ **To publish the Product Idea Response form**

1 On the **Tools** menu, select **Forms,** and then click **Publish Forms As**.

2 Double-click on Product Idea Response in the forms window.

3 Close the Product Idea Response form. Select **No** in the **Save Changes?** message box.

Create the Product Category View

Custom views organize information in folders so the information is meaningful and can be analyzed more quickly. For example, take a look at the Messages view in Figure 4.20. In this view, items are listed chronologically according to the order they were posted in the folder. With this flat presentation of information, you'd never know that discussions are taking place within the folder.

Figure 4.20   The Product Ideas folder with the Messages view selected

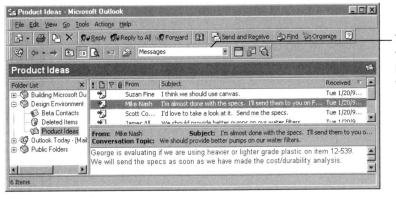

The Messages view shows items in the order they were received.

Now take a look at the same information in Figure 4.21. With the custom Product Category view applied to the folder, items are grouped first by the Product Category field, and then by the Conversation field. In addition, each item in a conversation group is sorted by the Conversation Index field, so you can see the history of responses to each item.

Figure 4.21   The Product Ideas folder with the Product Category view selected

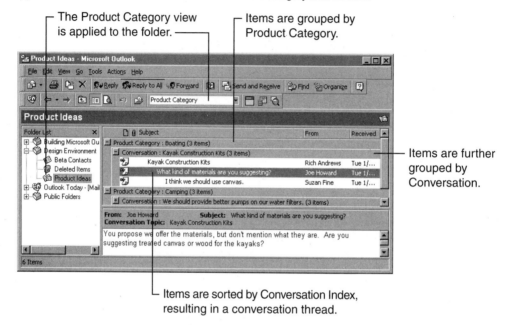

The Product Category view is applied to the folder.

Items are grouped by Product Category.

Items are further grouped by Conversation.

Items are sorted by Conversation Index, resulting in a conversation thread.

▶ **To create the Product Category view**

1   Click the **Product Ideas** folder in the Folder List.

2   On the **View** menu, select **Current View**, and then click **Define Views**.

3   Click **New**.

4   In the **Name of new view** text box, type **Product Category**, click **OK** twice, and then click **Apply View**.

Remove Fields

Now you remove the fields that aren't necessary for the Product Category view.

▶ **To remove fields**

- Drag the following column headings away from the **Column Heading** row until an **X** appears through the column heading, and then release the mouse button.
    - Importance (the **!** column heading)
    - Flag Status (the column heading with the flag symbol)

Group Items

For the Product Category view, you group items first by the Product Category field, and then by the Conversation Topic field.

When you group items in a view by Product Category, all items in the Product Ideas folder that have the value Camping selected in the **Product Category** drop-down list box are grouped together. Similarly, all items that have the value Fishing selected in the **Product Category** drop-down list box are grouped together.

When a user first submits a Product Idea item, the Subject of the item becomes the **Conversation Topic** property. Any response items to the item, whether a direct response, or a response to a response, inherit this **Conversation Topic** property. As a result, all items about a particular conversation topic are grouped together.

▶ **To group items by Product Category, then by Conversation**

1 On the **View** menu, select **Current View**, and then click **Customize Current View**.

2 Click **Group By** in the **View Summary** box.

3 In the **Select available fields from** drop-down list box near the bottom, click **User-defined fields in folder**.

4 In the **Group items by** drop-down list box, click **Product Category**.

5 In the **Select available fields from** drop-down list box, click **Frequently-used fields**.

6 In the **Then by** drop-down list box, click **Conversation**.

7 Click **OK** twice.

Sort Items

The Conversation Index field is the field that makes conversation threading come to life. When you group items by Conversation Topic, and then sort them by Conversation Index, you can suddenly see the relationship between items in a discussion application because a response to an item immediately follows the item. Plus, the response is indented from the associated item, so it's easy for a user who hasn't been part of the online conversation to quickly come up to speed on an issue by simply following the thread of conversation up to the last posted item.

▶ **To sort items by the Conversation Index field**

1 On the **View** menu, select **Current View**, and then click **Customize Current View**.

2 Click **Sort** in the **View Summary** box.

3 In the **Select available fields from** drop-down list box, click **Frequently-used fields**.

4 In the **Sort items by** drop-down list box, click **Conversation Index**, and then click **OK** twice.

Arrange the Column Heading Order

Usually for discussion applications, the **Subject** column heading precedes the **From** column heading. In Outlook, you can make adjustments to the view directly in the folder, so changing the column heading order is a simple matter of drag-and-drop editing.

▶ **To arrange the column heading order**

• Drag the **Subject** column heading to the left until the double arrow appears, and then drop the column heading.

Specify the Default Form for the Folder

Now you make the Product Idea form the default form for the Product Ideas folder so that when the user clicks the **New** button on the Outlook **Standard** toolbar, the Product Idea form appears.

▶ **To specify that the Product Idea form is the default form**

1 In the Folder List, right-click the Product Ideas folder.

2 Click **Properties**.

3 Click the **General** tab.

4 In the **When Posting to this folder, use** drop-down list box, click **Product Idea**, and then click **OK**

Set the Hidden Property for the Product Idea Response Form

Before you test the Product Ideas application to make sure it's working as expected, you set the **Hidden** property for the Product Idea Response form. This ensures that users can only open the Product Idea Response form by first selecting or opening a posted item. Therefore, the Product Idea Response form can be used only for posting responses, not for creating new items to start a conversation topic.

When you set the **Hidden** property of the Product Idea Response form, you remove the **Product Idea Response** command from the Outlook **Actions** menu. With the **Hidden** property set, the Product Idea Response form can only be opened by clicking one of the action commands you specified for the Product Idea and Product Idea Response forms.

▶ **To set the Hidden property for the Product Idea Response form**

1   In the Folder List, right-click the **Product Ideas** folder.

2   Click **Properties**.

3   Click the **Forms** tab, and then click **Manage**.

4   In the forms list box on the right, click **Product Idea Response**, and then click **Properties**.

5   Select the **Hidden** check box, and then click **OK**.

6   Click **Close** twice.

Test the Application

Before you copy the Product Ideas application to Public Folders and make it available to other users, it's a good idea to test the application to make sure everything is working as expected.

▶ **To test the Product Ideas application**

1 With the Product Ideas folder open, click **New Product Idea** on the Outlook **Actions** menu.

2 Fill in the form, and then click **Post**.

The new item is posted in the Product Ideas folder.

3 Double-click the Product Idea item you posted.

4 When the Product Idea form appears, click the **Product Idea Response** button on the form.

5 Fill in the Product Idea Response form, and then click **Post**.

6 Close the Product Idea form.

7 In the Product Ideas folder, double-click the Product Idea Response item you just posted.

8 When the Product Idea Response form appears, click the **Product Idea Response** button.

9 Fill in the Product Idea Response form, and then click **Post**.

10 Close the Product Idea Response form.

11 Repeat Steps 1–7 several times. Each time you perform step 2, click a different value in the **Product Category** box and enter different text in the **Subject** text box.

Copy the Folder to Public Folders

Now that you've created forms and a custom view for the Product Ideas folder, and you've tested the folder to make sure it works as planned, you copy the folder from the Design Environment personal folder to Public Folders so the folder can be shared by a workgroup or across the entire organization. Before you copy the folder, you might want to contact your administrator to find out the best location for the folder. In addition, you might need to contact your administrator to get the appropriate permissions to copy the folder to its destination in Public Folders.

▶ **To copy the Product Ideas folder**

1 In the Folder List, click the **Product Ideas** folder.

2 Delete any test items or draft forms from the folder, before copying. Select the items and press the DELETE key.

3 On the **File** menu, point to **Folder**, and then click **Copy "Product Ideas"**.

4 In the **Copy the selected folder to the folder** list box, click the location you want the folder copied to, such as All Public Folders.

5 Click **OK**.

About Folder Permissions

When you create the Product Ideas folder, you are automatically given owner permissions for the folder. In addition, all users are given Publishing Author permissions so they can post and open items in the folder, and modify and delete items they create. At this time, you can leave the folder permissions alone.

See Also   For more information about how to set permissions, see Chapter 8, "Folders."

Release the Application

Before you make the application available to co-workers, you set the **Initial View on Folder** property to Product Category. This is the view users first see when they open the folder.

▶ **To set administration properties**

1   In the Folder List, right-click the Product Ideas folder, and then click **Properties**.

2   Click the **Administration** tab.

3   In the **Initial view on folder** drop-down list box, select **Product Category**. Click **OK**.

Now that the folder is ready for use, you can send a message to your co-workers to notify them that the application is available.

See Also   For more information about releasing applications, see Chapter 13, "Distribute and Maintain Applications."

What's Next

In this chapter, we've taken a quick look at how to build an information-sharing groupware application based on the Post form. In the next chapter, "Forms," we'll take an in-depth look at the forms design environment, the different types of forms you can create, how forms work, and how to set form properties.

Building Blocks of Applications

Contents

Chapter 5   Forms   97

Chapter 6   Controls, Fields, and Properties   139

Chapter 7   Actions   183

Chapter 8   Folders   221

Forms

In This Chapter

Become Familiar with Designing Forms and Form Components 98

Learn How Forms Work 112

Create a Folder 116

Open the Form and Switch to Design Mode 116

Edit Form Pages 118

Add Controls 123

Create and Bind Fields 124

Polish the Layout 128

Create Help (Optional) 129

Edit the Read Page 130

Set Action Properties 131

Set Form Properties 132

Publish the Form 134

Test and Release the Form 137

With Outlook forms in Design mode, you can build custom forms to streamline request processes, collect and distribute information, and save and show information that is structured so it's not only easy to find, but easy to read. For example, you can create travel request forms to automate the approval of business travel plans. You can create product feedback forms to collect valuable feedback from your customers. Or you can create job candidate forms to post information about a potential employee, so that other members of your organization can view the candidate's background before interviewing the candidate. After the interview, interviewers can post their impressions of the candidate in a public folder, so a manager can quickly get an overall impression of the candidate.

This chapter discusses form design concepts, introduces the form design process, and then covers fundamental form design tasks such as adding controls and fields, creating new actions, setting form properties, and publishing forms. When you're done with this chapter, you should have the basic knowledge and skills you need to create and publish forms in your organization.

Throughout this chapter, there are numbered graphic blocks, such as Step 1 below, that represent major steps in the form design process. Within each step, you can find detailed information that can help you complete the subtasks involved in the step.

Become Familiar with Designing Forms and Form Components

This section covers the components of forms in Design mode and discusses the parts of an Outlook form.

Outlook Forms in Design Mode

The following elements are available while Outlook forms are in Design mode:

- **Form Design** window, to show the various pages of the form and the form properties and actions.

- **Control Toolbox**, to add new controls (such as buttons) to the form.

- **Field Chooser**, to select fields for the form.

- **Properties** dialog box, to modify a control or field.

- **Script Editor**, to program or automate the forms.

For more information on how to open a form in Design mode, see "Outlook Design Mode" in Chapter 2, "Outlook Design Tools."

Figure 5.1   Outlook design environment

Click to open the **Field Chooser**, **Control Toolbox**, **Properties** dialog box of the selected control, or **Script Editor**.

Click here to switch between **Read** and **Compose** pages of a form.

Click here to publish a form in a forms library.

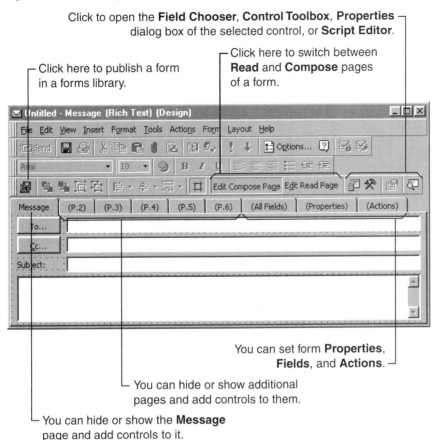

You can set form **Properties**, **Fields**, and **Actions**.

You can hide or show additional pages and add controls to them.

You can hide or show the **Message** page and add controls to it.

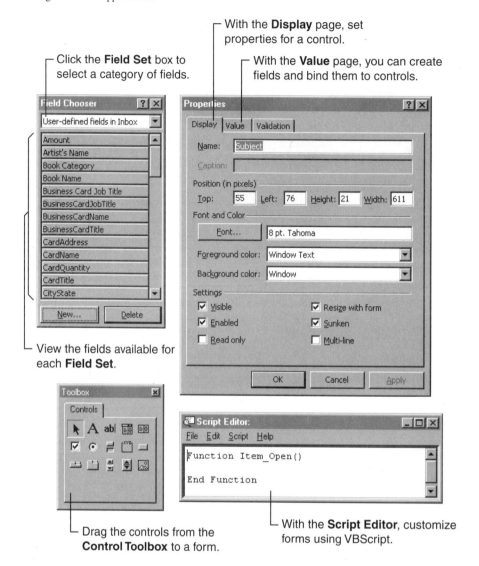

With the **Display** page, set properties for a control.

Click the **Field Set** box to select a category of fields.

With the **Value** page, you can create fields and bind them to controls.

View the fields available for each **Field Set**.

Drag the controls from the **Control Toolbox** to a form.

With the **Script Editor**, customize forms using VBScript.

Types of Forms

Outlook provides four basic types of forms you use as starting points for all forms that you build. To effectively design forms, you need to know the basic characteristics of these four types: Message, Post, Office Document, and built-in forms.

Message and Post forms are fully customizable. While Office Document forms can't be directly modified, you can add VBScript to the form to modify it.
Task, Appointment, and Journal forms can be customized by adding additional pages to the forms, but the existing pages cannot be modified. This also applies to the Contact form, but you can modify the first page of a Contact form.

For a detailed description of form components, see "Parts of a Form" later in this chapter.

Message Form

You use the Message form as a starting point for building forms that let users send information to another user, distribution list, or folder. The Message form is fully customizable. When Message forms are sent, they travel through the messaging transport agent and are routed to the specified address. Examples of Message forms are the Vacation Request form, the While You Were Out form, and the Business Card Request form.

Figure 5.2   The Mail Message form is the starting point for Message forms.

Post Form

You use the Post form as a starting point for building forms that enable users to post, open, and respond to information in a personal or public folder. The Post form is fully customizable. Post forms submit items directly to the active folder. As such, Post forms are tightly integrated with folders. Examples of Post forms are the Product Idea and Product Idea Response forms found in the Product Ideas application, which is discussed in Chapter 4, "Design a Custom Application."

Figure 5.3   The Post form is the starting point for forms that are integrated with a personal or public folder.

Office Document Form

You use the Office Document form as a starting point for building forms that have an Office 97 document—Word, PowerPoint, or Microsoft Excel—embedded in them. Office Document forms are essentially an Office document wrapped in either a Message or Post form. You can create Office Document forms to send documents to other users and to post documents in a folder. For instance, expense reports may be sent to your Accounting department on Microsoft Excel spreadsheets embedded in an Outlook form.

Figure 5.4   The New Office Document form is the starting point for Office Document forms.

Important   Office Document forms do not contain pages you can customize. However, you can customize the document embedded in the Document page of the form. To create a form in a Microsoft Office 97 document, see Help for the specific application you want to create a form for.

Built-in Forms

You can modify built-in forms in Calendar, Contacts, Journal, and Tasks modules by showing additional pages on the form. You can then add controls and fields to the form to suit the needs of your application. The default page cannot be modified, with the exception of the Contact form's default page.

The characteristics of each built-in form vary, depending on the application. For example, with the Task Request form, users send a Task Request to another user. With the Task form, however, users save the task in the current folder.

Figure 5.5   The built-in Appointment form can be customized to meet your personal needs or those of your workgroup or organization.

You can show additional pages and add controls to them.

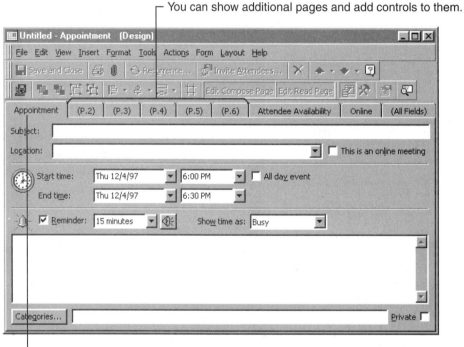

The first page of built-in forms cannot be modified with the exception of the first **Contact** page.

Parts of a Form

Before you get started designing forms, you need to know about the different components of a form and what each component is used for. This section dissects a form and discusses the purpose of each of its components.

The Compose and Read Pages

An Outlook form can consist of one page. But in most cases it consists of two pages: a **Compose** page and a **Read** page. Although the **Compose** and **Read** pages are often similar in appearance, they serve very different purposes. The **Compose** page enables users to create items and to send or post items. The **Read** page enables users to open and read submitted items in a folder, and to respond to items.

Figure 5.6   The Outlook form consists of a Compose page and a Read page.

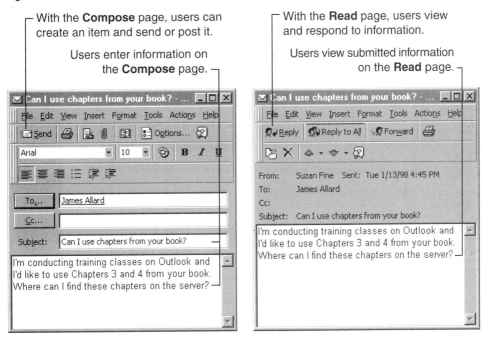

Pages

Forms also have a series of pages that you view by clicking their respective tabs. In addition to the default **Message** or **General** page, forms have five custom pages that you can add controls to. Forms also have pages such as the **Properties** and **Actions** pages that enable you to set properties for the form to define how it functions, as shown in Figure 5.7. The **All Fields** page allows you to view all fields and field values for the form. You can even update some of these properties, which is useful for testing.

Figure 5.7   Pages of the Message form

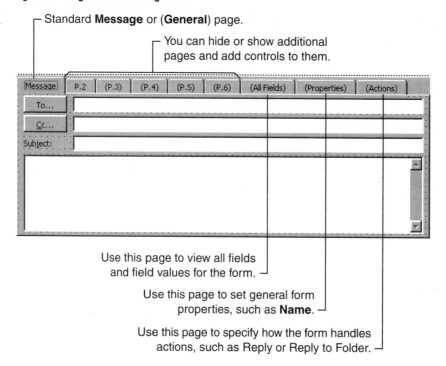

Standard **Message** or (**General**) page.

You can hide or show additional pages and add controls to them.

Use this page to view all fields and field values for the form.

Use this page to set general form properties, such as **Name**.

Use this page to specify how the form handles actions, such as Reply or Reply to Folder.

Controls

Controls are the components of a form that enable users to enter information and view information. Controls are the means through which users interact with the form. You add controls to the form by dragging them from the **Control Toolbox**.

Figure 5.8 Controls and the Control Toolbox

The Label control is used to show text that users cannot change.

The TextBox control enables users to enter and view text.

Users can add controls to the form by dragging them from the **Control Toolbox**.

The Frame control groups similar information, such as OptionButton controls.

The ComboBox control lets users enter values or select from a list.

Fields

A form field is a field that defines how information in a control or in a folder is saved and displayed in messaging applications. In addition, the field is a physical storage location in the item where the specified data is saved. To specify that the information in a control is to be saved, you bind the control to a field. For example, as shown in Figure 5.9, the TextBox control is bound to the Name field, so that the information in the control is saved to the field when an item is sent, saved, or posted. When the item is opened, the information is loaded from the field into the control.

Figure 5.9   The TextBox control is bound to the Name field.

Properties

Properties define the characteristics of form components. With Outlook, you can define properties for forms, controls, and fields. Figure 5.10 shows display properties that are set for the Name control.

Control properties are accessed by right-clicking on the control or field, and then selecting **Properties**. Form properties are modified on the **Properties** page while in Design mode.

Figure 5.10   Properties of the Name control

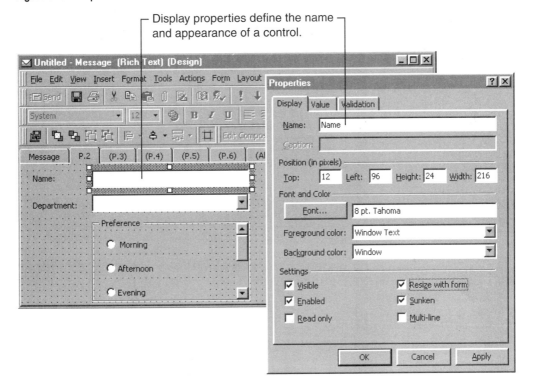

Actions

Actions define how a form handles responses. You can modify existing actions or create new actions. For example, you can modify an action that specifies that a custom form is opened when the user clicks the **Reply** button on a form. Or you can create a new action that adds a custom response button to the form. As shown in Figure 5.11, new actions have been created for the Vacation Request form that enable users to respond to a Vacation Request item by clicking an **Approve Vacation** or **Deny Vacation** button on the form.

Figure 5.11   The Actions page for the Vacation Request form

This action sends a Vacation Approved reply to the requester.

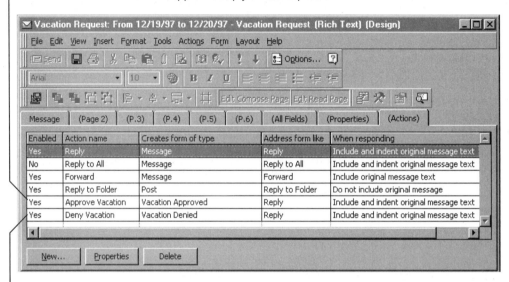

This action sends a Vacation Denied reply to the requester.

Form Scripts

With the Script Editor, you can use Microsoft Visual Basic Scripting Edition (VBScript) to add functionality to a form. You can add code for a command button that creates and sends a response item, you can launch other applications from a form using Automation, and you can create procedures that automatically fill in or clear values on the form, as shown in Figure 5.12.

Figure 5.12   The Script Editor shows code that automates a Business Card Request form.

The AutoFill_Click procedure automatically fills in Address field values.

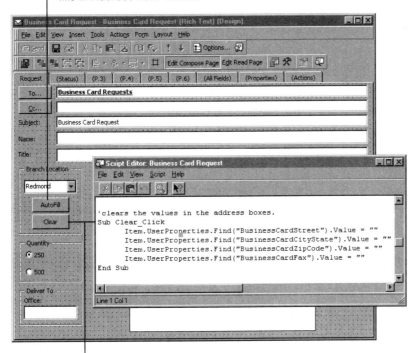

The Clear_Click procedure automatically clears values from the fields.

Learn How Forms Work

 This section briefly covers some fundamental form concepts, such as the meaning of the term *item*, how saving the form definition with an item affects the form, and how shared fields work.

What Is an Item?

Throughout the book, the term *item* is often used. In the past, an item was simply called a message. So why change the terminology? Because the term message can no longer encompass the vast array of information that can be included in an item. In Outlook, an item is a container for information. In addition to text and number values entered by users, this container known as an item can hold just about anything, including Uniform Resource Locators (URLs), voice mail, office documents, video clips, PowerPoint presentations, and so on. An item also contains properties that define the item, such as message class, and that associate the item with a specific form.

Note   You may be wondering where items are stored. Public folder items are stored on a server. Personal folder (.pst) and mailbox items are stored in the location specified by the user. When you click **Save** on the **File** menu to save a Message, Post, or Office Document form, Outlook saves the form in the Drafts folder.

What Happens When the Form Definition Is Saved with the Item?

In Design mode, Outlook provides an option on the form **Properties** page called **Send form definition with item**. The **Send form definition with item** option serves two purposes.

- **It enables users to send Message forms to other users.**   When the **Send form definition with item** option is selected for a Message form, the form definition is included in the item. This enables users who receive the item to view the item in the custom form, even though they do not have the custom form published in a forms library on their system. As such, it provides a useful way to send items created with custom forms to locations outside your immediate system. For example, you may want to send a customer feedback item over the Internet to a customer site. If the **Send form definition with item** option is selected, the customer sees the item in the custom form when they open it, even though they do not have the form published on their system. This also has a side effect of not giving your item a unique message class.

- **It provides a security measure.** If a user opens a Message form that has the **Send form definition with item** option selected, and the form is not available on the server or on the user's Outlook system, and the form has VBScript included with it, then the user sees the **Warning** message box, as shown in Figure 5.13. In this case, the **Send form definition with item** option provides a security measure to prevent a user from opening a potentially harmful form. When you finish designing a Message form, you can:

  - Clear the **Send form definition with item** option and publish the form in the Personal Forms Library or a forms library in a folder.

  - Submit the form to an administrator who checks it for harmful macros. If none exist, the administrator clears the **Send form definition with item** check box and then publishes the form to the Organizational Forms Library.

Figure 5.13 Users see this message box when they try to open an item that contains the form definition and VBScript.

Important   By default, the **Send form definition with item** option is turned off to keep form size small and reduce network traffic and form loading time. Users are given the choice to turn it on when the form is published.

See Also   For more information about the **Send form definition with item** option, see Step 12, "Set Form Properties," later in this chapter.

How Is a Form Opened?

By default, the **Send form definition with item** check box is cleared. The question then arises: If the form definition doesn't travel with the item, how is the form opened? The answer is that the form is launched from a Personal or Organizational Forms Library, or forms library of a folder, when the user attempts to create or view an item associated with the form. The form is associated with the item by its message class. Each form has a message class that identifies it internally to the server. For example, the standard Post form has the message class IPM.Post, while the standard

Contact form has the message class IPM.Contact. When an item is created, the message class of the form used to create the item is saved as one of the attributes of the item. When the user double-clicks an existing item to open it, the message class of the item is passed to the server, and is used to locate and launch the form associated with the item.

Publishing a form registers its definition. If the form definition doesn't exist in the user's forms libraries, Outlook will substitute the next class in common. For example, if IPM.Note.Myform.ThisForm does not exist, Outlook will try to open IPM.Note.Myform. If that does not exist, IPM.Note will load and the user will see a standard message form.

As shown in Figure 5.14, when a user opens the form to create a Volunteer Registration item, the form is launched from the Organizational Forms Library. The item, and not the form, is then sent to a recipient. When the recipient opens the item in his or her Inbox, the Volunteer Registration form is launched and the information from the item is shown in the form.

Figure 5.14 The Compose page creates and sends the item. The Read page shows the item. The form is loaded from the Organizational Forms Library.

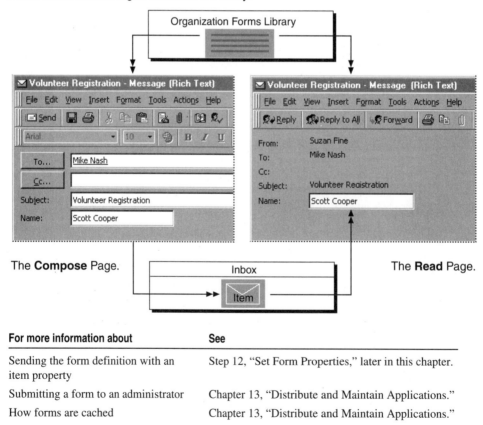

The **Compose** Page.

The **Read** Page.

For more information about	See
Sending the form definition with an item property	Step 12, "Set Form Properties," later in this chapter.
Submitting a form to an administrator	Chapter 13, "Distribute and Maintain Applications."
How forms are cached	Chapter 13, "Distribute and Maintain Applications."

How Do Shared Fields Work?

If you're new to designing forms, it helps to understand how the form saves information in the item and how it loads information from the item to the form. One of the central concepts behind the storing and loading of information is shared fields. A shared field is a field that is bound to controls on both the **Compose** and **Read** pages of a form. As shown in Figure 5.15, the Name control is bound to the Name field on the Volunteer Registration form.

Figure 5.15 When the item is created and sent, the information is saved from the control to the field. When the item is opened, the information is loaded from the field into the control.

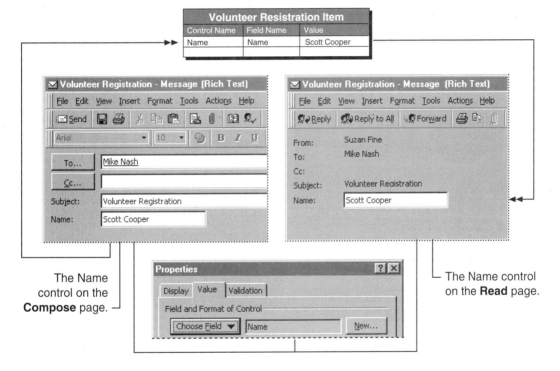

Shared fields can also be used between forms. For example, when a user creates a response to an item, the information in fields that are common between both forms is copied from the first-opened form to the response form.

See Also For more information about creating shared fields, see Chapter 6, "Controls, Fields, and Properties."

Create a Folder

Generally, it is a good idea to create a form in a personal folder. This method offers a couple of advantages. First, it lets you store forms in a central and private location while you're designing them. Second, it enables you to easily test the form. To do this, you can open the form by clicking the menu command that Outlook adds to the **Actions** menu of the folder when you publish the form in the folder's forms library.

See Also   If you have not yet created a personal folder (.pst) file, see "Create New Folders" in Chapter 3, "Customize Built-in Modules."

▶ **To create a personal folder**

1   In the Folder List, right-click a personal folder under which you want to create a folder, and then click **New Folder**.

2   In the **Name** text box, enter a name for the folder.

3   In the **Folder contains** drop-down list box, do one of the following:

- Click **Mail Items** to create a folder that will contain items created with Message, Post, or Office Document forms.

- Click **Appointment Items**, **Contact Items**, **Journal Items**, **Note Items**, or **Task Items** to create a folder for items of that type. For example, if you click **Appointment Items**, Outlook creates a Calendar folder.

4   Click **OK**.

See Also   For more information about creating folders, see Chapter 8, "Folders."

Open the Form and Switch to Design Mode

When you design an Outlook form, you always start with an existing form. Outlook gives you a variety of standard and custom forms to choose from. In addition to forms supplied in Outlook, you can design a form based on custom templates created by someone in your organization.

- To open a form and switch to Design mode, first click the folder in which you want to create the form. Then select the type of form you want to open, such as those in the following sections.

- To close a form, click the **Close** button. When you save Message, Post or Office Document forms, they become items in the Drafts folder of your Mailbox. Other forms are saved to the current folder.

▶ **To create a Message form**

1   On the Outlook **Actions** menu, click **New Mail Message**.

   To create a Message form, you must be in the Inbox folder or a folder that contains Mail items.

2   On the **Tools** menu of the form, select **Forms**, then click **Design This Form**.

▶ **To create a Post form**

1   On the Outlook **File** menu, select **New**, and then click **Post in This Folder**.

   To create a Post form, you must be in the Inbox folder or a folder that contains Mail items.

2   On the **Tools** menu of the form, select **Forms**, and then click **Design This Form**.

▶ **To create an Office Document form**

1   Click the folder in which you want to create the form.

2   On the **File** menu, point to **New**, and then click **Office Document**.

3   Select the document type, for example a Word document, and then click **OK**.

4   Do one of the following:

   • To create an Office Document form for posting items, click **Post the document in this folder**. Reply items will be posted to the current folder.

   • To create an Office Document form for sending items, click **Send the document to someone**. Reply items will be sent as a mail message.

To modify the Office Document, the **Lock** button on the **Forms** toolbar should be off.

▶ **To create a Calendar, Contacts, Tasks, Journal, or Notes form**

1   On the **Actions** menu, click the menu command associated with the form you want to modify.

   For example, to modify the Beta Contacts form in the Beta Contacts folder, click **New Beta Contacts** on the **Actions** menu.

2   On the form **Tools** menu, select **Forms**, and then click **Design This Form**.

▶ **To create a form based on a custom Outlook template**

1 On the **File** menu, select **New**, and then click **Choose Form**.

2 In the **Look in** drop-down list box, select **Templates in File System**.

3 Double-click the template you want.

4 If the template is a Post template, select the folder the form will be associated with.

5 On the form **Tools** menu, select **Forms**, and then click **Design This Form**.

For more information about	See
Creating a Message form	Chapter 10, "The Business Card Request Application."
Creating a Post form	Chapter 4, "Design a Custom Application," and Chapter 11, "The Help Desk Application."
Modifying a built-in form	Chapter 3, "Customize Built-in Modules."

Edit Form Pages

Usually forms consist of two pages: a **Compose** page and a **Read** page. There are other pages contained within the **Compose** or **Read** pages, such as **(P.2)-(P.6)**, that you can customize or use to set properties on the form. These pages are covered later in the chapter. Each of these individual pages of the form has its own **Compose** and **Read** pages, depending on if **Separate Read Layout** has been selected for that page.

The **Compose** page appears when the user opens the form to create an item. The **Read** page appears when the user double-clicks an existing item and opens it. When you create forms, you usually edit both the **Compose** and **Read** pages. In fact, when you first start designing forms, it's a common mistake to make adjustments to the **Compose** page, but forget to make the same adjustments to the **Read** page. When working with forms, you can switch back and forth between the **Read** and **Compose** pages by clicking the **Edit Compose Page** or **Edit Read Page** buttons on the **Form Design** toolbar, as shown in Figure 5.16. While the **Compose** and **Read** pages look very similar, they both have unique characteristics that you need to be aware of.

Figure 5.16 The Edit Compose Page and Edit Read Page buttons

Click here to show the **Compose** page. ⌐   ⌐ Click here to show the **Read** page.

The Compose Page

The **Compose** page of a form contains controls in which the user enters information. For example, in Figure 5.17, the user can enter information in the **Starting** and **Ending** text boxes. When the item is sent or posted, the information in these controls is saved in the item. In addition, the **Compose** page of Message forms provides controls such as the **To** button and **To** text box that enable users to specify an address for an item.

Figure 5.17   The user enters information in the controls on the Compose page.

When clicked, the **To** button shows the Address Book so users can select recipients.

Users can type recipient names in the **To** box.

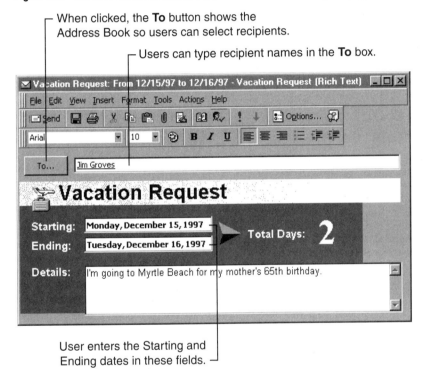

User enters the Starting and Ending dates in these fields.

The Read Page

The **Read** page of a form lets the user open and read an item. Quite often, many controls on the **Read** page are read-only, especially when the form involves money or sensitive information. As shown in Figure 5.18, the **Starting** and **Ending** text boxes on the **Read** page of the Vacation Request form are read-only, so the reader cannot change them.

Figure 5.18   The Read page of the Vacation Request form. Many of the controls on the Read page are read-only, so they cannot be changed by the reader.

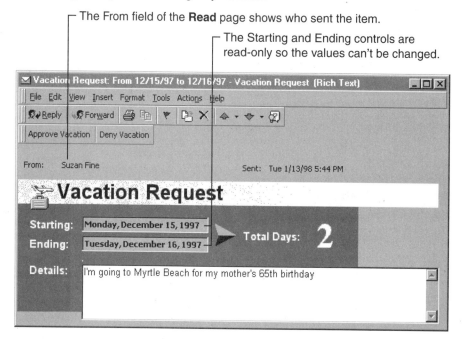

┌ The From field of the **Read** page shows who sent the item.

┌ The Starting and Ending controls are
read-only so the values can't be changed.

About Separate Read Layout

While a form is in Design mode, Outlook provides a **Separate Read Layout** option that lets you specify if an individual form page has a **Read** page layout that is different than the **Compose** page layout. By default, the **Separate Read Layout** option, located on the **Form** menu, is selected for the **Message** page of Message and Post forms. However, for a custom page, this option is not automatically selected.

Most often when designing forms, you edit the **Compose** page first, and then edit the **Read** page. When you open a Message or Post form, the **Message** page is visible. For many of the forms you create, the **Message** page may be the only page you edit. However, you can also edit pages **P. 2** through **P. 6**, as shown in Figure 5.19.

Important If you decide to add controls to a custom form page, you must select the **Separate Read Layout** option (**Form** menu) if you want the **Compose** layout of this page to differ from the **Read** layout, as shown in Figure 5.19.

Figure 5.19 For the Message form, the Separate Read Layout option is selected for the custom page.

When a control is added to a page, the page is automatically visible in Run mode.

Pages in parentheses are visible in Design mode but not in Run mode.

When you add controls to an additional page, click **Seperate Read Layout** if you want the **Read** page layout to differ from the **Compose** page layout.

Note If the **Separate Read Layout** option is not selected for a page, then you cannot switch between the **Compose** and **Read** pages when the individual page is active.

▶ **To view either the Read or Compose page**

1 Open the form and put it in Design mode.

2 Click the **Edit Compose Page** or **Edit Read Page** button on the **Form Design** toolbar.

▶ **To specify the Separate Read Layout option for a page**

1 Click the page for which you want to specify the **Separate Read Layout** option.

2 On the **Form** menu, click **Separate Read Layout**.

3 Repeat for each individual page of the form.

Hide or Show a Page

Outlook uses parentheses to designate the pages that are hidden at run time. For example, in the preceding Figure 5.19, notice the text is in parentheses for pages 3 through 6 to specify that these pages are hidden.

The capability to hide and show pages gives you great flexibility when designing forms. For example, quite often there isn't enough room on the **Message** page for all the controls you need to add. In this case, you can add additional controls to a custom form page. When you add controls to a page, the parentheses are removed from text in the page's tab, indicating that the page is visible at run time.

For some forms, you may want to hide the **Message** page. This can be especially useful for preaddressing forms. For example, you can specify an address in the To field of a form at design time, and then hide the page. This prevents the user from changing the address and also lets users submit items without ever seeing the destination address on the form. In addition, you may also want to hide a second page of the form. Keep in mind, however, that at least one page must be visible on the form.

▶ **To hide or show a page at run time**

1   In Design mode, click the desired page.

2   On the **Form** menu, click **Display This Page**.

Note   If you drag a field or a control to a hidden page, **Display This Page** will turn on automatically. To hide the page, deselect **Display This Page** on the **Form** menu.

For more information about	See
Preaddressing forms	"To Field" in Chapter 6, "Controls, Fields, and Properties"
Hiding and showing pages	"Hiding and Showing a Form Page" in Chapter 9, "Use Visual Basic Scripting Edition with Outlook," and Chapter 11, "The Help Desk Application"

Rename a Page

When you make a page visible, you should rename it to convey the purpose of the page.

▶ **To rename a page**

1   In Design mode, click the page.

2   On the **Form** menu, click **Rename Page**.

3   Type the new name for the page.

Add Controls

Controls are the means through which users enter and view information on the form. When creating forms with Outlook, you usually add controls to the **Compose** page of the form first. Then, if you want the information in the controls to be saved to the item, you create a field for the control and bind the field to the control. Binding fields is covered in Step 7.

To add controls to the form, you use the **Control Toolbox**.

▶ To show the Control Toolbox

- In Design mode, on the **Form Design** toolbar, click **Control Toolbox**.

With Outlook, you can add .ocx controls and Microsoft ActiveX® controls to the toolbox to provide added flexibility on your forms.

▶ To add additional controls to the Control Toolbox

1 Right-click the bottom of the **Controls** page on the **Control Toolbox**, and then click **Custom Controls** on the shortcut menu.

2 Under **Available Controls**, click the controls you want, and then click **OK**.

▶ To add a control to a form

- Drag the control from the **Control Toolbox** to the form.

▶ To set Display properties for a control

1 Right-click the control, and then click **Properties**.

2 On the **Display** page, set the properties you want.

▶ To set advanced properties for a control

1 Right-click the control, and then click **Advanced Properties**.

2 In the **Properties** window, set the properties you want and then close the window.

Create and Bind Fields

Fields are the means through which information in a control gets saved and shown in an item. Therefore, you only need to create fields for those controls that contain information that you want to save in the item. For example, you generally don't need to create an associated field for a Label control, as shown in Figure 5.20, because there's no reason to save the values in such controls to the item. However, for controls in which users enter information, such as the TextBox and ComboBox controls, you usually create a new field or bind an existing field to the control so that the value in the control is saved to the item.

Figure 5.20   Fields in which the user enters or selects information are generally bound to fields. Label and Image controls are usually not bound to fields.

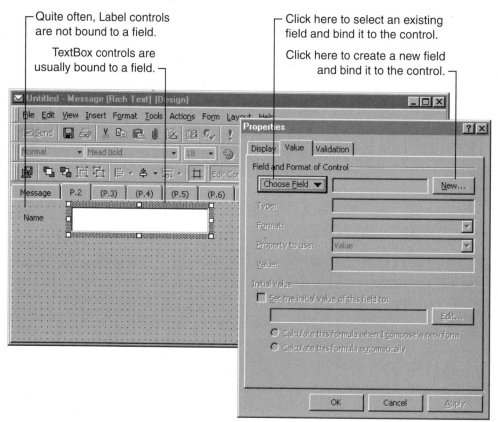

Create a New Field and Bind It to a Control

When you create a new field by using the **Properties** dialog box, the field you create is automatically bound to the currently selected control. In addition, the field you create is automatically added to the User-defined fields in *Folder* field set.

▶ **To create a new user-defined field**

1 Right-click the control, and then click **Properties**.

2 Click the **Value** page.

3 Click **New**.

4 In the **Name** text box, type the field name.

5 If necessary, change the **Type** and **Format** of the field, and then click **OK** twice.

See Also   For more information about specifying the type and format for a field, see Chapter 6, "Fields, Controls, and Properties."

Bind a Control to an Existing Field

In addition to the user-defined fields that you create, Outlook supplies several different sets of fields that you can use. These sets include Frequently-used fields, Address fields, Date/Time fields, and All Mail fields. These are built-in fields that in most cases perform advanced functions not easily attained with user-defined fields. To select an existing field to bind to a control, you use the **Properties** dialog box, as shown in the preceding illustration in Figure 5.20.

▶ **To bind a control to an existing field**

1 Right-click the control, and then click **Properties**.

2 Click the **Value** page.

3 Click **Choose Field**, point to the set of fields you want, and then click the field.

4 If necessary, change the **Format** and **Set Initial Value** of the field, and then click **OK**.

Select Fields from Other Forms

Outlook conveniently categorizes fields by the forms with which they're associated. This is often very useful if you want to create a form that has many of the same fields as another form. Rather than looking through the User-defined fields in *Folder* field set, you can view a shortened list of fields for a form.

▶ **To add a field set from a form to the field list**

1 Right-click the control, and then click **Properties**.

2 Click the **Value** tab.

3 Click **Choose Field**, and the click **Forms**.

4   In the upper left-hand library drop-down list box, click the forms library that contains the forms you want, as shown in Figure 5.21.

5   In the left-hand forms list box, double-click the form to add it to the **Selected Forms** box.

6   Click **Close** and then click **OK**.

Figure 5.21   You can add a field set from another form to the field list.

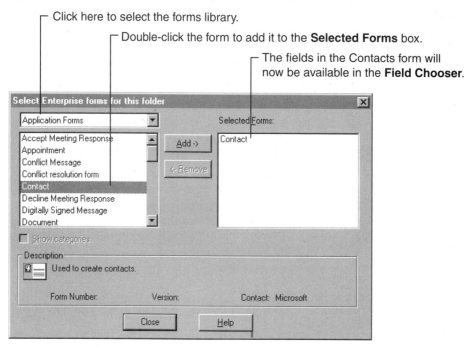

┌ Click here to select the forms library.

┌ Double-click the form to add it to the **Selected Forms** box.

┌ The fields in the Contacts form will now be available in the **Field Chooser**.

When to Use the Field Chooser

The **Field Chooser** enables you to view fields, add fields, and delete fields. You add a field from the **Field Chooser** by dragging it from the **Field Chooser** to the form. When you drag a field from the **Field Chooser**, Outlook adds a control and a control label to the form and automatically binds the control to the associated field. In addition, it automatically positions the controls on the form if the **AutoLayout** option is selected on the **Layout** menu. The control added to the form depends on the field you add. For example, if you add a Yes/No type field to a form from the **Field Chooser**, a CheckBox control is added to the form. If you add a Text type field, a TextBox control is added to the form.

In addition to providing a shortcut for adding TextBox and CheckBox controls to a form, the **Field Chooser** provides several other purposes:

- If you accidentally delete a standard control such as a Message, To, or From control on a form, you can add it back to the form by dragging it from the **Field Chooser**.
- The **Field Chooser** enables you to delete fields.
- The **Field Chooser** enables you to view fields available in the active folder and in other forms, as shown in Figure 5.22.

▶ To add a field from the Field Chooser

1 On the **Field Chooser**, click the set of fields you want.

2 Drag the field from the **Field Chooser** to the form, as shown in Figure 5.22.

Figure 5.22 You can drag fields directly from the Field Chooser to the form.

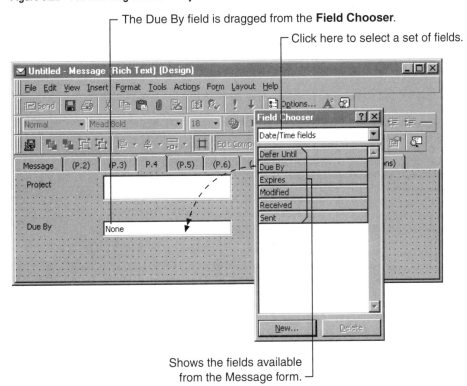

The Due By field is dragged from the **Field Chooser**.

Click here to select a set of fields.

Shows the fields available
from the Message form.

Delete a Field

To delete a field, you use the **Field Chooser**.

▶ **To delete a field**

1   On the **Field Chooser**, click the set of fields you want from the drop-down list box.

2   Click the field you want to delete, and then click **Delete**.

3   In the message box, click **Yes**.

Polish the Layout

After you add controls to the form, you can use Outlook's layout options to add professional polish to your forms. Outlook provides a great set of layout options that will save you countless hours of finish work. This section covers how to select, edit, align, and space controls. However, you are encouraged to experiment with the remainder of the layout options.

Select and Edit Controls

To select a control on a form, you click the control. To edit the control, you click it again. For example, to select a Label control, you click it once. To type text into the label, you click it again, and then type the text. To exit Edit mode, you click outside the Label control.

Align Controls

With Outlook alignment options, you can align the borders of a control. When you align controls, the alignment is always based on the last control selected. The sizing handles of the last control selected are white, as opposed to black sizing handles on the other controls, to indicate the control upon which the alignment is based.

▶ **To align controls**

1   Hold down CTRL and then click the controls you want to align.

2   On the **Layout** menu, point to **Align**, and then click one of the alignment menu commands.

Space Controls

After you align the controls, you can space them so they are evenly separated.

▶ **To space controls**

1 Hold down CTRL and then click the controls you want to space.

2 On the **Layout** menu, point to **Horizontal Spacing** or **Vertical Spacing**, and then click one of the spacing options.

Set Tab Order

The tab order defines the sequence in which the controls become active on the form when a user presses the TAB key. When you add controls to the form, the control name is added to the bottom of a list of controls in the **Tab Order** box.

Label controls, such as ConversationLabel and SubjectLabel, are listed in the **Tab Order** box but are not included in the tab order at run time. Also, when the Message control is active, pressing the TAB key will cause the Insert bar to advance to the next tab stop in the control. Therefore, it's usually best, if possible, to put the Message control as the last control in the tab order.

▶ **To set the tab order for the Compose page**

1 In Design mode, on the **Layout** menu, click **Tab Order**.

2 In the **Tab Order** list box, click **Move Up** or **Move Down** to put the controls in the proper tab sequence. Click **OK**.

Tip   You can select more than one control at a time in the **Tab Order** box. To do this, hold down the CTRL key, and then click the controls you want in the **Tab Order** list box.

View the Form in Run Mode

When you've finished with the layout of a page, it's a good idea to switch from Design mode to Run mode to see how the form will look at run time.

▶ **To switch between Design mode and Run mode**

1 On the **Form** menu, click **Run This Form**.

2 Click the **Close** button to return a form to Design mode.

Create Help (Optional)

 Not all forms require Help. In fact, most forms should be simple enough that Help is not required. However, in some cases, you may want to specify Control TipText for a control. With Control TipText, the TipText appears when the user positions the pointer over the control.

▶ **To create Control TipText**

1 In Design mode, right-click the control you want to specify Control TipText for, and then click **Advanced Properties** on the shortcut menu.

2 Double-click the **ControlTipText** cell, and then type the text you want in the text box next to the **Apply** button.

3 Click the **Apply** button to insert the text into the cell.

4 Close the **Advanced Properties** dialog box.

Edit the Read Page

Quite often, the **Compose** and **Read** pages of a form are very similar. As a result, you can design most of the **Read** page by copying controls from the **Compose** page. As a rule, you must edit the pages of the **Read** page if the page has a separate read layout.

Important   Each individual page of the form has its own **Read** or **Compose** page if **Separate Read Layout** was selected for that page.

▶ **To copy controls to the Read page**

1 On the **Form Design** toolbar, click **Edit Read Page**.

2 Click the individual page you want to edit.

3 Adjust or remove any unnecessary controls on the page to make room for the controls you want to copy from the **Compose** page.

4 On the **Form Design** toolbar, click **Edit Compose Page**.

5 Click the individual page that contains the controls you want to copy.

6 Hold down CTRL and click the fields that you want to copy.

7 Click the **Copy** button.

8 Click **Edit Read Page**.

9 Click the **Paste** button.

10 Repeat steps 2–9 for each **Read** page you want to edit.

Set Properties for Controls on the Read Page

Quite often, you make many of the controls on the **Read** page read-only. This prevents readers from changing the contents of an item after it has been sent or posted.

▶ **To make a control read-only**

1   In Design mode, hold down CTRL, and then click the fields you want to be read-only.

2   Right-click a control, and then click **Properties**.

3   On the **Display** page, select the **Read only** check box.

Set the Tab Order for the Read Page

With Outlook forms, you must set the tab order for the **Compose** and **Read** pages separately. In addition, you must the set the tab order for each individual page separately. For instructions on setting the tab order for a page, see Step 8, "Polish the Layout," earlier in this chapter.

About Viewing the Read Page in Run Mode

To view the **Read** page in Run mode, you must first send or post an item with the form, or for some built-in forms, you must save an item. For this reason, you should test the **Read** page after you publish the form. Publishing and testing the **Read** page of the form is covered later in this chapter.

▶ **To switch between Design mode and Run mode**

1   On the **Form** menu, click **Run This Form**.

2   Close the form in Run mode to return to the form in Design mode.

Set Action Properties

With form action properties, you specify how a form handles responses. Form actions are one of the most important aspects of Outlook because they enable users to respond to existing items in an Outlook folder.

Important   Throughout this book, the term *response* is used to encompass Reply, Forward, Reply to All, Reply to Folder, and all user-defined response actions.

With Outlook actions, you can specify:

- Whether a **Reply**, **Reply to All**, **Forward**, **Post to Folder**, or custom menu command appears on the Outlook **Actions** menu and the form **Actions** menu.

- Whether an action button appears on the form toolbar.

- The form to activate to enable the user to send or post a response.

- Whether the action opens the response form, sends the response immediately, or whether the user is prompted to open the response form.

▶ **To create actions**

- See "Create a New Action" in Chapter 4, "Design a Custom Application."

▶ **To set actions**

- See Chapter 7, "Actions." It provides a detailed look at how to set actions for Message and Post forms, and provides several detailed examples to help you understand how actions can be applied in applications.

Set Form Properties

With the form **Properties** page, you give the form a name and a description and you specify who to contact for questions about the form.

▶ **To set form properties**

- With the form open in Design mode, click the **Properties** page, as shown in Figure 5.23.

Figure 5.23   The form Properties page

Shows who is responsible for maintaining the form.

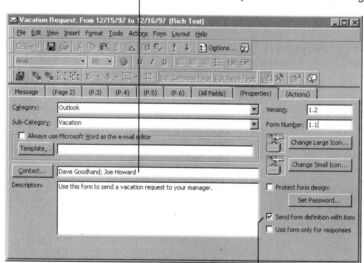

When checked, this causes the **Warning** dialog box to appear when the form is not available on the Outlook system, and VBScript is included in the form when the form is opened.

Category   Lets you create or specify a category for forms to help organize the forms in the **New Form** dialog box.

Sub-Category   Lets you create or specify a sub-category for the form.

Always Use Microsoft Word as the E-mail Editor   Lets you specify that Microsoft Word runs in the Message control of the form, so users have spell checking, thesaurus, and full formatting options that are available with Microsoft Word. The Word editing features are only available to recipients who use Word as their e-mail editor.

Template   Enables you to specify the Microsoft Word template that is used to format the text in the Message control of the form.

Contact   Click the **Contact** button to select the names of those people who are responsible for maintaining and upgrading the form. When the form is published, contact information shows in the form **Properties** page and the **Form Properties** dialog box selected from the **Form Manager**.

Description   Type a description for the form. The form description shows in the form **About** dialog box on the **Help** menu and also in the **Properties** dialog box for the form.

Change Large Icon   Click to change the icons for the form. Large icons appear in the form **Properties** dialog box.

Change Small Icon   Click to change the icons that appear in the Outlook folder to represent an item of the type created with the form.

Protect Form Design   Select this check box to have password protection for your form. This prevents other users from changing the form after you've published it.

Send Form Definition with Item   Specifies that the form definition is included with the item. By default, to speed opening the form, this check box is cleared. However, it may be selected when the form is published.

This option provides convenience and security for forms. It provides convenience because it enables you to send items to other users. Those users can then open the item in the form on their computer, even though the form is not installed on their Outlook system.

It provides a security measure for this reason: If a form contains VBScript and is not available on the user's Outlook system, and the **Send form definition with item** option is checked, the user sees a **Warning** dialog box, as shown earlier in this chapter in Figure 5.13. It prevents users from opening an unauthorized form that contains macros that can potentially delete or copy their mail, or send mail from their mailbox to another user.

After you create a Message form that is intended for general use, you submit it to an administrator for approval. The administrator checks the form for viruses and potentially harmful code. If the administrator approves the form, he clears the **Send form definition with item** check box, and then publishes the form in the Organizational Forms Library.

See Also For more information about form security and managing forms in your organization, see Chapter 13, "Distribute and Maintain Applications."

Use Form Only for Responses Certain forms, such as the Approve Vacation and Deny Vacation forms, are used solely for responding to existing items. As a result, these forms are opened only if a related item is first selected or opened. They also don't appear in the dialog boxes allowing you to compose a new form.

See Also For more information about this option and creating response forms, see Chapter 7, "Actions."

Publish the Form

When you finish designing a form, you publish it to a forms library. Optionally, you can make a backup copy of the form, although it is not required.

- When you publish a form, you register the form in a forms library and expose the form to the Outlook user interface. For example, after the form is published, the form menu commands and form name are visible in the Outlook user interface.

- When you make a backup copy of the form, you save the form definition as an .oft file.

Outlook forms are interpreted, not compiled. Therefore, there's no source code to worry about. And because only the form definition is saved, rather than the form and all of its associated controls, the file size is only about 10K on average.

Make a Backup Copy of the Form

Before you publish the form, you may want to make a backup copy of the form on your hard disk or on your organization's server. When you make a copy of the form, you save it as an .oft file in much the same manner as you save a Microsoft Word template.

▶ **To make a backup copy of a form**

1   With the form open, click **Save As** on the **File** menu.

2   In the **Save In** list box, select the default Outlook template folder, such as C:\Program Files\Microsoft Office\Templates.

3   In the **File name** text box, type a name for the form.

4   In the **Save as type** drop-down list box, select **Outlook Template (.oft)**.

5   Click **Save**.

▶ **To open your backup copy of a form**

1   Select **New** on the **File** menu, and then click **Choose Form**.

2   Click **Templates in File System** in the **Look In** drop-down list box, and then click on the form you'd like to open.

Publish the Form

When you publish a form, you accomplish three things:

- You make the form available to be run in Outlook.

- You register the form in the designated form library.

- You expose the form's properties, such as form name, description, and menu commands in Outlook.

About the Form Name and Message Class

When you click the **Publish Form As** button on the **Form Design** toolbar, and type a name in the **Display name** text box, Outlook automatically adds the name to the **Form name** text box and sets the message class for the form by appending the form name to IPM.*xxx*. For example, if the form is a Message form, and you type **Business Card Request** in the **Form name** text box, Outlook constructs the message class for the form by appending the form name to IPM.Note. Thus, the message class is IPM.Note.Business Card Request. The message class is the internal identifier of the form, and is used to locate and activate a form when an item associated with the form is created or opened.

▶ **To specify the form name**

1   On the **Form Design** toolbar, click **Publish Form As**.

2   Type a name in the **Form name** text box.

▶ **To change the message class**

- In the **Form Name** text box, change the name of the form.

    The **Message class** is automatically updated.

Publish to a Forms Library

When you publish a form, you publish it to a forms library. After the form is published in a library, you can then open the form to compose, submit, and read items in a folder. Where you publish the form determines how the form will be available to other users. The following table provides a description of the forms libraries where you can publish forms.

Important   When publishing and naming forms, the form names should be unique, or unpredictable results may occur. Also, if the form is published in more than one forms library and you make changes to the form, the form must be updated in all the forms libraries in which it is published, unless the form definition is sent with the item. To update forms libraries, use the Forms Manager. To synchronize offline forms libraries, use **Synchronize** on the **Tools** menu. For more information, see the sections "Forms Manager" and "How folders are synchronized" in Chapter 13, "Distribute and Maintain Applications."

Location	Description	Advantage
Organizational Forms Library	A public container of forms that is located on a server. It is not connected with a folder.	Allows forms to be used by anyone who has access to the server.
Personal Forms Library	A private container of forms. It is not connected with a folder.	Allows forms to be available for personal use. Also handy for designing and testing forms.
Public Folders Forms Library	A public container of forms. Each folder has its own forms library. The container exists in the folder on server.	Allows forms to be used by anyone who has access to the server and has permissions to use the folder.
Personal Folders Forms Library (in a .pst file)	A private container of forms. Each folder has its own forms library attached. Located on the local hard disk drive.	Allows forms to be organized in a personal folder. Also enables designers to distribute a large number of forms and folders by using a .pst personal folder file.
Offline Folder Forms Library (in an .ost file)	A private container of forms. Each folder has its own forms library attached. Synchronized manually with server.	Allows forms to be organized in a personal folder. Users in remote locations can use forms as if they were connected directly to the server. Folders can then be synchronized between the local hard disk and the server.

See Also   For more information on updating or synchronizing forms published in multiple locations, see Chapter 8, "Folders." For more information on publishing and distributing forms see Chapter 13, "Distribute and Maintain Applications."

▶ **To publish a form**

1 In Design mode, select **Forms** on the **Tools** menu, and then click **Publish Form As**.

2 In the **Display name** text box and **Form name** text box, type the name for the form.

3 To change the location (library) where the form is stored, click **Look In**, and then do one of the following:

   • To publish a form in the Organizational Forms Library, click **Organizational Forms Library** in the **Look in** drop-down list box, and then click **OK**.

   • To publish a form in the Personal Forms Library, click **Personal Forms Library** in the **Look in** drop-down list box, and then click **OK**.

   • To publish a form in a Public or Personal folder, choose **Outlook Folders**, click the **Browse** button, select the folder in the **Look in** drop-down list box, and then click **OK**.

4 Click **Publish**.

5 In the message box, choose **No** for most cases where users have access to the same libraries as you. Choose **Yes** if this form will be sent to someone outside your system, who needs the definition to view the form.

See Also   For more information about how to make forms available to users, see Chapter 13, "Distribute and Maintain Applications."

Test and Release the Form

After you publish the form, you need to test it to make sure it works as expected.

▶ **To test a Message form in the Personal or Organizational Forms Library**

1 On the Folder List, click **Inbox**.

2 On the Outlook **Tools** menu, select **Forms** and then click **Choose Form**.

3 Select the forms library from the **Look in** drop-down list box, and double-click it.

4 Fill out the form options, and then send the form to yourself.

5 When the item arrives in your Inbox, double-click it to make sure the **Read** page of the form works as expected.

▶ **To test a Post form in a forms library in a folder**

1   In the Folder List, click the folder that contains the form you want to test.

2   On the Outlook **Actions** menu, click the form's associated menu command to open the form.

3   Fill out the form options, and then click **Post**.

4   After the item is posted in the folder, double-click it to open it and make sure the **Read** page of the form works as expected.

Release the Form

See Also   For more information about releasing forms, see Chapter 13, "Distribute and Maintain Applications."

CHAPTER 6

Controls, Fields, and Properties

In This Chapter

Set Control Display Properties   140

Layer Controls   143

Set Advanced Control Properties   143

Bind a Control to an Existing Field   144

Create User-Defined Fields   146

Set Initial Field Values   156

Validate and Restrict Data   156

Set Field-Specific Properties   160

Set Control-Specific Properties   167

In this chapter, you'll cover the fundamental skills and information you need to effectively use controls, fields, and properties on a form. In addition, you'll take a look at the unique features of each commonly used control and then get some strategies for implementing these controls and fields in an application.

Specifically, we'll cover how to:

Set display properties for controls   including foreground and background colors.

Set advanced properties   such as the **BackStyle**, **BorderStyle**, **ControlTipText**, and **WordWrap** properties for a control.

Create combination fields   that show the results of combined text strings.

Create formula fields   that automatically perform calculations and show the results in the field. For example, for a Grand Total field, you can create a formula to show the result of adding the value of the Total field to the value of the SubTotal field.

Set initial values   in a field to determine the value that appears in the field when the form first appears at run time.

Validate and restrict information in a field and learn how to create validation formulas that Microsoft Outlook checks before it closes the form. For example, you can create a validation formula that shows a message box if a value in a field exceeds a certain number.

Use the To, Subject, and Message fields and see how to preaddress a form by setting the initial value of a To field. You will also take a look at how the Subject field works, and how to insert files, items, and hyperlinks to World Wide Web pages in the Message field.

Set control-specific properties and learn about creating check boxes, how to bind option buttons to a field, and how to create list boxes so users can select multiple values.

Set Control Display Properties

Each control, regardless of whether it is bound to a field or not, has a unique set of display properties that you can change. With display properties, you can change the name of the control, specify its exact position on the form, set its foreground or background color, and specify settings such as read-only or multi-line, as shown in Figure 6.1.

Since the Vacation Request form is the example used in this chapter, select the Vacation Request folder from the Folder List. Click the **Actions** menu, and choose the Vacation Request form from those listed at the bottom of the menu.

▶ **To view the display properties for a control on the Vacation Request form**

1 In Design mode, right-click the control, and then click **Properties** on the shortcut menu.

2 Click the **Display** tab.

Figure 6.1   Display properties for the StartDate TextBox control

— Name of the control.

— Shows an example of the font and foreground and background color of the control.

— Specifies that the control resizes when the form is resized.

— Enables users to enter multiple lines of text in a control.

Tip   When you add a control to a form, the control is given a default name such as TextBox1, Label1, and so on. If you'll be referencing the control in Microsoft Visual Basic Scripting Edition (VBScript) procedures for the form, it's a good idea to give the control a unique name, as shown in Figure 6.1.

Change Foreground and Background Colors

The background or foreground color for a control corresponds to the color specified for the component on the **Appearance** tab of the Display icon in Microsoft Windows® Control Panel. As shown earlier in Figure 6.1, the foreground color of the StartDate control is set to Window Text, so the color of the foreground text in the StartDate control matches the color of Window text in the **Display Properties** dialog box in Windows. Similarly, the background color of the StartDate control matches the color defined for Window. If you have Window defined as green on your system, the background of the control is green.

▶ **To set foreground and background colors for a control**

1   Right-click the control, and then click **Properties**.

2   Click the **Display** tab.

3   In the **Foreground color** or **Background color** drop-down list box, click the component that you wish to map the control to.

The Vacation Request form, as shown in Figure 6.2, provides a good example of how color effects can be achieved on a form. The background color for the Label8 control is set to Button Shadow, so it will have a dark gray color for almost all users. Also, many of the controls on the form have a white background. In this case, the background color is set to Window, which maps to white in Windows Control Panel. Notice that most of the controls actually sit on top of the Label8 control. Controls are layered in Design mode, using **Bring to Front** and **Send to Back** options from the icons in the **Form Design** toolbar. For this form, the Label8 control is sent to the back layer of the page.

Figure 6.2   The Vacation Request form

The StartDate and
EndDate controls sit on
top of the Label8 control. ⌐

┌ The background color of the Label8
  control is set to Button Shadow.

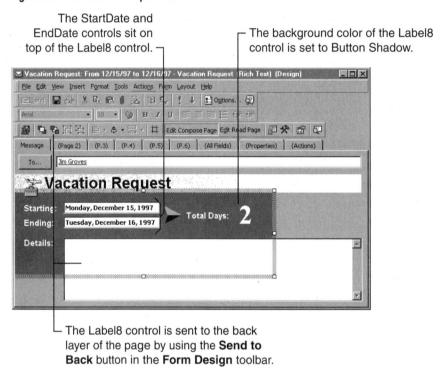

└ The Label8 control is sent to the back
  layer of the page by using the **Send to
  Back** button in the **Form Design** toolbar.

Tip   Generally, you can make a dark gray background for a control by setting the background color to Button Shadow. You can make the background color white by setting the background color to Window.

Layer Controls

The Label8 control on the Vacation Request form provides a good example of how you can layer controls on a form. As shown earlier in Figure 6.2, several controls, such as StartDate and EndDate, are located on top of the Label8 control. This is done by using the **Send to Back** and **Bring to Front** buttons on the **Form Design** toolbar. With these buttons, you can layer controls by bringing them to the front layer or sending them to the back layer.

▶ **To send a control to a back layer**

- Click the control, and then click the **Send to Back** button on the **Form Design** toolbar, or select **Order** from the **Layout** menu.

▶ **To bring a control to a front layer**

- Click the control, and then click the **Bring to Front** button on the **Form Design** toolbar, or select **Order** from the **Layout** menu.

See Also   For more information about setting control display properties, see "Set Control-Specific Properties" later in this chapter.

Set Advanced Control Properties

The **Advanced Properties** window provides even more capabilities for customizing a control. For example, with the **Advanced Properties** window, you can:

- Define a transparent background for a control.
- Specify the **ControlTipText** property—the text that appears when the user moves the pointer over the control.
- Specify if the control has the **WordWrap** property turned on.
- Specify the **BorderStyle** property for the control.

▶ **To open the Advanced Properties window**

- Right-click the control, and then click **Advanced Properties** on the shortcut menu.

In the example shown in Figure 6.3, the Label2 control sits on top of the textured Image1 control. However, the Label2 text appears to be part of the image because the Label2 **BackStyle** property is set to Transparent. The **BackStyle** property for a control can only be set in the **Advanced Properties** dialog box.

Figure 6.3   The BackStyle property of the Label2 control is set to Transparent so the control appears to be part of the Image1 control behind it.

The textured Image1 control
sits on the back layer.

The Label2 control has a transparent background
and sits on top of the Image1 control.

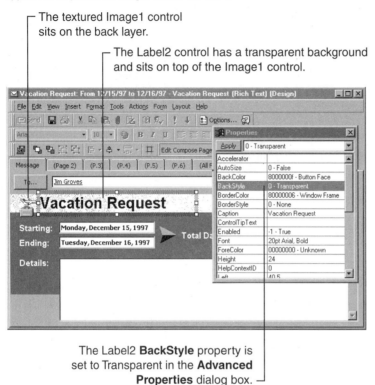

The Label2 **BackStyle** property is
set to Transparent in the **Advanced
Properties** dialog box.

Bind a Control to an Existing Field

In many cases, you can bind a control to an existing field, rather than creating a new field. For example, you can bind a control to a field supplied by Outlook, or you can bind a control to an existing user-defined field. You can view a list of available fields in the field list in the **Properties** dialog box, as shown in Figure 6.4.

Figure 6.4   The field set and field list in the Properties dialog box

— Click this button to view
  available field sets.

— The field list shows the
  fields you can select.

Properties [?][X]

Display | Value | Validation

Field and Format of Control

[Choose Field ▼] [   ] [New...]

Frequently-used fields	▶	Attachment
Address fields	▶	Categories
Date/Time fields	▶	Cc
All Mail fields	▶	Conversation
User-defined fields in Inbox	▶	Created
Contact	▶	Do Not AutoArchive
Forms...		Download State

Due By
Flag Status
Follow Up Flag
From
Icon
Importance
Junk E-mail Type
Read
Received
Sensitivity
Sent
Size
Subject
To

— When creating a message form, all
  user-defined fields are created in the
  Inbox, regardless of the active folder.

[ ] Set the initial value of this field

○ Calculate this formula when
○ Calculate this formula autom

[OK]

— Click **Forms** to add a new
  set of fields to a list.

▶ **To bind a control to an existing field**

1   Right-click the control you want to define a field for, and then click **Properties** on
    the shortcut menu.

2   Click the **Value** tab.

3   Click **Choose Field**, point to the set of fields you want, and then click the field.

The sets of fields available in the field list in the **Properties** dialog box differ for each
type of form. For example, if you create a Message form, the field list does not show
the field categories for built-in forms, such as All Contact fields, All Appointment
fields, and All Task fields. In addition, when creating a Message form, all user-defined
fields are created in the Inbox, regardless of the active folder.

The following table shows the field sets that are available for each type of form, and
shows where the user-defined fields are created for the form. It also shows if the **Field
Chooser** is available for the form type.

Form type	Available field categories	User-defined fields are created in	Field Chooser available
Message	Field sets from built-in forms, such as Appointment, are not available	Inbox	Yes
Post	All	Active folder	Yes
Office Document	N/A	N/A	N/A
Built-in	All	Active folder	Yes

Important   For Office Document forms, you must create fields in the document itself using the application (Microsoft Word, Microsoft Excel, or Microsoft PowerPoint) **Forms** toolbar. For example, for a Word document, you use the Word **Forms** toolbar to add fields directly to the document.

See Also   For more information about creating fields or properties in an Office 97 document, see the Help for the specific application.

Create User-Defined Fields

With Outlook, there are two ways to create fields. You can use the **Field Chooser**, which offers the advantage of automatically creating and positioning controls for you when you drag the field on the form. Or you can use the **Properties** dialog box, which enables you to edit field properties. In this section, we cover using the **Properties** dialog box to create new user-defined fields. Before you can create a field using the **Properties** dialog box, however, you must first select a control on the form that you want to bind the field to.

Note: When creating a Message form, all user-defined fields are created in the Inbox, regardless of the active folder.

▶ **To create a user-defined field**

1   Right-click the control you want to define a field for, and then click **Properties** on the shortcut menu.

2   Click the **Value** tab.

3   Click **New**.

4   In the **Name** text box, type a name for the field.

5   In the **Type** drop-down list box, click a field type.

6   In the **Format** drop-down list box, click a format, as shown in Figure 6.5.

Figure 6.5   You can create user-defined fields from the Properties dialog box.

Click here to create a user-defined field and bind it to a control.

Click here to select the **Type** of the field.

Click here to select the **Format** for the field and see an example of how the format presents data.

Note   After you create a field, you cannot change its type. Rather, you must create a new field with a different name with the desired properties. You can then delete the old field. To delete a field, use the **Field Chooser**.

Specify Field Type

When you create a new field, you use the **Type** property to specify the type of data stored in a field in the item. The following table describes the uses for the various field types.

Field types	Description
Text	Text or numbers that don't require calculations, such as phone numbers.
Number	Numeric data used in mathematical calculations, with the exception of currency.
Percent	Numeric data as a percentage.
Currency	Numeric data as currency or mathematical calculations that involve money.
Yes/No	Fields that are bound to a CheckBox control.
Date/Time	Date and time data.
Duration	Use to show time expired. This control has no inherent intelligence built in.
Keywords	Fields that are bound to a ListBox control from which the user can select multiple values.
Combination	Fields that show the result of combined text strings. Combination fields are read-only.
Formula	Fields that show the result of a formula. For example, a Totals field might contain a formula that multiplies the value of the Hours field by the Hourly Rate field. Formula fields are read-only.
Integer	Nondecimal numeric data.

Specify Field Formats

Field formats determine how information is saved and shown in a control. Each field type has a different set of formats that you can choose from. Each format in the field **Format** drop-down list box, as shown earlier in Figure 6.5, includes an example of how the format presents information in the control.

Create Combination Fields

With Combination fields, you can create a formula for a field that combines string values from other fields and shows the results in the control bound to the field. This section describes the general procedure for creating Combination fields, and then provides several examples of the types of Combination fields you can create.

▶ **To create a Combination field**

1 Right-click the control that you want to bind to a Combination field, and then click **Properties** on the shortcut menu.

2 Click the **Value** tab.

3 Click **New**.

4 In the **Name** text box, type a name for the field.

5 In the **Type** drop-down list box, click **Combination**.

6 Click **Edit**.

7 Do one of the following:

  • Click **Joining fields and any text fragments to each other** to show combined string values in the field.

  • Click **Showing only the first non-empty field, ignoring subsequent ones** if you want only the first value entered in the specified fields to show in the Combination field.

8 Type text in the **Formula** text box or click **Field** to specify the fields you want inserted in the expression. Click **OK**.

9 To make the formula update automatically, select the **Calculate this formula automatically** button on the **Value** page.

Note   The **Showing only the first non-empty field, ignoring subsequent ones** option is generally used in the context of folder fields. For example, when you have a folder that contains different types of items, one type of item may have the user name in the Author field, while another type of item might have the user name in the From field. To combine these two field values into one field in the folder, you can use the **Showing only the first non-empty field, ignoring subsequent ones** option.

Combine Field Strings

With the Visual Basic Expression Service provided with Outlook, you can easily build expressions for Combination fields without worrying about concatenating values. As shown in Figure 6.6, the FullName control shows the combined values from the FirstName and LastName fields.

Figure 6.6 The formula for the FullName field combines the values from the FirstName and LastName fields and shows the results in the FullName control. Notice the field is read-only.

The formula for the FullName field combines the values of the FirstName and LastName fields.

The FullName control, bound to the FullName field, shows the results of the formula.

Combine Field Value Strings with Text Fragments

Quite often, you combine text fragments that you type into the **Formula** text box with string values from other fields. In the following example, the Combination field named UserName is located on the **Read** page of a form. At run time, when the user opens a submitted item, the value of the From field is combined with the User Name: fragment to create the result shown in Figure 6.7.

Figure 6.7   The User Name: [From] formula automatically combines the text fragment with the value in the From field.

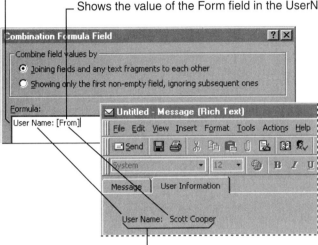

Shows the User Name: text fragment in the UserName field.

Shows the value of the Form field in the UserName field.

The UserName control is bound to the UserName field in the form. Notice the field is read-only.

Combine Field Values by Showing Only the First Non-Empty Field

In general, this option makes more sense when applied to a folder than when applied to a form. In fact, it is described in detail in Chapter 8, "Folders." However, it can have some use when applied to a form. For example, let's assume a folder contains items created with a form that has a variety of phone number fields, such as home phone, car phone, business phone, and fax number. Also assume that you want to create a new form that consolidates the numbers so that only the primary phone number shows on the form. To do this, you can create a Combination field named Primary Phone that combines the phone numbers, but only displays the value in the first non-empty phone field in the item.

See Also   For more information about using Combination fields in folders, see Chapter 8, "Folders."

Create Formula Fields

With Formula fields, you can create formulas that automatically calculate values and show the result in a control. Here are a few examples:

- For a Time Card form, you can create a formula for a field that totals the hours for the day, and then totals the hours for the week and shows the results in the Totals field.

- For the sample While You Were Out form supplied in Outlook, the Subject field contains a formula that combines the values from several fields into a message that shows in the Subject field.

- For the Vacation Request form supplied in Outlook, the TotalDays field contains a formula that automatically calculates the number of vacation days by finding the difference between the Starting date and the Ending date.

- For an Invoice form, you can create a Totals field that contains a formula to show the result of the number of hours multiplied by the hourly rate.

Although you can create a Formula field using the **Type** property, it's just as easy to create a formula for a Text, Number, or Currency field. As a result, there is no compelling reason to create a Formula field. Instead, it's preferable to create the type of field you want, and then create the formula for the field. As you'll see in the examples in this section, the fields include formulas, but are not defined as Formula fields.

▶ **To create a Formula field when you create the field**

1 In Design mode, right-click the control you want to bind to the Formula field, and then click **Properties** on the shortcut menu.

2 Click the **Value** tab.

3 Click **New**.

4 In the **Name** text box, type a name for the field.

5 In the **Type** drop-down list box, click the type of field you want. You do not have to select **Formula**. You can select any type of field—Currency, Number, Date/Time—and then click **OK**.

6 On the **Value** page, click **Edit**.

7 In the **Formula** text box, type in the formula or use the **Field** or **Function** buttons to insert the field or function you want. Some samples follow.

Specify That the Field Automatically Calculates the Results

After you create the formula for the field, you must set the **Calculate this formula automatically** option so the field is updated when field values referenced in the formula are changed. For example, for the Invoice form shown in Figure 6.8, the TOTAL field automatically updates when the values in the Hours or Hourly Rate controls change.

▶ **To specify that the field automatically calculates the result**

1 Right-click the control that you want to create a formula for, and then click **Properties** on the shortcut menu.

2 On the **Value** page, select the **Set the initial value of this field to** check box.

3 Click **Calculate this formula automatically**.

4 To make the control read-only, click the **Display** tab, and then select the **Read only** check box.

Calculate Totals

In Figure 6.8, the TOTAL field is a formula field that shows the result of the expression:

```
[Hours] * [Hourly Rate]
```

This expression multiplies the number of hours in the Hours field by the value in the Hourly Rate field and shows the result in the TOTAL field.

Figure 6.8   The TOTAL field automatically multiplies the hours by the hourly rate and shows the results.

Build Text Strings

The While You Were Out form, as shown in Figure 6.9, provides an example of a Formula field that shows the results of combined values in the Subject field, which is not visible on the form at run time. When the While You Were Out item is created, the values from the You Received and Please Contact fields are combined with the You Received text fragment to create the value in the Subject field. This is the value that appears in the user's Inbox when they receive the message.

Figure 6.9   The While You Were Out form. The Subject field is hidden on the form at run time.

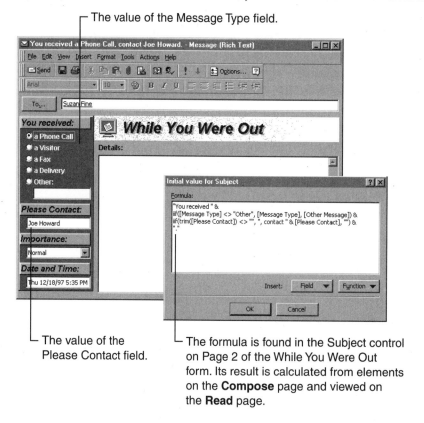

The value of the Message Type field.

The value of the Please Contact field.

The formula is found in the Subject control on Page 2 of the While You Were Out form. Its result is calculated from elements on the **Compose** page and viewed on the **Read** page.

When the item arrives in the user's Inbox, the Subject field shows the following result:

You received a Phone Call, contact Joe Howard.

In the formula, as shown earlier in Figure 6.9, the **IIf** function evaluates the expression and returns one of two parts, based on whether the expression evaluates as True or False. For example, if the Message Type field value is not Other, then the Subject field shows the value of the Message Type field (a Phone Call). In the next line, if the Please Contact field is not empty, then the value of the Please Contact field is added to the Subject field.

For more information, see Outlook Customization and Forms Help.

Calculate Date Differences

On the Vacation Request Form, as shown in Figure 6.10, the Total Days field contains a formula that automatically calculates the difference between the Starting and Ending fields and shows the result.

Figure 6.10 The Total Days field calculates the difference between the StartDate and EndDate fields and adds 1.

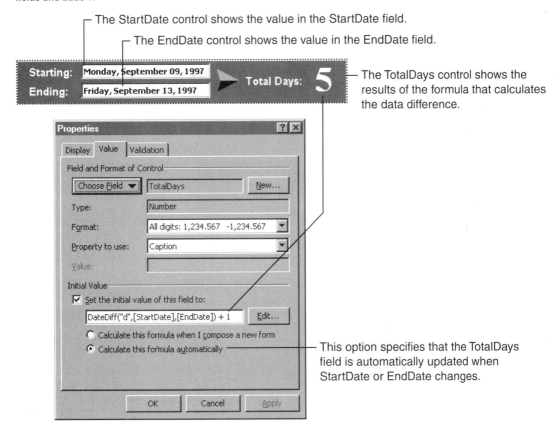

The StartDate control shows the value in the StartDate field.

The EndDate control shows the value in the EndDate field.

The TotalDays control shows the results of the formula that calculates the data difference.

This option specifies that the TotalDays field is automatically updated when StartDate or EndDate changes.

Tip The StartDate and EndDate fields in the Vacation Request form offer Microsoft IntelliSense®. For example, if you enter "Next Tuesday" into the EndDate field, Outlook translates "Next Tuesday" into the correct date.

Set Initial Field Values

When you create an initial value for a field, you specify the values that are available in the field when the user opens the form to create a new item. With Outlook, the way the initial value is set is handled somewhat differently based on the control to which the field is bound. As a result, we'll cover the general concept of initial values in this section, and then cover how to set the initial value for each control separately.

Here are a few examples of why you set initial values for fields:

- To set the default values in Label, TextBox, ComboBox, ListBox, CheckBox, and OptionButton controls.

- To set the initial value of the Subject field of a form to summarize the content of the form. For example, for an Art Approval form, you can set the initial value of the Subject field to "Art Approval".

- To set the initial value of the To field on a Message form to preaddress the form. For example, for an Employee Feedback form, you can preaddress the To field to an Employee Feedback public folder so all responses are automatically routed to that folder.

The following table lists the sections in this chapter that explain how to set initial values for the control to which the field is bound. Therefore, each control contains a separate section on how to set the initial value.

To set the initial value for a	See later in this chapter
To field	"To Field"
Subject field	"Subject Field"
Message field	"Message Field"
Field bound to a Label control	"Label Controls"
Field bound to a TextBox control	"TextBox Controls"
Field bound to an OptionButton control	"OptionButton Controls"
Field bound to a CheckBox control	"CheckBox Controls"
Field bound to a ComboBox control	"ComboBox Controls"
Field bound to a ListBox control	"ListBox Controls"

Validate and Restrict Data

Outlook provides a couple ways to validate and control how information is entered into a form.

- At the simplest level, you can specify that a value is required for a field. As a result, if the user tries to submit or save the item and no value is in the field, the user sees a message saying a value is required in the field.

- You can create a validation formula for a field. If the field validation fails, the users see a message box showing the types of values allowed in the field.

Specify That a Value Is Required for a Field

Many forms contain Text fields in which the user is required to enter information. For example, on the Business Card Request form, as shown in Figure 6.11, the Name field requires a value. If a value is not entered in the Name field when the user attempts to send the form, Outlook shows a message box that tells the user that a field on the form requires a value.

Figure 6.11   On the Business Card Request form, a value is required in the Name field. If no value is entered, users see a message when they attempt to send the item.

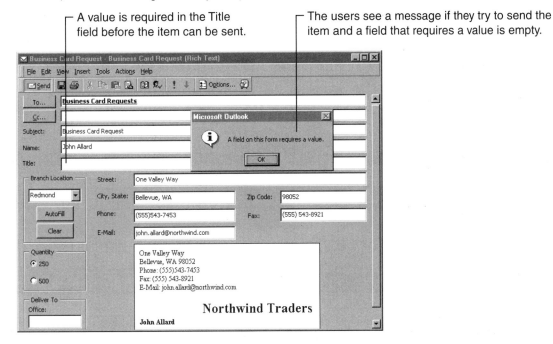

┌ A value is required in the Title
field before the item can be sent.

┌ The users see a message if they try to send the
item and a field that requires a value is empty.

▶ **To specify that a value is required for a Text field**

1 Right-click the control that is bound to the field, and then click **Properties** on the shortcut menu.

2 Click the **Validation** tab.

3 Select the **A value is required for this field** check box.

Important   Many of the Outlook field types automatically supply a value in the field by default. For example, the Date field automatically has the value "None" by default. For field types such as Date, Currency, and Number that automatically supply a value, you must create a formula or use a script to validate that the field contains the specified information.

Create Validation Formulas

Outlook performs field validation when the user attempts to save, send, or post an item. In addition, Outlook performs field validation when the user attempts to close a form. With validation formulas, you can limit the type of information that can be saved to the item. For example, you can define:

```
>=10 And <=100
```

as the validation formula for a Number field that accepts only values from 10 to 100. When users attempt to submit or save the item, they see a message only if the number entered in the field does not fall within the range of 10 to 100.

Tip If you want to validate the field immediately after the user enters information in the field, you can do so using the PropertyChange event or CustomPropertyChange event in Visual Basic Scripting Edition. For more information, see Chapter 9, "Use Visual Basic Scripting Edition with Outlook." Samples are also given in "The PropertyChange Event" or "The CustomPropertyChange Event" in Chapter 11, "The Help Desk Application."

▶ To create a validation formula

1 Right-click the control you want to create a validation expression for, and then click **Properties** on the shortcut menu.

2 Click the **Validation** tab, and then under **Validation Formula**, click the **Edit** button.

3 Type the validation formula or use the **Field** or **Function** button to build the formula. Click **OK.**

4 In the **Display this message if the validation fails** text box, type the message you want to appear in the message box that the user sees if the validation fails.

Formulas That Validate Amounts

For many forms, you can create validation formulas for fields to check if a value in the field is more or less than a specified value. For example, in Figure 6.12, the validation formula for the Amount field in the Charity Donation form specifies that the value in the field must be at least one dollar. If the user enters a value less than one dollar in the Amount field, a message appears.

Figure 6.12   The Amount field contains a value that is less than one dollar. When the user attempts to send the form, a message box appears indicating what is acceptable in the field.

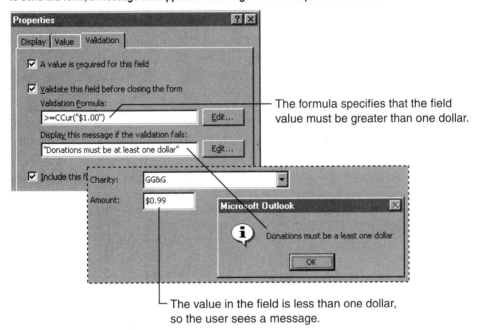

The formula specifies that the field value must be greater than one dollar.

The value in the field is less than one dollar, so the user sees a message.

See Also   Note that the **CCur** function (Currency Conversion) is used in the validation formula. For more information on the **CCur** function, see Outlook Customization and Forms Help.

Validation Formulas That Compare One Field Value with Another

In some cases, you might want to create a validation formula that compares one field value against another field value. For example, for the Vacation Request form as shown in Figure 6.13, the value of the StartDate field is compared to the value of the EndDate field to make sure the EndDate value falls after the StartDate value.

Figure 6.13   The validation formula for the Amount field specifies that the validation passes if the value is equal to or greater than one day.

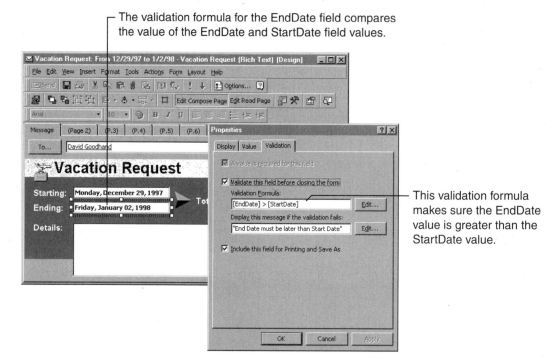

The validation formula for the EndDate field compares the value of the EndDate and StartDate field values.

This validation formula makes sure the EndDate value is greater than the StartDate value.

Set Field-Specific Properties

The **Message** page of standard Message and Post forms contains three Outlook-supplied fields that provide fundamental functionality on the form. These fields are:

To field   Used to address the form.

Subject field   Used to summarize the message. The text in the Subject field appears in the title bar of the form window. The value in the Subject field also sets the value of the Conversation field in the item.

Message field Used to enter text or insert files, items, or objects or insert shortcuts to them.

This section describes how the To, Subject, and Message fields work, and then describes strategies for effectively using these fields in a form.

To Field

With Outlook, you can preaddress forms by setting the initial value of the To field. Preaddressing a form is much like providing a self-addressed envelope. Because the address is already provided on the form, the user just fills in the form and clicks the **Send** button.

Preaddress a Form to a Distribution List or Person

In some cases, you want to preaddress a Message form to a distribution list or to a user. For example, you want to preaddress a form such as a Weekly Schedule form to a distribution list. In addition, you may want to preaddress a Reply form so the item created with the form is sent to your Inbox.

▶ **To set the initial value of the To field**

1   On the Outlook **Actions** menu, click **New Mail Message**.

2   On the form, click the **To** button.

3   Double-click the desired names or distribution list name to select recipients, and then click **OK**.

If the distribution list you want to specify does not exist, you must ask your administrator to create it. If you create a Personal Distribution List or use an existing Personal Distribution List, the form will work correctly only on your computer.

4   On the **Tools** menu, select **Forms**, and then click **Design This Form** to switch to Design mode.

5   Make additional modifications to your form, then save and exit.

Preaddress a Form to a Folder

In some cases, you might want to preaddress a form to a folder. For example, the Business Card Request form, as shown in Figure 6.14, can be opened from the Organizational Forms Library. However, the form is preaddressed to the Business Card Request folder, so the user can automatically submit the item simply by clicking the **Send** button.

Figure 6.14   The Business Card Request form is preaddressed to the Business Card Request folder.

The user simply clicks the **Send** button to send the item to the folder.

The To field is preaddressed to the Business Card Requests folder.

Before you can preaddress a form to a folder, the folder address must exist in the Global Address Book or your Personal Address Book. If the folder address does not exist in the Global Address Book, you can ask your administrator to make the folder address available in the Global Address book or you can publish the folder address to your Personal Address Book.

Important   To publish a folder address in your Personal Address Book, the folder must be located in Public Folders.

▶ **To add a folder address to your Personal Address Book**

1 In the Folder List, right-click the folder, and then click **Properties** on the shortcut menu.

2 Click the **Administration** tab. (You will see the **Summary** tab if you do not have owner permissions to modify this folder.)

3 Click **Personal Address Book** to add this item to your Personal Address Book.

▶ **To preaddress the To field to a folder**

1 On the Outlook **Actions** menu, click **New Mail Message**.

2 On the Message form, click the **To** button.

3 In the **Show Names from the** drop-down list box, click **Personal Address Book**.

4 Double-click the folder name in the list, and then click **OK**. The folder name should appear in the To field.

5 On the **Tools** menu, select **Forms**, and then click **Design This Form** to switch to Design mode.

6 Modify the form as desired, then save and exit.

See Also   For more information, see "Add Folder Address to Personal Address Book" in Chapter 8, "Folders."

Subject Field

The Subject field provides several important functions on a form:

- It summarizes the information in the item.
- It sets the value of the Conversation field. The Conversation field is the field used to create threaded conversations in views.
- The value in the Subject field appears in the title bar of the window.

Figure 6.15   Shows how the Subject field functions in the New Product Idea form

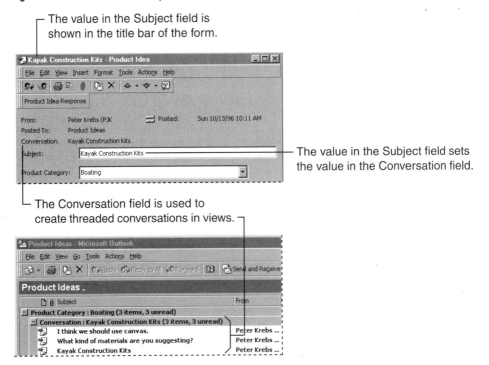

The value in the Subject field is shown in the title bar of the form.

The value in the Subject field sets the value in the Conversation field.

The Conversation field is used to create threaded conversations in views.

Set the Initial Value of the Subject Field

In some cases, you may want to set the initial value of the Subject field. For example, for single-purpose forms such as the Business Card Request form, you can set the initial value of the Subject field to "Business Card Request."

▶ **To specify the initial value of the Subject field**

1   Right-click the Subject control, and then click **Properties** on the shortcut menu.

2   Click the **Value** tab.

3   In the **Value** text box, type a value or click **Edit** to build an initial value formula for the Subject field.

Message Field

With the Message field, you can:

- Insert file attachments and shortcuts. For example, for a Copier Request form, the user can insert attached files into the Message field. If the files are too large to send through the Microsoft Exchange Server system, the user can insert shortcuts to the attached files instead. In addition, you, the designer, can insert files or shortcuts, and hyperlinks. For example, you may want to insert attachments for ReadMe files that explain how to use the form or application. Or you may want to insert a hyperlink to a file or folder address.

- Insert item attachments and shortcuts. For example, this enables users to insert messages from other users into the Message field.

- Insert a shortcut to a World Wide Web page. Recipients must have a Web browser installed on their computer to use the shortcuts.

- Insert linked or embedded objects. These objects can be Word documents, Microsoft Excel workbooks, and PowerPoint presentations.

Figure 6.16   At design time or run time, you can insert files, items, and objects in the Message field. You can also insert shortcuts.

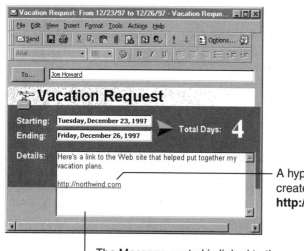

A hyperlink is automatically created when the user types **http://** in the Message control.

The Message control is linked to the Message field—the only field in which you can insert files, objects, items, and hyperlinks.

Each of these scenarios is covered in more detail in the following sections.

Restrictions and Rules for the Message Control Usage

When working with the Message field and control, there are a few guidelines you should be aware of:

- The Message control is automatically bound to the Message field.

- Each form can contain one Message control per page. For example, the **Compose** page of a form can contain a Message control and the **Read** page can contain a Message control.

- You cannot have a Message control on the **Message** page and a duplicate control on page 2 or following of the **Compose** or **Read** pages.

- If the form does not have the **Separate Read Layout** option selected on the **Form** menu for the page that contains the Message control, the form can only contain one Message control.

- The Message control is the only control on a form in which you or the user can insert files, items, or objects.

- The form must be in Run mode to enter information into the Message control.

▶ **To insert a file attachment or shortcut in the Message control**

1   In Run mode, click in the Message control where you want to insert the file attachment or shortcut.

2   On the **Insert** menu, click **File**.

3   Locate and click the file you want to insert.

4   Under **Insert as**, click an option.

5   Click **OK**.

▶ **To insert an item in the Message control**

1   In Run mode, click in the Message control where you want to insert the item.

2   On the **Insert** menu, click **Item**.

3   In the **Look in** drop-down list box, click the folder that contains the item you want to insert, and then click the item.

4   Under **Insert as**, click an option.

5   Click **OK**.

▶ **To insert a folder shortcut in the Message control**

- In Run mode, with the right mouse button, drag the folder from the Folder List to the Message control.

▶ **To insert a URL shortcut in the Message control**

1 First create the Universal Resource Locator (URL) shortcut using your Web browser.

2 In Run mode, drag the URL shortcut icon from desktop to the Message control.

▶ **To insert a hyperlink in the Message control**

1 In Run mode, type the hyperlink in the Message control. When you type **http://** or one of the supported protocols, the text is automatically underlined and the color is changed to blue. For example, to create a hyperlink to the Building Microsoft Outlook 98 Applications folder using the Outlook protocol, you specify the following hyperlink in the Message control:

<Outlook://Building Microsoft Outlook 98 Applications>

If the hyperlink includes spaces, you must enclose the entire address in angle brackets (< >).

Here are the supported protocols:

Protocol	Description
file://	A protocol used to open files on an intranet.
ftp://	File Transfer Protocol (FTP), the most common method used to transfer files over the Internet.
gopher://	Gopher protocol, by which hyperlinks and text are stored separately.
http://	Hypertext Transfer Protocol (HTTP).
https://	Hypertext Transfer Protocol Secure; a protocol designed to provide secure communications using HTTP over the Internet.
mailto://	A protocol used to send mail to an e-mail address. When the recipient clicks this hyperlink, a new message opens with the mailto e-mail address filled in.
news://	A protocol used to open an Internet newsgroup for recipients who are connected to an NNTP server.
nntp://	Network News Transfer Protocol: a protocol used to distribute, inquire, retrieve, and post Usenet articles over the Internet.
Outlook://	A protocol used to open an Outlook folder or an item or file in Outlook. This protocol is supported only in Outlook.
prospero://	A protocol used to organize Internet resources in your personal set of hyperlinks that go to information on remote file servers, for your personal virtual file system.
telnet://	The Internet standard protocol for logging on from remote locations.
wais://	Wide Area Information Servers Protocol: a distributed information system used to retrieve documents based on keywords you supply.

▶ **To insert an object in the Message control**

1   In Run mode, click in the Message control where you want to insert the object.

2   On the **Insert** menu, click **Object**.

3   In the **Insert Object** dialog box, click the **Create from File** button.

4   In the **Create from File** text box, type the name of the file that you want to link or embed in the Message control, or click **Browse** to select from a list.

- To create a linked object, select the **Link to file** check box.

- To show the object as an icon, select the **Display as icon** check box.

You can see the **Link to file** check box, when **Create from File** is selected.

Set Control-Specific Properties

Each of the controls in the Outlook **Control Toolbox** serves a unique purpose. As a result, the properties for each control are set in a slightly different way. This section covers setting the properties for the most commonly used controls.

▶ **To use controls**

1   Open the form in Design mode by selecting **Forms** on the **Tools** menu, and then clicking **Design This Form**.

2   Click the **Control Toolbox** button on the **Advanced** toolbar.

3   Drag the desired control to the form page.

4   Modify the control using the following guidelines.

Label Controls

Label controls can be used to show text on the page. As such, they are useful for company logos, address information, or a heading on a form page, as shown in Figure 6.17.

When to Bind a Label Control

Generally, you bind Label controls to fields when you want to save the value to the item. For example, in the Vacation Request form, as shown in Figure 6.17, the Total Days label is bound to the TotalDays field. In this way, the value in the field is saved to the item when the item is saved or sent. However, also notice that Label2 and Label5 are not bound. As a result, the value in the Vacation Request field is not saved to the item. Rather, it exists in the form definition and is recreated each time an instance of the form is activated.

Figure 6.17   Label controls on the Vacation Request form

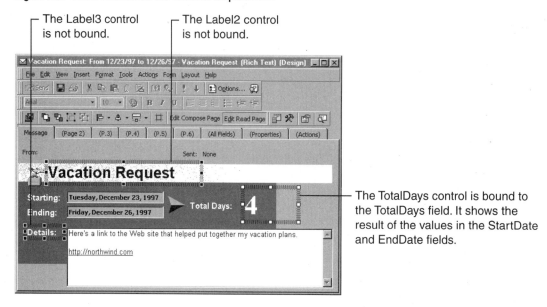

The Label3 control is not bound.

The Label2 control is not bound.

The TotalDays control is bound to the TotalDays field. It shows the result of the values in the StartDate and EndDate fields.

Set the Initial Value of a Label Control

In some cases, you may want to set the initial value of a Label control. For example, in the Vacation Request form, the TotalDays Label control on the **Compose** page contains a formula that automatically shows the result in the field.

▶ **To set the initial value of a Label control**

1   In Design mode, right-click the control, and then click **Properties** on the shortcut menu.

2   Click the **Value** tab, and then type the initial value in the **Initial Value** text box or click **Edit** to create an initial value formula.

   • To automatically calculate a formula, click **Calculate this formula automatically**.

   • To show the initial value in the Label control when the form is opened to create an item, click **Calculate this formula when I compose a new form**.

Note   Before you can set the initial value of a Label control, the control must be bound to a field. See also "Bind a Control to an Existing Field," earlier in this chapter.

TextBox Controls

Use TextBox controls on a form to let the user enter, edit, and view information, as shown in Figure 6.18. For example, you can place a TextBox control on a **Compose** page to let the user enter information and on the **Read** page to let the user view information.

Note In some cases, you may want to insert attachments, shortcuts, or hyperlinks. To do this, you must use the Message control. For more information about the Message control, see "Message Field" earlier in this chapter.

Figure 6.18   TextBox controls on the Business Card Request form

TextBox controls on the Business Card Request form.

The TextBox control has a variety of display properties that give you great flexibility in determining how the TextBox control looks and functions. For example, you can specify the **Multi-line** property so the user can enter more than one line of text in the control. Before you can specify the initial value for a control, it must be bound to a field.

▶ **To specify the Multi-line option for a TextBox control**

1 In Design mode, right-click the control, and then click **Properties** on the shortcut menu.

2 Click the **Display** tab, and then select the **Multi-line** check box.

Initial values for text boxes can be specified on the **Value** page of the **Properties** dialog box for that control.

▶ **To specify the initial value for a TextBox control**

• On the **Value** page, type a value in the **Initial Value** text box or click **Edit** to build an initial value formula for the field.

Frame Controls

Use the Frame control to contain controls that are logically related, as shown in Figure 6.19. Frame controls are often used to contain OptionButton controls, but they can also contain other controls such as CheckBox, ComboBox, Label, and TextBox controls.

Tip You can use the Frame control to create a line on the form. Set the height or width to 2, depending on whether it's a horizontal or vertical line.

Figure 6.19   The Frame control

Use the Frame control to group related controls on the form.

▶ **To add a Frame control**

- Drag the control from the **Control Toolbox** to the form.

Controls within the Frame can be easily removed by dragging and deleting.

▶ **To add or remove controls from a Frame control**

- To add a control, drag the control into the frame. To remove a control, drag it outside the borders of the frame, right-click the control, and then choose **Delete** on the shortcut menu.

▶ **To change the caption of the Frame control**

1   Right-click the border of the Frame control, and then click **Properties** on the shortcut menu.

2   In the **Caption** text box on the **Display** page, type a new caption for the Frame control.

OptionButton Controls

Use OptionButton controls on a form when you want to present a limited number of choices to the user. For example, on the Business Card Request form, OptionButton controls are used to enable the user to select the quantity of cards they want, as shown in Figure 6.20.

Figure 6.20   OptionButton controls on the Business Card Request form

OptionButton controls offer a choice
of mutually exclusive options.

▶ **To specify a caption for an OptionButton control**

1   In Design mode, drag the OptionButton control from the **Control Toolbox** to the form.

2   Click the OptionButton control. When the insertion pointer appears, type the caption for the control.

Set Value Properties for an OptionButton Control

For OptionButton controls that you want to group together, you bind the controls to the same field. For example, the OptionButton controls in the earlier Figure 6.20 are bound to the Quantity field. When you bind one OptionButton control to a field, all other option buttons in the group are automatically bound to the same field. Option buttons on a page that are not included in a container, such as a Frame or MultiPage control, are automatically grouped together. Option buttons in a container control are grouped with the option buttons in that container.

▶ **To bind an OptionButton control to a field**

1   Right-click the control, and then click **Properties** on the shortcut menu.

2   Click the **Value** tab.

3   Do one of the following:

• Click **New** to create a new field. You can create a Currency, Text, or Number field. Choose the type of field to match the data in the control. In this example, the Quantity field is a Number field.

• Click **Choose Field**, point to **User-defined fields in** *folder*, and then click the field that you want to bind the OptionButton control to. In this example, the OptionButton control is bound to the Quantity field. The *folder* name changes depending on which form is being designed.

When you bind one option button in the group to a field, all option buttons in the group are automatically bound to the same field.

Set the Value Property of Each Option Button Separately

After you bind the option buttons in a group to an existing field, you must set the **Value** property of each option button separately. The **Value** property is the value that is written to the field when the option button is selected at run time. As such, this value appears in folder views to represent the option button if it is selected in an item.

▶ **To set the Value property of an OptionButton control**

1 Right-click the OptionButton control that you want to set the **Value** property for, and then click **Properties** on the shortcut menu.

2 Click the **Value** tab.

3 In the **Initial Value** text box, type a value for the option button.

4 Click **OK**.

▶ **To set the initial value of an OptionButton control**

1 Right-click the OptionButton control that you want as the default button, when the form first appears at run time. Then, click **Advanced Properties** on the shortcut menu.

2 Click the **Value** cell, and then type **True**.

3 Click **Apply**, and then close the **Advanced Properties** window.

CheckBox Controls

Use CheckBox controls to give the user an On/Off or Yes/No choice, as shown in Figure 6.21. Because check boxes work independently of each other, the user can select any number of check boxes at one time.

Figure 6.21   A CheckBox control

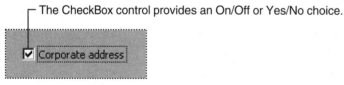

The CheckBox control provides an On/Off or Yes/No choice.

▶ **To bind a CheckBox control to a field**

1 Right-click the control, and then click **Properties** on the shortcut menu.

2 On the **Value** page, do one of the following:

• Click **New** to create a new field. You can create a Yes/No, On/Off, True/False, or Icon field. When you select a Yes/No field, the selected value appears in the cell in the folder. If you select Icon, the CheckBox icon appears in the folder as selected or cleared.

- Click **Choose Field**, point to **User-defined fields in** *folder*, and then choose the field that you want to bind the CheckBox control to. In this example, the CheckBox control in Figure 6.21 is bound to the Corporate field.

Note The CheckBox control must be bound to a Yes/No field type for the check box to operate properly.

▶ **To set the initial value of a CheckBox control**

1 Right-click the CheckBox control, and then click **Advanced Properties** on the shortcut menu.

2 Click the **Value** cell, and then type **True**.

3 Click **Apply**, and then close the **Advanced Properties** window.

ComboBox Controls

Use ComboBox controls so users can either choose a value from the list portion of the control or enter text in the edit box portion of the control, as shown in Figure 6.22. When working with the ComboBox control, you create the control, bind it to a field, and then specify the values for the items in the combo box list.

Figure 6.22 A Dropdown ComboBox control

▶ **To bind the ComboBox control to a field**

1 Right-click the control, and then click **Properties** on the shortcut menu.

2 On the **Value** page, do one of the following:

- To create a new field, click **New**.

- To bind the ComboBox control to an existing field, click **Choose Field**, point to **User-defined fields in** *folder,* and then click the field you want to bind the ComboBox control to.

▶ **To select a list type**

- In the **List Type** drop-down list box on the **Value** page, click either **Dropdown** or **Droplist**.

  Outlook provides two types of combo boxes that you can use.

List type	Description
Dropdown	. Users can either select a value from the list or type a value in the text box.
Droplist	Users must select a value from the list.

▶ **To add values to the combo box list**

- In the **Possible values** text box on the **Value** page, type the values you want to appear in the list. Separate each value with a semicolon (;), as shown in Figure 6.23.

▶ **To set the initial value of a ComboBox control**

- In the **Initial Value** text box on the **Value** page, type in the value that you want to appear in the edit box portion of the control when the form first appears, as shown in Figure 6.23.

Figure 6.23   A ComboBox control

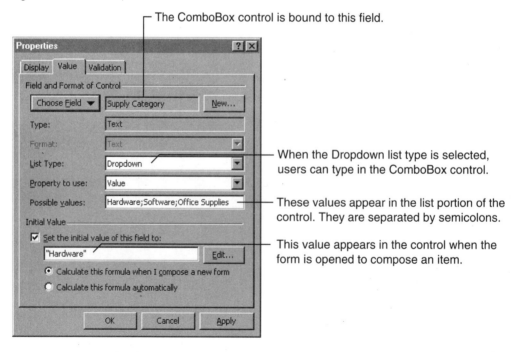

The ComboBox control is bound to this field.

When the Dropdown list type is selected, users can type in the ComboBox control.

These values appear in the list portion of the control. They are separated by semicolons.

This value appears in the control when the form is opened to compose an item.

ListBox Controls

Use ListBox controls to show a list of values from which the user can select one or many values. To create a list box that enables users to select more than one value, you must bind the ListBox control to a Keywords field. List boxes that are bound to Keywords fields have check boxes that enable users to select multiple values, as shown in Figure 6.24. When the user selects multiple values in the ListBox control, the values appear in the view in an Outlook folder as comma-separated values.

Figure 6.24   Values selected in a list box bound to a Keywords field are shown as comma-separated values in an Outlook view.

When a ListBox control is bound to a Keywords field, multiple values can be selected in the control.

Multiple values in a Keywords field appear as comma-seperated values in an Outlook view of the folder the user-defined field was created in. If this is in a **Message** form, the user-defined fields are created in the author's inbox.

▶ **To bind the ListBox control to a field**

1   In Design mode, right-click the control, and then click **Properties** on the shortcut menu.

2   On the **Value** page, do one of the following:

- To bind the ListBox control to an existing field, click **Choose Field**, point to **User-defined fields in** *folder*, and then click the field that you want to bind the ListBox control to. Items selected from this list will appear in the field this list is bound to.

- To create a Keywords field, click **New**, and then click **Keywords** in the **Type** drop-down list box. With Keywords you can place several values in a single field, depending on what the user selects. These values can be used to group items within a folder, similar to the Categories field of Task items.

- To create a ListBox control without a Keywords field, click **Text**, **Number**, **Currency**, or **Date/Time** in the **Type** drop-down list box, and then in the **Format** box, click a format. This information is transient and not stored in a field, but it could be accessed and acted on using VBScript For more information, see Chapter 9, "Use Visual Basic Scripting Edition with Outlook."

Note   Do not bind the ListBox control to a Yes/No, Combination, or Formula field.

▶ To add values to the ListBox control

- In the **Possible values** text box on the **Value** page, type the values you want to appear in the list. Separate each value with a semicolon, as shown in Figure 6.25.

▶ To set the initial value of a ListBox control

- In the **Initial Value** text box on the **Value** page, do one of the following:
  - To set the initial value to a single value, type the value that you want to appear as checked in the ListBox control when the user opens the form to compose an item, as shown in Figure 6.25.
  - To set the initial value to multiple values, type the values that you want to appear as checked in the ListBox control when the user opens the form to compose an item. Separate each value in the **Initial Value** text box with a semicolon.

Figure 6.25   The values that you want to appear in the list are typed in the Possible Values text box.

The ListBox control is bound to Platforms, a Keywords field type.

Multiple values appear as check boxes in the ListBox control.

This value is checked in the ListBox control when the user opens the form to compose an item.

CommandButton Controls

The CommandButton control, when clicked, triggers the Click event. As such, you can write VBScript Click event procedures in the Script Editor for each CommandButton control, as shown in Figure 6.26.

Important   Outlook only supports the Click event for controls.

Figure 6.26   CommandButton controls on the Business Card Request form

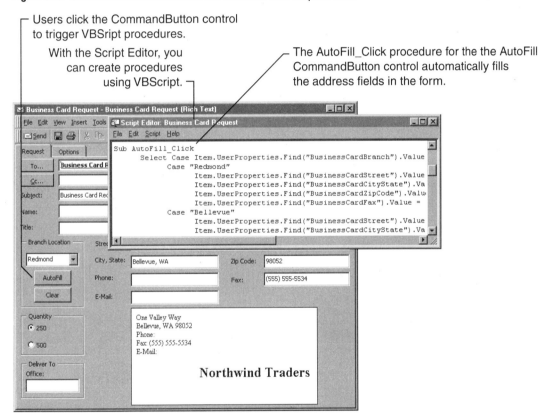

┌─ Users click the CommandButton control
│ to trigger VBSript procedures.

    With the Script Editor, you   ┌─ The AutoFill_Click procedure for the the AutoFill
      can create procedures   CommandButton control automatically fills
        using VBScript. ─┐   the address fields in the form.

▶ **To add a CommandButton control**

1   In Design mode, drag the control from the **Control Toolbox** to the form.

2   To set the caption for a CommandButton control, click the control. When the edit pointer appears, type the name in the control.

3   To specify a name for the CommandButton control, right-click the control, and then click **Properties** on the shortcut menu.

4   In the **Name** text box on the **Display** page, type a name, and then click **OK**.

▶ **To create a procedure for a CommandButton control**

1 Click the **View Code** button on the **Form Design** toolbar.

2 In the Script Editor window, type **Sub** followed by a space, followed by **CommandButton1_Click**, where CommandButton1 is the name of the control. Add the necessary code to the procedure. End the procedure with an **End Sub** statement, as shown in the following example:

```
Sub CommandButton1_Click
    MsgBox "This is a procedure for a CommandButton control."
End Sub
```

3 Close window.

▶ **To test a CommandButton control Click procedure**

1 On the **Form** menu, click **Run This Form** to switch the form into Run mode.

2 Click the command button.

3 To switch back to Design mode, close the Run window.

See Also For more information about creating procedures for forms using Visual Basic Scripting Edition, see Chapter 9, "Use Visual Basic Scripting Edition with Outlook."

MultiPage Controls

Use MultiPage controls to provide multiple pages of information on a form, as shown in Figure 6.27.

Figure 6.27 The MultiPage control on the Compose page of the Get User Info form.

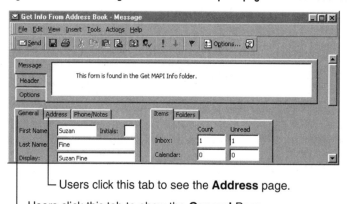

└─ Users click this tab to see the **Address** page.

└─ Users click this tab to show the **General** Page.

▶ **To add a MultiPage control**

- Drag the MultiPage control from the **Control Toolbox** to the form.

▶ **To add controls to the MultiPage control**

- Switch to the page you want to add controls to, and then drag the controls you want from the **Control Toolbox** to the MultiPage control.

▶ **To insert, rename, delete, or move a page**

- Right-click a tab on the MultiPage control, and then click **Insert**, **Delete**, **Rename**, or **Move** on the shortcut menu, as shown in Figure 6.28.

Figure 6.28   The shortcut menu of the MultiPage control

Right-click on a tab on the MultiPage control to show the shortcut menu.

How the TabStrip Control Differs from the MultiPage Control

With a MultiPage control, each page on the control usually contains a different set of controls. However, with the TabStrip control, each page contains the same controls. For example, you might use a TabStrip control to present the addresses of various companies. You set the title of each tab to the name of the company, and then you write code that, when you click a tab, updates the controls to show the address of that company.

See Also   For more information about the TabStrip control, see Outlook Customization and Forms Help.

Image Controls

Use Image controls to contain graphic images, as shown in Figure 6.29.

Figure 6.29 Image controls on the Vacation Request form

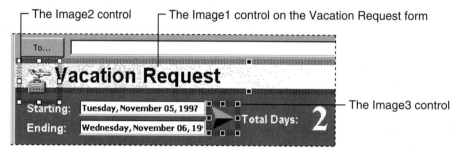

▶ To add a picture to an Image control

1 Right-click the Image control, and then click **Advanced Properties** on the shortcut menu.

2 Double-click the **Picture** cell, and then select the image.

▶ To delete the picture in the Image control

• You must delete the Image control, so click the Image control, and then press the DELETE key.

▶ To size an image in the Image control

1 Right-click the Image control, and then click **Advanced Properties**.

2 Do one of the following

To	Do this
Automatically size the control to the picture	In the **AutoSize** cell, click **True**.
Maintain the size of the picture, regardless of the size of the Image control	In the **PictureSizeMode** cell, click **Clip**.
Stretch the picture to fill the Image control	In the **PictureSizeMode** cell, click **Stretch**.
Enlarge the picture, but still maintain the **PictureAlignment** property setting	In the **PictureSizeMode** cell, click **Zoom**.

SpinButton Control

Use the SpinButton control to enable the user to increment or decrement numbers in a control. Although you can write script for the SpinButton control, it is not required to create a SpinButton control. To create a spin button for a control, you can bind the spin button to the same field that a TextBox control is bound to. Here is an example of how you can create a SpinButton control.

▶ **To add the TextBox control and bind it to a field**

1 From the **Control Toolbox**, drag a TextBox control to the form.

2 Right-click the TextBox control, and then click **Properties** on the shortcut menu.

3 Click the **Value** tab, and then click **New**.

4 In the **Name** text box, type a name for the field.

5 In the **Type** drop-down list box, click **Number**.

6 Click **OK**. If desired, select **Calculate this field automatically**, and then click **OK** again.

▶ **To add the SpinButton control and bind it to a field**

1 From the **Control Toolbox**, drag a SpinButton control to the form and position it to the right of the TextBox control you just added.

2 Right-click the SpinButton control, and then click **Properties** on the shortcut menu.

3 Click the **Value** tab.

4 Click **Choose Field**, point to **User defined fields in** *folder*, and then click the field you just added.

5 Click **OK**.

6 Hold down the CTRL key, and then right-click the SpinButton and TextBox controls.

7 On the shortcut menu, point to **Make Same Size**, and then click **Height**.

8 To test the SpinButton control, click **Run This Form** on the **Form** menu to enter Run mode, and then click the SpinButton control to increment or decrement the number in the TextBox control.

See Also   For more information about the SpinButton control, see Outlook Customization and Forms Help.

Controls that Require VBScript

In addition to the CommandButton control, the **Control Toolbox** provides several other controls that require VBScript to operate. These are the ToggleButton, TabStrip, and ScrollBar controls.

See Also   For more information about these controls, see Outlook Customization and Forms Help.

CHAPTER 7

Actions

In This Chapter

Voting Buttons for Message Forms   184

Reply Actions for Message Forms   193

Reply to Folder Actions for Post Forms   207

Action properties make it possible for you to define custom responses for forms, instead of using the standard Reply and Reply to Folder actions. For example, with the Vacation Request form, supervisors can reply to a vacation request item by choosing an Approve Vacation or Deny Vacation action, rather than using the standard Reply action.

In this chapter, we take a close look at the different ways of creating responses for forms. Specifically, we look at:

Voting buttons for Message forms   The easiest way to create responses for Message forms uses Voting buttons. As an example, we cover how Voting buttons are created for an Art Approval form.

Reply actions for Message forms   As an example, we cover how Reply actions are implemented for the Vacation Request form.

Reply to folder actions for Post forms   As an example, we take a look at how custom responses are designed for the Course Catalog Entry in the Training Management folder.

Voting Buttons for Message Forms

Voting buttons, which are only available with Message forms, provide an easy way for users to collect quick feedback from other users. When you specify Voting button options for a form, you cause two important things to happen.

- Voting buttons are added to the **Read** page, as shown in Figure 7.1.
- The location of the Tracking item is specified. The Tracking item contains the voting results and shows them on the **Tracking** page, as shown in Figure 7.2.

Figure 7.1   The Read page of the Art Approval form. This page is used by members of the Art Approval Committee to approve or reject the art submitted by the artist.

Voting buttons are added to the **Read** Page of the Art Approval form. Reviewers click **Approve** or **Reject** to send their response to the artist.

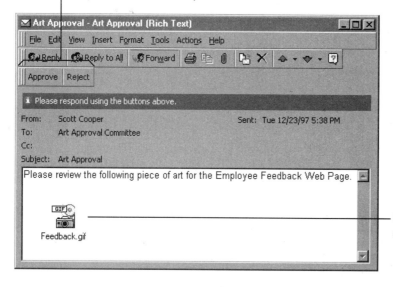

Reviewers can double-click the attached file to review the art.

Figure 7.2   The Tracking page of the Art Approval form tallies the results of the responses from the Art Approval Committee members.

The Tracking item is stored in the Art Approval folder in the user's Mailbox folder.

The Tracking item tallies the responses. The user double-clicks the Tracking item to open it.

The **Tracking** page of the Tracking item.

The reply totals are shown on the **Tracking** page.

In the following section, we create an Art Approval form that has Voting buttons and a Tracking item. When you're done, you will understand how Voting buttons work and how they can be used to collect feedback from other users.

Overview of the Art Approval Form

The Art Approval form illustrates the easiest way to create responses for Message forms. It uses voting buttons, which send responses to a folder for review. The Art Approval form, as shown in Figure 7.3, is for use by an artist to send an attached file of electronic art to users on the Art Approval Committee distribution list for review. The recipients review the attached file, and then vote to approve or reject. To see the voting results, the artist opens the Art Approval Tracking item in the Art Approval folder.

Figure 7.3 The Compose page of the Art Approval form

The To field is preaddressed to the Art Approval Committee distribution list.

The initial value of the Subject field is set to Art Approval.

The art file is attached in the Message box.

Create the Art Approval Folder

Before you create the Art Approval form, create an Art Approval folder in your Mailbox folder. That's where you'll store the Tracking item that tallies responses.

▶ **To create the Art Approval folder**

1 In the Folder List, right-click the Mailbox folder, and then click **New Folder**.

2 In the **Name** text box, type **Art Approval**, and then click **OK**.

3 If a prompt appears, click **No** in the **Add shortcut to Outlook bar?** dialog box.

Create the Art Approval Form

To create the Art Approval form, first open the standard Message form. Then, set the initial value of the To and Subject fields. Next, specify Voting button options for the form. Finally, publish the form in your Personal Forms Library.

Open the form in Run mode

This form should be built entirely in Run mode.

▶ **To open the standard Message form**

1   In the Folder List or Outlook Shortcut bar, click **Inbox**.

2   Select **New Mail Message** from the Outlook **Actions** menu.

Preaddress the To Field

Quite often, you'll want to preaddress a form to the people you send the form to on a regular basis. To preaddress a form, you set the initial value of the To field. In the example in this chapter, the initial value of the To field is set to the Art Approval Committee distribution list. For the form that you create, however, you preaddress the form to your own address. You must set the initial value of the To field at run time because you cannot open the Address Book from the To field at design time.

See Also   To create a distribution list, see Microsoft Outlook Help.

▶ **To preaddress the form**

1   On the opened form, click the **To** button.

2   Double-click the address you want to set as the initial value in the To field. (For this example, you can select your own address.)

3   Click **OK**.

Set the Initial Value of the Subject Field

For forms that serve a specific purpose, such as the Art Approval form, it makes sense to set the initial value of the Subject field. This saves the user the time of filling in the Subject field and ensures that a recipient sees a consistent Subject field each time he receives an Art Approval item in his Inbox.

▶ **To set the initial value of the Subject field**

•   Type **Art Approval** in the **Subject** text box.

You don't see the initial value in the Subject field immediately. It only appears when the form is opened to compose an item at run time.

Set Options for the Art Approval Form

Options are set by clicking on the **Options** icon on the form **Standard** toolbar, which opens the **Message Options** window. Here, you specify voting button and menu options and desired tracking and tallying information. Remember, the **Options** icon is only available in message forms.

Set Voting Button Options

Voting buttons appear on the **Read** page of the form and enable the user to respond to the Art Approval item by clicking the **Approve** or **Reject** button. The **Read** page of the form appears when the user double-clicks an Art Approval item in the Inbox.

▶ To specify voting buttons

1   Select the **Use voting buttons** check box.

2   In the **Use voting buttons** text box, type the text you want to appear on the Voting buttons or select the values from the list. If you type values, you must separate the values with a semicolon.

Specify Who the Replies Are Sent To

When you select the **Have replies sent to** check box, your address is automatically added to the text box. You can add additional addresses to the text box or you can replace your address with another.

▶ To specify the reply address

1   Select the **Have replies sent to** check box.

2   To specify additional names, click **Select Names**, and then double-click the names you want.

3   When the appropriate addresses appear in the **Message Recipients** box, click **OK**.

Note   When the approval committee votes, their replies will go to the Inbox(es) specified here. The tally of votes (tracking) will be stored in the folder specified in the **Save sent message to** text box.

Specify Where the Tracking Item is Stored

With forms that have Voting buttons, Outlook provides an automatic tally of the Voting button responses in a saved item in a folder. This folder must be located in your Mailbox folder. The default folder is the Sent Items folder. However, you can change it.

▶ To specify where the Tracking item is stored

1   On the **Message Options** window, choose **Save sent message to**, and then click **Browse**.

2   In the **Folders** list box, click the Art Approval folder, and then click **OK**.

3   Click **Close** to save your options.

As shown in Figure 7.4, the **Save sent message to** option is set to the Art Approval folder. So when an Art Approval item is sent, an Art Approval item is also saved in the Art Approval folder in your Mailbox folder. After you receive and open voting responses in your Inbox, the responses are written to the Tracking item in the Art Approval folder. If this seems a little confusing right now, don't worry. We'll go through the process step by step.

Figure 7.4 Voting button options for the Art Approval form

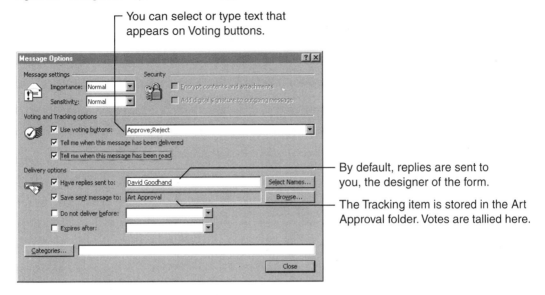

You can select or type text that appears on Voting buttons.

By default, replies are sent to you, the designer of the form.

The Tracking item is stored in the Art Approval folder. Votes are tallied here.

Publish the Form to the Personal Forms Library

After the form is created and modified, you publish the form to your Personal Forms Library so that you can open and test the form.

▶ **To publish the form**

1   Select **Forms** on the **Tools** menu, and then click **Publish Form As**.

2   If **Personal Forms Library** does not appear in the **Look in** drop-down list box, click it and select **Personal Forms Library**.

3   In the **Display name** text box and the **Form name** text box, type **Art Approval** or whatever you want to name the form, and then click **Publish**.

4   Close the form. At the **Do you want to save changes?** prompt, choose **No** for most cases, or **Yes** if you want a backup copy saved in the Drafts folder.

The form is 'saved' in its final form by publishing it. The **Save** prompt, on the other hand, creates a copy in the Drafts folder.

See Also For more information about where to publish forms, see Chapter 13, "Distribute and Maintain Applications."

How Actions are Automatically Set for Voting Buttons

When you specify Voting buttons and publish a form, Outlook automatically adds custom actions to the **Actions** page. There are two important points to remember about these actions. First, when you specify Voting buttons, the **Creates form of type** property is set to the standard Message form (IPM.Note). Second, the **Address form like** property is set to **Response**, as shown in Figure 7.5.

Figure 7.5   The Actions page of the Art Approval form. Approve and Reject actions are automatically added when you specify the Voting buttons on the Options page.

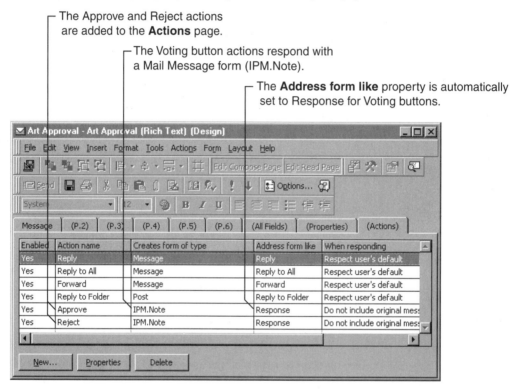

The Approve and Reject actions are added to the **Actions** page.

The Voting button actions respond with a Mail Message form (IPM.Note).

The **Address form like** property is automatically set to Response for Voting buttons.

Test the Art Approval Form

Now you open the Art Approval form and then send an Art Approval item to your Inbox.

Send an Art Approval Item

First, you open the Art Approval form from your Personal Forms Library. When you open the form, you see the **Compose** page of the form. Using the **Compose** page, you send an Art Approval item to your Inbox.

▶ **To send the Art Approval form**

1   On the Outlook **File** menu, select **New**, and then click **Choose Form**.

2   In the **Look in** drop-down list box, click **Personal Forms Library**, and then double-click **Art Approval**.

3   On the **Insert** menu, click **File**, and then double-click a file to insert in the message box on the Art Approval form.

4   Click the **Send** button.

Use the Voting Buttons to Respond

Now you open the Art Approval item in your Inbox. Then you click one of the Voting buttons.

▶ **To vote in the item**

1   Double-click the Art Approval item in the Inbox to which the form was addressed in the **To** box.

2   Normally, you open the attached item to review it. However, in this case, there is no need to.

3   Click **Approve**.

4   Click **Send the response now**, and then click **OK**.

5   Close the Art Approval form.

Review Replies

Now you open the Art Approval reply in your Inbox. Then, you open the Tracking item in the Art Approval folder.

Important   The Voting button responses are tallied in the Tracking item only after the response items are opened in your Inbox. If the items are not opened, the results are not tallied in the Tracking item. If no response items are opened, the **Tracking** page is not available on the Tracking form.

▶ **To open the response item in your Inbox**

- In your Inbox, double-click the Art Approval item.

▶ **To open the Tracking item**

1 In the Folder List, open the Art Approval folder.

2 Double-click the Tracking item, as shown in Figure 7.2 earlier in this chapter.

   The Tracking item is identified by an information icon, as shown in Figure 7.2, earlier in this chapter.

3 Click the **Tracking** tab.

Figure 7.6   The Tracking item is opened in the Art Approval folder.

This icon indicates the responses have been tallied in the Tracking items.

Click the **Tracking** page to view a tally of the responses.

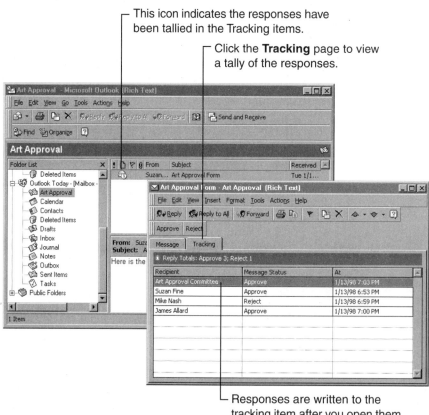

Responses are written to the tracking item after you open them in your Inbox. Only the most recent vote of the person is shown.

Reply Actions for Message Forms

When creating applications with Message forms, you often create Reply actions that open custom forms, instead of the standard Message form. For example, the Vacation Request form has two custom actions: the Approve Vacation action activates the Vacation Approved form and the Deny Vacation action activates the Vacation Denied form.

In this section, we create custom Reply actions for Message forms. Throughout this section, we use the Vacation Request application for examples of how to implement Reply actions with Message forms.

▶ To open the Vacation Request folder

- In the Folder List, expand the Building Microsoft Outlook 98 Applications folder, and then expand the Building Blocks folder. Then click the Vacation Request folder.

Note If you haven't installed the Building Microsoft Outlook 98 Applications folder, see the Introduction of this book for instructions.

Overview of the Vacation Request Application

The Vacation Request application consists of four forms: Vacation Request, Vacation Approved, Vacation Denied, and Vacation Report. All forms are intentionally left unhidden in this folder so you can view them.

▶ To view a Vacation Request form

1   On the **Actions** menu, view the forms at the bottom of the menu.

2   Click **New Vacation** *form name*.

Vacation Request form   The form opens in **Compose** page. The user can compose a Vacation Request item and send it to his supervisor. When the receiving supervisor opens the form from her Inbox, she sees the Vacation Request **Read** page. It contains the **Approve Vacation** and **Deny Vacation** buttons, as shown in Figure 7.7.

Figure 7.7   **The Read page of the Vacation Request form**

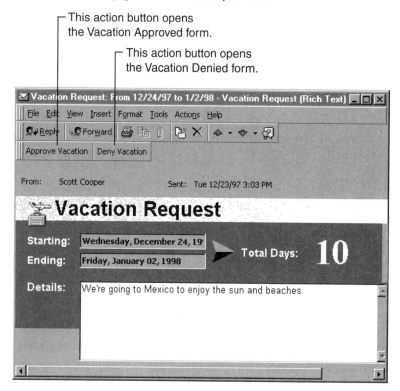

This action button opens
the Vacation Approved form.

This action button opens
the Vacation Denied form.

Vacation Approved form   The supervisor sees the **Compose** page of the Vacation Approved form when she clicks the **Approve Vacation** button on the Vacation Request form. She then clicks **Send** to route the approved vacation request to the user.

Vacation Denied form   The supervisor sees the **Compose** page of this form when she clicks the **Deny Vacation** button on the Vacation Request form. She can then click **Send** to route the denied vacation request to the user.

Vacation Report form   This form lets the user send the supervisor a report of the vacation days taken. The supervisor can then track the days available for each employee.

Because we're discussing actions, we focus primarily on the Vacation Request form and its associated actions in this part of the chapter. Along the way, we take a look at a custom Reply action.

Actions for the Vacation Request Form

To get familiar with actions, let's take a look at the **Actions** page for the Vacation Request form, as shown in Figure 7.8.

▶ **To view the Actions page for the Vacation Request form**

- In the Design mode of the Vacation Request form, click the Actions page.

Note   If you haven't installed the Building Outlook 98 Applications folder, see the instructions in the Introduction to this book.

Figure 7.8   The Actions page for the Vacation Request form

This action places an **Approve Vacation** button on the **Read** page. When the button is clicked, it opens the Vacation Approved form.

This action places a **Deny Vacation** button on the **Read** page. When the button is clicked, it opens the Vacation Denied form.

Click here to show the **Actions** page.

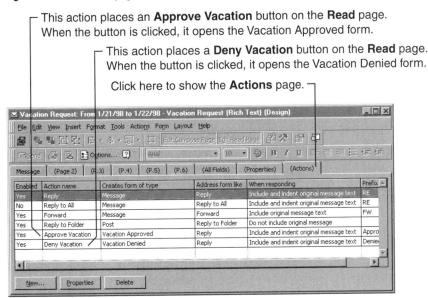

New Reply Actions

When you create new Reply actions, you specify that custom command buttons and menu commands are added to the form. The menu commands and buttons, when clicked, activate a custom form that lets the user reply to an item. For example, the Vacation Request form has a custom Approve Vacation action. When a supervisor opens a vacation request in his Inbox, he can click the **Approve Vacation** button to open the Vacation Approved form, as shown in Figure 7.9.

The supervisor can then click the **Send** button to send the Vacation Approved item to the person who requested it. When the Vacation Approved form is opened, the original message is copied from the Vacation Request form to the message box of the Vacation Approved form. Likewise, the From field is copied to the To field, and the values in the StartDate, EndDate, and TotalDays fields are copied from the Vacation Request form to the Vacation Approved form.

Figure 7.9 The Read page (partial) of the Vacation Request form and the Compose page of the Vacation Approved form

On the **Read** page of the Vacation Request form, the **Approve Vacation** button opens the Vacation Approved form.

The supervisor clicks the **Send** button to send the response to the requester.

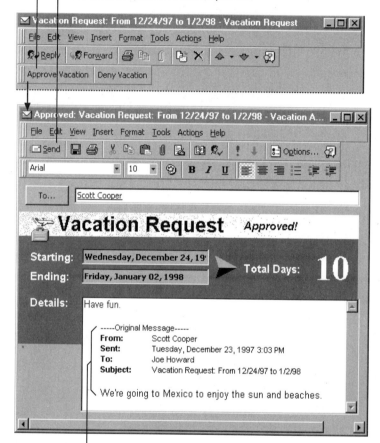

The original message is copied to the message box of the Vacation Approved form.

Approve Vacation Action

Now let's take a look at the properties associated with the Approve Vacation action.

▶ **To view the Approve Vacation action**

1 Open the Vacation Request form by selecting the **Vacation Request** folder from the Folder List. Then, click **New Vacation Request** on the **Actions** menu.

2 In Design mode, click on the **Actions** page, and then double-click the **Approve Vacation** action.

The **Form Action Properties** dialog box, as shown in Figure 7.10, enables you to create new actions and to modify existing actions. With this dialog box, you specify the text that appears on the **Action** button and menu, the form that appears when the button is clicked, and whether the original message is copied to the Reply item.

Figure 7.10 The Form Action Properties dialog box

This option determines if action buttons and menu commands are visible on the **Read** page.

Text that appears on the action button on the **Read** page of the form.

Form that is activated when the action button is clicked.

This option specifies if and how the original item is copied to the Reply item message box.

This option determines how the To, Cc, and Subject fields are set up in the Reply item.

These options specify if the Reply form is opened or if the item is sent immediately.

See Also To create a new Action Item, see "Create a New Action" in Chapter 4, "Design a Custom Application."

Action Name

The **Action name** text box, as shown in the preceding Figure 7.10, defines the name of both the menu command and command button that open the associated custom Reply form. The custom action button appears on the **Read** page of the form.

The custom menu command appears in two places:

- On the Outlook **Actions** menu when an item created with the associated form is selected in a folder. For example, with the Vacation Request form, the **Approve Vacation** command appears on the **Actions** menu when a Vacation Request item is selected in the Inbox.

- On the form **Actions** menu of the **Read** page.

Form Name and Message Class

The **Form name** box contains the name of the form that is opened when the menu command or command button is selected. The **Message class** box contains the internal identifier for the form. When you select a form in the **Form name** box, the message class automatically appears in the **Message class** box.

The **Form name** list contains the names of the forms published in the active folder. In addition, it contains a **Forms** value that you can use to select from forms in the Organizational, Personal, or Standard Forms Library.

▶ **To specify a form name**

- Do one of the following:

  - In the **Form name** drop-down list box, type a form name, and then click **Check** to search for the form.

    If Outlook cannot find the form, you see a message box. If this happens, I highly recommend you create the form before you specify the form name. After you create the form and publish it in a forms library, you can return to the original form and click the name of the form in the **Form name** drop-down list box.

  - In the **Form name** drop-down list box, click a form name from the drop-down list.

  - In the **Form name** drop-down list box, click **Forms** on the drop-down list. In the **Choose Form** box, double-click the form you want.

Characteristics of the New Form

Under **Characteristics of the new form**, you can specify how the original message is copied to the message box of the Reply form. In addition, you can specify how the values in the From, Cc, and Subject fields are copied from the original form to the Reply form.

When Responding

For Reply actions, you can specify if the contents of the original item are copied to the message box of the Reply item. You can also specify how the contents of the message box are copied. The default setting for this property is **Respect user's default**. In Outlook, the user can set the **When replying to a message** option on the **Email Options** page of the **Options** dialog box (**Tools** menu). By default, this property is set for the user to **Include and indent original message text**. Therefore, if you have **Respect user's default** selected in the **When responding** drop-down list box, you can assume that for most users the message box on the reply form includes and indents the original message. If you want to override the user's **When replying to a message** preference, click another option in the **When responding** drop-down list box to explicitly define how you want the contents of the message box to appear on the Reply form.

Here are a few general guidelines for setting the **When responding** option for Message forms.

- If the amount of information in the original message is small, click **Include and indent the original message text**. As shown in the preceding Figure 7.10, this is the option that is selected for the Approve Vacation action in the Vacation Request form.

- If you want to include a shortcut to the message in the response item, click **Attach link to original message**.

Address Form Like A

For Message forms, you almost always choose **Reply** for this option. When you choose **Reply**, the To field of the Reply form contains the contents of the From field of the original item, and the Cc field is empty. The Subject field, unless otherwise specified, contains **RE:**, followed by the contents of the Subject field of the original item.

The following table describes how the **Address form like a** options set up the Reply form.

Option	Description
Reply	This sets up the Reply form so the To field contains the contents of the From field of the original item. The Cc field is empty. The Subject field contains whatever is specified in the **Subject prefix** box of the **Form Actions Properties** dialog box, such as **RE:**. It is followed by the contents of the Subject field of the original item.
Reply to All	This sets up the Reply form so the To field contains the contents of the From and Cc fields of the original item. The Subject field contains **RE:**,or whatever you specify, followed by the contents of the Subject field of the original item.
Forward	This sets up the form so the To and Cc fields are empty and the Subject field contains **FW:**, or whatever you specify, followed by the contents of the Subject field of the original item.
Reply to Folder	This sets up the Reply form so the Post To field contains the active folder address, the Conversation field contains the subject of the original item, and the Subject field is empty. In most cases, the Conversation field is not visible on a form. The Conversation field contains the value of the Subject of the original item.
Response	This is used exclusively for Voting button actions.

Show Action On

Most of the time, you can leave the default **Menu and Toolbar** option for a form. However, there might be times when you want to control the placement of the custom action buttons on the form. For example, you might want to add a command button to the bottom of the form and then write a macro for the command button to activate the Reply form when the button is clicked. If this is the case, you can click the **Menu only** option, or uncheck the **Show Action On** box so it will not show in either the menu or the toolbar.

This Action Will

For the Vacation Request form, the Approve action, when initiated, opens the Vacation Approved form. For most actions, you specify **Open the form** under **This action will**. However, there might be cases when you choose the **Send the form immediately** option. For example, you might send a form to a user requesting their updated phone number and address. Rather than opening a Reply form, the user can fill in the fields on the original form, and then click the custom action button. The Reply form is then activated, but isn't visible to the user. Values from the originating form are then copied to the Reply form. If you specify the **Send the form immediately** option, you must still create the Reply form. And you must ensure that the fields you want filled in on the invisible Reply form are included on the original form.

Subject Prefix

Shows the prefix that appears in the **Subject** text box of the Reply form. The prefix is **RE:** by default. For example, for the Approve Vacation action, the **Approve** prefix appears in the **Subject** text box of the Vacation Approved form. When the person who requested the vacation receives the Approved Vacation item in his Inbox, the text in the Subject column in the folder tells him his vacation is approved.

How Field Values Are Copied to the Reply Form

Outlook does not provide a way to explicitly define the field values that are copied from custom fields on the original form to custom fields on the Reply form. Rather, you accomplish this by using the same fields for both forms, as shown in Figure 7.11. When the field is shared between the original and Reply form, the values are automatically copied from the original form to the Reply form at run time.

For example, the following fields are located on both the Vacation Request form and the Vacation Approved form. When an Approve Vacation action is initiated, the values in these fields are copied from the Vacation Request form to the Vacation Approved form.

- Subject
- TotalDays
- StartDate
- EndDate

Figure 7.11   Values between fields common to both the original and Reply form are copied to the Reply form.

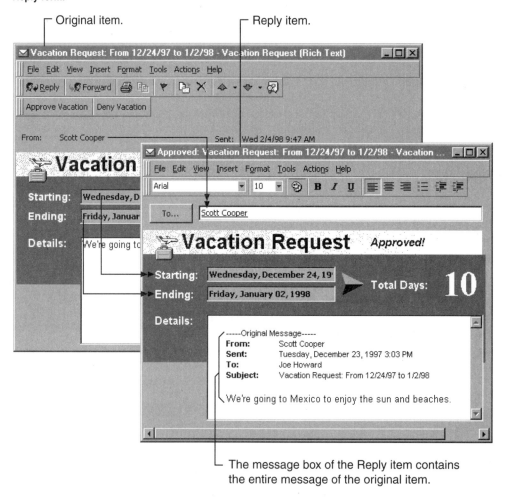

┌─ Original item.

┌─ Reply item.

└─ The message box of the Reply item contains the entire message of the original item.

Important   To ensure that field values are copied between the original form and the Reply form, use the same fields for both forms. For example, for the Vacation Request applications, the TotalDays, StartDate, and EndDate fields are used for the Vacation Request form.

Note   In Figure 7.11, the Subject field is not visible. Instead, it is located on Page 2, a hidden page. The Subject text, however, is copied from the original item to the Reply item and does appear in the **Subject** box on the **Read** page of the Reply item.

Vacation Request Reply Forms

In most cases, the custom Reply form is very similar to the original form. Quite often, you can use the original form as a template for the Reply form. For example, the Vacation Approved form is a Reply form based on the Vacation Request form. Only a few modifications have been made:

- The custom Reply actions are removed.
- The form **Description** is changed, as shown in Figure 7.12.

See Also   For more information on creating and modifying forms, see "Open the Form and Switch to Design Mode" in Chapter 5, "Forms."

Figure 7.12   The form description is changed for the Reply form.

Select this check box after you are sure the Reply form is working correctly.

When this check box is selected, the form is included with the item.

Publish Reply Forms

For Reply forms to work correctly, they must be available on the user's system. Before you publish the forms, however, it's a good idea to make a backup copy.

▶ **To make a backup copy of a form**

1 With the form open, click **Save As** on the **File** menu.

2 In the **Save in** drop-down list box, select the default Outlook template folder, such as C:\ Program Files\Microsoft Office\Templates.

3 In the **File name** text box, type a name for the form.

4 In the **Save as type** drop-down list box, select **Outlook Template (.oft)**.

5 Click **Save**.

▶ **To open your backup copy of a form**

1 Select **New** on the **File** menu, and then click **Choose Form**.

2 Click **Templates in File System** in the **Look In** drop-down list box, and then click on the form you'd like to open.

After you make a backup copy of the form, you can publish it to one of the following forms libraries:

Organizational Forms Library Publish the form in this library if you want the form to be available to all users in your organization.

Personal Forms Library Publish the form in this library if you intend to use the form for personal use. The Personal Forms Library is also a good place to publish forms when you want to test them.

The forms library of a folder Publish the form in the forms library of a folder if the form is integrated with a folder.

See Also For more information about where to publish forms, see Chapter 13, "Distribute and Maintain Applications."

▶ **To publish a form**

1 On the **Tools** menu, select **Forms**, and then click **Publish Form As**.

2 Click the **Look In** drop-down list box, and select the forms library you want to publish in.

3 In the **Display name** text box and the **Form name** text box, type a name for the form, and then click **Publish**.

Test the Forms

After you publish the forms to a forms library, you should run the forms to make sure they work as expected. For example, here's how you publish and test the Vacation Request forms.

▶ **To publish the Vacation Request forms**

1 In the Vacation Request folder, click **New Vacation Request** on the **Actions** menu.

2 On the **Tools** menu, select **Forms**, and then click **Design This Form** to switch to Design mode.

3 On the **Tools** menu, select **Forms**, and then click **Publish Form As**.

4 Click the **Look in** drop-down list box and then click **Personal Forms Library**.

5 Type a name for the form in the **Display name** text box and the **Form name** text box.

6 Click **Publish**.

7 Close the form.

8 On the **Actions** menu, click **New Vacation Approved**, and then repeat steps 2 through 7.

9 On the **Actions** menu, click **New Vacation Denied**, and then repeat steps 2 through 7.

▶ **To test the Vacation Request forms**

1 Select **New** on the **File** menu, and then click **Choose Form**.

2 In the **Look In** drop-down list box, select **Personal Forms Library** and click **Vacation Request**.

3 Address the form to yourself, and then click the **Send** button.

4 When the Vacation Request item arrives in your Inbox, double-click it to open it.

5 Click the **Approve Vacation** button.

6 Click **Send**.

7 When the Approved Vacation item arrives in your Inbox, double-click it to open it.

Note Remember to keep forms updated and synchronized with each other by performing upkeep:

- Keep fields uniform on both **Compose** and **Read** pages.

- If form names are changed, update the links between the action and form. See the section "The Create Offering Action" later in this chapter.

Set the Hidden Properties for Response Forms

After you publish and test the forms, you select the **Hidden** option for response forms, so the response forms can only be opened as a response to an item. For example, if the **Hidden** check box is selected for the Vacation Approved form and the form is published in the Personal Forms Library, the Vacation Approved form name does not appear in the forms list in the **New Form** dialog box. Users can only open the form when an associated Vacation Request item is selected in the Inbox or when the Vacation Request item is opened in Read mode.

▶ **To set the Hidden property for the Vacation Approved form**

1 On the Outlook **Tools** menu, click **Options**, and then click the **Other** tab.

2 Click the **Advanced Options** button.

3 Click the **Custom Forms** button.

4 Click the **Manage Forms** button.

5 Note that the upper-right form library text box is set to Personal Forms.

6 In the lower-right library list box, click **Vacation Approved**, and then click **Properties**.

7 Select the **Hidden** check box, and then click **OK**.

8 Repeat steps 4 and 5 for the Vacation Denied form.

9 Click **Close** and then click **OK**.

Note After forms are hidden, they are no longer visible in the following places:

- The **Choose Form** dialog box selected from **New** on the **File** menu.
- The **Actions** menu for that folder.

Custom Reply Forms for Users Not on Your Microsoft Exchange Server System

Sometimes, you may want to create forms that are used between your company and another company over the Internet. For example, let's assume you have a Legal Approval form and a Legal Approval Response form and you want to use the forms between your company and an attorney's office. Also assume that the attorney has Outlook, but is not on your Microsoft Exchange Server system. For this scenario to work correctly, the attorney must have both the Legal Approval form and the Legal Approval Response form installed on her system—either in the Organizational Forms or Personal Forms Library.

Note   If the Reply form specified by an action is not available on the user's system, Outlook opens the standard Message form in its place.

See Also   For more information about where to publish forms, see Chapter 13, "Distribute and Maintain Applications." For information on sending forms to other people, see "Learn How Forms Work" in Chapter 5, "Forms."

Reply to Folder Actions for Post Forms

When creating applications with Post forms, you can create custom actions so users can reply to items in a folder using custom forms, rather than the standard Post form. In this section, we use the Training Management application for examples of how to implement Reply to Folder actions for Post forms.

▶ **To open the Training Management folder**

- In the Folder List, expand the Building Microsoft Outlook 98 Applications folder, and then expand the Building Blocks folder. Then click the Training Management folder.

Overview of the Training Management Application

The Training Management application enables training personnel to create an entire course catalog in the Training Management folder. To create the catalog, administrators first post Course Catalog Entry items in the folder. Course Catalog Entry items contain a general description of the course. After Course Catalog Entry items have been posted, training administrators can post Course Offering items as responses to the Course Catalog Entry items, as shown in Figure 7.13. After students complete a course, they can post an Evaluation item as a response to the Course Offering item.

Figure 7.13   The Training Management folder

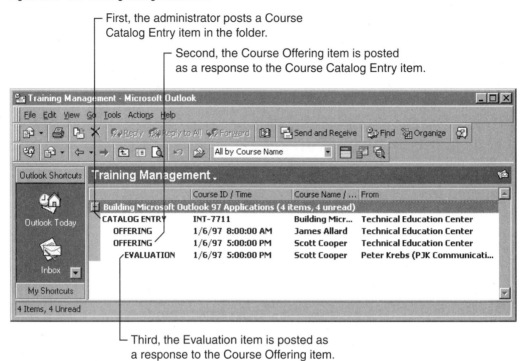

First, the administrator posts a Course
Catalog Entry item in the folder.

Second, the Course Offering item is posted
as a response to the Course Catalog Entry item.

Third, the Evaluation item is posted as
a response to the Course Offering item.

The Training Management application contains the following forms:

Course Catalog Entry form   This form enables the administrator to post an item that
contains general information about a course, such as the Course ID, cost, name, target
audience, and course description. The **Read** page of the form enables an administrator
to view the course offering information and to open a Course Offering response item.

Figure 7.14 The Read page of the Course Catalog Entry form

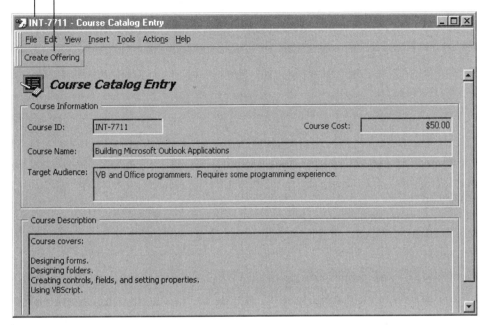

┌─ The Course Catalog Entry form contains the original item.

  ┌─ The training administrator clicks here
    to create a response to the original item.

Course Offering Form The Course Offering form enables an administrator to post a Course Offering item in the Training Management folder. The Course Offering item, which contains specifics about the course such as class time and instructor, is posted as a response to the Course Catalog Entry item. The **Read** page of the Course Offering form shows two custom buttons: a **Signup** button that lets students register for a class and a **Course Evaluation** button that lets students post a course evaluation in the Training Management folder. The **Compose** page shows a **Post** button that sends the form to the specified folder for public viewing.

Figure 7.15   The Compose page of the Course Offering form

The administrator clicks here to post the Course Offering
Response item in the Training Management folder.

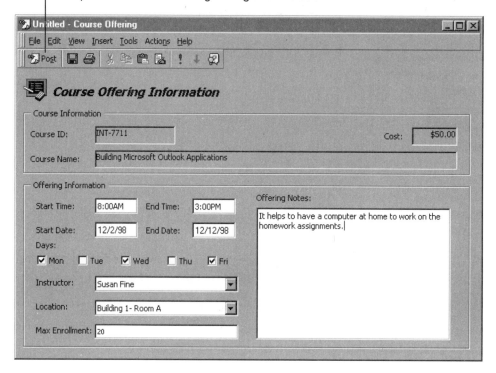

Signup form   This form enables a student to send a Signup item to the Course
Registration folder. We won't cover this part of the application in this section.

Evaluation form   This form enables students to post an Evaluation item as a response
to a Course Offering item. We won't cover this part of the application in this section.

In the rest of this section, we look at the custom actions of the Course Catalog Entry
form. First, we examine how the actions work in the folder. Then, we look at how the
fields are copied from the Course Catalog Entry form to the Course Offering form.
Finally, we look at how response items are organized in a custom view in the Training
Management folder.

Actions for the Course Catalog Entry Form

Now let's take a look at the **Actions** page for the Course Catalog Entry form, as
shown in Figure 7.16.

▶ **To view the Actions page of the Course Catalog Entry form**

1 On the **Actions** menu of the Training Management folder, click **New Course Catalog Entry**.

2 On the form **Tools** menu, select **Forms,** and then click **Design This Form**.

3 Click the **Actions** page, as shown in Figure 7.16.

Figure 7.16   The Actions page for the Course Catalog Entry form

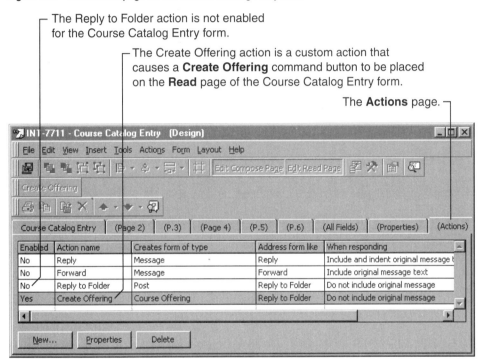

The Reply to Folder action is not enabled
for the Course Catalog Entry form.

The Create Offering action is a custom action that
causes a **Create Offering** command button to be placed
on the **Read** page of the Course Catalog Entry form.

The **Actions** page.

Make the Reply to Folder Action Unavailable

Here is a simple rule to remember:

Rule   If you create a custom Reply to Folder action for a form, set the Enabled option to No for the standard Reply to Folder so the action is not available.

As shown in Figure 7.16, the **Reply to Folder** command is not available for the Course Catalog Entry form. This is done to prevent the user from posting standard Post form items in the Training Management folder. You can also do this for the Reply and Forward actions.

▶ **To make the Reply to Folder action unavailable**

1 On the **Actions** page, double-click the **Reply to Folder** action.

2 Clear the **Enabled** check box.

New Post to Folder Actions

With new Post to Folder actions, you can specify that custom command buttons and menu commands are added to the form. The menu commands or buttons, when clicked, open a custom form that enables the user to post a response item to the folder. For example, the Course Catalog Entry form has a custom Course Offering action. When an administrator opens a Course Catalog Entry item in his Inbox, he can click the **Course Offering** button as shown in Figure 7.17.

Figure 7.17   The Create Offering button is added to the Read page of the Course Catalog Entry form. When clicked, it opens the Compose page of the Course Offering form.

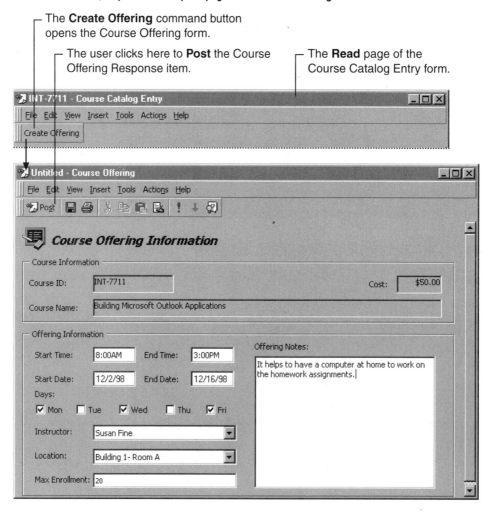

The **Create Offering** command button opens the Course Offering form.

The user clicks here to **Post** the Course Offering Response item.

The **Read** page of the Course Catalog Entry form.

The Create Offering Action

Now let's take a look at the options that make up the Create Offering action, as shown in Figure 7.18.

▶ **To view the Course Offering action options**

1   In the Design mode of the **Course Catalog Entry** form, click the **Actions** page.

2   Double-click the **Create Offering** action to open the **Form Action Properties** dialog box.

Figure 7.18   The properties for the Create Offering action

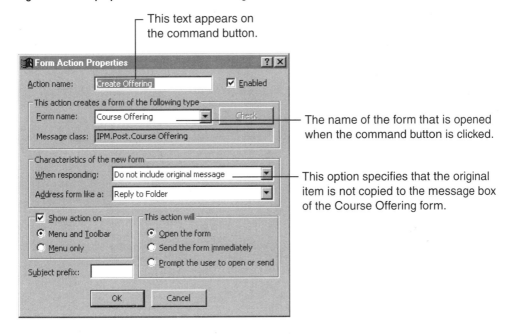

This text appears on the command button.

The name of the form that is opened when the command button is clicked.

This option specifies that the original item is not copied to the message box of the Course Offering form.

Action Name

On Post forms, the **Action Name** option defines the name of the menu command and action button that open the associated Reply to Folder form.

The custom **Create Offering** command button appears on the **Read** page of the Course Catalog Entry form. The custom menu command appears in the following places:

• On the Outlook **Actions** menu when an item created with the associated form is selected in a folder. For example, the **Create Offering** command appears on the **Actions** menu when a Course Catalog Entry item is selected in the Training Management folder.

- On the **Context** menu when you right-click on an item created with the associated form.

- On the **Actions** menu of the **Read** page of the Course Catalog Entry form.

Form Name and Message Class

The **Form name** option holds the name of the form that opens when the command button or menu command is clicked. The message class, the internal identifier for the form, is automatically supplied for you in the **Message class** text box. The **Form name** drop-down list box contains the names of the forms published in the current folder, so you see the Training Management forms in the **Form name** drop-down list box.

▶ To specify a form name

- Do one of the following:

  - In the **Form name** drop-down list box, type a form name, and then click **Check** to search for the form.

    If Outlook cannot find the form, you see a message box that explains that Outlook can't find the form. If this happens, you should create the Response form before you specify the **Form name** option. After you create the Response form and publish it in a forms library, you can then return to the original form and click the name of the Response form in the **Form name** drop-down list box.

  - In the **Form name** drop-down list box, click a form name to specify the form that is activated when the user clicks an action menu command or command button.

  - In the **Form name** drop-down list box, click **Forms** to open the **Choose Form** dialog box. In the first box, click the library, and then in the box below it double-click the form you want.

Characteristics of the New Form

Under **Characteristics of the new form**, you specify how values from the original item are copied to the Response item.

When Responding

When creating actions, remember that the original message can only be copied to the message box of the Response item. So, if the Response form does not have a message box, as is the case with the Course Offering form, then the message cannot be copied.

Rule   If the Response form does not have a message box, then specify **Do not include original message** in the **When responding** box.

Generally with Post forms you should be very careful about including the original message, especially if the message is very large.

Address Form Like A

For Post forms, you always choose **Reply to Folder** for the **Address form like a** option. **Reply to Folder** sets up the response form so the Post To field of the Response form contains the active folder address, the Conversation field contains the subject of the original item, and the Subject field is empty.

Show Action On

Most of the time, you can specify the default **Menu and Toolbar** option. However, there may be times when you want to place action buttons in a custom location on the form. To do this, you can add a command button to the form, and then create a procedure for the command button to open the Response form when the command button is clicked. If this is the case, you can click on the **Menu only** option or uncheck **Show Action On**.

See Also   For more information about creating procedures for forms, see Chapter 9, "Use Visual Basic Scripting Edition with Outlook."

This Action Will

For the Course Catalog Entry form, when the Create Offering action is initiated, it opens the Course Offering form. For most Reply to Folder actions, you specify **Open the form** under **This action will**.

Subject Prefix

When the **Reply to Folder** option is selected in the **Address form like a** box, the Subject field of the Response item is cleared. So, in most cases, you leave the **Subject prefix** box blank when **Reply to Folder** is selected.

How Field Values Are Copied to the Response Form

Earlier in this chapter, we learned that values from shared fields—those fields that are common between the original item and the Response item—are copied from the original item to the Response item.

When the **Reply to Folder** option is selected in the **Address form like a** box for an action, the same principles apply. Values from shared fields are copied from the original item to the Response item. However, there is one exception.

Important   When the **Reply to Folder** option is selected in the **Address form like a** box, the value from the Subject field is not copied from the original item to the Response item. Instead, the value of the Subject field of the original item is copied to the Conversation field of the Response item and the Subject field in the Response item is blank.

In Figure 7.19, there is no Subject field visible on either form. Instead the Subject field is hidden (on Page 2) and bound to the CourseID field, so when a form is opened, the value of the CourseID field appears in the title bar of the form. That's because the value in the item's Subject field always appears in the title bar of the form. Also, there is no message box on either form, so the original message is not copied to the Response message.

When the Create Offering action is started, as shown in Figure 7.19, the values in these fields are copied from the Course Catalog Entry form to the Course Offering form.

- CourseID
- CourseCost
- CourseName

Figure 7.19   Values between fields common to both the original and Response form are copied to the Response form.

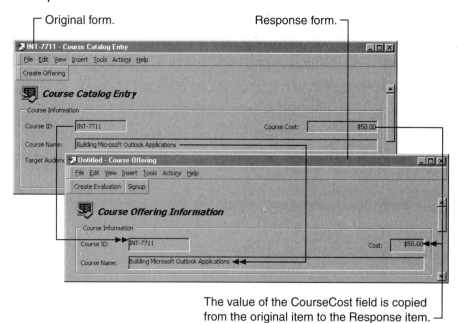

The value of the CourseCost field is copied from the original item to the Response item.

Rule   To make sure field values are copied between the original form and the Response form, use the same fields for both forms. For example, for the Training Management application, the CourseID, CourseCost, and CourseName fields are used for both the Course Catalog Entry form and the Course Offering Information form.

Create Response Forms

Generally, I recommend that you create all Response forms for an application before you create form actions. For example, for the Training Management application, you create the Course Catalog Entry form, and then you create the Course Offering form. After you've created the Course Offering form, you then return to the Course Catalog Entry form and create a Create Offering action that specifies the Course Offering form as the **Form name** option.

In some cases, the Response form is very similar to the original form, so you can use the original form as a template. Other times, it's quicker to start from scratch. In the case of the Course Offering Response form, either approach can be used.

See Also For more information on creating and modifying forms, see Chapter 5, "Forms."

Publish the Forms to the Forms Library of the Folder

When you create actions for a form, you must make sure that the forms that are opened as a result of the action are published in the forms library of the folder. Before you publish the forms, however, it's a good idea to make a backup copy of them.

▶ **To make a backup copy of a form**

1   With the form open, click **Save As** on the **File** menu.

2   In the **Save in** drop-down list box, select the default Outlook template folder, such as C:\ Program Files\Microsoft Office\Templates.

3   In the **File name** drop-down list box, type a name for the form.

4   In the **Save as type** drop-down list box, select **Outlook Template (.oft)**.

5   Click **Save**.

▶ **To open your backup copy of a form**

1   Select **New** on the **File** menu, and then click **Choose Form**.

2   Click **Templates in File System** in the **Look In** drop-down list box, and then click on the form you'd like to open.

▶ **To publish a form in the forms library of a folder**

1   On the **Tools** menu, select **Forms,** and then click **Publish Form As**.

2   If the text in the **Look In** box does not reflect the active folder, click **Browse**, select the forms library you want, and then click **OK**.

3   Type the name of the form in the **Display name** text box and the **Form name** text box.

4   Click **Publish**.

Test the Forms

After you create actions and custom forms to respond to the actions, you should run the forms to make sure they work as expected. For example, here is a quick way to test the forms and their actions in the Training Management application.

▶ **To test the forms in the Training Management application**

1 In the Folder List, click the **Training Management** folder.

2 On the **Actions** menu, click **New Course Catalog Entry**.

3 Fill in the Course Catalog Entry form, and then click **Post**.

4 In the **Training Management** folder, double-click the Course Catalog Entry item you just posted.

5 Click the **Create Offering** button.

6 Fill in the Course Offering form, and then click **Post**.

The Course Offering item is posted as a response to the Course Catalog Entry item. As such, it is indented in the folder.

7 Optionally, you can double-click the Course Offering item, and then click **Create Evaluation** or **Signup** on the form. Click **Post** to put it in the folder.

The Signup form is a Message form that routes course registration information to a course administrator or public folder. If you like, you can send the message to your Inbox as a test. The Course Evaluation form is a custom Response form that posts a Response Evaluation item in the Training Management folder.

Set the Hidden Property for Response Forms

After you publish and test forms, you set the **Hidden** property for the response forms. For example, the following procedure sets the **Hidden** property for the response forms in the Training Management folder.

▶ **To set the Hidden property for the Training Management Response forms**

1 In the Folder List, right-click the Training Management folder, and then click **Properties** on the shortcut menu.

2 Click the **Forms** page, and then click **Manage**.

3 In the lower-right list box, click **Course Offering**, and then click **Properties**.

4 Select the **Hidden** check box, and then click **OK**.

5 In the lower-right list box, click **Course Evaluation**, and then click **Properties**.

6 Select the **Hidden** check box, and then click **OK**.

7 In the lower-right list box, click **SignUp**, and then click **Properties**.

8 Select the **Hidden** check box, and then click **OK**.

9 Click **Close**, and then click **OK**.

Note After forms are hidden, they are no longer visible in the following places:

- The **Choose Form** dialog box selected from **New** on the **File** menu.
- The **Actions** menu for that folder.

In This Chapter

A Quick Reminder About Planning   222

Create or Select a Folder   223

Publish Forms in the Folder   226

Design Folder Views   230

Set General Properties   252

Test Forms and Views   253

Copy the Folder to Public Folders   254

Specify Internet Newsgroup   254

Set Administration Properties   254

Set Permissions   257

Design Rules   260

Test and Release the Folder   264

With Outlook, you can create a wide variety of folders to help users share, organize, and track information in your organization. Here are just a few examples:

- **Discussion folders that provide a public forum for users to submit, share, and respond to ideas and information** For example, you can create a discussion folder for posting job openings, job candidate information, and interview responses for a candidate. Or you can create a Technical Users Group folder, such as the HTML folder at Microsoft where writers and designers can post, read, and share information and solutions to problems.

- **Reference folders that provide a place to store and organize information** For example, you can create a Product Specification Library that stores Microsoft Word documents. In addition, you can create a Reference Library that stores Web addresses or a Project Library that stores a variety of materials such as data sheets, PowerPoint presentations, Visual Basic prototypes, or Microsoft Excel workbooks.

- **Tracking folders that enable users to record and review information that is constantly updated**   For example, you can create an application such as the sample Help Desk application, so users and help desk technicians can schedule appointments and track the status of help desk requests.

This chapter takes an in-depth look at creating public folders, discusses how to manage forms, and looks at creating custom views. It also covers how to set folder permissions and create rules for a folder. In this chapter, the folder design process is broken into steps. Each step is clearly marked with a numbered graphic block. Within each step, you can find detailed information that helps you to complete the step.

For the majority of examples in this chapter, the sample Classified Ads folder is used, as shown in Figure 8.1.

▶ **To open the Classified Ads folder**

- In the Folder List, expand the **Building Microsoft Outlook 98 Applications** folder, expand the **Building Blocks** folder, and then click the **Classified Ads** folder.

Figure 8.1   The Classified Ads folder

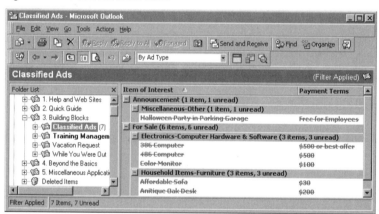

A Quick Reminder About Planning

To create folders that meet the needs of your users, it helps to first plan them. While planning processes differ with each organization and application, there are general steps you can follow when planning a public folder:

- Determine who will plan, design, and implement the folder.

- Identify folder users and their needs.

- Create a design plan that identifies the problems to be solved and how the folder will solve them. The design plan should include preliminary graphics of form windows or views to be created.

Create or Select a Folder

With Outlook, you can design a folder by using one of three methods.

Method	Use when
Create a new folder from scratch	You cannot find an existing folder in your organization that closely matches the folder you want to create. In this case, it's quicker to start from scratch.
Modify an existing folder that is in public use	You want to make minor changes to a folder, such as adding permissions or a view.
Copy the design of an existing folder to a new folder, and then modify the new folder	You want to create a new folder based on the design of an existing folder. Or you want to make changes to an existing folder and those changes will disrupt users' work.

Choose Where to Design the New Folder

If the method of folder design you choose requires that you create a new folder, you can create the folder in Public Folders, your Outlook Mailbox, or Personal Folders. The location determines whether the folder is public or private and determines the design properties you can set for the folder.

Designing a new folder in a personal folder is highly recommended. In a personal folder (.pst), you can create forms and design views, and then test them to make sure they work as expected. After you create forms and design views, you or the administrator can copy the folder to Public Folders where you can complete the design of the folder by setting permissions and administration properties.

The following table shows the attributes that you can set in each folder location.

Option	In a personal folder	In a mailbox folder	In a public folder
Copy or install forms	x	x	x
Design views	x	x	x
Designate the types of items allowed in the folder	x		x
Set permissions		x	x
Set administration properties	Some	Some	All
Define rules			x

Note Personal folders appearing on the Folder List are attached to personal folder (.pst) files saved on your hard disk drive. For more information on creating a personal folder (.pst) file, see "Create New Folders" in Chapter 3, "Customize Built-in Modules."

Create a Folder from Scratch

One way to design a folder is to create a new folder. After you create the folder, you can follow the design process outlined in this chapter, beginning with Step 2, "Publish Forms in the Folder."

▶ To create a folder

1   In the Folder List, right-click a personal folder you want to create a folder in, and then click **New Folder** on the shortcut menu.

2   In the **Name** text box, enter a name for the folder.

3   In the **Folder contains** a drop-down list box, do one of the following:

- Click **Mail Items** to create a folder that will contain items created with Message, Post, or Office Document forms.

- Click **Appointment Items**, **Contact Items**, **Journal Items**, **Note Items**, or **Task Items** to create a folder that will contain items of the associated type. For example, if you click **Appointment Items**, Outlook creates a Calendar folder.

4   Click **OK** to close. If a prompt appears, click **No** in the **Add shortcut to Outlook Bar?** message box.

Directly Modify a Folder

If a folder is in public use, it's best to directly modify the folder only if the changes are minor and will not disrupt users' work. Minor changes include adding permissions, adding a view, or changing a folder contact.

To make more significant changes such as modifying forms or rules, copy the design of the folder to another folder, modify the design, as described in "Copy a Folder Design" below, and then copy the modified design back to the original folder.

Note   To modify a folder, you must have owner permissions for the folder. To check your permissions for a folder, right-click the folder, and then click **Properties** on the shortcut menu. You can view your permissions on the **Permissions** page of a Mailbox or Public folder.

▶ To directly modify a Mailbox or Public folder

1   In the Folder List, right-click the folder, and then click **Properties** on the shortcut menu.

2   In the **Properties** dialog box, make the changes you want to the folder, and then click **OK**.

Copy a Folder Design

To create or modify a folder, you can copy the design of an existing folder to a new folder. You can then customize the design of the new folder.

Copying a folder design involves copying design components, such as forms and views, from one folder to another. When a folder design is copied, the folder permissions and rules are always maintained, regardless of whether the folder design is copied to or copied from a folder in a personal folder or a public folder.

When Outlook copies the design to a folder, it merges the design components of the source folder with design components of the destination folder. If two properties conflict—for example, the permissions for a user in the source folder are different from the permissions in the destination folder—the properties in the source folder take precedence. All of the design components in the destination folder are overwritten.

Note   To modify a Mailbox or Public folder, you must have owner permissions for the folder. To check your permissions for a folder, right-click the folder, and then click **Properties** on the shortcut menu. You can view your permissions on the **Permissions** page. To copy permissions, rules, forms, and views, you must have owner permissions for the folder.

▶ **To copy a folder design**

1   In the Folder List, click the folder you want to copy the design to.

2   On the **File** menu, point to **Folder**, and then click **Copy Folder Design**.

3   In the **Copy design from this folder** list box, select the folder you want to copy the design from.

4   Under **Copy design of**, select one or more of the following.

To	Select
Copy permissions from the source folder	**Permissions**
Copy the rules associated with the source folder	**Rules**
Copy the description of the source folder	**Description**
Copy forms and views that are stored in the source folder	**Forms & Views**

5   Click **OK**.

Publish Forms in the Folder

Not all folders require custom forms. But for those folders that do, you must first design the forms, and then publish them in an Outlook folder, such as a Mailbox folder, a Public folder, or a Personal folder. When you publish a form in a folder, you accomplish two things:

- You make the form available in the folder, so it can be opened by users to compose and view items in the folder.

- You expose the form properties, such as form name, description, and menu commands, in Outlook.

▶ To publish a form in an Outlook folder

1 With the form open, select **Forms** on the **Tools** menu, and then click **Publish Form As**.

2 In the **Display name** text box, type in the name of the form that will appear in the form caption, forms list, and menu command.

In the **Form Name** text box, type the name reflected in Message class, if different.

To change the location (library) where the form is published, click the **Look In** drop-down list box, and then select the folder where you want to publish the form.

3 Click **Publish**.

See Also   For more information about creating and publishing forms, see Chapter 5, "Forms."

Manage Forms

With the **Forms** page of the folder **Properties** dialog box, as shown in Figure 8.2, you can see the forms that are published in the forms library of the folder. In addition, you can specify the types of items that can be submitted in the folder. You can also use the **Forms** page to access the Forms Manager. With the Forms Manager, you can copy and delete forms, and view form properties.

▶ To view the Forms page

1 In the Folder List, right-click the folder, and then click **Properties** on the shortcut menu.

2 Click the **Forms** page.

Figure 8.2   The Forms page shows the forms that are published in the current folder.

Click here to open the Forms Manager.

Shows the forms published in the forms library of this folder.

Specifies the types of items that can be submitted in a public folder.

Tip   You can also access the Forms Manager by clicking **Options** on the Outlook **Tools** menu. This allows access to all forms, not just the ones in the current folder. Click the **Other** tab, then click the **Advanced Options** button, and then click the **Custom Forms** button. Finally, click the **Manage Forms** button to get to the Forms Manager.

Specify the Types of Items Allowed in the Folder

In many folders, you may want to control the types of items that can be submitted. For example, in the Classified Ads folder, you want to prevent the user from submitting standard post items to the folder because they are out of context and do not appear correctly in the custom views created for the folder.

▶ **To specify the types of items allowed in a public folder**

• On the **Forms** page of the folder's **Properties** dialog box, under **Allow these forms in this folder**, click one of the following.

To specify that	Click
Only items created with the forms specified in the **Forms associated with this folder** list box can be submitted in the folder.	**Only forms listed above**
Only items created with the forms in the **Forms associated with this folder** list box and standard Post and Message forms can be submitted in the folder.	**Forms listed above and the standard forms**
Any type of item can be submitted in the folder.	**Any form**

Copy and Delete Forms or Set the Hidden Property for a Form

You can use the Forms Manager, as shown in Figure 8.3, to copy and delete forms and to view form properties.

▶ **To open the Forms Manager**

• On the **Forms** page of the folder's **Properties** box, click **Manage**.

Figure 8.3   The Forms Manager dialog box

Click here to select the source forms library for a Copy operation.

Shows forms in the selected forms library.

Shows the active folder.

Click here to select the destination forms library for a Copy operation. When grey, it manages only the current folder.

Click to view properties of the selected form, such as the **Hidden** property.

If the form that you want to use already exists in your organization and is published in a forms library, you can copy it to the forms library of the folder you're designing. By default, the left-hand list box in the **Forms Manager** dialog box shows the contents of the Organization Forms Library and the right-hand list box shows the contents of the active folder's forms library. The left-hand list is the source forms library from which you can copy forms. The right-hand list box is the destination forms library where you copy the forms to. You can easily change the libraries shown in these boxes.

▶ **To change the library in the left or right list boxes of Forms Manager**

1 Choose **Set** for the list box that contains the library you want to change.

2 Do one of the following:

- In the **Forms Library** drop-down list box, click the library you want.
- In the **Folder Forms Library** list box, click the folder you want.

▶ **To copy a form to a folder**

- In the left list box, click the form you want to copy, and then click **Copy**.

You can copy a form from one forms library to another. You can delete any form from either forms library.

▶ **To delete a form**

- In the right or left list box, click the form you want to delete, and then click **Delete**.

To synchronize a form with an updated version, select the one you wish to update. For the update process to work, the form must be visible in both forms libraries (in both the right and left list boxes).

▶ **To update forms published in different forms libraries**

- In the right list box, click the form, and then click **Update**. Although you won't see an action, the forms will now be updated.

View Forms Properties or Set the Hidden Property for a Form

With the **Properties** dialog box, you can view a form's properties, and you can set the **Hidden** property for a form. When you select the **Hidden** property for a form, you specify that the form's associated menu command is not visible in the Outlook user interface, so users can only create response items with the form or view items with the form. In addition, forms published in the Personal Forms Library or the Organization Forms Library with the **Hidden** property selected are not visible to the user in the **Choose Form** dialog box. The **Choose Form** dialog box is available by selecting **New** on the **File** menu.

▶ **To view the properties of a form**

- In the right-hand list box of the **Forms Manager** dialog box, click the form whose properties you want to view, and then click **Properties**.

▶ **To set the Hidden property for a form**

1 In the right-hand list box of the **Forms Manager** dialog box, click the form that you want to set the **Hidden** property for, and then click **Properties**.

2 Select the **Hidden** check box, and then click **OK**.

Important   The **Install** and **Save As** buttons are not valid for Outlook forms. They are intended for use with forms created for Microsoft Exchange Client.

Design Folder Views

To help users organize and manage the information stored in folders, you can create folder views. With views, users can organize and view the same information in different ways within the folder. With Outlook, you can create table, timeline, card, day/week/month, and icon view types.

This chapter focuses on the most commonly used type of view, the table view. When creating table views, you work with the following view features of Outlook:

- **Columns**   As shown in Figure 8.4, columns show values for a particular field in an item under the column heading.

- **Groups**   With groups, you can create categories of items that share a common field value. As shown in Figure 8.4, items in the By Category view are grouped by the type of ad. Groups can be expanded or collapsed.

- **Sort**   You can sort the items in a group based on the criteria you specify. For example, you can sort items by the date received, by field values, or alphabetically.

- **Filter**   With Outlook filters, you create criteria that specify the items to be shown in the folder. For example, in Figure 8.4, the filter applied to the folder specifies that only items created with the Classified Ad form are shown in the folder.

- **Format**   With the **Format** dialog box, you can specify fonts, grid lines, and in-cell editing for a folder. With in-cell editing, users can change information in a cell in the folder.

Figure 8.4   The view chosen by the user determines how items are organized in the folder.

The column heading determines the values that appear in the column below.

The By Category view in the **Current View** box is applied to the folder.

The filter shows only items created with the Classified Ad form.

Items are grouped by type of ad, and then by category.

Items within each group can be sorted from least expensive to most expensive.

Create a New View

Each view you create is given a name that appears in the **Current View** drop-down list box on the **Advanced** toolbar, as shown in the preceding illustration in Figure 8.4. When the view name is clicked in the **Current View** drop-down list box, the view is applied to the folder and the items in the folder are arranged according to the criteria specified in the view.

▶ **To create a new view**

1 On the **View** menu, select **Current View**, and then click **Define Views**.

2 Click **New**.

3 In the **Name of new view** text box, type a name.

4 In the **Type of view** text box, click the type of view you want.

5 Under **Can be used on**, verify that **This folder, visible to everyone** is selected.

6 Click **OK** twice.

7 Click **Apply View**.

Show Only the Views Created for the Folder

For each folder you create, Outlook provides several standard views in the **Current View** drop-down list box. In many cases, these views are not relevant to your folder, so you can remove them from the **Current View** drop-down list box. If you want to remove the standard views from the **Current View** drop-down list box, and show only the custom views you create, you can select the **Only show views created for this folder** check box, as shown in Figure 8.5.

▶ **To show only the custom views created for the folder**

1   On the **View** menu, select **Current View**, and then click **Define Views**.

2   Select the **Only show views created for this folder** check box.

3   Click **Close**.

Figure 8.5   The Only show views created for this folder check box specifies that the standard views are not shown in the Current View drop-down list box on the Standard toolbar.

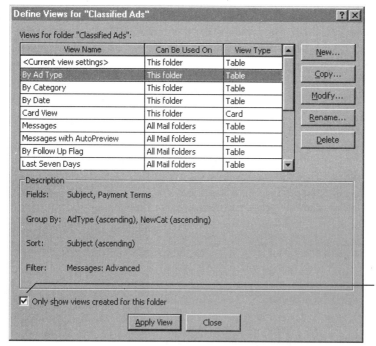

Select this check box to remove the standard views from the **Current View** box.

Create Columns

With Outlook, you can create columns by dragging fields from the **Field Chooser** to the column heading row. When you add a column to a view, the column shows the value of the field for each of the items in the view, as shown in Figure 8.6.

Figure 8.6   Columns for the By Ad Type view in the Classified Ads folder

Under this column heading, you see the values from the Subject field of each item.

Under this column heading, you see the values from the Payment Terms field of each item.

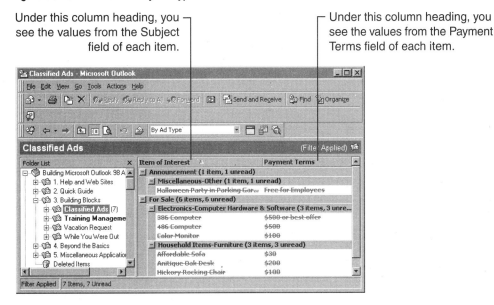

▶ **To add a column to a view**

1   On the **Advanced** toolbar, click the **Field Chooser** icon.

2   In the field set drop-down list box in the **Field Chooser**, click the field set you want to choose fields from.

3   Drag the field you want as the new column heading to the column heading row, as shown in Figure 8.7. Use the double-arrow marker to position the new column heading in the column heading row.

Figure 8.7   The Payment Terms field is added to the column heading row.

Fields can be dragged from the **Field Chooser**
to the column heading row to create columns.

▶ **To remove a column from a view**

• Drag the column heading away from the column heading row until an **X** appears
through the column heading, and then release the mouse button.

Format Columns

By default, a column heading has the same label as the field on which it is based. For
example, the **Payment Terms** column heading is identical to the Payment Terms field.
In some cases, however, you may want to change the column heading label so it is
different than the field name. Such is the case with the **Item of Interest** column
heading in the By Ad Type view.

On the Classified Ads form, the Subject field on the form is labeled Item of Interest, as shown in Figure 8.8. In this case, the Subject field is used for the form because the Subject field provides the unique ability to display its value in the caption on the form window. Much as the label for a field can be changed on the form, the label can also be changed in the column heading of the view. For example, for the By Ad Type view, as shown earlier in Figures 8.6 and 8.7, the column heading for the Subject field is **Item Of Interest**. This is accomplished by changing the label for the field in the **Format Columns** dialog box, as shown in Figure 8.8.

Figure 8.8 The Subject field is labeled Item of Interest. The value of the field appears in the window caption.

▶ **To change the format properties of a column**

1 Right-click the column heading you want to format, and then click **Format Columns** on the shortcut menu.

2 In the **Available fields** list box, click the field you want to format, and then make the changes you want.

3 Click **OK**.

Create Combination Columns

In some cases, you may want to add Combination fields to a view. To help demonstrate the point, this section shows you an example of a Volunteer Registration application. Note that this application is merely an example and is not included in the Building Microsoft Outlook 98 Applications folder.

With the fields on the Volunteer Registration form, as shown in Figure 8.9, a user can enter his or her first name, last name, address, city, and postal code in separate fields.

Figure 8.9   The Volunteer Registration form

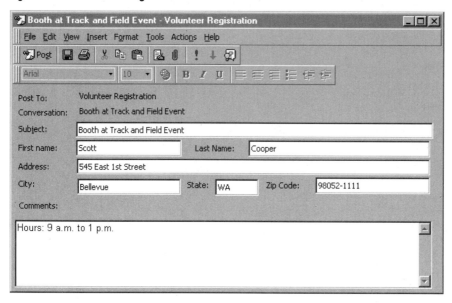

Now, assume you want to create a column in the Volunteer Registration view that combines the Fname and Lname field values and shows them in a single **Name** column, as shown in Figure 8.10. To do this, you create a combination column.

Figure 8.10   The Volunteer Registration folder

The **Name** column combines values from the Fname and Lname fields.

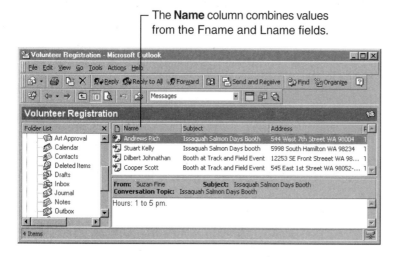

Create a Combination Column That Combines Text Fragments

There are two kinds of Combination fields you can create: those that combine text fragments and those that show the value of the first non-empty field. This section shows you how to create a combination column that combines text fragments. The next section shows you how to create a combination column that shows only the value of the first non-empty field.

▶ **To create a combination column**

1   On the **Advanced** toolbar, click the **Field Chooser** icon.

2   Click **New**.

3   In the **Name** text box, type the column name.

4   In the **Type** drop-down list box, click **Combination**.

5   Click **Edit**.

6   Click **Field** to add the fields you want to combine, and then click **OK** twice.

7   From the **Field Chooser**, drag the field you want as the new column heading to the column heading row. Use the double-arrow marker to position the new column heading in the column heading row.

   Message forms save **User-defined fields** in the Inbox.

   Other forms save **User-defined fields** in the current folder.

In some cases, you may want to change the label of the combination column so it is different from the field name. In addition, you may want to change the formula specified for the combination column. To do this, you use the **Format Columns** dialog box, as shown in Figure 8.11.

▶ **To change a combination column label or formula**

1   Select the folder, right-click the column heading, and then click **Format Columns** on the shortcut menu.

2   In the **Available fields** list box, select the combination field whose properties you want to set, and do one or both of the following:

   • To change the formula, click the button next to the **Formula** text box.

   • To change the column label, change the text in the **Label** text box.

3   Click **OK**.

Figure 8.11   The format properties for the Name column in the Volunteer Registration folder

The field in which the first and last names are combined.

The formula combines the values of the two fields.

The label that appears in the column heading row.

Create a Combination Column That Shows Only the Value of the First Non-Empty Field

In some cases, you may want to create a column that shows only the value of the first non-empty field in the item. For example, you may want to create a combination column if you have multiple item types in the folder, and the items have fields with similar values but different field names. Assume you have documents and standard post items in a folder and you want to create an **Author** column. Rather than creating a **From** column for post items and an **Author** column for document items, you can create an Author/From field, and then click the **Showing only the first non-empty field, ignoring subsequent ones** option.

▶ **To create a combination column that shows only the value of the first non-empty field**

1   On the **Advanced** toolbar, click the **Field Chooser** icon.

2   Click **New**.

3   In the **Name** text box, type a name.

4   In the **Type** drop-down list box, click **Combination**.

5   Click **Edit**.

6   Click **Showing only the first non-empty field, ignoring subsequent ones**.

7   Click **Field** to add the fields you want to combine, and then click **OK** twice.

8   From the **Field Chooser**, drag the field you want as the new column heading to the column heading row. Use the double-arrow marker to position the new column heading in the column heading row.

Create Formula Columns

For some views, you may want to show different field values in the folder. For example, in the sample Training Management folder, as shown in Figure 8.12, the Course ID/Time and Course Name/Instructor columns are formula columns. In the Course ID/Time column, the value of the CourseID field is shown in the column if the item is a Catalog Entry item. If the item is a Course Offering item, the value of the StartTime field is shown in the column.

Figure 8.12   The formula for the Course ID/Time column shows a different field value for each message class.

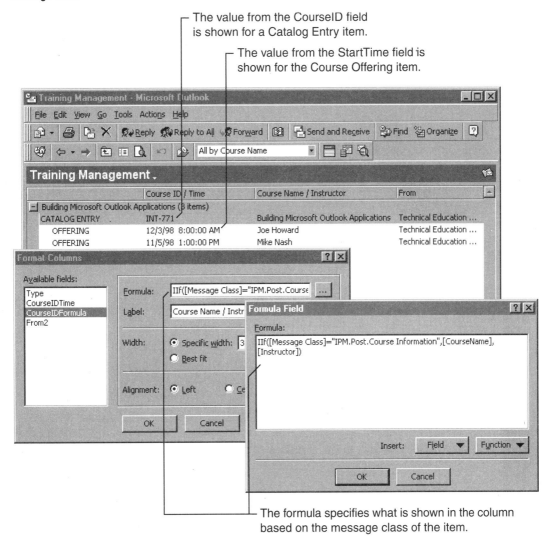

The value from the CourseID field is shown for a Catalog Entry item.

The value from the StartTime field is shown for the Course Offering item.

The formula specifies what is shown in the column based on the message class of the item.

▶ To create a formula column

1   On the **Advanced** toolbar, click the **Field Chooser** icon.

2   Click **New**.

3   In the **Name** text box, type a name.

4   In the **Type** drop-down list box, click **Formula**.

5   Click **Edit**.

6   In the **Formula** box, specify the formula you want for the column, and then click **OK** twice.

7   From the **Field Chooser**, drag the field you want as the new column heading to the column heading row. Use the double-arrow marker to position the new column heading in the column heading row.

You may want to change the label of the formula column so it reflects the field values shown in the column. In addition, you may want to change the formula specified for the column.

▶ To change a formula column label or formula

1   Right-click the column heading, and then click **Format Columns** on the shortcut menu.

2   In the **Available fields** list box, select the field whose properties you want to set, and do one or both of the following:

- To change the formula, click the button next to the **Formula** text box.

- To change the column label, change the text in the **Label** text box.

3   Click **OK**.

Group Items

Groups provide a convenient way to organize items that have the same field values in a folder. For example, in the By Ad Type view in the Classified Ads folder, items are grouped by ad type, and then by category. So items that have a "For Sale" value in the AdType field, as shown in Figure 8.13, are grouped together. In addition, items that have an "Electronics-Computer Hardware & Software" value in the Category field are grouped together.

Figure 8.13   The Classified Ads form

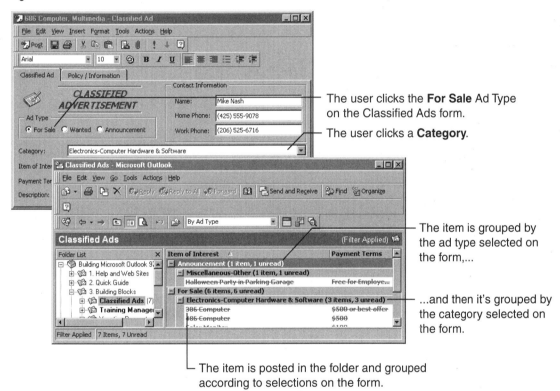

The user clicks the **For Sale** Ad Type on the Classified Ads form.

The user clicks a **Category**.

The item is grouped by the ad type selected on the form,...

...and then it's grouped by the category selected on the form.

The item is posted in the folder and grouped according to selections on the form.

▶ **To group items using Customize Current View**

1 On the **View** menu, select **Current View**, click **Customize Current View**, and then click **Group By**.

2 In the **Select available fields from** drop-down list box, click the field set that contains the field you want to group by.

3 Under **Group items by**, click the field you want to group items by.

4 Optionally, you can click the **Show field in view** check box. This option shows the field in the view above the column heading.

5 Click **Ascending** or **Descending**. When **Ascending** is selected, the groups are arranged alphabetically, starting with "A" at the top.

6 To group items into further subsets, click a field in the next available **Then by** drop-down list box, as shown in Figure 8.14.

7 Click **OK** twice.

Figure 8.14   The Group By dialog box for the By Ad Type view

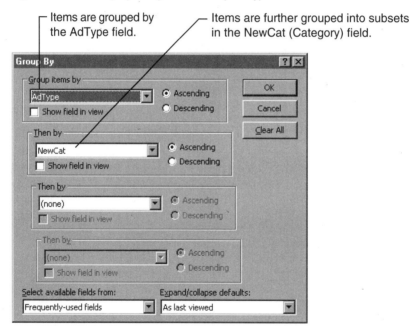

Show or Hide the Group By Box

An easy way to create groups for a view is to show the **Group By** box, and then drag column headings to the **Group By** box. You can then hide the **Group By** box.

▶ **To create groups by using the Group By box**

1 On the **Advanced** toolbar, click the **Group By Box** icon. The **Group By** box appears above the column heading area.

2 Drag the fields you want to group by from the **Field Chooser**, or from the column heading row, to the **Group By** box above the column heading row.

3 After you create the groups you want, click the **Group By Box** icon on the **Advanced** toolbar to hide the **Group By** box.

Sort Items

Sorting items provides a convenient way to organize information within a group. For example, you can sort items in a group by the date the items were received, or you can sort items alphabetically. When you specify a field to sort by, you can specify ascending or descending order. Ascending order sorts items in alphabetical order, with the oldest date (or the lowest value) at the top of the list. Descending order sorts items in alphabetical order, with the most recent date (or highest value) at the top of the list. Figure 8.15 shows the items in the By Ad Type view sorted by **Subject**. Remember that the label for the Subject field is changed in the column heading from **Subject** to **Item of Interest**, as discussed earlier in "Format Columns."

Figure 8.15 Items in each group are sorted alphabetically by Subject in the Item Of Interest column.

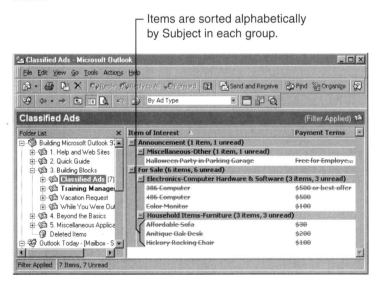

▶ **To sort items**

1   On the **View** menu, click **Current View**, and then click **Customize Current View**.

2   Click **Sort**.

3   In the **Select available fields from** drop-down list box, click the category of fields that contains the field you want to sort by.

4   Under **Sort items by**, click the field you want to sort items by.

5   Click either **Ascending** or **Descending** to choose the sort order.

6   To sort items into further subsets, click a field in the next available **Then by** drop-down list box, as shown in Figure 8.16.

7   Click **OK** twice.

Figure 8.16   Items are sorted alphabetically by the value in the Subject field.

Group by Conversation, Sort by Conversation Index

Conversation and **Conversation Index** are unique properties that you can use to create views for discussion folders so people can view the history of responses to an item, also known as a *conversation thread*. For this section, the Product Ideas folder covered in Chapter 3, "Customize Built-in Modules," is used to provide an example of grouping by **Conversation** and sorting by **Conversation Index**.

Grouping by Conversation

Conversation is a unique property that is inherited from the Subject field. For example, if you submit a standard post item to a folder, the Conversation field of the item is set to the value of the Subject field. Therefore, any responses made to the item automatically inherit the value of the Conversation field. As shown in Figure 8.17, the items in the Product Ideas folder are grouped by **Product Category**, and then by **Conversation**.

Figure 8.17 Items are grouped by Product Category, and then by Conversation. They are sorted by Conversation Index.

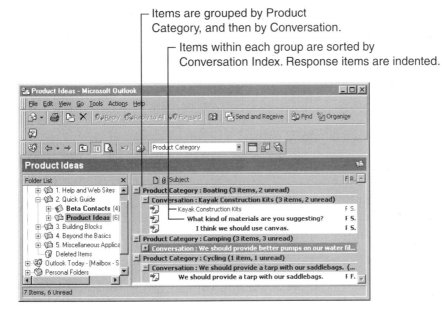

To group items by Conversation

1 On the **View** menu, select **Current View**, and then click **Customize Current View**.

2 Click **Group By**.

3 In the **Select available fields from** drop-down list box, click **Frequently-used fields**.

4 Under **Group items by**, click the field that you want to group items by.

5 In the **Then by** drop-down list box, click **Conversation**, as shown in Figure 8.18.

6 Click **OK** twice.

Figure 8.18   Items are grouped by Product Category, and then by Conversation.

Sorting by Conversation Index

The **Conversation Index** property is a way of keeping track of responses. When you sort by **Conversation Index**, the responses to each item are indented from, and follow directly after, the original item. In this way, users can track the history of responses to an item, as shown earlier in Figure 8.17.

▶ **To sort items by Conversation Index**

1   On the **View** menu, select **Current View**, and then click **Customize Current View**.

2   Click **Sort**.

3   Under **Sort items by**, click **Conversation Index**, as shown in Figure 8.19.

4   Click **OK** twice.

Figure 8.19   Items are sorted by Conversation Index, so response items are indented and follow the original item.

Filter Items

Filters provide a way to quickly and easily find information in a folder. When a filter is applied in a view, only the items that meet the filter conditions show in the folder. For example, as shown in Figure 8.20, the filter created for the By Ad Type view shows only items created with the Classified Ad form (IPM.Post.CreateAd) in the folder.

Figure 8.20 **The filter for the By Ad Type view shows only items created with the Classified Ad form (IPM.Post.CreateAd) in the folder.**

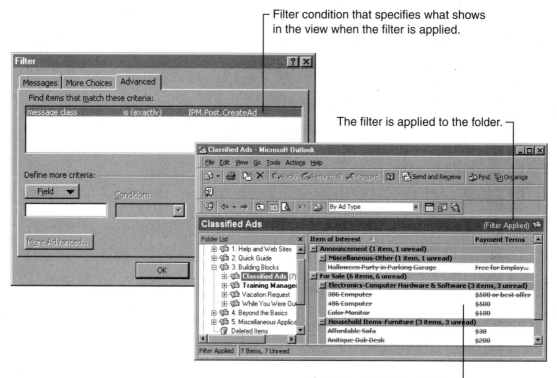

Filter condition that specifies what shows in the view when the filter is applied.

The filter is applied to the folder.

Only items created with the Classified Ad form show in the folder.

Filters consist of a condition or set of conditions that determine what items are shown in a folder. For example, a condition may be *From:Jim Hance*. Conditions can have multiple arguments. For example, *From:Jim Hance, Don Funk*. Here are a few simple guidelines to follow when creating conditions:

- Multiple conditions are AND values. For example, the condition *From:Jim Hance;Subject:GG&G* is true if the From field of the incoming item contains "Jim Hance" and the Subject field contains "GG&G."

- Multiple arguments within a condition are OR values. For example, the condition *From:Jim Hance;Karl Buhl;Don Funk;Max Benson* is true if the From field contains any of the names included in the expression.

Specify Simple Filter Conditions

In some cases, you may want to filter messages that meet specific criteria. For example, you may want to filter all incoming messages from a particular user or about a particular subject.

▶ **To filter simple message properties**

1   On the **View** menu, select **Current View**, and then click **Customize Current View**.

2   Click **Filter**.

3   On the **Messages** page, specify the properties you want for the filter. For example, to create a filter that shows only messages from a particular person, click **From**, and then double-click the person's name in the list.

4   Click **OK** twice.

Specify Advanced Filter Conditions

On the **Advanced** page, you can create a wide variety of filter conditions. For example, you can specify that only items with a specific message class show in the view. In addition, you can specify that only items with a specific value in a field show in the view.

Filter on Message Class

When you filter on message class, you specify that only items created with a particular form are visible in the folder. For example, in the By Ad Type view in the Classified Ads folder, only items created with the Classified Ad form show in the view.

▶ **To filter on message class**

1   On the **View** menu, select **Current View**, and then click **Customize Current View**.

2   Click **Filter**.

3   Click the **Advanced** page.

4   Click **Field**, point to **All Mail fields**, and then click **Message Class**.

5   In the **Condition** drop-down list box, click **is (exactly)**.

6   In the **Value** text box, type the message class, as shown in Figure 8.21.

7   Click **Add to List**.

8   Click **OK** twice.

Figure 8.21 The condition for the filter in the By Ad Type view specifies that only items with the message class IPM.Post.CreateAd show in the folder.

Shows the message class of the CreateAd form.

Click here to add the condition to the list.

Filter on Field Values

You can create a filter that shows only items that have a specific value in a field. For example, as shown in Figure 8.22, the conditions for the filter specify that only items created with the Classified Ad form, and that have the value "For Sale" in the AdType field and the value "Transportation-Cars" in the NewCat field show in the view.

Figure 8.22 Advanced filter conditions for the Ad Type view

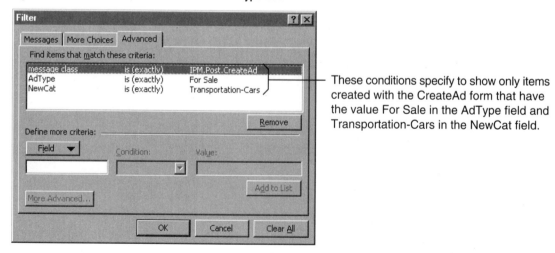

These conditions specify to show only items created with the CreateAd form that have the value For Sale in the AdType field and Transportation-Cars in the NewCat field.

▶ **To filter on a field value**

1 On the **View** menu, select **Current View**, and then click **Customize Current View**.

2 Click **Filter**.

3 Click the **Advanced** page.

4 Click **Field**, point to the field set you want, and then click the field you want.

5 Do one of the following:

- To filter a single field value, click **is (exactly)** in the **Condition** drop-down list box, and then type the value you want in the **Value** text box.

- To filter multiple values in a field, click **contains** in the **Condition** list box, and then type the values you want, separated by a comma, in the **Value** text box.

6 Click **Add to List**.

7 Click **OK** twice.

Format Views

By using the **Other Settings** dialog box, accessible from the **View Summary** dialog box, you can change the fonts in the view, specify grid lines for the view, specify if group headings are shaded, and turn on in-cell editing so users can enter and edit information in the cells in the folder, as shown in Figure 8.23.

Figure 8.23 Format options for the By Ad Type view

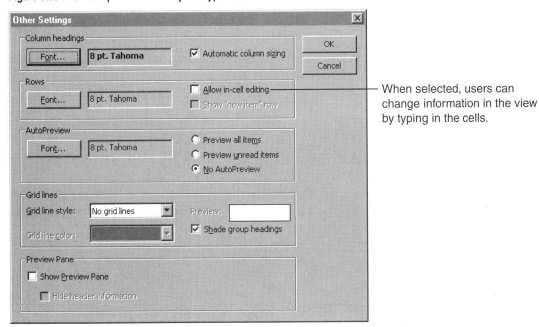

When selected, users can change information in the view by typing in the cells.

▶ **To format a view**

1   In the **Current View** drop-down list box on the **Advanced** toolbar, switch to the view you want to change.

2   On the **View** menu, select **Current View**, and then click **Customize Current View**.

3   Click **Other Settings**.

4   Select the options you want, and then click **OK** twice.

Set General Properties

On the **General** page of the **Properties** dialog box, as shown in Figure 8.24, you can specify the default form that appears when a user creates a new item in a folder. For example, for the Classified Ads folder, the Classified Ads form appears when the user clicks the **New Post in This Folder** command on the **Actions** menu.

Figure 8.24   The When posting to this folder, use option specifies that the Classified Ads form appears when the New Post in This Folder command is clicked.

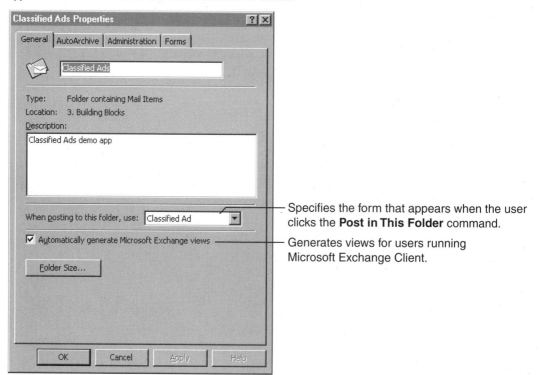

Specifies the form that appears when the user clicks the **Post in This Folder** command.

Generates views for users running Microsoft Exchange Client.

▶ **To set general properties**

1   In the Folder List, right-click the folder you want to set properties for, and then
    click **Properties** on the shortcut menu.

2   Click the **General** page.

▶ **To specify the form that appears when the user clicks the New Post in This Folder
command**

- In the **When posting to this folder, use** drop-down list box, click the form that you
  want to appear when the user clicks **Post in This Folder** after selecting **New** on the
  File menu.

  If you do not want a custom form to appear, click **Post** in the **When posting to this
  folder, use** drop-down list box.

▶ **To automatically generate Microsoft Exchange views**

- If your organization uses both Microsoft Exchange Client and Outlook, select the
  Automatically generate Microsoft Exchange views check box. This option
  generates Microsoft Exchange views for the folder so the views can be seen by
  users of Microsoft Exchange Client.

Note   This property is only available for Outlook table views.

Test Forms and Views

After you publish forms and define views for the folder, you need to test them to make
sure they work as expected.

- To test the forms, open the folder in which the forms are published, and then click
  the menu commands that are associated with the form on the **Actions** menu. In the
  form, enter the information you want, and then click the **Post** button. After posting
  the item in the folder, double-click it to open it and make sure it shows information
  correctly in the form. You should test each form in the folder.

- To test views, open the folder you want to test, and then click each of the views in
  the **Current View** drop-down list box on the **Advanced** toolbar. If the folder has
  multiple forms, you should post several types of items in the folder before testing
  the views.

When you finish testing the forms and views, you can delete the test items you posted
in the folder.

Copy the Folder to Public Folders

After adding forms, defining views, and testing their functionality, you are ready to copy your folder to Public Folders. You can then complete the folder design by designating types of items allowed in the folder, setting permissions, setting administration properties, and specifying rules. This step is only necessary if you started the folder design process with a personal folder or a mailbox folder, and not in a public folder.

Depending on the policies of your organization, you may not have permission to add a folder to Public Folders. You may be required to hand off the folder to your administrator who then copies the folder and completes the design task according to your specifications. Or, you may be given permissions to copy your folder to a specific public folder and then complete the task yourself. See your administrator for specific instructions.

▶ To copy the folder to a new location

1   In the Folder List, right-click the folder, and then click **Copy "*folder name*"** on the shortcut menu.

2   Click the public folder you want to copy the folder to, and then click **OK**.

Specify Internet Newsgroup

The **Internet News** page identifies the folder as an Internet newsgroup folder. Users of Internet newsreader software within a Microsoft Exchange environment can view and post items posted in the newsgroup folder, within Public Folders.

▶ To open the Internet News page of a Public Folder

1   In the Folder List, right-click the folder you want to identify as a newsgroup folder, and then click **Properties** on the shortcut menu.

2   Click the **Internet News** page.

Set Administration Properties

After you copy a folder to a public folder, it's a good idea to restrict access to the folder while you set folder permissions and test the folder. To restrict access to the folder, you can use the **This folder is available to** option on the **Administration** page, as shown in Figure 8.25.

▶ **To restrict access to the folder**

1 In the Folder List, right-click the folder, and then click **Properties** on the shortcut menu.

2 Click the **Administration** page.

3 Click **Owners only**.

Figure 8.25   Administration options for the Classified Ads folder

Click this option if you want to preaddress the To field of a form to a specific folder.

Click this option to restrict access to the folder while it's under construction.

Click this option to create or edit rules for the folder.

Click this option to forward all posted items to a designated recipient or public folder.

Initial View on Folder

You use this option to specify the folder view that you want to display when the user first opens the folder. By default, this view is the Messages or Normal view, depending on the type of items the folder contains.

Drag/Drop Posting Is A

You use this option to specify how Outlook formats items that are dragged to a folder. You can specify that the drag/drop operation formats the posted item in one of the following ways:

- **Move/Copy**   This option specifies that when an item is dragged to a folder, Outlook does not reformat the item. For example, if Eric Lang drags an item, sent by Clair Hector, from his Inbox to the Employee Feedback folder, the item appearing in the Employee Feedback folder is shown as sent by Clair Hector.

- **Forward**   This option specifies that when an item is dragged to a folder, Outlook reformats the item to show that is has been forwarded by the user who dragged it to the folder. For example, if Eric Lang drags an Inbox item from Clair Hector to the Employee Feedback folder, the item in the Employee Feedback folder appears as though it has been forwarded by Eric Lang.

Add Folder Address to Personal Address Book

You use this option to preaddress forms. When you click the **Personal Address Book** button, the folder address is automatically added to your Personal Address Book. You can then use the folder address in your Personal Address Book to preaddress a Message form to a folder or to create a rule that automatically forwards items to the folder.

Tip   Another way to make the folder address available for preaddressing a form is to ask your administrator to add the folder address to the Global Address Book. You can then select the folder name from the Global Address Book to preaddress a form.

See Also   For more information about preaddressing a Message form to a folder address, see "To Field" in Chapter 6, "Controls, Fields, and Properties."

This Folder Is Available To

You use this option to make a folder unavailable while it's under construction.

You can click **Owners only** if you are modifying or creating a folder design. This gives only those people with the Owner role permission to access the folder. After the folder is tested and is ready for general use, you can click **All users with access permission** and make the folder available for public use.

Tip   The **Owners only** option prevents access to the specified folder, but does not prevent access to subfolders. This way, users can post items in a subfolder while the parent folder is disabled.

Folder Assistant

You can click the **Folder Assistant** button to create rules that automatically process incoming folder items. Rules are described in more detail in "Design Rules" later in this chapter.

Moderated Folder

You can use a moderated folder to cause all posted items to be forwarded to a designated recipient or public folder for review. Permissions must be granted to move these items back into the folder for general viewing once they have been reviewed and approved.

Set Permissions

You assign permissions to users to define the functions they can perform in the folder. You determine who can view and use the folder by adding the user names, distribution list names, or public folder names to the **Name** list box on the **Permissions** page. After the names are added to the **Name** list box, you can assign roles to define the permissions for each user or distribution list, as shown in Figure 8.26.

Note Permissions can be set for folders in your Mailbox or Public folders. Permissions cannot be set for Personal folders.

Figure 8.26   Permissions for the Classified Ads folder

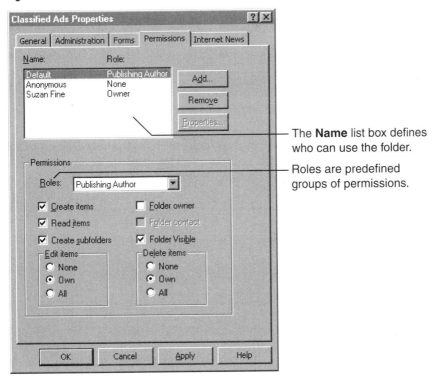

The **Name** list box defines who can use the folder.

Roles are predefined groups of permissions.

▶ **To open the Permissions page**

1   In the Folder List, right-click the folder you want to set permissions for, and then click **Properties** on the shortcut menu.

2   Click the **Permissions** page.

Modify the Name List

The names in the **Name** text box determine who can view and use the folder. If you create the folder, you are automatically given owner permissions for the folder. With owner permissions, you can add users to, and remove users from, the **Name** text box. You can also change permissions for selected users.

One name in the **Name** text box is Default. The permissions defined for Default are granted to all users who have access to the folder. If you want to give a particular user permissions other than Default, add the user name to the **Name** text box, and then set permissions for that user.

When you test the folder, it's a good idea to set the Default permissions to None in the **Roles** drop-down list box. Then, grant access to a limited number of users. When you are sure that everything is working correctly in the folder, you can change the Default permissions and add names to the **Name** text box.

You can remove any name from the **Name** text box except Default and, if you are the sole owner of the folder, your name. If you remove Default or your name, they will reappear the next time you view the **Permissions** page.

About Distribution Lists

Distribution lists provide a convenient way to assign permissions to a group of users. For example, rather than enter 50 names in the **Name** list box, you can enter the distribution list name to assign permissions to all users on the list.

▶ **To add a user, distribution list, or folder name to the Name box**

1   On the **Permissions** page, click **Add**.

2   Click the user, distribution list, or folder you want to add, and then click **Add**.

3   Click **OK**.

Assign Roles

XE " " \r "roles" roles, assigning XE " " roles, assigning XE " " roles, assigning XE " " \r "roles" roles, assigning XE " " \r "roles" roles, assigningWhen you set permissions for a user, you define the functions they can perform within the folder. You can set permissions by using predefined roles or by using custom roles:

- **Predefined Roles** Predefined groups of permissions that are available from the **Roles** drop-down list box.

- **Custom Roles**   Permissions you set for the user that do not match any of the predefined roles.

▶ To assign roles to users

1   In the **Name** text box on the **Permissions** page, click the user name you want to set permissions for.

2   In the **Roles** drop-down list box, click a role for the user.

3   The following table lists the roles and the predefined permissions that are assigned to each role.

Role	Description
Owner	Create, read, modify, and delete all items and files and create subfolders. As the folder owner, you can change permissions others have for the folder.
Publishing Editor	Create, read, modify, and delete all items and files and create subfolders.
Editor	Create, read, modify, and delete all items and files.
Nonediting Author	Create and read items. This person or group cannot edit, but can delete items and files you create.
Publishing Author	Create and read items and files, create subfolders, and modify and delete items and files you create.
Author	Create and read items and files, and modify and delete items and files you create.
Reviewer	Read items and files only.
Contributor	Create items and files only. The user cannot open the folder.
None	The user cannot open the folder.
Custom	Perform activities defined by the folder owner, from options selected on the **Permissions** page.

▶ To assign a custom Role

1   In the **Name** list box, click the user name whose permissions you want to set.

2   In the **Roles** drop-down list box, click the role that most closely resembles the permissions you want to grant to the user.

3   Under **Permissions**, select the options you want. If the permissions do not match a role, you see **Custom** in the **Roles** drop-down list box. If the permissions match a role, the role will show in the **Roles** drop-down list box.

Design Rules

Rules automatically process items as they arrive in a folder. A rule consists of two parts: A set of conditions that are applied to an incoming item, and the actions that are taken if the conditions are met, as shown in Figure 8.27.

Figure 8.27 Rules for the Training Management folder

If the incoming item matches
the conditions of the rule ...

... then the action for
the rule is triggered.

You can use rules to:

- Specify that specific types of items are automatically returned to the sender.
- Automatically delete items based on the specified conditions.
- Automatically reply to specific kinds of items with a reply template.
- Automatically forward specific types of items to another folder or user.

▶ **To create rules**

1 In the Folder List, right-click the folder, and then click **Properties** on the shortcut menu.

2 Click the **Administration** tab, and then click **Folder Assistant**.

Note Folder Assistant is only available for public folders.

Specifying Conditions of a Rule

The conditions of a rule identify the items that are to be processed by the rule. These conditions can range from very simple to relatively advanced. An example of a simple condition is *From:James Allard*. This condition states that if an item is submitted to the folder and the item is from James Allard, then a specified action is taken. A more advanced set of conditions is *Only Messages That Do Not Match This Criteria; From:James Allard;Joe Howard;Scott Cooper*. These conditions state that if the items submitted to the folder are not from James Allard, Joe Howard, or Scott Cooper, then a specified action is taken.

Rules Syntax

Before you create rules, there are a few fundamental concepts you need to know:

- A rule consists of conditions and a corresponding action. A rule can have one condition or multiple conditions. For example, *From:James Allard* is a single condition and *From:James Allard;Subject:GG&G* are two conditions. Each condition is delimited by a semicolon. A condition can consist of an argument or multiple arguments. For example, *From:James Allard* is a condition with a single argument and *From:James Allard; Joe Howard* is a condition with multiple arguments.

- Multiple conditions within a rule are AND values. For example, the condition *From:James Allard;Subject:GG&G* is true if the From field of the incoming items contains "James Allard" and the Subject field contains "GG&G."

- Multiple arguments within a condition are OR values. For example, the condition *From:James Allard;Joe Howard;Max Benson* is true if the From field of the incoming item contains any one of the names included in the expression.

Specifying Simple Conditions

With simple conditions, you can specify conditions based on the contents of the From, Sent, To, Subject, and Message fields of an incoming item.

▶ **To specify simple conditions**

1 From the **Folder Assistant** dialog box on the **Administration** page, click **Add Rule**, or select the rule you want and then click **Edit Rule**.

2 Under **When a message arrives that meets the following conditions**, type the criteria in the associated boxes.

Specifying Advanced Conditions

With the **Advanced** dialog box, you can specify a wide range of conditions, including conditions based on values in user-defined fields in the folder.

▶ **To specify advanced conditions**

1 In the **Folder Assistant** dialog box on the **Administration** page, click **Add Rule**, or select the rule you want and then click **Edit Rule**.

2 Click **Advanced**.

3 Type the criteria in the appropriate boxes.

Specifying That a Rule Applies to Items That Do Not Match the Conditions

You can create rules that take actions if conditions are met and rules that take actions if the conditions are not met.

▶ **To specify that a rule applies only to items that do not match the conditions**

- In the **Advanced** dialog box, click the **Only items that do not match these conditions** check box.

Specifying Conditions with User-Defined Fields

In some cases, you may want to create conditions based on user-defined fields in the folder. For example, for the Training Management folder, you may want to create a rule that forwards a Course Offering item to a distribution list when a Course Offering item that pertains to a specific subject is posted in the folder.

▶ **To specify custom fields as conditions**

1 In the **Advanced** dialog box, under **Show properties of**, do one of the following.

To	Click
Show custom fields of the currently selected forms	**Selected forms**, click **Forms**, and then select the forms you want
Show the standard document fields	**Document**
Show the custom fields of the currently selected folder	**Folder:** *folder name*

2 Under **Properties**, select the check box of the property that you want to use to create a condition.

3 In the list or text boxes to the right of the check boxes, do one or more of the following:

- If the field to the right of the selected check box is a text box, you can type one or more values in the text box. For example, if you want to create a rule that forwards Training Management items that have the value "Building Microsoft Outlook 98 Applications" in the CourseDescription field, then type **Building Microsoft Outlook 98 Applications** in the text box to its right, as shown in Figure 8.28. If you specify multiple values in the text boxes, separate the values with a semicolon.

- If a drop-down list box and a text box are to the right of the check box, click the value in the list box first. Then type or click the criteria in the box to its right.

4 Click **OK**.

Figure 8.28   With Advanced properties, you can build conditions based on specific field values in a field.

Click the check box of the field that you want to specify conditions for.

This condition identifies items with the value Building Microsoft Outlook Applications in the CourseDescription field.

Specifying Actions for a Rule

Actions occur when the conditions of a rule are met.

▶ **To specify an action**

• In the **Edit Rule** dialog box, under **Perform these actions**, do one of the following.

To	Click
Return the item to the sender if the conditions of the rule are met	**Return to Sender**
Delete the item if the conditions of the rule are met	**Delete**
Specify the Reply message that is sent if the conditions of the rule are not met	Click **Reply with**, click **Template**, and then fill out the message box of the form with the Reply message you want to send.
Forward an item if the conditions of the rule are not met	Click **Forward**, click **To**, and then select the user name, distribution list, or folder.

See Also   For more information about specifying actions, see Chapter 7, "Actions."

Test and Release the Folder

After you create or modify a folder, you should pilot test it with a few users. When testing the folder, you and the users involved in the pilot test should compose, submit, and open items in the folder and check views, permissions, and rules to make sure they work as planned.

When you're sure the folder is working properly, you can open the **Administration** page in the folder **Properties** dialog box and make the folder available to the general public.

▶ **To make the folder available to all users with access permission**

1 In the Folder List, right-click the folder, and then click **Properties** on the shortcut menu.

2 Click the **Administration** page.

3 Click **All users with access permission**.

4 Click **OK**.

If you plan to replicate the folder application between servers, define replication settings and test the folder on a small scale before replicating it between a large number of servers.

When the folder is ready for public use, send out an announcement to the users who will be using the folder to let them know the folder is available. You can include a link to the folder in your announcement message so users can easily find the folder.

For more information about	See
Setting permissions	"Set Permissions" earlier in this chapter
Distributing and maintaining folders	Chapter 13, "Distribute and Maintain Applications"
Replicating folders	The Microsoft Exchange Server documentation

Beyond the Basics

Contents

Chapter 9   Use Visual Basic Scripting Edition with Outlook   267

Chapter 10   The Business Card Request Application   341

Chapter 11   The Help Desk Application   389

Chapter 12   The Document Tracking Application   429

Chapter 13   Distribute and Maintain Applications   477

Use Visual Basic Scripting Edition with Outlook

In This Chapter

The Outlook Script Editor   268

Troubleshooting Code Using the Script Debugger   270

How to Open an Item That Contains VBScript   273

Information Resources for Using VBScript in Outlook 98   273

Object Libraries   276

Object Models   279

The Application Object   284

The NameSpace Object   287

The Outlook Window (Explorer Object)   288

The AddressLists Collection Object   289

The AddressList Object   290

The AddressEntries Collection Object   290

The AddressEntry Object   291

The Folders Collection Object   295

The MAPIFolder Object   296

The Items Collection Object   298

The PostItem Object   301

The MailItem Object   303

The AppointmentItem Object   306

The MeetingItem Object   311

The TaskItem Object   315

The TaskRequestItem Object   316

The Inspector Object   318

The Pages Collection Object   320

The Page Object   321

The Controls Collection Object   321

(continued on next page)

(continued from previous page)
The Control Object 323
The UserProperties Collection Object 325
The Recipients Collection Object 326
Events 328
A Quick Tutorial — the Library Order Application 336
Automation 340

By using Microsoft Visual Basic Scripting Edition (VBScript) in Outlook, you can create procedures that control Outlook folders, forms, items, pages, properties, actions, events, and controls. For example, with VBScript, you can create procedures that use code to create and send or post items. You can also use VBScript to modify Outlook events. For example, you can modify the Write event of a Post form so that it automatically sends a notification message to a distribution list when a new item is posted in a folder. You can also use VBScript to write information from an Outlook item to a database, or you can display information from a database in an Outlook item. In addition, you can use VBScript to automate processes. For example, you can create a procedure for a Bulk Mailer Announcement form that automatically addresses an announcement item to all users in a specified Contacts folder.

This chapter is designed to give you the fundamental skills and knowledge you need to create industrial strength applications by using VBScript. This chapter covers how to use VBScript to:

- Reference a folder collection or a folder in the Folder List.

- Create, open, send, and post standard and custom items.

- Open and close standard and custom forms.

- Set and change field values in items.

- Hide or show a form page.

- Change the properties of a control on a page.

- Specify the recipients of an item.

- Modify Outlook events.

The Outlook Script Editor

With the Script Editor, which is available for each form, you can add procedures to forms to control an Outlook application or another application such as Microsoft Word or Microsoft Excel. In addition, you can create procedures to control Outlook folders, forms, and items, and controls and properties in items. For example, you can create a procedure to automatically set a folder as the active folder, and then create and post an item in the folder. Or, you can create a procedure that creates a collection of items in a folder based on a specified filter, and then changes a field value for each item in the collection.

▶ **To view the Outlook Script Editor**

1 In Inbox, click **New Mail Message** on the **Actions** menu.

2 On the **Tools** menu of the form, click **Forms**, and then click **Design This Form**.

3 On the **Form Design** toolbar, click **View Code**.

An Introduction to Using the Script Editor

As an introduction to using the Script Editor, this section describes how to add code to the PropertyChange event to show a message whenever you change a standard field value on a Mail Message form. The PropertyChange event is triggered any time you change a standard field value on the form. For example, if you change the standard **Importance** or **Sensitivity** options on a Message form, the PropertyChange event is triggered because a field value has been changed.

▶ **To create and test a PropertyChange event**

1 On the Script Editor **Script** menu, click **Event Handler**.

2 In the **Insert Event Handler** dialog box, double-click **PropertyChange**.

3 Add the code you want, as shown in Figure 9.1.

4 On the **Form** menu of the form, click **Run This Form**.

5 On the **Standard** toolbar of the form in Run mode, click **Importance: High**.

6 Click **OK** to close the message.

7 On the **File** menu of the form in Run mode, click **Close**.

Figure 9.1   The PropertyChange event in the Script Editor

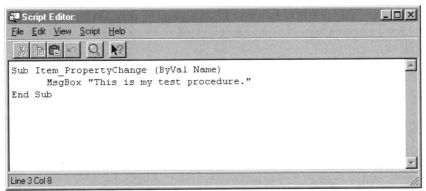

If there is an error in the syntax of the code when you run the form, Outlook displays a message and immediately stops executing the code.

Changes you make to a script do not affect forms that are currently running. If you want to compare the effect of a code change, run one form, change the procedure you want to test, and then run a second instance of the form (from the form that is in Design mode). You can then compare the two forms in Run mode to see how the code change affects the second instance.

Jumping to a Line of Code

When you test procedures, you sometimes see an error message that refers to a line of code. The Script Editor provides a way to jump to a particular line of code.

▶ **To jump to a line of code**

1   On the Script Editor **Edit** menu, click **Go To**.

2   In the **Line Number** text box, type the line number, and then click **OK**.

Troubleshooting Code Using the Script Debugger

The Microsoft Script Debugger is a tool that helps you control the execution of a script so you can observe where run-time errors occur. You can view and change the value of a variable while the script is running, letting you observe how different values affect the execution of the script. You can also see all the names of all the procedures that are currently executing.

The Script Debugger is included in the Outlook 98 Development Tools component, which you must install after installing Outlook 98.

▶ **To install Microsoft Outlook Development Tools**

1   Insert the companion CD-ROM into your CD-ROM drive.

2   Click **Start**, click **Settings**, and then click **Control Panel**.

3   Double-click **Add/Remove Programs**.

4   On the **Install/Uninstall** page, click Microsoft Outlook 98, and then click **Add/Remove**.

5   In the **Outlook 98 Active Setup** dialog box, click **Add New Components**.

6   On the **Outlook 98 Components** page in Microsoft Internet Explorer, select **Development Tools**, and then click **Next**.

7   Click **Install Now**.

8   When Setup finishes, click **Restart Now**.

The Development Tools component also includes Microsoft Outlook 98 Customization and Forms, and Visual Basic Reference Help files.

▶ **To open the Script Debugger**

• With a form in Run mode, on the **Tools** menu, click **Forms,** and then click **Script Debugger**.

Figure 9.2   The Script Debugger

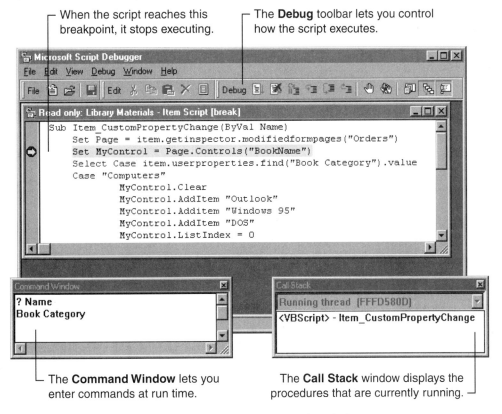

┌ When the script reaches this breakpoint, it stops executing.

┌ The **Debug** toolbar lets you control how the script executes.

└ The **Command Window** lets you enter commands at run time.

The **Call Stack** window displays the procedures that are currently running. ┘

The Script Debugger lets you view the script and copy text from it, but you cannot use the debugger to edit the script.

Controlling How a Script Executes

The **Debug** toolbar lets you control the execution of your script at run time. Using this toolbar, you can:

- Set and clear breakpoints that halt execution of the script at the breakpoint.

- Step through the script, executing each line one at a time.

- Resume normal execution after stopping for a breakpoint.

See Also For more information about controlling script execution, see Microsoft Script Debugger Help.

Entering Commands at Run Time

Using the **Command Window** of the Script Debugger, you can execute script commands any time that the script is halted at a breakpoint or has stepped to another statement. The command reflects or affects the state of the script at the point where execution has halted.

▶ **To enter script commands**

1 On the **Debug** toolbar, click **Command Window**.

2 In the **Command Window**, type the command you want executed, and then press ENTER.

For example, to display the current value of the variable *Name*, type the following in the **Command Window**:

```
? Name
```

To change the value of the variable, use an assignment statement, as in this example:

```
Name = "New Name"
```

Viewing the Call Stack

The **Call Stack** window lets you see the names of all the procedures that are currently executing. This is especially useful if your script contains nested procedures, that is, procedures that are called within other procedures.

▶ **To view the call stack**

- On the **Debug** toolbar, click **Call Stack**.

How to Open an Item That Contains VBScript

When designing and editing forms, you can prevent VBScript code from executing when you open a form, by holding down the SHIFT key when you select the form. For example, to open a form in your Personal Forms Library, click **Forms** on the Outlook **Tools** menu, select **Choose Form**, select **Personal Forms Library**, and then hold down the SHIFT key and double-click the form you want to open.

The form opens but the VBScript code does not execute. This method helps to ensure that values are not inadvertently written to the fields in the form when the Open event is fired when the form opens. It also helps to ensure that the fields do not contain unwanted data in them when you publish the form.

Information Resources for Using VBScript in Outlook 98

In the 1. Help and Web Sites folder in the Building Microsoft Outlook 98 Applications folder, you can find folders containing items that tell you how to install Help files or to visit Web sites. These Web sites can assist you in your VBScript programming tasks. Here is an overview of the Web sites available:

- **http://www.microsoft.com/vbscript/**   The Microsoft VBScript Web site. If you are using Microsoft Internet Explorer version 3.0 or above, you can get to this site by opening the 1. Help and Web Sites folder in the Building Microsoft Outlook 98 Applications folder. You can then open the **Web Sites** folder and double-click the **Microsoft Visual Basic Scripting Edition** item.

- **http://www.microsoft.com/outlook/**   The Microsoft Outlook Web Site. This site contains VBScript samples, form samples, and valuable tips and techniques for creating Outlook applications. If you are using Microsoft Internet Explorer 3.0 or above, you can get to this site by opening the **1. Help and Web Sites** folder in the Building Microsoft Outlook 98 Applications folder. You can then open the **Web Sites** folder and double-click the **Microsoft Outlook** item.

The VBScript Samples folder in the 4. Beyond the Basics folder provides sample items that let you view and run VBScript code snippets.

▶ **To open the VBScript folder**

1   In the Folder List, open the **Building Microsoft Outlook 98 Applications** folder, and then open the **4. Beyond the Basics** folder.

2   Open the **VBScript** folder, and then open the **VBScript Samples** folder.

3   Double-click the item you want to open, and then click a command button to execute the sample procedure.

4   To view the sample code, click **Forms** on the **Tools** menu, click **Design This Form**, and then on the **Form Design** toolbar, click **View Code**.

Microsoft Outlook Visual Basic Help

You can use the Microsoft Outlook Visual Basic Reference Help file to view the methods and properties for each object, as shown in Figure 9.3.

▶ **To use Microsoft Outlook Visual Basic Reference Help**

1   On the Script Editor **Help** menu, click **Microsoft Outlook Object Library Help**.

2   Click the **Contents** page, and then double-click **Microsoft Outlook Visual Basic Reference**.

3   Double-click **Objects**, and then double-click the object you want.

Figure 9.3   Help for the Application object

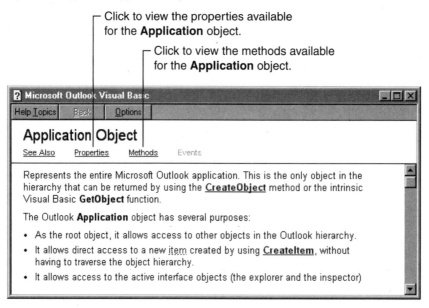

┌ Click to view the properties available
for the **Application** object.

┌ Click to view the methods available
for the **Application** object.

A Caution About Microsoft Outlook Visual Basic Help

Many of the code examples in Microsoft Outlook Visual Basic Reference Help (Vbaoutl.hlp) were written for Visual Basic for Applications. These code examples will run in VBScript with these slight modifications:

- Substitute the **Application** object for the **CreateObject("Outlook.Application")** statement.

- Replace constants with their numeric values.

▶ **To view the numeric values for Outlook constants**

1 On the Script Editor **Help** menu, click **Microsoft Outlook Object Library Help**.

2 Click the **Contents** page.

3 In the **Contents** list, double-click **Microsoft Outlook Visual Basic Reference**.

4 Double-click **Microsoft Outlook Constants**.

For example, a code example for the **GetDefaultFolder** method in the Microsoft Outlook Visual Basic Reference Help file is as follows:

```
Set myOlApp = CreateObject("Outlook.Application")
Set myNameSpace = myOlApp.GetNameSpace("MAPI")
Set myCalendar = myNameSpace.GetDefaultFolder(olFolderCalendar)
```

To make this work in VBScript, you must change the code as follows:

```
Set myNameSpace = Application.GetNameSpace("MAPI")
Set myCalendar = myNameSpace.GetDefaultFolder(9)
```

The Implied Item Object

Another difference between VBA and VBScript is how the context of the code affects how you can access objects. Because a VBA procedure is running in the context of another application, all object references must be explicit. In VBScript, however, when you reference the active item in Outlook, the **Item** object is implied. As such, you do not need to set the **Item** object when referencing the active item. For example, to set the value of an active item's Subject field, you can use the following statement:

```
Item.Subject = "This is a test"
```

You can also leave out the reference to the item, as shown in this example:

```
Subject = "This is a test"
```

▶ To test this example

1 On the Outlook **Actions** menu, click **New Mail Message**.

2 On the form **Tools** menu, click **Forms**, and then click **Design This Form**.

3 On the **Form Design** toolbar, click **Control Toolbox**.

4 Resize the **Message** control on the form to make room for a CommandButton control.

5 Drag a CommandButton control to the form. By default, the CommandButton control is given the name CommandButton1.

6 On the **Form Design** toolbar, click **View Code**.

7 In the Script Editor window, replace the current CommandButton1_Click procedure with the following:

```
Sub CommandButton1_Click
    Subject = "The item is implied."
End Sub
```

8 On the **Form** menu of the form in Design mode, click **Run This Form**.

9 Click **CommandButton1**.

10 In the **Subject** box of the form, you now see **The item is implied**.

Object Libraries

An object library is a file with an .olb file name extension that provides information to programs such as VBScript and Visual Basic for Applications about available objects. For example, the Microsoft Outlook 98 Object Model (Msoutl85.olb) contains the methods, events, properties, and constants that can be used to program the available objects. Sometimes object libraries are contained within dynamic-link library (.dll) files, such as Fm20.dll, which contains the Microsoft Forms 2.0 Object Library.

When you use VBScript in Outlook, there are two primary object libraries that you use:

- **The Microsoft Outlook 98 Object Model**   This library contains the objects, methods, events, and properties for almost all the objects that you work with in Outlook, with the exception of the **Page** object, the **Controls** collection object, and the **Control** object.

- **The Microsoft Forms 2.0 Object Library**   This library contains the objects, methods, properties, and constants that you use to work with a **Page** object, a **Controls** collection object, and a **Control** object.

To view the objects available in the Microsoft Outlook 98 Object Model and the Microsoft Forms 2.0 Object Library, you can use the Help files described earlier in this chapter, or you can use an object browser.

Using an Object Browser

An object browser shows the objects, properties, and methods available from object libraries. Outlook provides an object browser that you can use to view the Outlook object model. Outlook does not provide an object browser that lets you view the Microsoft Forms 2.0 Forms Library, but you can use the Microsoft Excel 97 Object Browser or the Visual Basic or Visual C++ Developer Studio Object Browser in its place. For more information about using these object browsers, see the accompanying Help.

▶ **To use the Microsoft Excel 97 Object Browser to view the forms object model**

1   On the **File** menu, click **New**.

2   On the **General** page, double-click **Workbook**.

3   On the **Tools** menu, point to **Macro**, and then click **Visual Basic Editor**.

4   On the **View** menu, click **Object Browser**.

Note   Although you can view the Outlook object library using another object browser, the Outlook Object Browser is specifically designed to work with the Outlook Script Editor and Outlook Visual Basic Reference Help

▶ **To use the Outlook Object Browser to view the Outlook 98 Object Model**

- On the Outlook Script Editor **Script** menu, click **Object Browser**.

Moving Around in the Outlook Object Browser

With the Outlook Object Browser, you can browse through all available objects in the Microsoft Outlook 98 Object Library and see their properties and methods, as shown in Figure 9.4. In addition, you can get Help for any component in the library.

▶ **To move around in the object browser**

1   In the **Classes** list box, click an object to view the methods and properties for the object.

2   In the **Members of** *object name* list box, click a method or property to view further details, as shown in Figure 9.4.

Figure 9.4   The Microsoft Outlook Object Browser

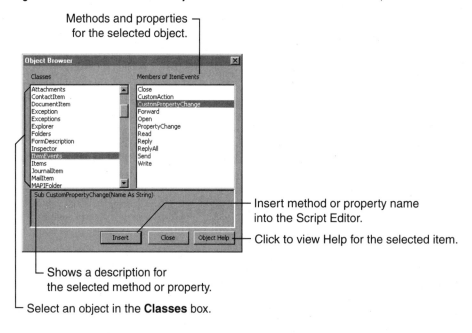

Methods and properties
for the selected object.

Insert method or property name
into the Script Editor.

Click to view Help for the selected item.

Shows a description for
the selected method or property.

Select an object in the **Classes** box.

To view the Outlook Visual Basic Reference Help topic for the selected item, click **Object Help**. To place the name of the item in your code, click **Insert**.

Object Models

An object model provides a visual representation of the hierarchical structure and relationship of objects in an object library, as shown in Figure 9.5. As such, it provides a way for you to quickly see how an object library is designed.

▶ **To view the Microsoft Outlook object model**

1 On the Script Editor **Help** menu, click **Microsoft Outlook Object Library Help**.

2 Click the **Contents** page.

3 Double-click **Microsoft Outlook Visual Basic Reference**, double-click **Objects**, and then double-click **Outlook Object Hierarchy**.

Figure 9.5   The Microsoft Outlook object model

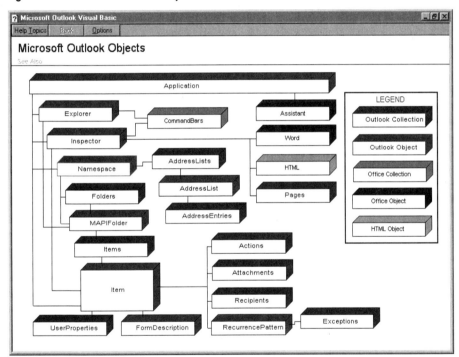

▶ **To view the Microsoft Forms 2.0 object model**

1 On the **Help** menu of the Microsoft Excel 97 Object Browser, click **Contents and Index**, and then click the **Index** tab.

2 Type **object models**, and then double-click **Microsoft Forms**.

3 Double-click **Object Model Overview**.

Using the Object Hierarchy

In an object library, all objects have a unique set of methods, properties, and events. Properties are attributes of the object that define the object. Methods are actions that can be performed on an object. Events occur when specific actions are performed on an object (when it is opened or clicked, for example).

To use the object model, you must often move down through the object hierarchy to reference the particular object you want. For example, assume you want to display the Outlook window, which is represented by the **Explorer** object. Since the **Application** object sits at the top of the hierarchy, you must first reference the **Application** object before you reference the **Explorer** object.

In the following procedure, the **ActiveExplorer** method of the **Application** object is used to return the currently active Outlook window (the **Explorer** object). The **Display** method of the **Explorer** object is then used to make the Outlook window the active window on the desktop.

```
Sub CommandButton1_Click
    Set MyExplorer = Application.ActiveExplorer
    MyExplorer.Display
End Sub
```

▶ **To test the code samples in this chapter**

1 On the Outlook **Actions** menu, click **New Mail Message**.

2 On the form **Tools** menu, click **Forms**, and then click **Design This Form**.

3 On the **Form Design** toolbar, click **Control Toolbox**.

4 Resize the **Message** control on the form to make room for a CommandButton control.

5 Drag a CommandButton control to the form. By default, the CommandButton control is given the name CommandButton1.

6 On the **Form Design** toolbar, click **View Code**.

7 Type the sample code in the Script Editor window.

8 Click **Run This Form** on the **Form** menu, and then click **CommandButton1**.

9 Repeat steps 7 and 8 for each code sample you want to test.

The following example moves further down the object hierarchy and returns a **Folder** object. It then uses the **Name** property of the **Folder** object to display the name of the folder in a message.

```
Sub CommandButton1_Click
    Set MyFolder = Application.ActiveExplorer.CurrentFolder
    MsgBox MyFolder.Name
End Sub
```

Getting and Setting Properties

This section covers how you either get or set the properties of an object. To get or set a property, you must reference both the object name and the property name.

Getting an Object Property

In certain cases, you want to get the properties of an object. The following procedure retrieves the text in the message box of an item and shows it in a message. Before you click CommandButton1, type some text in the message box of the form.

```
Sub CommandButton1_Click
    BodyText = Item.Body
    MsgBox BodyText
End Sub
```

Tip Notice in the preceding example that the active item is referenced without moving through the object hierarchy. In this case, the item is implied, as discussed in "The Implied Item Object" earlier in this chapter.

Setting an Object Property

In this example, the body text of the item is set.

```
Sub CommandButton1_Click
    Item.Body = "This text appears in the message box."
End Sub
```

Using Variables

Variable names follow the standard rules for naming anything in Microsoft VBScript. A variable name:

- Must begin with an alphabetic character.
- Cannot contain an embedded period.
- Must not exceed 255 characters.
- Must be unique in the scope in which it's declared.

Generally, when you declare a variable within a procedure, only code within that procedure can reference or change the value of that variable; it has *local* scope and is known as a *procedure-level* variable. When you declare a variable outside a procedure, you make it recognizable to all the procedures in your script; it has *script-level* scope and is known as a *script-level* variable.

When you're using variables in VBScript, the following limitations apply:

- There can be no more than 127 procedure-level variables (arrays count as a single variable).
- Each script is limited to no more than 127 script-level variables.

The length of time a variable exists is called its *lifetime*. A script-level variable's lifetime extends from the time it's declared until the time the script is finished running. A local variable's lifetime begins when its declaration statement is encountered as the procedure begins, and it ends when the procedure concludes. Local variables are ideal as temporary storage space while a procedure is running. You can have local variables with the same name in different procedures, because each variable is recognized only by the procedure in which it's declared.

A variable's scope is determined by where you declare the variable. At a script level, the lifetime of a variable is always the same; it exists while the script is running. At a procedure level, a variable exists only while the procedure is running; when the procedure exits, the variable is destroyed.

Using the Variant Data Type

Microsoft VBScript in Outlook uses only the **Variant** data type: a special kind of data type that can contain different types of information, depending on how the value is used. The **Variant** data type can contain either numeric or string information. The **Variant** data type behaves as a number when it's used in a numeric context and as a string when it's used in a string context. If you're working with data that resembles numeric data, VBScript treats it as such and processes it accordingly. If you're working with data that's string data, VBScript treats the data as a string. Numbers enclosed in quotation marks are treated as strings.

The **Variant** data type can make distinctions about the specific nature of numeric information, such as information that represents a date or time. When used with other date or time data, the result is always expressed as a date or a time. The **Variant** data type can contain numeric information ranging in size from **Boolean** values to huge floating-point numbers. These various categories of information that can be contained in a **Variant** data type are called *subtypes*. Usually, you can put the type of data you want in a **Variant**, and it will most likely behave in a way that's suited to the data it contains.

Assigning Objects to Variables

When assigning variables, you assign object variables in a slightly different way than for other variables. For example, if a variable is shared between procedures, you declare the variable as a script-level variable. In this procedure, the ItemChanged variable is declared as a script-level variable. ItemChanged is set to **True** whenever a standard property is changed in an item.

```
Dim ItemChanged    ' Script-level variable.
Sub Item_PropertyChange(ByVal Name)
    ItemChanged = True
End Sub
```

An object variable is a variable that is used to refer to an object. As shown in the following example, you don't need to declare the variable. Instead, you use the **Set** statement to assign an object to a variable. The first line of code in this example assigns the object variable to the newly created item. Once you've set an object, you can then use the object's methods and properties to control the object. This example creates a new mail item, and then displays the item.

```
Sub CommandButton1_Click
   Set MyItem = Application.CreateItem(0)
   MyItem.Display
End Sub
```

Referencing Collections and Single Objects

Some objects in Outlook are collection objects, while others are single objects. For example, all the items in a folder can be contained in an **Items** collection object. However, a single item in an **Items** collection object may be represented by a **MailItem** object or a **PostItem** object.

The following code uses the **Items** property to reference the collection of items in your Inbox. It then shows the number of items in the **Items** collection object.

```
Sub CommandButton1_Click
   Set MyFolder = Application.GetNameSpace("MAPI").GetDefaultFolder(6)
   Set MyItems = MyFolder.Items
   MsgBox MyItems.Count
End Sub
```

In the next example, the items in the **Items** collection object are referenced by index number. In this case, the code iterates through the **Items** collection and shows the text in the Message field for the first three items in the your Inbox. (Note that items in the Inbox do not necessarily appear in the order received.)

```
Sub CommandButton1_Click
   Set MyFolder = Application.GetNameSpace("MAPI").GetDefaultFolder(6)
   Set MyItems = MyFolder.Items
   For i = 1 to 3
      MsgBox MyFolder.Items(i).Subject
   Next
End Sub
```

After you set a collection object, you can reference objects in the collection by index, as shown in the preceding example, or by name. For example, to reference an item in an **Items** collection by name, you specify the value of the Subject field.

Before you run this example, do the following:

Click **New Mail Message** on the Outlook **Actions** menu. Address the message to yourself, and type **VBScript Test** in the **Subject** box. Click **Send**. Add the code in this example to the Script Editor, and then click **CommandButton1**.

```
Sub CommandButton1_Click
    Set MyFolder = Application.GetNameSpace("MAPI").GetDefaultFolder(6)
    Set MyItems = MyFolder.Items
    Set MyItem = MyItems("VBScript Test")
    MyItem.Display
End Sub
```

Generally, you don't reference an item in an **Items** collection by name. However, you almost always reference a field property in a **UserProperties** collection by name, as shown in this example that sets the name of the user-defined field called Customer Name to James Allard.

Before you run this example, do the following:

Make sure the form is in Design mode, and then click **Field Chooser** on the **Form Design** toolbar. In the **Field Chooser**, click **New**, type **Customer Name** in the **Name** text box, and then click **OK**. Drag the **Customer Name** field from the **Field Chooser** to the form. Add the code in the example to the Script Editor. Click **Run This Form** on the **Form** menu to switch to Run mode, and then click **CommandButton1**.

```
Sub CommandButton1_Click
    UserProperties.Find("Customer Name").Value = "James Allard"
End Sub
```

The Application Object

The **Application** object sits at the top of the object model and represents the entire Microsoft Outlook application.

The Outlook **Application** object has several purposes:

- As the root object, it enables you to reference other objects in the Outlook object hierarchy.

- It provides methods such as **CreateItem** and **CreateObject** so that you can create new items and reference them without moving through the object hierarchy.

- It provides methods for directly referencing the active Outlook window or form.

See Also For a complete list and description of the methods and properties for the **Application** object, see Microsoft Outlook Visual Basic Reference Help.

Application Object Methods

This section covers the **ActiveExplorer**, **CreateItem**, **CreateObject**, and **GetNameSpace** methods.

Returning the Active Window

You can use the **ActiveExplorer** method of the **Application** object to return the active Outlook window.

The following example sets the **MyExplorer** object to the currently active Outlook window, and then activates the window on the desktop when the CommandButton1 control is clicked. To make this example work, add a CommandButton1 control to the form, and then add the example code to the Script Editor.

```
Sub CommandButton1_Click
   Set MyExplorer = Application.ActiveExplorer
   MyExplorer.Display
End Sub
```

Creating a Standard Item

You can use the **CreateItem** method of the **Application** object to create and return Outlook standard items, such as a message item, a post item, or an appointment item.

This example creates a message item and shows it when CommandButton1 is clicked.

```
Sub CommandButton1_Click
   Set MyItem = Application.CreateItem(0)
   MyItem.Display
End Sub
```

The following table lists the numeric values that you use as arguments for the **CreateItem** method.

Type of item	Value
Mail message	0
Appointment	1
Contact	2
Task	3
Journal	4
Note	5
Post	6

See Also   For more information about creating custom items, see "Items Collection Methods" later in this chapter.

Creating an Automation Object

You can use the **CreateObject** method of the **Application** object to create Automation objects, such as Microsoft Excel, Microsoft Access, or Microsoft Word objects.

This example is taken from the Document Tracking application, which is covered in Chapter 12. It uses the **CreateObject** method to create a database engine automation object. It then calls the FieldValues procedure that writes the values from the item to the Microsoft Access 97 database.

See Also   For more information about this procedure and how it's used, see Chapter 12, "The Document Tracking Application."

Important   Data Access Objects (DAO) will only work if the user has Microsoft Office 97 (not stand-alone Outlook) installed. In addition, the user must install "Data Access Objects for Visual Basic" (DAO 3.5) during Office 97 Setup.

```
Sub AddNewDatabaseRecord
    DbOpenTable = 1
    On Error Resume Next
    Set Dbe = Item.Application.CreateObject("DAO.DBEngine.35")
    If Err.Number <> 0 Then
        Msgbox Err.Description & "—Some functions may not work correctly" & Chr(13) _
            & "Please make sure that DAO 3.5 or greater is installed on this machine."
        Exit Sub
    End If
    Set MyDb = Dbe.Workspaces(0).OpenDatabase("C:\My Documents\Document Tracking.mdb")
    Set Rs = MyDb.OpenRecordset("Tracking Information", DbOpenTable)
    Rs.AddNew
    Rs("Status") = Item.Status
    Call FieldValues
    Rs.Update
    Rs.MoveLast
    Rs.Close
    MyDb.Close
End Sub
```

Returning a MAPI NameSpace Object

You can use the **GetNameSpace("MAPI")** method of the **Application** object to return the MAPI message store.

In this example, the **GetNameSpace** method returns the **NameSpace** object. The **CurrentUser** property of the **NameSpace** object is then used to show your name in a message box.

```
Sub CommandButton1_Click
    Set MyNameSpace = Application.GetNameSpace("MAPI")
    MsgBox MyNameSpace.CurrentUser
End Sub
```

Important   The only data source currently supported is MAPI, which allows access to all Outlook data stored in MAPI. For this reason, the **GetNameSpace** method must always appear in Outlook as **GetNameSpace("MAPI")**.

The NameSpace Object

In Outlook, the **NameSpace** object represents the MAPI message store. The **NameSpace** object provides methods for logging on to or logging off Outlook, referencing a default folder, and returning objects directly by ID. In addition, the **NameSpace** object provides access to a variety of methods and properties that are not available with the **Application** object.

See Also   For a complete list and description of the methods and properties for the **NameSpace** object, see Microsoft Outlook Visual Basic Reference Help.

NameSpace Object Methods

This section covers the **GetDefaultFolder** method of the **NameSpace** object.

Returning a Default Folder

You can use the **GetDefaultFolder** method of the **NameSpace** object to access folders in the root folder—also known as the Mailbox. To reference a folder in the Mailbox, you must specify a numeric value as the argument in the **GetDefaultFolder** method. The following table lists these numeric values.

Folder	Value
Deleted Items	3
Outbox	4
Sent Items	5
Inbox	6
Calendar	9
Contacts	10
Journal	11
Notes	12
Tasks	13

This example uses the **GetDefaultFolder** method of the **NameSpace** object to return the Contacts folder and then show it.

```
Sub CommandButton1_Click
    Set MyFolder = Application.GetNameSpace("MAPI").GetDefaultFolder(10)
    MyFolder.Display
End Sub
```

Properties of the NameSpace Object

The **NameSpace** object provides two properties that you use quite often. These are the **CurrentUser** and **Folders** properties.

Returning the Name of the Current User

You can use the **CurrentUser** property of the **NameSpace** object to return the name of the currently logged-on user.

This example shows the current user's name in the message box when the CommandButton1 control is pressed.

```
Sub CommandButton1_Click
    Set MyNameSpace = Application.GetNameSpace("MAPI")
    MsgBox MyNameSpace.CurrentUser
End Sub
```

Referencing a Folder Collection

You can use the **Folders** property of the **NameSpace** object to reference the collection of folders in the MAPI name space.

This example references the highest level folders in the Folder List and then shows the count in a message.

```
Sub CommandButton1_Click
    Set MyNameSpace = Application.GetNameSpace("MAPI")
    Set MyFolders = MyNameSpace.Folders
    MsgBox MyFolders.Count
End Sub
```

The Outlook Window (Explorer Object)

The Outlook window is represented by the **Explorer** object. The following sections cover some of the methods and properties for the **Explorer** object.

See Also   For a complete list and description of the methods and properties for the **Explorer** object, see Microsoft Outlook Visual Basic Reference Help.

Explorer Methods

This section covers the **Display** method of the **Explorer** object.

Showing the Active Outlook Window

You can use the **Display** method of the **Explorer** object to activate the Outlook window.

This example returns the active Outlook window, and then shows it on the desktop.

```
Sub CommandButton1_Click
    Set MyExplorer = Application.ActiveExplorer
    MyExplorer.Display
End Sub
```

Explorer Properties

This section explains how to use the **CurrentFolder** property.

Returning the Active Folder

You can use the **CurrentFolder** property of the **Explorer** object to return the active folder in the Outlook window.

This example shows the name of the active folder in the message box when the CommandButton1 control is clicked.

```
Sub CommandButton1_Click
    Set MyExplorer = Application.ActiveExplorer
    MsgBox MyExplorer.CurrentFolder
End Sub
```

The AddressLists Collection Object

Outlook users often have several address books from which they can select recipients for a message. The **AddressLists** collection object contains all the address books available to a user; through it, you can reference one or more **AddressList** objects, each of which represents a single address book.

The **AddressLists** collection object is always referenced from the **NameSpace** object.

AddressLists Collection Methods

This section covers the **Item** method of the **AddressLists** collection object.

Iterating Through a Collection of Address Lists

You can use the **Item** method of the **AddressLists** collection object to iterate through a collection of address books.

This example uses the **Count** property of the **AddressLists** collection object to determine the number of **AddressList** objects referenced by the collection. It then uses the **Item** method of the **AddressLists** collection object to return and display the name of each address book.

```
Sub CommandButton1_Click
    Set MyNameSpace = Application.GetNameSpace("MAPI")
    Set MyAddressLists = MyNameSpace.AddressLists
    MsgBox "There are " & MyAddressLists.Count & " address lists."
    For i = 1 to MyAddressLists.Count
        Set MyAddressList = MyAddressLists.Item(i)
        MsgBox MyAddressList.Name & " is " & i & " of " & MyAddressLists.Count
    Next
End Sub
```

The AddressList Object

The **AddressList** object represents a single Outlook address book that contains a set of **AddressEntry** objects. The **AddressEntry** objects, in turn, can be accessed through the **AddressEntries** property of the **AddressList** object.

The AddressEntries Collection Object

The **AddressEntries** collection object is provided by the **AddressEntries** property of the **AddressList** object. It provides access to each of the **AddressEntry** objects contained within a given address book.

AddressEntries Collection Methods

This section covers the **Add** and **Item** methods of the **AddressEntries** collection object.

Adding an Address Entry

You can use the **Add** method of the **AddressEntries** collection object to create a new item in an address book.

This example uses the **Add** method to create a new entry in the Personal Address Book. The **Update** method of the **AddressEntry** object is required to commit the new item to the address book.

```
Sub CommandButton1_Click
    Set MyNameSpace = Application.GetNameSpace("MAPI")
    Set MyAddressList = MyNameSpace.AddressLists("Personal Address Book")
    Set MyEntries = MyAddressList.AddressEntries
    Set myEntry = MyEntries.Add ("SMTP","James Allard","jamesallard@microsoft.com")
    myEntry.Update
End Sub
```

Iterating Through a Collection of Address Entries

You can use the **Item** method of the **AddressEntries** collection object to iterate through the items in an address book.

This example uses the **Count** property of the **AddressEntries** collection object to return the number of items in the user's Personal Address Book. It also uses the **Item** method of the **AddressEntries** collection object to return each item in the address book and then display its name.

```
Sub CommandButton1_Click
    Set MyNameSpace = Application.GetNameSpace("MAPI")
    Set MyAddressList = MyNameSpace.AddressLists("Personal Address Book")
    Set MyAddressEntries = MyAddressList.AddressEntries
    For i = 1 to MyAddressEntries.Count
        Set MyEntry = MyAddressEntries.Item(i)
        MsgBox MyEntry.Name
    Next
End Sub
```

The AddressEntry Object

The **AddressEntry** object represents an individual item in an address book. The **AddressEntry** object contains information about one or more individuals or processes to which the messaging system can send messages. If the **AddressEntry** object represents a distribution list (that is, if its **DisplayType** property is set to **olDistList** or **olPrivateDistList**, it can contain additional **AddressEntry** objects that can be accessed through its **Members** property.

AddressEntry Object Methods

This section covers the **Details**, **Update**, **Delete**, and **GetFreeBusy** methods of the **AddressEntry** object.

Displaying Details of an Address Entry

The **Details** method of the **AddressEntry** object displays a modal dialog box that lets a user see (and, if permissions allow, change) the information stored in the address book item represented by the object.

The following example steps through the items in a user's Personal Address Book, using the **Details** method to display the information contained in each item. If the user clicks **OK** in the dialog box, the next entry is displayed. If the user clicks the **Cancel** button in the dialog box, an error is produced. For this reason, an **On Error** statement is included to prevent the routine from exiting immediately, and the **err** global variable is tested to determine if it is not zero (which would indicate that the user clicked **Cancel** or that an error has occurred).

```
Sub CommandButton1_Click
    Set MyNameSpace = Application.GetNameSpace("MAPI")
    Set MyAddressList = MyNameSpace.AddressLists("Personal Address Book")
    Set MyAddressEntries = MyAddressList.AddressEntries
    On Error Resume Next
    For i = 1 to MyAddressEntries.Count
        Set MyEntry = MyAddressEntries.Item(i)
        MyEntry.Details
        If err <> 0 Then Exit Sub
    Next
End Sub
```

Changing an Address Entry

If you have the appropriate permissions, you can change the **Address**, **Name**, and **Type** properties of an **AddressEntry** object. To commit the change to the address book, you use the object's **Update** method.

The following example converts the **Name** property of an **AddressEntry** object to all uppercase characters.

```
Sub CommandButton1_Click
    Set MyNameSpace = Application.GetNameSpace("MAPI")
    Set MyAddressList = MyNameSpace.AddressLists("Personal Address Book")
    Set MyEntries = MyAddressList.AddressEntries
    Set MyEntry = MyEntries.Item(1)
    MyEntry.Name = Ucase(MyEntry.Name)
    MyEntry.Update
End Sub
```

Deleting an Address Entry

The **Delete** method of the **AddressEntry** object removes an item from the address book.

The following example steps through the items in the Personal Address Book and deletes the first item for which the type is set to "SAMPLE".

```
Sub CommandButton1_Click
    Set MyNameSpace = Application.GetNameSpace("MAPI")
    Set MyAddressList = MyNameSpace.AddressLists("Personal Address Book")
    Set MyEntries = MyAddressList.AddressEntries
    Set MyEntry = MyEntries.GetFirst
    Do While TypeName(MyEntry) <> "Nothing"
        If MyEntry.Type = "SAMPLE" Then
            MsgBox "Deleting "& MyEntry
            MyEntry.Delete
            Exit Sub
        End If
        Set MyEntry = MyEntries.GetNext
    Loop
    MsgBox "No sample entries found."
End Sub
```

Getting Free/Busy Information for a User

You can determine whether someone is available at a given time using the **GetFreeBusy** method of the **AddressEntry** object. This method returns a string representing 30 days of free/busy information, starting at midnight on a specified date. Each character in the string is a digit that indicates whether the person is available during a specified time period. You can specify whether the string should indicate only whether the person is available, or you can specify that you want the string to indicate whether a busy time is marked as "tentative" or "out of office."

For example, the following returns a string 1440 characters long (48 half-hour periods over 30 days) containing a "0" for each half-hour period the person is free, a "1" for each period the person has a busy time marked "tentative," a "3" for each period the person has a busy time marked "out of office," and a "2" for other busy periods:

```
MyStatus = MyAddressEntry.GetFreeBusy("7/1/98",30,True)
```

The following returns a string 720 characters long (24 one-hour periods over 30 days) containing a "0" for each hour the person is free and a "1" for each hour the person is busy, regardless of how the busy periods are designated:

```
MyStatus = MyAddressEntry.GetFreeBusy("7/1/98",60,False)
```

The following example displays the next time a person is busy. In addition to Outlook objects and methods, it uses the following VBScript functions:

- **InputBox**, to prompt the user for the name of the person whose first busy time is to be checked.

- **Date**, to retrieve the current date.

- **FormatDateTime**, to convert the retrieved date to the format required by **GetFreeBusy.**

- **InStr**, to determine the location (offset) of the first "1" character in the string returned by **GetFreeBusy.**

```
Sub CommandButton1_Click
    Set MyNameSpace = Application.GetNameSpace("MAPI")
    Set MyAddressList = MyNameSpace.AddressLists("Global Address List")
    Set MyEntries = MyAddressList.AddressEntries
    MyName = InputBox("Find first busy time for:")
    If MyName <> "" then
        Set MyEntry = MyEntries(MyName)
        StartDate = FormatDateTime(Date,2)
        MyBusyTime = MyEntry.GetFreeBusy(StartDate,60)
        MsgBox MyEntry.Name & " is busy " & InStr(MyBusyTime,"1")-1 _
            & " hours after 12:00 am " & StartDate
    End If
End Sub
```

AddressEntry Properties

You can use such properties as **Name**, **Address**, **Members**, **Type**, and **Manager** to retrieve useful information contained in the item.

See Also For a complete list and description of the methods and properties for the **AddressEntry** object, see Microsoft Outlook Visual Basic Reference Help.

The following example uses the **Members**, **Name**, and **Address** properties of the **AddressEntry** object to display the name and address of each member of a private distribution list named Department.

```
Sub CommandButton1_Click
    Set MyNameSpace = Application.GetNameSpace("MAPI")
    Set MyAddressList = MyNameSpace.AddressLists("Personal Address Book")
    Set MyDistList = MyAddressList.AddressEntries("Department")
    Set MyAddressEntries = MyDistList.Members
    For i = 1 to MyAddressEntries.Count
        Set MyEntry = MyAddressEntries.Item(i)
        MsgBox MyEntry.Name & " " & MyEntry.Address
    Next
End Sub
```

The Folders Collection Object

The Outlook 98 Object Model provides two folder objects: a **Folders** collection object and a **MAPIFolder** object. The **Folders** collection object represents multiple folders. The **MAPIFolder** object, covered later in this chapter, represents a single folder.

The **Folders** collection object can contain one or multiple folders. The **Folders** collection object is always referenced from the **NameSpace** object.

See Also   For a complete list and description of the methods and properties for the **Folders** collection object, see Microsoft Outlook Visual Basic Reference Help.

Folders Collection Methods

This section covers the **Add** and **Item** methods of the **Folders** collection object.

Adding a Folder to the Folder List

You can use the **Add** method of the **Folders** collection object to add a folder to the Folder List.

This example uses the **Add** method of the **Folders** collection object to add a folder called My New Folder to the Building Microsoft Outlook 98 Applications personal folder (.pst).

```
Sub CommandButton1_Click
    Set MyNameSpace = Application.GetNameSpace("MAPI")
    Set MyFolder = MyNameSpace.Folders("Building Microsoft Outlook 98 Applications")
    Set MyNewFolder = MyFolder.Folders.Add("My New Folder")
End Sub
```

Iterating Through a Collection of Folders

You can use the **Item** method of the **Folders** collection object to iterate through a collection of folders.

This example uses the uses the **Count** property of the **Folders** collection object to return the number of folder items in the folders collection. It also uses the **Item** method of the **Folders** collection object to return each folder in the collection and then display its name.

```
Sub CommandButton1_Click
   Set MyNameSpace = Application.GetNameSpace("MAPI")
   Set MyFolders = MyNameSpace.Folders("Building Microsoft Outlook 98 Applications")
   Set MyCollection = MyFolders.Folders
   For i = 1 to MyCollection.Count
      Set MyFolder = MyCollection.Item(i)
      MsgBox MyFolder.Name
   Next
End Sub
```

Note When moving through a collection of folders or items, the folders or items are not always ordered in the collection based upon the date they are received in the folder. If your code depends on a particular order in the collection, use the **Sort** method of the collection object to control the order of the collection.

The MAPIFolder Object

The **MAPIFolder** object represents a single Outlook folder. A **MAPIFolder** object can contain other **MAPIFolder** objects, as well as Outlook items. This section explains how to move through the Folder List by using the **MAPIFolder** object and its **Folders** property.

See Also For a complete list and description of the methods and properties for the **MAPIFolder** object, see Microsoft Outlook Visual Basic Reference Help.

MAPIFolder Object Methods

This section covers the **CopyTo** and **Display** methods of the **MAPIFolder** object.

Copying a Folder

You can use the **CopyTo** method of the **MAPIFolder** object to create a copy of a folder in another folder.

This example copies the Notes folder to Inbox.

```
Sub CommandButton1_Click
   Set MyNameSpace = Application.GetNameSpace("MAPI")
   Set MyInboxFolder = MyNameSpace.GetDefaultFolder(6)
   Set MyCurrentFolder = MyNameSpace.GetDefaultFolder(12)
   Set MyNewFolder = MyCurrentFolder.CopyTo(MyInboxFolder)
End Sub
```

Displaying a Folder

You can use the **Display** method of the **MAPIFolder** object to display the folder represented by the **MAPIFolder** object.

```
Sub CommandButton1_Click
    Set MyNameSpace = Application.GetNameSpace("MAPI")
    Set MyFolder = MyNameSpace.Folders("Public Folders")
    MyFolder.Display
End Sub
```

MAPIFolder Object Properties

This section covers the **Folders**, **Items**, **EntryID**, and **StoreID** properties. The **Folders** property is useful for accessing a folder in the Folder List. The **Items** property is useful for retrieving a collection of items in the folder.

Referencing a Folder in the Folder List

You can use the **Folders** property with the **MAPIFolder** object to return another **MAPIFolder** object.

In this procedure, the **Folders** property is used to move through the various branches of a personal folders list.

```
Sub CommandButton1_Click
    Set MyNameSpace = Application.GetNameSpace("MAPI")
    Set MyFolder = MyNameSpace.Folders("Building Microsoft Outlook 98 Applications")
    Set BeyondFolder = MyFolder.Folders("4. Beyond the Basics")
    Set VBScriptFolder = BeyondFolder.Folders("VBScript")
    MsgBox VBScriptFolder.Name
End Sub
```

Iterating Through a Collection of Items in a Folder

You can use the **Items** property of the **MAPIFolder** object to return a collection of items in the folder.

The following example uses the **Items** property of the **MAPIFolder** object to return the collection of items in the Inbox folder. It then shows the Subject value of the first five items in the **Items** collection.

```
Sub CommandButton1_Click
    Set MyNameSpace = Application.GetNameSpace("MAPI")
    Set MyInboxFolder = MyNameSpace.GetDefaultFolder(6)
    Set MyItems = MyInboxFolder.Items
    For i = 1 to 5
        Set MyItem = MyItems(i)
        Msgbox MyItem.Subject
    Next
End Sub
```

The EntryID and StoreID Properties

The **EntryID** and **StoreID** properties of the **MAPIFolder** object can be used to identify a folder in Outlook. These properties are useful when you are working with multiple-folder applications.

This example sets the value of the entry ID for the Folder field to the entry ID of the folder and the value of the entry ID for the Store field to the store ID.

Before you run this example, do the following:

Make sure the form is in Design mode, and then click **Field Chooser** on the **Form Design** toolbar. In the **Field Chooser**, click **New**, type **Entry ID for Folder** in the **Name** text box, and then click **OK**. Drag the **Entry ID for Folder** field from the Field Chooser to the form. In the **Field Chooser**, click **New**, type **Entry ID for Store** in the **Name** text box, and then click **OK**. Drag the **Entry ID for Store** field from the Field Chooser to the form. Add the code in the example to the Script Editor. Click **Run This Form** on the **Form** menu to switch to Run mode, and then click **CommandButton1**.

```
Sub CommandButton1_Click
    Set MyFolder = Application.ActiveExplorer.CurrentFolder
    UserProperties.Find("Entry ID for Folder") = MyFolder.EntryID
    UserProperties.Find("Entry ID for Store") = MyFolder.StoreID
End Sub
```

The Items Collection Object

Items are the discrete packages of information represented by a mail message, a post item, a contact item, a journal item, a meeting request, a note, or a task item. You use the **Items** property to return the **Items** collection of a **MAPIFolder** object. The single item object is represented by the following objects:

- **AppointmentItem** object—an appointment item
- **ContactItem** object—a contact item
- **DocumentItem** object—a document item
- **JournalItem** object—a journal item
- **MailItem** object—a mail message item
- **MeetingItem** object—a meeting item
- **NoteItem** object—a note item

- **PostItem** object—a post item
- **ReportItem** object—a mail-delivery report item
- **TaskItem** object—a task item
- **TaskRequestAcceptItem**—an item sent to accept a task request
- **TaskRequestDeclineItem**—an item sent to decline a task request
- **TaskRequestItem**—an item sent to assign a task
- **TaskRequestUpdateItem**—an item sent to update a task request

This section covers some of the methods and properties of the **Items** collection object. Sections that follow this section cover the methods and properties of specific item objects.

See Also   For a complete list and description of the methods and properties for the **Items** collection object, see Microsoft Outlook Visual Basic Reference Help.

Items Collection Methods

This section covers the **Add**, **Find**, and **Restrict** methods of the **Items** collection object.

Creating a Custom Item

With Outlook, there are two basic methods of creating items. Standard items such as message items (IPM.Note), post items (IPM.Post), and contact items (IPM.Contact) are created by using the **CreateItem** method of the **Application** object, as discussed earlier in this chapter.

To create custom items, however, such as an IPM.Post.Product Idea item, you use the **Add** method of the **Items** collection object. For example, to create a Product Idea item (IPM.Post.Product Idea) for the Products Ideas folder, you must first return the **Items** collection object, and then use the **Add** method of the **Items** collection object to add the new item to the collection. The custom item has the methods and properties of the item upon which is it based. For example, an item with the message class IPM.Post.Product Idea contains the methods and properties of the **PostItem** object in addition to the custom UserProperties defined for IPM.Post.Product Idea. If you create an item with the message class IPM.Note.Orders, you use the **MailItem** object.

Important   Before you can create a custom item, the form associated with the item must exist in the forms library of the folder that the item is created from. For example, to create a Product Idea item, the Product Idea form must exist in the Product Ideas folder forms library or in the Personal or Organizational forms libraries.

The following example references the Product Ideas folder, and then creates a Product
Idea item and displays it. Note that the Product Idea form exists in the Product Ideas
folder forms library.

```
Sub CommandButton1_Click
    Set MyNameSpace = Application.GetNameSpace("MAPI")
    Set BuildFolder = MyNameSpace.Folders("Building Microsoft Outlook 98 Applications")
    Set QuickFolder = BuildFolder.Folders("2. Quick Guide")
    Set ProductIdeasFolder = QuickFolder.Folders("Product Ideas")
    Set MyItems = ProductIdeasFolder.Items
    Set MyItem = MyItems.Add("IPM.Post.Product Idea")
    MyItem.Subject = "VBScript Test"
    MyItem.Body = "This is a test"
    MyItem.Display
End Sub
```

Important   Notice in the preceding procedure that the **Body** property of the single item object
corresponds with the Message field on the form. For more details about the properties of
standard items, see "Properties of the MailItem and PostItem Objects" later in this chapter.

Finding an Item in a Folder

You can use the **Find** method of the **Items** collection object to find an item in a folder
based on the conditions that you specify.

This example uses the **Find** method of the **Items** collection object to return the first
item in the Product Ideas folder with the value "Boating" in the Product Category
field.

```
Sub CommandButton1_Click
    Set MyNameSpace = Application.GetNameSpace("MAPI")
    Set BuildFolder = MyNameSpace.Folders("Building Microsoft Outlook 98 Applications")
    Set QuickFolder = BuildFolder.Folders("2. Quick Guide")
    Set ProductIdeasFolder = QuickFolder.Folders("Product Ideas")
    Set MyItem = ProductIdeasFolder.Items.Find("[Product Category] = 'Boating'")
    MyItem.Display
End Sub
```

Creating a Filtered Collection of Items from a Folder

You can use the **Restrict** method of the **Items** collection object to create filters that
return only those items in a folder that match the conditions you specify.

See Also   For more information about filter expressions, see "Find Method" in
Microsoft Outlook Visual Basic Reference Help.

This example returns the collection of items from the Product Ideas folder, and then creates a filtered collection of items with only the value "Boating" in the Product Category field.

```
Sub CommandButton1_Click
    Set MyNameSpace = Application.GetNameSpace("MAPI")
    Set BuildFolder = MyNameSpace.Folders("Building Microsoft Outlook 98 Applications")
    Set QuickFolder = BuildFolder.Folders("2. Quick Guide")
    Set ProductIdeasFolder = QuickFolder.Folders("Product Ideas")
    Set MyItems = ProductIdeasFolder.Items
    Set MyFilter = MyItems.Restrict("[Product Category] = 'Boating'")
    MsgBox MyFilter.Count
End Sub
```

Properties of the Items Collection Object

This section explains how to use the **Count** property.

Returning the Count of Items in the Items Collection

You can use the **Count** property of the **Items** collection object to return the number of items in the **Items** collection. This provides an easy way to loop through collections to process a large number of items, as shown in the previous example.

This example returns the number of items in your Inbox and shows the number in a message box.

```
Sub CommandButton1_Click
    Set MyFolder = Item.Application.GetNameSpace("MAPI").GetDefaultFolder(6)
    Set MyItems = MyFolder.Items
    MsgBox "You have " & MyItems.Count & " items in your Inbox."
End Sub
```

The PostItem Object

The **PostItem** object represents a message posted in a public folder. Unlike a **MailItem** object, a **PostItem** object is not sent to a recipient. This section covers some of the methods of the **PostItem** object. Properties of the **PostItem** object are similar to the properties of the **MailItem** object, so they are discussed together in "Properties of the MailItem and PostItem Objects," later in this chapter.

Methods of the PostItem Object

The **PostItem** object provides a variety of methods that you can use to control the actions of an item. This section covers the **Copy**, **Move**, **Display**, and **Post** methods.

Copying and Moving an Item

You can use the **Copy** method of the **PostItem** object to create a copy of an item. You can then use the **Move** method to move the copied item to a new location.

This example returns the first item in the Product Ideas folder with the value "Boating" in the Product Category field. It then uses the **Copy** method to create a copy of the item returned from the Product Ideas folder. The **Move** method is then used to move the copied item from the Product Ideas folder to the Inbox.

```
Sub CommandButton1_Click
    Set MyNameSpace = Application.GetNameSpace("MAPI")
    Set BuildFolder = MyNameSpace.Folders("Building Microsoft Outlook 98 Applications")
    Set QuickFolder = BuildFolder.Folders("2. Quick Guide")
    Set ProductIdeasFolder = QuickFolder.Folders("Product Ideas")
    Set MyItem = ProductIdeasFolder.Items.Find("[Product Category] = 'Boating'")
    Set MyCopiedItem = MyItem.Copy
    Set DestinationFolder = MyNameSpace.GetDefaultFolder(6)
    MyCopiedItem.Move DestinationFolder
End Sub
```

Creating and Displaying a Custom Post Item

You can use the **Display** method of the **PostItem** object to display an item on the desktop. As discussed earlier, you use the **Add** method of the **Items** collection object to create a new custom post item.

This example returns the Product Ideas folder, and then creates a new custom **PostItem** object by using the **Add** method of the **Items** collection object. It then displays the item in the Product Idea form. If you click the **Post** button on the form, the item is posted in the Product Ideas folder.

```
Sub CommandButton1_Click
    Set MyNameSpace = Application.GetNameSpace("MAPI")
    Set BuildFolder = MyNameSpace.Folders("Building Microsoft Outlook 98 Applications")
    Set QuickFolder = BuildFolder.Folders("2. Quick Guide")
    Set ProductIdeasFolder = QuickFolder.Folders("Product Ideas")
    Set MyItem = ProductIdeasFolder.Items.Add("IPM.Post.Product Idea")
    MyItem.Subject = "This is a test."
    MyItem.Body = "This is Message text."
    MyItem.Display
End Sub
```

Posting an Item

You can use the **Post** method of the **PostItem** object to post an item in a folder.

The following example sets the folder to the Product Ideas folder. It then creates a new item with the message class IPM.Post Product Idea, which is added to the Product Ideas **Items** collection. In this procedure, the object returned to MyItem by the **Add** method is a **PostItem** object. The **Subject** and **Body** properties of the MyItem object are set, and then the item is posted to the Product Ideas folder. To run this example, use the names of the folders in your Folder List.

```
Sub CommandButton1_Click
    Set MyNameSpace = Application.GetNameSpace("MAPI")
    Set BuildFolder = MyNameSpace.Folders("Building Microsoft Outlook 98 Applications")
    Set QuickFolder = BuildFolder.Folders("2. Quick Guide")
```

```
      Set ProductIdeasFolder = QuickFolder.Folders("Product Ideas")
      Set MyItem = ProductIdeasFolder.Items.Add("IPM.Post.Product Idea")
      MyItem.Subject = "This is a test of the Post method."
      MyItem.Body = "This is Message text."
      MyItem.Post
End Sub
```

The MailItem Object

The **MailItem** object represents a message in a mail folder. This section covers some of the methods and properties of the **PostItem** object. Properties of the **PostItem** object are similar to the properties of the **MailItem** object, so they are discussed together.

Methods of the MailItem Object

This section covers the **Send**, **Reply**, and **Close** methods of the **MailItem** object.

Sending a Message

You can use the **Send** method of the **MailItem** object to send a message to a recipient.

This example creates a mail message item, sets the Subject and message Body fields, and then sets the To field to your name. It then uses the **Send** method to send the item to the specified recipient.

```
Sub CommandButton1_Click
    Set MyItem = Application.CreateItem(0)
    MyItem.Subject = "This is a test"
    MyItem.Body = "This is Message Body text."
    MyItem.To = Application.GetNameSpace("MAPI").CurrentUser
    MyItem.Send
End Sub
```

Replying to a Message

You can use the **Reply** method of a **MailItem** object to return a reply item.

This example creates a reply item based on the current item, and then returns the reply item, which is represented by the MyReply object. The reply item is then displayed. To run this example, you must first put a CommandButton1 control on the **Read** page of a Mail Message form. Exit Design mode and send the item to your Inbox, and then open the item in the Inbox and click **CommandButton1**. The reply item is displayed.

```
Sub CommandButton1_Click
    Set MyFolder = Application.GetNameSpace("MAPI").GetDefaultFolder(6)
    Set MyItem = MyFolder.Items.Item(1)
    Set MyReply = MyItem.Reply
    MyReply.Display
End Sub
```

Closing an Item

You can use the **Close** method of the **MailItem** object to close an item. When you close the item, you also close the item's associated form.

This example closes the current item when CommandButton1 is clicked.

```
Sub CommandButton1_Click
    Item.Close(2)
End Sub
```

You can use one of the following arguments with the **Close** method.

Save option	Value
Save all changes without prompting	0
Discard all changes without prompting	1
Prompt to save or discard all changes	2

Properties of the MailItem and PostItem Objects

This section covers the **GetInspector**, **Body**, **HTMLBody**, **To**, and **SenderName** properties of the **MailItem** and **PostItem** objects.

Using GetInspector to Reference the Form

You can use the **GetInspector** property of the **MailItem** object or the **PostItem** object to reference the form associated with an item. You can then reference the page on the form, and then the controls on the page.

This example uses the **GetInspector** property of the **MailItem** object to return the form associated with the item. It references the **Message** page on the form, and then sets the **Visible** property of the TextBox1 control to **False**.

Before you run this example, do the following:

If you don't have a TextBox1 control on the form, click **Design This Form** from **Forms** on the **Tools** menu to switch to Design mode. Then, drag a TextBox control from the **Control Toolbox** to the form. Click **Run This Form** on the **Form** menu to switch to Run mode, and then click **CommandButton1** to hide the TextBox1 control.

```
Sub CommandButton1_Click
    Set MyPage = GetInspector.ModifiedFormPages("Message")
    MyPage.TextBox1.Visible = False
End Sub
```

Setting the Message Text of an Item

You can use the **Body** property of a **MailItem** object or a **PostItem** object to specify the text that appears in the Message control of a mail message.

The following example creates a reply item, enters text in the Message control of the reply item, and then sends the form. To run this example, you must first put a CommandButton1 control on the **Read** page of a Mail Message form. Then switch to Run mode and send the item to your Inbox. Open the item in the Inbox, and then click **CommandButton1**. The reply item appears.

```
Sub CommandButton1_Click
    Set MyReply = Item.Reply
    MyReply.Body = "It rains a lot here. "
    MyReply.Display
End Sub
```

Note   The **Body** property does not support Rich Text Format (RTF) or Hypertext Markup Language (HTML).

You can also use the **HTMLBody** property of a **MailItem** object or a **PostItem** object to specify formatted text in the Message control. When you set this property, Outlook automatically sets the **EditorType** property of the associated **Inspector** object to **olEditorHTML** (2).

The following example displays the current editor type, sets the **HTMLBody** property of the item, and then displays the new editor type.

```
Sub CommandButton1_Click
    MsgBox "EditorType = " & Item.GetInspector.EditorType
    Item.HTMLBody = "<H1>This is HTML text.</H1>"
    MsgBox "EditorType is now = " & Item.GetInspector.EditorType
End Sub
```

Note   Setting the **Body** property of the item causes Outlook to reset the editor type to be the user's default.

Setting the To Field of an Item

You can use the **To** property of the **MailItem** object to set the value of a To field.

This example creates a new item, and then sets the To field and Subject field values of the item.

```
Sub CommandButton1_Click
    Set MyItem = Application.CreateItem(0)
    MyItem.To = "James Allard"
    MyItem.Subject = "How to set the To field"
    MyItem.Display
End Sub
```

Getting the Sender Name of an Item

You can use the **SenderName** property of the **MailItem** object to return the name of the person who sent the message. This example gets the first item in the Inbox and sets the Recip variable to the value of the **SenderName** property. It then creates a new message item and sets its To field to the value of the Recip variable. When the item is displayed, the value of the **SenderName** property shows in the **To** box of the form.

```
Sub CommandButton1_Click
    Set MyFolder = Application.GetNameSpace("MAPI").GetDefaultFolder(6)
    Set MyItem = MyFolder.Items(1)
    Recip = MyItem.SenderName
    Set MyNewItem = Application.CreateItem(0)
    MyNewItem.To = Recip
    MyNewItem.Display
End Sub
```

Note   In the preceding example, the name in the To field is not resolved. To resolve a name, the name must be added to the **Recipients** collection object. For more information, see "The Recipients Collection Object" later in this chapter.

The AppointmentItem Object

An **AppointmentItem** object represents an appointment in the Calendar folder. An **AppointmentItem** object can represent a one-time appointment, a meeting, or a recurring appointment or meeting. A meeting usually involves more than one person, and is created when an **AppointmentItem** is sent to other users, who receive it in the form of a **MeetingItem** object in their respective Inbox folders.

An appointment or meeting can be recurring, that is, set to occur more than once on a regularly repeating basis. When this occurs, a **RecurrencePattern** object is created for the **AppointmentItem** object. An instance of a recurring appointment can be changed or deleted. This creates an exception to the recurrence pattern, and this exception is represented by an **Exception** object. All **Exception** objects associated with a given **AppointmentItem** object are contained in an **Exceptions** collection object associated with the **AppointmentItem**.

This section covers working with recurring appointments, including how to create a recurring appointment and how to deal with exceptions to the recurrence pattern. The section that follows covers creating a meeting from an appointment.

Working with Recurring Appointments

Creating a Recurring Appointment

A recurring appointment is represented by an **AppointmentItem** object with the **IsRecurring** property set to **True**. However, you cannot set this property directly; instead, you create a recurring appointment by calling the **GetRecurrencePattern** method of the **AppointmentItem** object and then saving the item.

The following example illustrates how to create an appointment named "Test Appointment" and then call the **GetRecurrencePattern** method to make it a recurring appointment.

```
Sub CommandButton1_Click
    Set MyItem = Application.CreateItem(1)
    MyItem.Subject = "Test Appointment"
    Set MyPattern = MyItem.GetRecurrencePattern
    MyItem.Save
End Sub
```

The **GetRecurrencePattern** method returns a **RecurrencePattern** object. You can change the recurrence pattern of the appointment by setting properties of the appointment's **RecurrencePattern** object.

Setting the Recurrence Pattern of an Appointment

When a new recurring appointment is created, it inherits a default recurrence pattern based on the time that the appointment was created. To change the recurrence pattern of an appointment, set the appropriate properties of the appointment's **RecurrencePattern** object.

See Also   For more information about the properties of the **RecurrencePattern** object that affect the recurrence pattern, see Microsoft Outlook Visual Basic Reference Help.

The following example shows how to create a one-hour recurring appointment that occurs at noon on the second Tuesday of each month for two months, starting July, 1998.

```
Sub CommandButton1_Click
    Set MyItem = Application.CreateItem(1)
    MyItem.Subject = "Monthly Appointment"
    Set MyPattern = MyItem.GetRecurrencePattern
    MyPattern.RecurrenceType = 3 ' Monthly, on a specific weekday
    MyPattern.Interval = 1 ' Every month (2 would be every other month)
    MyPattern.DayOfWeekMask = 4 ' Which day of week (Tuesday)
    MyPattern.Instance = 2 ' Which instance (second Tuesday)
    MyPattern.StartTime = "12:00 pm" ' Time each appointment begins
    MyPattern.EndTime = "1:00 pm" ' Time each appointment ends
    MyPattern.PatternStartDate = #7/1/98# ' Earliest date appointment can occur
    MyPattern.PatternEndDate = #9/1/98# ' Latest date appointment can occur
    MyItem.Save
End Sub
```

Working with a Single Appointment in a Series

To determine whether an instance of a recurring appointment occurs at a particular time, use the **GetOccurrence** method of the **RecurrencePattern** object. This method returns an **AppointmentItem** object representing the instance of the recurring appointment.

Important   The **GetOccurrence** method produces an error if an instance of the recurring appointment does not start at the date and time you provide. If it is possible that your script can supply a date and time that does not match an instance of a recurring appointment (because of user input, for example), the script should be able to handle the error appropriately. Otherwise, the script procedure will fail and Outlook will display an error message.

The following example illustrates how to use the **GetOccurrence** method to determine whether a recurring appointment (created by the code in the previous section) starts on a date and time provided by the user. The **On Error Resume Next** statement ensures that the procedure will continue if the user enters anything that does not match the start date and time of an instance of the recurring appointment. After calling the **GetOccurrence** method, the script tests the **MyAppointment** variable to determine whether it is set to **Nothing**, indicating that the method failed and so did not return an **AppointmentItem** object.

```
Sub CommandButton1_Click
    Set MyNameSpace = Application.GetNameSpace("MAPI")
    Set MyCalendarFolder = MyNameSpace.GetDefaultFolder(9)
    Set MyItem = MyCalendarFolder.Items("Monthly Appointment")
    Set MyPattern = MyItem.GetRecurrencePattern
    On Error Resume Next
    MyDate = InputBox ("Enter a date and time (m/d/yy hh:mm): ")
    Do While MyDate <> ""
        Set MyAppointment = Nothing
        Set MyAppointment = MyPattern.GetOccurrence(MyDate)
        If TypeName(MyAppointment) <> "Nothing" Then
            MsgBox "This instance of " & MyAppointment.Subject _
                & " occurs on " & MyAppointment.Start
        Else
            MsgBox MyItem.Subject & " does not occur on " & MyDate
        End If
        MyDate = InputBox ("Enter another date and time (m/d/yy hh:mm):")
    Loop
End Sub
```

Once you retrieve the **AppointmentItem** object representing an instance of a recurring appointment, you can delete or change the appointment instance. When this happens, Outlook creates an **Exception** object. The properties of this object describe the changes that were made to the instance. All of the **Exception** objects for a recurring appointment are contained in an **Exceptions** collection object associated with the appointment's **RecurrencePattern** object.

The **AppointmentItem** property of the **Exception** object returns the **AppointmentItem** object that constitutes the exception to the original recurrence pattern of the recurring appointment. You can use the methods and properties of the **AppointmentItem** object to work with the appointment exception.

The following example changes the subject of an instance of the recurring appointment created by the script in the previous section. It then uses the **AppointmentItem** property of the resulting **Exception** object to change the start time of the appointment exception.

```
Sub CommandButton1_Click
    Set MyNameSpace = Application.GetNameSpace("MAPI")
    Set MyCalendarFolder = MyNameSpace.GetDefaultFolder(9)
    Set MyItem = MyCalendarFolder.Items("Monthly Appointment")
    Set MyPattern = MyItem.GetRecurrencePattern
    Set MyInstance = MyPattern.GetOccurrence(#8/11/98 12:00 pm#)
    MyInstance.Subject = "Monthly Pattern (exception)"
    MsgBox MyInstance.Subject & " starts on " & MyInstance.Start
    MyInstance.Save
    Set MyNewPattern = MyItem.GetRecurrencePattern
    Set MyException = MyNewPattern.Exceptions.Item(1)
    Set MyNewInstance = MyException.AppointmentItem
    MyNewInstance.Start = (#8/11/98 1:00 pm#)
    MsgBox MyNewInstance.Subject & " now starts on " & MyNewInstance.Start
    MyNewInstance.Save
End Sub
```

The following two sections describe how to use the **Exception** object to work with changed or deleted instances of a recurring appointment.

Determining the Original Date of an Exception

The **OriginalDate** property of the **Exception** object returns the start date and time of the changed appointment before it was changed.

The following example uses the **OriginalDate** property to retrieve the original start date of the appointment exception created in the previous section. In addition, it uses the **Start** property of the **AppointmentItem** associated with the **Exception** object to provide the new start date of the appointment.

```
Sub CommandButton1_Click
    Set MyNameSpace = Application.GetNameSpace("MAPI")
    Set MyCalendarFolder = MyNameSpace.GetDefaultFolder(9)
    Set MyItem = MyCalendarFolder.Items("Monthly Appointment")
    Set MyPattern = MyItem.GetRecurrencePattern
    Set MyException = MyPattern.Exceptions.Item(1)
    MsgBox "The changed appointment originally occurred on " _
        & MyException.OriginalDate & Chr(13) & "It now occurs on "_
        & MyException.AppointmentItem.Start
End Sub
```

Determining Whether an Appointment Instance was Deleted

When an appointment in a recurring series is deleted, an **Exception** object representing the deleted appointment is created, and the **Deleted** property of the **Exception** object is set to **True**.

The following example uses the **Delete** method of the **AppointmentItem** object to delete the appointment instance changed in the previous section. It then tests the value of the **Deleted** property of the **Exception** object representing the deleted appointment to determine whether the appointment was actually deleted.

```
Sub CommandButton1_Click
    Set MyNameSpace = Application.GetNameSpace("MAPI")
    Set MyCalendarFolder = MyNameSpace.GetDefaultFolder(9)
    Set MyItem = MyCalendarFolder.Items("Monthly Appointment")
    Set MyPattern = MyItem.GetRecurrencePattern
    Set MyAppointment = MyPattern.GetOccurrence(#8/11/98 1:00 pm#)
    MyAppointment.Delete
    Set MyException = MyPattern.Exceptions.Item(1)
    If MyException.Deleted Then MsgBox "The appointment was deleted."
End Sub
```

The MeetingItem Object

A **MeetingItem** object represents a request for a meeting received in a user's Inbox mail folder. You cannot create a **MeetingItem** object directly. Instead, Outlook creates a **MeetingItem** object in each recipient's Inbox folder when a user sends an **AppointmentItem** object with its **MeetingStatus** property set to **olMeeting** (1).

The following example shows how to create an appointment and then send the appointment as a meeting request to a required attendee and an optional attendee.

```
Sub CommandButton1_Click
    Set myItem = Application.CreateItem(1) ' Create an appointment
    myItem.MeetingStatus = 1 ' Appointment is a meeting
    myItem.Subject = "Marketing Strategy Meeting"
    myItem.Location = "Conference Room B"
    myItem.Start = #9/24/98 1:30:00 PM#
    myItem.Duration = 90
    Set myRequiredAttendee = myItem.Recipients.Add("James Allard")
    myRequiredAttendee.Type = 1 ' Required
    Set myOptionalAttendee = myItem.Recipients.Add("Jim Hance")
    myOptionalAttendee.Type = 2 ' Optional
    myItem.Send
End Sub
```

The **MeetingItem** object replaces the **MeetingRequestItem** object provided by Outlook 97.

Working with Meeting Requests

Most often, you will not work directly with a **MeetingItem** object. For example, you do not use the **MeetingItem** object to accept or decline the meeting. Instead, you use the appointment associated with the meeting request.

The **GetAssociatedAppointment** method of the **MeetingItem** object returns an **AppointmentItem** object that you can use to accept or refuse the meeting request or to directly add the meeting (as an appointment) to the Calendar folder.

You can also directly access an **AppointmentItem** that has its **MeetingStatus** property set to **olMeeting** (1) to determine which recipients have accepted or declined the meeting request.

The following sections illustrate how to work with a meeting request through the appointment associated with the meeting.

Retrieving the Associated Appointment of a Meeting

The **MeetingItem** object is a message containing a request to add an appointment to the recipient's calendar—it is not the appointment itself. To access the appointment associated with the meeting request, you use the **GetAssociatedAppointment** method of the **MeetingItem** object. This method requires a Boolean argument that specifies whether the appointment is added to the user's Calendar.

The following example calls the **GetAssociatedAppointment** method of each **MeetingItem** in the user's Inbox and then uses the returned **AppointmentItem** object's **Display** method to open the appointment. Note that the argument of **GetAssociatedAppointment** is set to **False** so the appointment is not added to the user's Calendar.

```
Sub CommandButton1_Click
    Set myNameSpace = Application.GetNameSpace("MAPI")
    Set myFolder = myNameSpace.GetDefaultFolder(6)
    Set myItems = myFolder.Items
    Set myMeetingRequest = _
    myItems.Find("[MessageClass] = 'IPM.Schedule.Meeting.Request'")
    Do While TypeName (myMeetingRequest)<> "Nothing"
        myMeetingRequest.GetAssociatedAppointment(False).Display
        Set myMeetingRequest = myItems.FindNext
    Loop
End Sub
```

Responding to a Meeting Request

To respond to a meeting request, you use the **GetAssociatedAppointment** method of the **MeetingItem** object to obtain the **AppointmentItem** object associated with the meeting request. You then use the **Respond** method of the **AppointmentItem** object to notify the meeting organizer whether the meeting has been accepted, declined, or tentatively added to the receiving user's Calendar.

The **Respond** method allows you to send the notification without user intervention, or it can allow the user to edit the response before sending it. The **Respond** method accepts three parameters. The first specifies the actual response (accept, decline, or tentative), while the second two are Boolean values that determine whether the user will be given the opportunity to edit the response.

To send the notification without requiring action by the user, you call the **Respond** method with the second parameter set to **True** and then send the **AppointmentItem**, as shown in the following example.

```
Sub CommandButton1_Click
    Set myNamespace = Application.GetNamespace("MAPI")
    Set myFolder = myNamespace.GetDefaultFolder(6)
    Set myMtgReq = _
        myFolder.Items.Find("[MessageClass] = 'IPM.Schedule.Meeting.Request'")
    If TypeName(myMtgReq) <> "Nothing" Then
        Set myAppt = myMtgReq.GetAssociatedAppointment(True)
        myAppt.Respond 3, True
        myAppt.Send
        MsgBox "The " & myAppt.Subject & " meeting on " & myAppt.Start _
            & " has been accepted."
    Else
        MsgBox "You have no meeting requests in your Inbox."
    End If
End Sub
```

If you want to allow the user to choose how to respond (that is, whether to send a
response and whether to edit the body of the response before sending), call the
Respond method with the second parameter set to **False** and third parameters set to
True, as shown:

```
Sub CommandButton1_Click
    Set myNamespace = Application.GetNamespace("MAPI")
    Set myFolder = myNamespace.GetDefaultFolder(6)
    Set myMtgReq = _
        myFolder.Items.Find("[MessageClass] ='IPM.Schedule.Meeting.Request'")
    If TypeName(myMtgReq) <> "Nothing" Then
        Set myAppt = myMtgReq.GetAssociatedAppointment(True)
        myAppt.Respond 3, False, True
    Else
        MsgBox "You have no meeting requests in your Inbox."
    End If
End Sub
```

In this example, the **Respond** method displays a dialog box giving the user three
choices:

- Edit the response before sending

- Send the response now

- Don't send a response

Outlook immediately sends the **AppointmentItem** to the meeting organizer if the user
chooses **Send the response now**. If the user chooses **Edit the response before
sending**, Outlook opens the item to allow the user to change recipients, the subject, or
the body text before sending the response.

Instead of giving the user the choice of how to respond, you can call the **Respond**
method with the second and third parameters both set to **False**. This has the same
result as the user choosing **Edit the response before sending**.

Determining the Status of a Recipient of a Meeting Request

An **AppointmentItem** object created from a **MeetingItem** object has a **Recipients** collection object associated with it. You can use the **MeetingResponseStatus** property of the **Recipient** objects in this collection to determine whether a given recipient has accepted or declined the requested meeting.

The script in the following example retrieves each meeting that the user has requested and then checks the **MeetingResponseStatus** property for each recipient of the meeting. A description of the status for each recipient is added to a text string that is displayed in a message box once the status of all the recipients has been checked.

```
Sub CommandButton1_Click
    Set myNamespace = Application.GetNamespace("MAPI")
    Set myFolder = myNamespace.GetDefaultFolder(9)
    Set myItems = myFolder.Items
    Set myMeeting = myItems.Find("[MeetingStatus] = 1")
    Do While TypeName(myMeeting) <> "Nothing"
        TextStr = "The following is the status of recipients for " _
            & MyMeeting.Subject & " on " & MyMeeting.Start & ":" & chr(13)
        Set myRecipients = myMeeting.Recipients
        For x = 1 To myRecipients.Count
            TextStr = TextStr & chr(13)& myRecipients(x).Name
            Select Case myRecipients(x).MeetingResponseStatus
                Case 0
                    TextStr2 = " did not respond."
                Case 1
                    TextStr2 = " organized the meeting."
                Case 2
                    TextStr2 = " tentatively accepted."
                Case 3
                    TextStr2 = " accepted."
                Case 4
                    TextStr2 = " declined."
            End Select
            TextStr = TextStr & TextStr2
        Next
        If MsgBox(TextStr,1) = 2 then Exit Sub ' Use OK/Cancel; exit if Cancel
        Set myMeeting = myItems.FindNext
    Loop
End Sub
```

See Also   For more information about the **MeetingResponseStatus** property and the values it returns, see Microsoft Outlook Visual Basic Reference Help.

The TaskItem Object

The **TaskItem** object represents a single item in the user's Tasks folder. A task is similar to an appointment in that it can be sent to others (much like a meeting request) and can be recurring. Unlike an appointment, however, an uncompleted recurring task has only a single instance. When an instance of a recurring task is marked as complete, Outlook creates a second instance of the task for the next time period in the task's recurrence pattern.

This section shows you how to work with a **TaskItem** object. A later section, "The TaskRequestItem Object," demonstrates how to work with assigned tasks.

Methods of the TaskItem Object

This section covers the **GetRecurrencePattern** and **Assign** methods of the **TaskItem** object.

Creating a Recurring Task

You can use the **GetRecurrencePattern** method of the **TaskItem** object to create a recurring task, in much the same manner as creating a recurring appointment (for more information, see "Creating a Recurring Appointment" earlier in this chapter).

The following example shows how to create a task and then call the **GetRecurrencePattern** method to make the task a recurring task.

```
Sub CommandButton1_Click
    Set MyItem = Application.CreateItem(3)
    MyItem.Subject = "Test Task"
    Set MyPattern = MyItem.GetRecurrencePattern
    MyItem.Save
End Sub
```

As with a recurring meeting, you use the **RecurrencePattern** object associated with the task to specify how often and when the task will recur. Unlike a recurring appointment, however, a recurring task does not have multiple occurrences; instead, when a recurring task is marked as completed, Outlook creates a copy of the task for the next date in the recurrence pattern. Consequently, the **RecurrencePattern** object of a task does not support the **GetOccurrence** method or the **Exceptions** property.

Delegating a Task

In much the same way as you can invite others to a meeting by sending them an **AppointmentItem** object, you can delegate a task to others by sending them a **TaskItem** object. Before sending the object, however, you must first use the **Assign** method to create an assigned task.

The following example shows how to create and delegate a task using the **Assign** and
Send methods:

```
Sub CommandButton1_Click
    Set myItem = Application.CreateItem(3)
    myItem.Assign
    Set myDelegate = myItem.Recipients.Add("James Allard")
    myItem.Subject = "Develop order confirmation form"
    myItem.DueDate = #6/4/98#
    myItem.Send
End Sub
```

When a task is assigned and sent to another user, the user receives a
TaskRequestItem object. You can use this object to access the task associated with
the request and to respond to the task request.

The TaskRequestItem Object

A **TaskRequestItem** object represents a request to assign a task in the Inbox of the
user to whom the task is being assigned.

The following example displays a message box containing the subject of each task
request in the user's Inbox folder.

```
Sub CommandButton1_Click
    Set myNameSpace = Application.GetNameSpace("MAPI")
    Set myFolder = myNameSpace.GetDefaultFolder(6)
    Set myItems = myFolder.Items
    Set myTaskRequest = _
        myItems.Find("[MessageClass] = 'IPM.TaskRequest'")
    Do While TypeName (myTaskRequest)<> "Nothing"
        myMessage = myMessage & chr(13) & myTaskRequest.Subject
        Set myTaskRequest = myItems.FindNext
    Loop
    If myMessage = "" then
        MsgBox "You have no pending task requests"
    Else
        MsgBox "Your pending task requests are:" & chr(13) & myMessage
    End If
End Sub
```

Working with Task Requests

As with a **MeetingItem** object, usually you will not work directly with a **TaskRequestItem** object. For example, you do not use the **TaskRequestItem** object to accept or decline the task. Instead, you use the task associated with the task request.

The **GetAssociatedTask** method of the **TaskRequestItem** object returns a **TaskItem** object that you can use to accept or refuse the task.

Retrieving the Associated Task of a Task Request

Using the **GetAssociatedTask** method, you can access the task associated with a **TaskRequestItem**. Properties of the **TaskItem** returned by this method contain additional information about the assigned task, such as its due date.

Important Before you call the **GetAssociatedTask** method for a **TaskRequestItem** object, you must first process the **TaskRequestItem** object. By default, this is done automatically (unless the user has cleared the **Process requests and responses on arrival** check box on the **Advanced Email** dialog box available through the **Options** dialog box). You can also process a **TaskRequestItem** object by calling its **Display** method. Note that when a **TaskRequestItem** object is processed, its associated task is added to the user's Tasks folder.

The following code example displays a message box containing the subject and due date of every task request in the user's Inbox. This example is identical to the one in the previous section, but uses the **GetAssociatedTask** method to access the **DueDate** property of the task associated with the task request. Note that this example assumes that the **TaskRequestItem** objects have already been processed.

```
Sub CommandButton1_Click
    Set myNameSpace = Application.GetNameSpace("MAPI")
    Set myFolder = myNameSpace.GetDefaultFolder(6)
    Set myItems = myFolder.Items
    Set myTaskRequest = _
    myItems.Find("[MessageClass] = 'IPM.TaskRequest'")
    Do While TypeName (myTaskRequest)<> "Nothing"
        myMessage = myMessage & chr(13) _
            & myTaskRequest.Subject & " due on " _
            & myTaskRequest.GetAssociatedTask(False).DueDate
        Set myTaskRequest = myItems.FindNext
    Loop
    If myMessage = "" then
        MsgBox "You have no pending task requests"
    Else
        MsgBox "Your pending task requests are:" & chr(13) & myMessage
    End If
End Sub
```

Responding to a Task Request

To accept, decline, or modify a task request, use the **Respond** method of the **TaskItem** object returned by the **GetAssociatedTask** method of a **TaskRequestItem** object.

The following example retrieves the first **TaskRequestItem** in the user's Inbox and accepts it.

```
Sub CommandButton1_Click
    Set myNameSpace = Application.GetNameSpace("MAPI")
    Set myFolder = myNameSpace.GetDefaultFolder(6)
    Set myItems = myFolder.Items
    Set myTaskRequest = _
    myItems.Find("[MessageClass] = 'IPM.TaskRequest'")
    If TypeName(myTaskRequest) <> "Nothing" then
        Set myTask = MyTaskRequest.GetAssociatedTask(False)
        myTask.Respond 2, True,False
        myTask.Send
        msgbox "Accepted: " & MyTask.Subject
    Else
        MsgBox "You have no pending task requests"
    End If
End Sub
```

Note that if you set the second parameter of the **Respond** method to **True**, you must call the **Send** method of the **TaskItem.**

When the **Respond** method is used to respond to a task request, the initiating user receives a **TaskRequestAcceptItem**, **TaskRequestDeclineItem**, or **TaskRequestUpdateItem** object, depending on the type of response. You work with these objects in much the same way as a **TaskRequestItem** object in that you use the object's **GetAssociatedTask** method to retrieve the **TaskItem** object associated with the request and then call the methods and access the properties of the **TaskItem** object.

The Inspector Object

Forms in the Outlook object model are referenced by the **Inspector** object. This section covers only some of the methods and properties of the **Inspector** object.

See Also   For a complete list and description of the methods and properties for the **Inspector** object, see Microsoft Outlook Visual Basic Reference Help.

Methods of the Inspector Object

This section covers the **SetCurrentFormPage**, **HideFormPage**, and **ShowFormPage** methods of the **Inspector** object.

Setting the Current Form Page

You can use the **SetCurrentFormPage** method of the **Inspector** object to set the current form page of a form.

This example shows the **Details** page as the current form page of a Contact form when you click **CommandButton1**. (To use this example, you must add a command button to a Contact form in Design mode, add the code in the Script Editor, and then run the form.)

```
Sub CommandButton1_Click
    Set MyInspector = Item.GetInspector
    MyInspector.SetCurrentFormPage("Details")
End Sub
```

Hiding and Showing a Form Page

You can use the **HideFormPage** method of the **Inspector** object to hide a form page.

In this example, the **All Fields** page of the Contact form is hidden.

```
Sub CommandButton1_Click
    Set MyInspector = Item.GetInspector
    MyInspector.HideFormPage("All Fields")
End Sub
```

To show a form page, you use the **ShowFormPage** method of the **Inspector** object. Add a second button to the Contact form, add the following code, and then click **CommandButton2** to show the **All Fields** page.

```
Sub CommandButton2_Click
    Set MyInspector = Item.GetInspector
    MyInspector.ShowFormPage("All Fields")
End Sub
```

Properties of the Inspector Object

This section covers the **ModifiedFormPages** property of the **Inspector** object. The **ModifiedFormPages** property returns the entire collection of pages for a form. The **Pages** collection object is covered in more detail in the next section.

Referencing a Form Page and Its Controls

You can use the **ModifiedFormPages** property of the **Inspector** object to return the **Pages** collection that represents the pages on a form that have been modified. Note that standard pages on a form, such as a **Message** page, are also included in the collection if the standard pages can be customized. You must use the **Pages** collection object to switch to the page, which then allows you to gain access to controls on the page.

The following example uses the **ModifiedFormPages** property of the **Inspector** object to return the **Message** page in the **Pages** collection object. It then uses the **Controls** property of the **Page** object to reference the ToggleButton1 control. When the toggle button is down, the Label2 control is visible. When the toggle button is up, the Label2 control is not visible.

Before you run this example, do the following:

Switch to Design mode and drag a ToggleButton control from the **Control Toolbox** to the **Message** page of the form. Then drag a Label control from the **Control Toolbox** to the **Message** page. This example assumes that the Label control is named Label2. If it's not, change the name by right-clicking the Label control, and then click **Properties** on the shortcut menu. Click the **Display** tab, type **Label2** in the **Name** box, and then click **OK**. Note that the procedure uses ToggleButton1_Click instead of CommandButton1_Click. To run the example, click **Run This Form** on the **Form** menu to switch to Run mode, and then click **ToggleButton1**.

```
Sub ToggleButton1_Click
    Set MyPage = Item.GetInspector.ModifiedFormPages("Message")
    Set MyControl = MyPage.ToggleButton1
    If MyControl.Value = True Then
        MyPage.Label2.Visible = True
    Else
        MyPage.Label2.Visible = False
    End If
End Sub
```

The Pages Collection Object

To reference a page or controls on a page, you use the **ModifiedFormPages** property of the **Inspector** object to reference the **Pages** collection object, and then reference the individual page by name or number.

This procedure uses the **ModifiedFormPages** property of the **Inspector** object to return the number of modified form pages in the **Pages** collection. Note that the pages are not added to the collection until the page is clicked at design time.

```
Sub CommandButton1_Click
    Set PagesCollection = Item.GetInspector.ModifiedFormPages
    MsgBox "The number of modified form pages in the Pages collection is " _
        & PagesCollection.Count & "."
End Sub
```

The Page Object

Important The **Page** object is contained in the Microsoft Forms 2.0 Object Library. To view the methods and properties for the **Page** object, use the Microsoft Excel 97 Object Browser.

You can use the **ModifiedFormPages** property to return the **Pages** collection from an **Inspector** object. You use **ModifiedFormPages(index)**, where index is the name or index number, to return a single page from a **Pages** collection.

This example references the **Message** page, and then references the CommandButton1 control on the page. When clicked, the CommandButton1 control moves to the left.

```
Sub CommandButton1_Click
    Set MyPage = GetInspector.ModifiedFormPages("Message")
    Set MyControl = MyPage.CommandButton1
    MyControl.Left = MyControl.Left + 20
End Sub
```

The Controls Collection Object

To access controls on Outlook forms, you use the **Controls** collection object. The **Controls** collection object contains the collection of controls on a form page. To access an individual control in the **Controls** collection, you use the index value of the control or the name of the control. The **Controls** collection object is contained in the Microsoft Forms 2.0 Object Library. This section discusses how to reference control collections and controls on a form.

Methods of the Controls Collection Object

Important The **Controls** collection object is contained in the Microsoft Forms 2.0 Object Library. To view the methods and properties for the **Controls** collection object, use the Microsoft Excel 97 Object Browser.

The **Controls** collection object offers a variety of methods that enable you to manipulate the controls on a form. For example, you can use the **Move** method to move all the controls on a page. Or you can use the **SendToBack** method to send the controls in the **Controls** collection to the back layer of the page.

You can use the **Controls** property to return the **Controls** collection from a **Page** object. You use **Controls(index)**, where index is the name or index number, to return a control from a **Controls** collection.

Adding a Control to the Form Page

You can use the **Add** method of the **Controls** collection object to add a control to the form.

This example uses the **Add** method to add a new CommandButton control to the **Message** page to the right of the CommandButton1 control.

```
Sub CommandButton1_Click
    Set MyPage = GetInspector.ModifiedFormPages("Message")
    Set MyControl = MyPage.Controls.Add("Forms.CommandButton.1")
    MyControl.Left = MyPage.CommandButton1.Left + 150
    MyControl.Top = MyPage.CommandButton1.Top
    MyControl.Width = 50
    MyControl.Height = 20
    MyControl.Caption = "New Button"
End Sub
```

See Also   For more information about using the **Add** method of the **Controls** collection object, see Microsoft Outlook Customization and Forms Help.

Properties of the Controls Collection Object

The **Controls** collection object provides only the **Count** property. With the **Count** property, you can use the **For...Next** statement to loop through the controls in a collection.

This example returns the collection of controls on the **Test** page. It then displays the name of each control contained on the page. To test this example, rename a custom page "Test," and then add several controls to the page.

```
Sub CommandButton1_Click
    Set Page = Item.GetInspector.ModifiedFormPages("Test")
    Set MyControls = Page.Controls
    For i = 0 to MyControls.Count - 1
        MsgBox MyControls(i).Name
    Next
End Sub
```

Important   Notice that the **For...Next** statement starts at 0. You must use 0 to reference the first item in the collection. However, Outlook returns a count of 3. Therefore, you must specify the *Count -1* argument for the **For...Next** statement in Outlook.

The Control Object

Important   The **Control** object and the individual control objects, such as CheckBox and TextBox, are contained in the Microsoft Forms 2.0 Object Library. To view the methods and properties for the **Controls** collection object, use the Microsoft Excel 97 Object Browser. For an up-to-date reference of the supported methods and properties for controls, see "Control Reference" in Microsoft Outlook Customization and Forms Help. To access Microsoft Outlook Customization and Forms Help, click **Microsoft Outlook Forms Help** on the Outlook **Help** menu. If this menu is not available, see "Information Resources for Using VBScript in Outlook 98" earlier in this chapter.

In the Visual Basic Forms object model, the control objects are generically represented by a **Control** object. Further, they are individually represented by the objects that represent the names of the individual control components, such as TextBox, CheckBox, and so on. As discussed in the preceding section, to reference a control, use the **Controls** property to return the **Controls** collection from a **Page** object, and then use **Controls(index)**, where index is the name or index number, to return a control from a **Controls** collection.

Properties of Control Objects

The properties available for a control will differ for each type of control. This section covers the **Value** property for the CheckBox control and the **Enabled** property for the TextBox control.

Setting the Enabled Property of a Control

This example uses a CheckBox control called CheckBox1 and a TextBox control called TextBox1. When the CheckBox1 control is clicked, the procedure evaluates the state of CheckBox1. If the value of CheckBox1 is **True**, then TextBox1 is enabled; otherwise, it is not enabled.

Before you run this example, do the following:

With the form in Design mode, drag a CheckBox control from the **Control Toolbox** to the **Message** page of the form. If you don't have a TextBox control named TextBox1 already on the form, drag a TextBox control to the form. This example assumes it's named TextBox1. Switch the form to Run mode and then click **CheckBox1** to enable or disable the TextBox1 control.

```
Sub CheckBox1_Click
    Set MyPage = Item.GetInspector.ModifiedFormPages("Message")
    Set MyControls = MyPage.Controls
    If MyControls("CheckBox1").Value = True Then
        MyControls("TextBox1").Enabled = True
    Else
        MyControls("TextBox1").Enabled = False
    End If
End Sub
```

Setting the PossibleValues Property of a ComboBox or ListBox

Rather than use the **AddItem** method to add items to a ListBox or ComboBox control, you can use the **PossibleValues** property. Note that the **PossibleValues** property is an undocumented property.

In this example, the **PossibleValues** property is used to add the values Red, Green, and Blue to the ComboBox1 control when **CommandButton1** is clicked.

```
Sub CommandButton1_Click
    Set MyPage = Item.GetInspector.ModifiedFormPages("Message")
    MyPage.ComboBox1.PossibleValues = "Red;Green;Blue"
End Sub
```

Resizing a Control Vertically and Horizontally

Quite often, you want controls on a form to adjust horizontally and vertically when the form is resized. To do this, you must set an invisible property called **LayoutFlags**. This example sets the **LayoutFlags** property for the TextBox1 control when you click **CommandButton1**.

To run this example, do the following:

In Design mode, add a TextBox1 control to the **P.2** page of a form. Resize the TextBox1 control so that its bottom border is near the bottom border of the form and its right border is near the right border of the form. (Don't obscure the CommandButton1 control.) Add the following code for the CommandButton1 control. Switch to Run mode, resize the form, and notice what happens. Then click **CommandButton1** and resize the form. After the **LayoutFlags** property is set, the controls adjust to the size of the form.

```
Sub CommandButton1_Click
    Item.GetInspector.ModifiedFormPages("P.2").TextBox1.LayoutFlags = 68
End Sub
```

After you set the **LayoutFlags** property, you can delete the procedure from the Script Editor.

Resizing a Control Vertically

Quite often, you want controls on the form to vertically resize when the form is vertically resized. To do this, you set the **LayoutFlags** property to 65.

To run this example, do the following:

Delete the TextBox1 control from the **P.2** page and then add a new TextBox1 control. Resize the TextBox1 control so that its bottom border is near the bottom border of the form. (Don't obscure the CommandButton1 control.) Add the following code for the CommandButton1 control. Switch to Run mode, and resize the form vertically. Then click **CommandButton1**, and vertically resize the form again.

```
Sub CommandButton1_Click
    Item.GetInspector.ModifiedFormPages("P.2").TextBox1.LayoutFlags = 65
End Sub
```

After you set the **LayoutFlags** property, you can delete the procedure from the Script Editor.

Binding a Control to a Field at Run Time

You can use the **ItemProperty** property to bind a control to a field at run time.

To run this example, do the following:

Add a new TextBox1 control (or use the existing one if it's already on the form) to the **P.2** page of the form. Add the following code for the CommandButton1 control. Switch to Run mode, click the **Message** page, and type **Test** in the **Subject** box. Then click **CommandButton1**. Notice the value in the **Subject** box appears in the TextBox1 control because the control is now bound to the Subject field.

```
Sub CommandButton1_Click
    Item.GetInspector.ModifiedFormPages("P.2").TextBox1.ItemProperty = "Subject"
End Sub
```

The UserProperties Collection Object

The **UserProperties** collection object represents the custom fields contained in an item. To return a collection of user-defined fields for an item, you can use the **UserProperties** method of the **MailItem** object, the **PostItem** object, and so on. The **UserProperty** object represents a single field in the item.

See Also   For a complete list and description of the properties and methods for the **UserProperties** collection object, see Microsoft Outlook Visual Basic Reference Help.

Note   Standard properties in Outlook, such as **Subject**, **To**, and **Body**, are properties of the individual item object. For more information, see "Properties of the MailItem and PostItem Objects" earlier in this chapter.

Methods of the UserProperties Collection Object

This section covers the **Find** method of the **UserProperties** collection object.

Getting the Value of a User Property

You can use the **Find** method of the **UserProperties** collection object to get the value of a user-defined field in an item.

The following example uses the **Find** method of the **UserProperties** collection object to return the value of the Customer Name field when the CommandButton1 control is clicked.

Before you run this example, do the following:

Drag the Customer Name field you created earlier in this chapter to the **Message** page of the form. If you didn't create a Customer Name field, do so now by clicking **New** in the **Field Chooser**, typing **Customer Name**, and then clicking **OK**. Click the **All Fields** tab on the form, and then in the **Value** cell for **Customer Name**, type **James Allard**. Click the **Message** page, and then click **CommandButton1**.

```
Sub CommandButton1_Click
    MsgBox "The value of the Customer Name field is " _
        & UserProperties.Find("Customer Name").Value & "."
End Sub
```

Setting the Value of a User Property

You can also use the **Find** method of the **UserProperties** collection object to set the value of a field.

This examples uses the **Find** method of the **UserProperties** collection object to set the value of the Customer Name field, and the ComboBox control to which it is bound, to the value "Scott Cooper."

```
Sub CommandButton1_Click
    UserProperties.Find("Customer Name") = "Scott Cooper"
End Sub
```

The Recipients Collection Object

The **Recipients** collection object represents the names that appear in the To field of the **MailItem**, **MeetingRequestItem**, and **TaskRequestItem** objects.

Methods of the Recipients Collection Object

This section covers the **Add** and **ResolveAll** methods of the **Recipients** collection object.

See Also   For a complete list and description of the properties and methods for the **Recipients** collection object and the **Recipient** object, see Microsoft Outlook Visual Basic Reference Help.

Adding Recipients to the Collection

You can use the **Add** method of the **Recipients** collection object to add recipient names to the **Recipients** collection.

This example creates a new message item, and then uses the **Recipients** property of the **MailItem** object to return the **Recipients** collection object which, in this case, is empty. It then adds two names to the **Recipients** collection object, uses the **ResolveAll** method to resolve the recipient names, and then displays the Message form.

For this example, you can replace the names "David Goodhand" and "Rich Andrews" with names of people in your organization.

```
Sub AddRecipientsToCollection_Click
    Set MyItem = Application.CreateItem(0)
    Set MyRecipient = MyItem.Recipients
    MyRecipient.Add("David Goodhand")
    MyRecipient.Add("Rich Andrews")
    MyRecipient.ResolveAll
    MyItem.Display
End Sub
```

Automatically Addressing an Item to All Contacts in a Contacts Folder

This example uses the **Add** method and the **ResolveAll** method to show how you can use the **Recipients** collection object to create a procedure that enables you to automatically address a message to all the users in the Contacts folder in your Mailbox. In this procedure, the Contact's e-mail addresses are added to the **Recipients** collection object.

```
Sub CommandButton1_Click
    Set MyNameSpace = Application.GetNameSpace("MAPI")
    Set MyFolder = MyNameSpace.GetDefaultFolder(10)
    Set MyItems = MyFolder.Items
    Set MySendItem = Application.CreateItem(0)
    Set MyRecipients = MySendItem.Recipients
    MyCount = MyItems.Count
    For i = 1 To MyCount
       If MyItems(i).EMaillAddress > " " Then
          MyRecipients.Add MyItems(i).EMaillAddress
          MsgBox MyItems(i).EMaillAddress
       End If
    Next
    MyRecipients.ResolveAll
    MySendItem.Display
End Sub
```

Events

By using the Script Editor, you can add code to Outlook events to modify the behavior of the event. For example, for the Open event, you can add code to specify the current form page, or you can add code to write data from a database into a ComboBox control. For the Click event, you can create a procedure that creates a custom item, includes an attachment to the current item, and then posts the item in a folder. In addition to modifying events, you can prevent events from occurring.

▶ **To add or modify an event**

1 With the form in Design mode, click **View Code** on the **Form Design** toolbar.

2 On the Script Editor **Script** menu, click **Event Handler**.

3 In the **Insert Event Handler** list box, double-click the event you want.

With an event procedure, the word *Item* refers to the current Outlook item associated with the form. For example, the following Item_PropertyChange procedure sets the value of the Subject field in the item when the value in the **Sensitivity** drop-down list box in the **Message Options** dialog box is changed.

```
Sub Item_PropertyChange(ByVal PropertyName)
    Select Case PropertyName
    Case "Sensitivity"
       Item.Subject = "The sensitivity value has changed."
    End Select
End Sub
```

▶ **To test the preceding example code**

1 On the Outlook **Actions** menu, click **New Mail Message**.

2 On the form **Tools** menu, select **Forms**, and then click **Design This Form**.

3 On the **Form Design** toolbar, click **View Code**.

4 Add the preceding sample code to the Script Editor window.

5 On the form **Form** menu, click **Run This Form**.

6 Click the **Options** button on the **Standard** toolbar, and then click a new value in the **Sensitivity** drop-down list box.

7 Close the **Message Options** dialog box.

   The text is now added to the **Subject** box.

The Firing Sequence of Events

You should be aware that an item's events will fire if the item is created through code (VBScript or VBA automation code) or through the Outlook user interface. When an Outlook form is opened to compose an item or to read an item, events are fired in the sequences described in the following sections.

Note   An item's events fire whether the item is created through program code (VBScript or VBA) or through the Outlook user interface.

When You Create a New Item

When you create a new item, the Item_Open event is fired. In Outlook, you generally create a new item by opening a form. However, for certain folders such as the Tasks folder, you can create a new item by clicking the **New Item** row in the folder. In either case, the Item_Open event is fired.

When You Send an Item

When you send an item, the Item_Send event is fired, followed by the Item_Write event, and the Item_Close event.

Note   The message class, IPM.Note, is used for sending items.

When You Post or Save an Item

In Outlook, posting an item performs the same task as saving an item. When you post or save an item, the Item_Write event is fired. There are several cases in which an Item_Write event may occur. For example, a post item is created and the **Post** button is clicked on the form; a contact item is created and the **Save and Close** button is clicked on the form; a task item is created by clicking the **New Item** row, and then the item is saved when the user clicks outside the **New Item** row.

When you post or save an item, the Item_Write event is fired, followed by the Item_Close event.

When You Open an Existing Item

In Outlook, an item can be opened in a couple of ways. If the item exists in a view that allows in-cell editing, the item can be opened simply by clicking the item in the view. In addition, an existing item can also be opened by double-clicking the item and viewing it in a form. When either case occurs, the Item_Read event is fired. If the item is viewed in a form, the Item_Read event is followed by the Item_Open event.

When You Close an Item

When you close an item, the Item_Close event is fired. If changes have been made to the item when you attempt to close it, you are asked if you want to save the item. If you click **Yes**, the Item_Write event is fired, followed by the Item_Close event.

Preventing Events from Firing

In some cases, you may want to prevent events from occurring. For example, for a Reply event, you may want to add code that opens a custom form rather than the default Message form. To do this, you must first prevent the default behavior from occurring. To prevent the default behavior from occurring, you assign **False** to the function value.

This example prevents the standard Reply event from occurring in a Mail Message form. Instead, it opens a custom Orders form when the **Reply** button is clicked.

```
Function Item_Reply(ByVal Response)
    Item_Reply = False
    Set MyFolder = Application.GetNameSpace("MAPI").GetDefaultFolder(6)
    Set MyItem = MyFolder.Items.Add("IPM.Note.Orders")
    MyItem.To = Item.To
    MyItem.Subject = "RE: " & MyItem.Subject
    MyItem.Display
End Function
```

Events that can be interrupted include Item_Close, Item_CustomAction, Item_Forward, Item_Open, Item_Reply, Item_ReplyAll, Item_Send, and Item_Write.

The Click Event

The Click event occurs when a user clicks a control, such as a command button, on a form. You can create as many Click procedures as you have controls on the form.

Important   The Click event is the only VBScript control event supported in Outlook.

▶ To create a Click event procedure

- In the Script Editor, type the name of the control that you are creating the Click event for, followed by an underscore character (_) and the word "Click."

This example creates an item and displays the standard Message form when **CommandButton1** is clicked on the form.

```
Sub CommandButton1_Click
    Set MyItem = Application.CreateItem(0)
    MyItem.Subject = "This is a test."
    MyItem.To = "David Goodhand"
    MyItem.Display
End Sub
```

See Also   For more information about working with controls, see "The Controls Collection Object" and "The Control Object" earlier in this chapter.

The Close Event

The Close event occurs when the form associated with the item is being closed. When the Close event occurs, the form is still open on the desktop. You can prevent the form from closing by setting the function value to **False**.

The following example shows the code used in the Close event for the Document Tracking form in the Document Tracking application, which is covered in Chapter 12. In this code sample, if the value of the NewItemCreated variable is **True**, then the SendNotification procedure is called. The SendNotification procedure sends a notification message to users to indicate that a new item has been posted in the Document Tracking folder.

```
Function Item_Close()
   If NewItemCreated = True Then
      Call SendNotification
      NewItemCreated = False
   End If
End Function
```

See Also   For more information about how this event works, see "The Item_Close Event Procedure" in Chapter 12, "The Document Tracking Application."

The CustomAction Event

The CustomAction event occurs when a custom action defined in the form is carried out. You define custom actions on the **Action** page of a form by creating a new action. When a CustomAction event is fired, both the name of the custom action being carried out and the newly created response item are passed to the CustomAction event. You can prevent the custom action from occurring by setting the function value to **False**.

This example shows a CustomAction event procedure that is used in the Assigned Help Task form in the Help Desk application, which is covered in Chapter 11. In this case, the Discussion action is created at design time with the **Form Action Properties** dialog box. The action is triggered when the user clicks the **Discussion** button on the Assigned Help Task form.

```
Function Item_CustomAction(ByVal MyAction, ByVal MyResponse)
   Select Case MyAction.Name
      Case "Discussion"
         MyResponse.Body = "For more information about this ticket, " _
            & "double-click the link." & Chr(10)
         MyResponse.Display
   End Select
End Function
```

To trigger an action from a command button, you can use the **Execute** method of the **Action** object. For example, when the **Discussion** button is clicked on the Assigned Help Task form, the custom Discussion action is triggered.

```
Sub Discussion_Click
   Item.Save
   Item.Actions("Discussion").Execute
End Sub
```

See Also   For more information about how this event works, see "Create a Task Discussion Item" in Chapter 11, "The Help Desk Application."

Tip   You can also use the CustomAction event as a custom method. For example, you can set the CustomAction event to **False** so that the response form is not loaded. You can then add code to the CustomAction event procedure to accomplish the task you want. For example, you can add code to the CustomAction event to automatically create an announcement message and send it to a distribution list.

The CustomPropertyChange Event

The CustomPropertyChange event occurs when the value changes in one of the item's user-defined fields. The field name is passed to the procedure, so you can create a **Select Case** statement to determine which field value has changed.

The following example is used in the Document Tracking application in Chapter 12. In this example, the field name is passed as an argument to the FieldName parameter. The **Select Case** statement is then used to evaluate the field that is changed. In this example, the Format Other field is linked to the Format Other check box. If the field is Format Other and its value is **True**, then the OtherComments text box is enabled. If the value of the Format Other field is **False**, then the OtherComments text box is cleared, and the text box is not enabled.

```
Sub Item_CustomPropertyChange(ByVal FieldName)
    ItemChanged = True
    Select Case FieldName
        Case "Format Other"
            Set MyPage = Item.GetInspector.ModifiedFormPages("Production Information")
            Set MyOtherComments = MyPage.Controls("OtherComments")
            If Item.UserProperties.Find("Format Other").Value = True Then
                MyOtherComments.Enabled = True
            Else
                MyOtherComments.Enabled = False
                Item.UserProperties.Find("Other Comments").Value = ""
            End If
    End Select
End Sub
```

See Also   For more information about this example, see "The Item_CustomPropertyChange Event Procedure" in Chapter 12, "The Document Tracking Application."

The Forward Event

The Forward event occurs when the user initiates the Forward action on a form—usually by clicking the **Forward** button. You can prevent the default Forward behavior from occurring by setting the function value to **False**.

In this example, the Forward event is prevented from firing if the message is confidential.

```
Function Item_Forward(ByVal MyForwardItem)
    If Item.Sensitivity = 3 Then
        MsgBox "This message is confidential and cannot be forwarded."
        Item_Forward = False
    End If
End Function
```

The Open Event

The Open event occurs when an Outlook form is opened to either compose an item or read an item. When the Open event occurs, the form is initialized but not yet displayed. You can prevent the form from opening by setting the function value to **False**.

The following example checks the **ReceivedTime** property of a message to determine if the form is in Compose or Read mode. If the **ReceivedTime** property is not set, then the **Message** page is shown. If the **ReceivedTime** property is set, then the **P.2** page is shown, so that the person processing the order can view the order.

Before you run this example, do the following:

Add a Message field to the **P.2** page, add this example code in the Script Editor, and then click **Publish Form As** on the **Form Design** toolbar. In the **Display name** text box, type **TestEvent**, and then publish the form to the Personal Forms Library. On the Outlook **File** menu, select **New**, and then click **Choose Form**. Next, select the **TestEvent** form in the Personal Forms Library. Notice the **Message** page is shown. Now address the form to yourself and click **Send**. Then double-click the sent item in your Inbox. Notice that the **P.2** page is shown.

```
Function Item_Open()
    If Item.ReceivedTime <> "1/1/4501" Then
        Item.GetInspector.SetCurrentFormPage("P.2")
        Item.GetInspector.HideFormPage("Message")
    Else
        Item.GetInspector.SetCurrentFormPage("Message")
        Item.GetInspector.HideFormPage("P.2")
    End If
End Function
```

Important   Notice in the preceding example that the **If** statement checks to see if the ReceivedTime field is set to "1/1/4501." In Outlook, Date fields that show "None" in the field will return a value of "1/1/4501."

The PropertyChange Event

The PropertyChange event occurs when one of the item's standard fields, such as Subject, To, Importance, or Sensitivity, is changed. The field name is passed to the procedure, so you can use the **Select Case** statement to determine which field value has changed.

In this example, a message box shows the value of the Importance or Sensitivity field if the values in the fields are changed. To test this example, add the following code to the Script Editor, exit Design mode, and then change the values in the **Importance** and **Sensitivity** drop-down list boxes in the **Message Options** dialog box.

```
Sub Item_PropertyChange(ByVal FieldName)
   Select Case FieldName
      Case "Importance"
         MsgBox "The value of the Importance field is " & Item.Importance & "."
      Case "Sensitivity"
         MsgBox "The value of the Sensitivity field is " & Item.Sensitivity & "."
   End Select
End Sub
```

The Read Event

The Read event occurs when an existing Outlook item is opened for editing by a user. The Read event differs from the Open event in that the Read event occurs whenever a user selects the item in a view that supports in-cell editing, as well as when the item is being opened in an inspector. The Read event is fired before the Open event.

In this example, the value of the Date Opened user-defined field is set when the submitted item is first opened.

Before you run this example, do the following:

Click **New** in the **Field Chooser**, and then type **Date Opened** in the **Name** text box. In the **Type** drop-down list box, click **Date/Time**, and then click **OK**. Drag the Date Opened field to the **Message** page, and then click **Edit Read Page** on the **Form Design** toolbar. Resize the Message control to make room for the Date Opened control, and then drag the Date Opened field from the **Field Chooser** to the **Read** page. Click **Publish Form As** and publish the form in your Personal Forms Library. Then, on the Outlook **File** menu, select **New**, click **Choose Form**, and then select the form. Address the form to yourself and click **Send**. Double-click the sent item in your Inbox. Notice that the current date is now in the Date Opened field.

```
Function Item_Read()
   If Item.UserProperties.Find("Date Opened").Value = "1/1/4501" Then
      Item.UserProperties.Find("Date Opened").Value = Now
   End If
End Function
```

The Reply Event

The Reply event occurs when a user clicks the **Reply** button on the form. When the Reply event occurs, the newly created reply item is passed to the procedure. You can prevent the item from being sent by setting the function value to **False**.

This example prevents the standard Reply event from occurring, and creates an item with a custom Task form. It then copies the values from the item's Subject and To fields to the task response item.

```
Function Item_Reply(ByVal Response)
   Item_Reply = False
   Set MyFolder = Application.GetNameSpace("MAPI").GetDefaultFolder(13)
   Set MyItem = MyFolder.Items.Add("IPM.Task.Test")
   MyItem.To = Item.To
   MyItem.Subject = "RE: " & MyItem.Subject
   MyItem.Display
End Function
```

The ReplyAll Event

The ReplyAll event occurs when a user clicks the **ReplyAll** command on a form. When a user clicks **ReplyAll**, the response is sent to the sender and to all recipients in the **To** and **Cc** boxes on the form. You can prevent the item from being sent by setting the function value to **False**.

The following example reminds the user that he or she is replying to all the original recipients of an item and makes it possible for the user to cancel the action.

```
Function Item_ReplyAll (ByVal MyResponse)
   MyResult = MsgBox("Do you really want to send this reply to all " _
      & "the recipients in the To and Cc boxes? ", 289, "Flame Protector")
   If MyResult = 1 Then
      Item_ReplyAll = True
   Else
      Item_ReplyAll = False
   End If
End Function
```

The Send Event

The Send event occurs when a user sends an item. You can prevent the item from being sent by setting the function value to **False**. If you prevent the event from occurring, the form remains open.

This example automatically sets the expiration date on the item when the item is sent.

```
Function Item_Send()
   Item.ExpiryTime = Date + 7
End Function
```

The Write Event

The Write event occurs when the user either sends, posts, or saves an item.

You can prevent an item from being saved by setting the function value to **False**. Quite often, you can include code that writes to external objects such as databases or spreadsheets when the Write event is fired.

This example is taken from Chapter 12, "The Document Tracking Application," and shows how the Item_Write event is used to create or update a database record. For the Document Tracking form, the Item_Write event calls the AddNewDatabaseRecord procedure if a database record for the item has not been created. If the item has been created and the item is changed, the procedure calls the UpdateDatabaseRecord procedure.

```
Function Item_Write()
    If Item.UserProperties.Find("Database Record Created") = "No" Then
        Call AddNewDatabaseRecord
        Item.UserProperties.Find("Database Record Created") = "Yes"
    Else
        If ItemChanged = True Then
            Call UpdateDatabaseRecord
        End If
    End If
End Function
```

See Also   For more information, see "The Item_Write Event Procedure" in Chapter 12, "The Document Tracking Application."

A Quick Tutorial — the Library Order Application

So far, this chapter has covered a sampling of the objects and methods in VBScript. Now, let's look at how Outlook objects, methods, and properties can be applied in the Library Order application. This application is designed to be simple in order to demonstrate how VBScript can be used to build and enhance applications.

To run this application, you must have the Building Microsoft Outlook 98 Applications.pst file installed on your system.

Overview

The Library Order application consists of a Library Materials Order message form, a Library Materials post form, and a Library Orders folder. To submit a Library Materials item, you open the Library Materials Order form from your Personal Forms Library. The Open event of the Library Materials Order form, as shown in the following example, sets the Library Orders folder as the active folder, and then opens the Library Materials form. It then closes the Library Materials Order item, which is never visible.

The Item_Open Event of the Library Materials Order Form

The Item_Open event of the Library Materials Order form contains code, as shown in the following example, that sets the Library Orders folder as the active folder, and then creates and displays the Library Materials item. It then closes the Library Materials Order form. The Library Materials Order form is never visible to the user.

```
Function Item_Open()
   Set MyNameSpace = Application.GetNameSpace("MAPI")
   Set BuildFolder = MyNameSpace.Folders("Building Microsoft Outlook 98 Applications")
   Set BeyondFolder = BuildFolder.Folders("4. Beyond the Basics")
   Set VBScriptFolder = BeyondFolder.Folders("VBScript")
   Set LibraryOrdersFolder = VBScriptFolder.Folders("Library Orders")
   Set MyItems = LibraryOrdersFolder.Items
   Set MyItem = MyItems.Add("IPM.Post.Library Materials")
   MyItem.Display
   Item.Close 1
End Function
```

The Library Materials Post Form

When the Library Materials post form opens, as shown in Figure 9.6, you can select the Book Category and Book Name fields, and then click the **Submit Book Order** button to post the item to the Library Orders folder.

Figure 9.6   The Library Materials post form

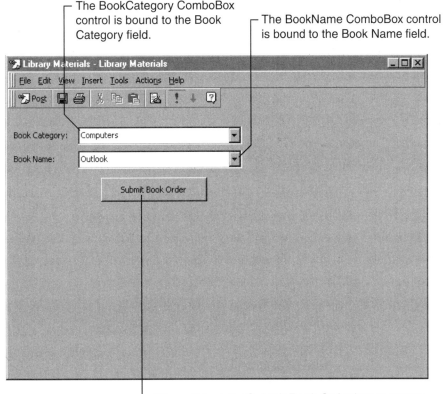

The BookCategory ComboBox control is bound to the Book Category field.

The BookName ComboBox control is bound to the Book Name field.

When clicked, the **Submit Book Order** button creates an item and posts it in the Library Orders folder.

The CustomPropertyChange Event

The CustomPropertyChange event of the Library Materials Order form is passed the name of the user-defined field when a value in the field is changed.

This procedure determines if the changed field is the Book Category field. If so, it calls the ChangeBookNameValues procedure.

```
Sub Item_CustomPropertyChange(ByVal MyPropertyName)
    Select Case MyPropertyName
        Case "Book Category"
            Call ChangeBookNameValues
    End Select
End Sub
```

The ChangeBookNameValues Procedure

The ChangeBookNameValues procedure returns the **Orders** page so you can gain access to the controls on it. It then checks the value of the Book Category field. If the field value is "Computers," it loads one list of values into the BookName control. If the value is "Gardening," it loads a different list.

```
' Changes the values in the Book Name field when the Book Category field changes.
Sub ChangeBookNameValues
    Set Page = Item.GetInspector.ModifiedFormPages("Orders")
    Set MyControl = Page.Controls("BookName")
    Select Case Item.UserProperties.Find("Book Category").Value
        Case "Computers"
            MyControl.Clear
            MyControl.AddItem "Outlook"
            MyControl.AddItem "Windows 95"
            MyControl.AddItem "DOS"
            MyControl.ListIndex = 0
        Case "Gardening"
            MyControl.Clear
            MyControl.AddItem "Roses"
            MyControl.AddItem "Tools"
            MyControl.AddItem "Shrubs"
            MyControl.ListIndex = 0
    End Select
End Sub
```

The SubmitBookOrder_Click Procedure

For the SubmitBookOrder_Click procedure, the **Post** method of the **PostItem** object is carried out.

```
' Post an order in the Library Orders folder.
Sub SubmitBookOrder_Click
    Item.Post
End Sub
```

Setting Up the Library Order Application

To set up this application, you must copy the Library Materials Order form from the Library Orders Folder forms library to your Personal Forms Library.

▶ **To copy the Library Materials Order form**

1   On the Outlook **Tools** menu, click **Options**, and then click the **Other** tab.

2   Click the **Advanced Options** button.

3   Click the **Custom Forms** button.

4   Next to the upper left-hand text box, click **Set**.

5   In the **Folder Forms Library** list box, select the **Library Orders** folder. It's located in the VBScript folder in the 4. Beyond the Basics folder in the Building Microsoft Outlook 98 Applications folder.

6   Click **OK**.

7   The upper right-hand text box should be set to **Personal Forms**. (If it's not, click the **Set** button, and change the setting to the Personal Forms Library.)

8   In the right-hand list box in the **Forms Manager**, click **Library Materials Order**, and then click **Copy**.

The Library Materials Order form is now copied to your Personal Forms Library.

Running the Library Order Application

Now you can run the Library Order application and test it by submitting a sample book order.

▶ **To run the Library Order application**

1   On the Outlook **File** menu, select **New**, click **Choose Form**, and then click **Library Materials Order** in the Personal Forms Library.

2   In the **Book Category** drop-down list box, click **Gardening**.

3   In the **Book Name** drop-down list box, click **Roses**, and then click **Submit Book Order**.

The Library Order application also consists of the Library Orders folder. In this case, the Library Orders folder is a folder in the VBScript personal folder (.pst). However, for a real application, create this folder in Public Folders.

Automation

In addition to using VBScript to program Outlook objects, you can use it to program Outlook objects remotely. You use Automation when you want to control an entire session. For example, you may want to automatically send a message from within a Visual Basic or Microsoft Excel application.

To automate Outlook from another application, such as Visual Basic or Microsoft Excel, you must first reference the Microsoft Outlook 98 Object Model. You can then use the **GetObject** function to automate a session that's already running, or the **CreateObject** function to open a new Outlook session. After the Outlook **Application** object is returned, you can then write code that uses the objects, properties, methods, and constants in the Outlook 98 Object Model.

This example creates a mail item from a Microsoft Excel 97 worksheet when the **MailSalesReport** button is clicked.

```
Sub MailSalesReport_Click
    Set MyOlApp = CreateObject("Outlook.Application")
    Set MyItem = MyOlApp.CreateItem(OlMailItem)
    MyItem.Subject = "Sales Results - " & Now()
    MyItem.Body = " Click the icon to open the Sales Results." & Chr(13)
    Set MyAttachments = MyItem.Attachments
    MyAttachments.Add "C:\My Documents\005.doc", OlByReference, 1, _
        "4th Quarter 1996 Results Chart"
    MyItem.To = "Sales"
    MyItem.Display
End Sub
```

Note   As shown in the preceding example, the constants in the Outlook 98 Object Model are valid when used in Visual Basic or Visual Basic for Applications.

Important   If you use Automation to control Outlook, you cannot write event procedures to respond to the events supported by Outlook items.

The Business Card Request Application

In This Chapter

Overview of the Business Card Request Application   342

Create the Business Card Requests Folder   345

Preaddress a Message Form   346

Design the Form   346

Create Views   381

Set Permissions   384

Test the Application   385

Send the Form to the Administrator   386

Check the Form for Viruses and Harmful Code   386

Release the Application   387

The Business Card Request application covered in this chapter provides a good example of the kinds of processes that you can streamline with Outlook applications. It can also serve as a template for other similar request processes in your organization, such as copier services requests, audio/visual equipment requests, or move requests. In the course of designing the Business Card Request application, we cover some important design concepts, such as how to:

- Preaddress a Message form to a public folder.

- Create separate layouts for **Compose** and **Read** pages.

- Use Visual Basic Scripting Edition (VBScript) to hide and show a page based on whether the form is submitted or not.

- Use VBScript to create a delivery notification message.

- Create a folder view that groups request items into Request Pending or Request Processed groups.

- Submit the Business Card Request form to an administrator who checks the form for harmful macros and viruses and then publishes the form in the OrganizationalForms Library.

Overview of the Business Card Request Application

The Business Card Request application consists of the following components:

- Business Card Requests folder
- Business Card Request form
- Custom views
- Permissions
- VBScript

Business Card Requests folder   The Business Card Requests folder, as shown in Figure 10.1, contains Business Card Request items. Items in the folder are grouped by their request status.

Figure 10.1   The Business Card Requests folder

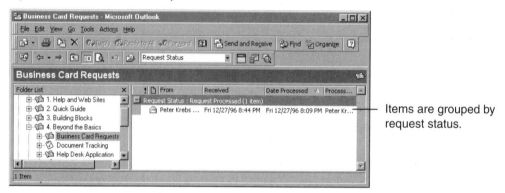

Items are grouped by request status.

Business Card Request form   The Compose window of the Business Card Request form, as shown in Figure 10.2, lets users create and submit a Business Card Request to the Business Card Requests folder.

Figure 10.2   The Compose window of the Business Card Request form

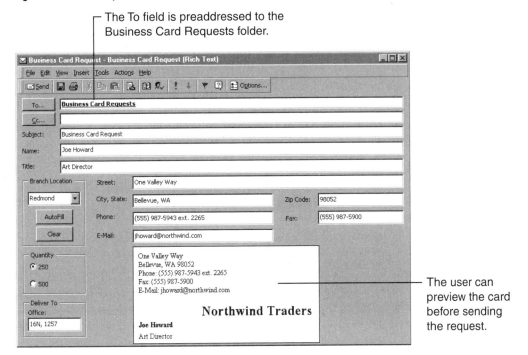

— The To field is preaddressed to the Business Card Requests folder.

— The user can preview the card before sending the request.

When the administrator who is responsible for processing the Business Card Request double-clicks the submitted request in the Business Card Requests folder, she sees the **Read** page of the Business Card Request form. With the controls on the **Status** page of the form, the administrator updates the status of the request and sends a confirmation to the user, as shown in Figure 10.3.

Figure 10.3   The Status page on the Read page of the Business Card Request form

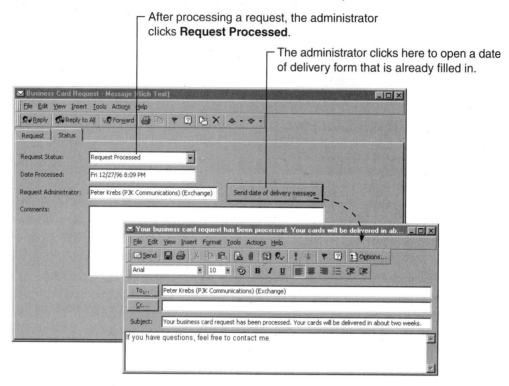

Custom views   The Business Card Requests folder provides two custom views. The Request Status view, as shown in Figure 10.1, indicates which requests are processed. Processed orders are in one group, unprocessed orders are in the other. The By Requester Name view groups request items by the From field, so users can easily find their request in the folder by searching for their name.

Permissions   Business Card Request administrators are given Editor permissions so they can edit items in the folder, while the general public is given Contributor permissions so they can submit items in the folder, but cannot change them after they are submitted. Application designers are given Owner permissions.

VBScript   The Business Card Request form contains several procedures written with VBScript, which automate the request process. One procedure automatically fills in the address boxes on the Business Card Request form when the user clicks the **AutoFill** button. Another procedure automatically fills in the text of the delivery notification item that is sent to the requester.

Create the Business Card Requests Folder

In earlier chapters, you started your applications in a personal folder (.pst). For the Business Card Request application, however, you create the folder in Public Folders so you can publish the public folder address to your Personal Address Book. Later you use this address to preaddress the Business Card Request form to the Business Card Requests public folder.

▶ To create the Business Card Requests folder

1 In the Folder List, click Public Folders, right-click the folder you want to create the Business Card Requests folder in, and then click **New Folder** on the shortcut menu.

2 In the **Name** text box, type **Business Card Requests**, and then click **OK**.

3 If a prompt appears, select an option in the **Add shortcut to Outlook Bar?** box.

4 Click **OK**.

Publish the Folder Address and Restrict Access to the Folder

You use the **Administration** page of the **Properties** dialog box to publish the folder address to your Personal Address Book. Later, when you design the Business Card Request form, you preaddress the form by specifying the Business Card Requests folder in the **To** text box of the form. You also select the **Owners only** option to prevent users from opening the folder while it's under construction.

▶ To publish the folder address to your Personal Address Book

1 In the Folder List, right-click the Business Card Requests folder, and then click **Properties** on the shortcut menu.

2 Click the **Administration** page, and then click **Personal Address Book**.

Although you don't receive confirmation, the folder address is published to your Personal Address Book.

3 Keep the **Properties** dialog box open.

▶ To prevent users from opening the folder

• On the **Administration** page, click **Owners only**, and then click **OK**.

Preaddress a Message Form

To start the form design process, you preaddress a Message form to the Business Card Requests folder you just published in your Personal Address Book. With this method, you can be sure Business Card Request items always arrive in the intended folder. And it makes it easy for users to submit requests because all they need to do is fill in the form and then click the **Send** button.

Important   To preaddress the form, you must be in Run mode.

▶ **To preaddress the form to the Business Card Requests folder**

1   On the **Actions** menu, click **New Mail Message**.

2   Click the **To** button.

3   In the **Show names from the** drop-down list box, click **Personal Address Book**.

4   In the list box, select **Business Card Request**.

5   Click **To**, and then click **OK**.

Design the Form

Now you switch to design mode and add controls and fields to create the Business Card Request form.

▶ **To switch to design mode**

•   On the form **Tools** menu, select **Forms**, and then click **Design This Form**.

Edit the Compose Page

When you design a form, you start by editing the **Compose** page. For the **Compose** page of the Business Card Request form, you change the name of the **Message** page to **Request**, and then you add controls to the page. When you're done, the **Compose** page looks like the illustration in Figure 10.4.

Figure 10.4   The Compose page of the Business Card Request form

The **Message** page is renamed **Request**.

Rename the Message Page

When you've completed the Business Card Request form, the form will have two pages. There's a **Request** page that the user fills out and sends to the Business Card Requests folder and a **Status** page that the administrator uses to indicate a request has been processed. For now, we'll focus on the **Request** page.

▶ **To rename the Message page**

1   In the form Design mode, click the **Message** page.

2   On the **Form** menu, click **Rename Page**.

3   In the **Page name** text box, type **Request** and then click **OK**.

Set the Initial Value of the Subject Field

The Business Card Request form is used for only one purpose, so you set the initial value of the Subject field to Business Card Request.

▶ **To set the initial value of the Subject field**

1 Right-click the **Subject** control, and then click **Properties** on the shortcut menu.

2 Click the **Value** page.

3 Select the **Set the initial value of this field to** check box, and then type **Business Card Request**.

4 Click **OK**.

Remove Controls

You don't use the Message control on the Business Card Request form, so you remove it, as shown in Figure 10.5.

▶ **To remove the Message control**

• Click the Message control, and then press the DELETE key.

Figure 10.5   The selected Message control on the Request page

Click the Message control and then delete it. ¬

Add the BusinessCardName Control

The BusinessCardName control is a TextBox control you add to the form by dragging the control from the **Control Toolbox**. After you add a TextBox control, you set its display properties to name the control. For this application, we'll set the exact sizes for the Top, Left, and Height properties of the controls. The Width property is up to you. You can use the illustrations provided in this chapter as a guideline.

▶ **To add the BusinessCardName control and set its Display properties**

1   On the **Form Design** toolbar, click the **Control Toolbox** button.

2   Drag another TextBox control from the **Control Toolbox** to the form.

3   Right-click the control, and then click **Properties** on the shortcut menu.

4   On the **Display** page, set the following properties.

Property	Setting
Name	BusinessCardName
Top	82
Left	76
Height	24
Width	*User-defined*
Resize with form	Selected

When you've finished setting properties, leave the **Properties** dialog box open.

Bind the BusinessCardName Control to the BusinessCardName Field

Now you switch to the **Value** page of the **Properties** dialog box and create a field called BusinessCardName. When you create the field, the BusinessCardName control is automatically bound to the BusinessCardName field. At run time, users enter information in the BusinessCardName control. The information in the control is saved to the BusinessCardName field.

▶ **To create a field called BusinessCardName**

1   In the **Properties** dialog box, click the **Value** page.

2   Click **New**.

3   In the **Name** text box, type **BusinessCardName**, and then click **OK**.

4   Leave the **Properties** dialog box open.

Set Validation Properties

You set Validation properties for the BusinessCardName field so users can't send the form unless there is text in the BusinessCardName field.

▶ **To set Validation properties**

1 Click the **Validation** page.

2 Select the **A value is required for this field** check box, and then click **OK**.

Add a Label for the Name Field

You add a label for the BusinessCardName control so users know what to type into the control.

▶ **To add a label for the BusinessCardName control**

1 Drag a Label control from the **Control Toolbox** to the form.

2 Click the Label control, and then type **Name:**.

3 Resize the label and position it on the form as shown in Figure 10.6.

Figure 10.6   The BusinessCardName control and its label

A label is added for the BusinessCardName control.

The BusinessCardName control.

Add the BusinessCardTitle Control

Now you add another TextBox control to the form. This control serves as the BusinessCardTitle control.

▶ **To add the BusinessCardTitle control**

1 Drag a TextBox control from the **Control Toolbox** to the form.

2 Right-click the control, and then click **Properties** on the shortcut menu.

Bind the Control to the BusinessCardTitle Field

Now you create a field called BusinessCardTitle that you bind the control to. Then you switch to the **Display** page and set Display properties for the control.

▶ To create a field called BusinessCardTitle

1 In the **Properties** dialog box, click the **Value** page.

2 Click **New**.

3 In the **Name** text box, type **BusinessCardTitle**, and then click **OK**.

4 Click the **Display** tab, and then set the following properties.

Property	Setting
Name	BusinessCardTitle
Top	112
Left	76
Height	24
Width	*User-defined*
Resize with form	Selected

5 Click **OK**.

Add a Label for the BusinessCardTitle Control

Now you add a label for the BusinessCardTitle control.

▶ To add a label to the BusinessCardTitle Control

1 Drag a Label control from the Control Toolbox to the form.

2 Click the Label control, and then type **Title:**.

3 Resize the label and position it on the form as shown in Figure 10.7.

Figure 10.7   The BusinessCardTitle control and its label

┌ The label for the BusinessCardTitle control.

  ┌ The BusinessCardTitle control.

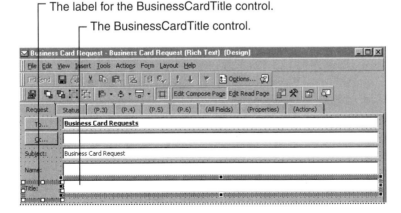

Add the BusinessCardStreet Control

1 Add a TextBox control to the form.

2 Right-click the control, and then click **Properties** on the shortcut menu.

3 On the **Value** page, click **New**.

4 In the **Name** text box, type **BusinessCardStreet**, and then click **OK**.

5 On the **Validation** page, select the **A value is required for this field** check box.

6 On the **Display** page, set the properties as shown in the following table.

Property	Setting
Name	BusinessCardStreet
Top	143
Left	207
Height	24
Width	*User-defined*
Resize with form	Selected

7 Click **OK**.

8 Drag a Label control from the **Control Toolbox** to the form.

9 Click the Label control, and then type **Street:**.

10 Resize and position the label as shown in Figure 10.4.

Add the BusinessCardCityState Control

1 Add a TextBox control to the form.

2 Right-click the control, and then click **Properties** on the shortcut menu.

3 On the **Value** page, click **New**, type **BusinessCardCityState** in the **Name** text box, and then click **OK**.

4 On the **Validation** page, select the **A value is required for this field** check box.

5 On the **Display** page, set the properties as shown in the following table.

Property	Setting
Name	BusinessCardCityState
Top	175
Left	207
Height	24
Width	*User-defined*
Resize with form	Selected

6 Click **OK**.

7 Drag a Label control from the **Control Toolbox** to the form.

8 Click the Label control, and then type **City, State:**.

9 Resize and position the label as in Figure 10.4.

Add the BusinessCardZipCode Control

1 Add a TextBox control to the form.

2 Right-click the control, and then click **Properties** on the shortcut menu.

3 On the **Value** page, click **New**, type **BusinessCardZipCode** in the **Name** text box, and then click **OK**.

4 On the **Validation** page, select the **A value is required for this field** check box.

5 On the **Display** page, set the properties as shown in the following table.

Property	Setting
Name	BusinessCardZipCode
Top	143
Left	553
Height	24
Width	*User-defined*
Resize with form	Selected

6 Click **OK**.

7 Drag a Label control from the **Control Toolbox** to the form.

8 Click the Label control, and then type **Zip Code:**.

9 Resize and position the label as in Figure 10.4.

Add the BusinessCardPhone Control

1 Add a TextBox control to the form.

2 Right-click the control, and then click **Properties** on the shortcut menu.

3 On the **Value** page, click **New**.

4 In the **Name** text box, type **BusinessCardPhone**, and then click **OK**.

5 On the **Validation** page, select the **A value is required for this field** check box.

6 On the **Display** page, set the properties as shown in the following table:

Property	Setting
Name	BusinessCardPhone
Top	206
Left	207
Height	24
Width	*User-defined*
Resize with form	selected

7 Click **OK**.

8 Drag a Label control from the **Control Toolbox** to the form.

9 Click the Label control, and then type **Phone:**.

10 Resize and position the label as needed.

Add the BusinessCardFax Control

1 Add a TextBox control to the form.

2 Right-click the control, and then click **Properties** on the shortcut menu.

3 On the **Value** page, click **New**.

4 In the **Name** text box, type **BusinessCardFax**, and then click **OK**.

5 On the **Display** page, set the properties as shown in the following table:

Property	Setting
Name	BusinessCardFax
Top	175
Left	553
Height	24
Width	*User-defined*
Resize with form	Selected

6 Click **OK**.

7 Drag a Label control from the **Control Toolbox** to the form.

8 Click the Label control, and then type **Fax:**.

9 Resize and position the label as needed.

Add the BusinessCardEMail Control

1 Add a TextBox control to the form.

2 Right-click the control, and then click **Properties** on the shortcut menu.

3 On the **Value** page, click **New**.

4 In the **Name** text box, type **BusinessCardEMail**, and then click **OK**.

5 On the **Display** page, set the properties as shown in the following table.

Property	Setting
Name	BusinessCardEMail
Top	237
Left	207
Height	24
Width	*User-defined*
Resize with form	Selected

6 Click **OK**.

7 Drag a Label control from the **Control Toolbox** to the form.

8 Click the Label control, and then type **E-Mail:**.

9 Resize and position the label.

Your form should now look like the form shown in Figure 10.8.

Figure 10.8   The Business Card Request form with the address controls added to the form

┌─ The address controls are added to the form.

Add the BusinessCardBranchLocation Control

The BusinessCardBranchLocation control is a Frame control that contains other controls.

▶ **To add the BusinessCardBranchLocation control**

1   Add a Frame control to the form.

2   Right-click the control, and then click **Properties** on the shortcut menu.

3   On the **Display** page, set the properties as shown in the following table.

Property	Setting
Name	BusinessCardBranchLocation
Caption	Branch Location
Top	141
Left	8
Height	122
Width	User-defined

4   Click **OK**.

5   Resize and position the control, as in Figure 10.4.

Add the BusinessCardBranch Control

The BusinessCardBranch control is a ComboBox control that shows a list of branch locations at run time.

▶ **To add the BusinessCardBranch control**

1 Drag a ComboBox control into the BusinessCardBranchLocation frame.

2 Right-click the control, and then click **Properties** on the shortcut menu.

3 On the **Value** page, click **New**.

4 In the **Name** text box, type **BusinessCardBranch**, and then click **OK**.

5 In the **List Type** drop-down list box, click **Droplist**.

6 In the **Possible values** text box, type: **Bellevue; Redmond; Seattle**.

7 In the **Initial Value** text box, type **Redmond**.

8 Click the **Display** page, and then set the following properties.

Property	Setting
Name	BusinessCardBranch
Top	18
Left	7
Height	24
Width	*User-defined*

9 Click **OK**.

Add the AutoFill Control

The AutoFill control is a CommandButton control. Later in this chapter, you create a procedure for this control that automatically loads address values into the address boxes based on the value in the BusinessCardBranchLocation field.

▶ **To add the AutoFill control**

1 Drag a CommandButton control into the BusinessCardBranchLocation frame.

2 Right-click the control, and then click **Properties** on the shortcut menu.

3 On the **Display** page, set the following properties.

Property	Setting
Name	AutoFill
Caption	AutoFill
Top	49
Left	22
Height	26
Width	*User-defined*

4 Click **OK**.

Add the Clear Control

The Clear control is also a CommandButton control. Later in this chapter, you create a procedure for this control that clears the values in the address boxes.

▶ **To add the Clear control**

1 Drag a CommandButton control into the BusinessCardBranchLocation frame.

2 Right-click the CommandButton control, and then click **Properties** on the shortcut menu.

3 On the **Display** page, set the following properties.

Property	Setting
Name	Clear
Caption	Clear
Top	79
Left	22
Height	26
Width	*User-defined*

4 Click **OK**.

Resize the labels so that the form looks like the form shown in Figure 10.9.

Figure 10.9   The BusinessCardBranchLocation frame is added to the form.

The BusinessCardBranchLocation frame.

The BusinessCardBranch control.

Add the Quantity Control

The Quantity control is a Frame control that will contain option buttons.

▶ **To add the Quantity control**

1   Add a Frame control to the form.

2   Right-click the control, and then click **Properties** on the shortcut menu

3   On the **Display** page, set the following properties.

Property	Setting
Name	Quantity
Caption	Quantity
Top	271
Left	8
Height	76
Width	*User-defined*

4   Click **OK**.

Add the CardQuantity1 Control

The CardQuantity1 control is an OptionButton control that the user clicks to specify an order of 250 business cards.

▶ **To add the CardQuantity1 control**

1   Drag an OptionButton control into the Quantity frame.

2   Right-click the OptionButton control, and then click **Properties** on the shortcut menu.

3   On the **Value** page, click **New**.

4   In the **Name** text box, type **CardQuantity**, and then click **OK**.

5   In the **Value** text box, type **250**.

6   On the **Display** page, set the following properties.

Property	Setting
Name	CardQuantity1
Caption	250
Top	8
Left	8
Height	24
Width	*User-defined*

7   Click **OK**.

8   Right-click the CardQuantity1 control, and then click **Advanced Properties** on the shortcut menu.

9   Click the **Value** cell, and then type **True**.

10 Close the **Advanced Properties** dialog box.

Add the CardQuantity2 Control

The CardQuantity2 control is an OptionButton control that the user clicks to specify an order of 500 business cards. When you add this OptionButton control to the frame, the OptionButton control is automatically bound to the CardQuantity field.

▶ **To add the CardQuantity2 control**

1   Drag an OptionButton control into the Quantity frame.

2   Right-click the OptionButton control, and then click **Properties** on the shortcut menu.

3   On the **Value** page, type **500** in the **Value** text box.

4   On the **Display** page, set the following properties.

Property	Setting
Name	CardQuantity2
Caption	500
Top	38
Left	8
Height	24
Width	*User-defined*

5 Click **OK**.

Add the DeliverTo Control

The DeliverTo control is a Frame control that will contain a TextBox control that users type their office location into.

▶ To add the DeliverTo control

1 Add a Frame control to the form.

2 Right-click the control, and then click **Properties** on the shortcut menu.

3 On the **Display** page, set the following properties.

Property	Setting
Name	DeliverTo
Caption	Deliver To
Top	355
Left	8
Height	68
Width	*User-defined*

4 Click **OK**.

Add the BusinessCardOffice Control

1 Drag a TextBox control into the DeliverTo frame.

2 Right-click the TextBox control, and then click **Properties** on the shortcut menu.

3 On the **Value** page, click **New**.

4 In the **Name** text box, type **BusinessCardOffice**, and then click **OK**.

5 On the **Display** page, set the following properties.

Property	Setting
Name	BusinessCardOffice
Top	25
Left	6
Height	24
Width	97

6 Click **OK**.

7 Drag a Label control to the form. Don't drag it into the Deliver To frame yet.

8 Click the Label control, and then type **Office:**.

9 Make the label small enough to fit into the Deliver To frame, and then drag the label into the Deliver To frame.

Your form should now look like the form shown in Figure 10.10.

Figure 10.10   The Business Card Request form with the address controls added to the form

The CardQuantity1 and CardQuantity2 controls.

The BusinessCardOffice control.

Add the BusinessCardImage Control

1   Add an Image control to the form.

2   Right-click the control, and then click **Properties** on the shortcut menu.

3   On the **Display** page, set the following properties.

Property	Setting
Name	BusinessCardImage
Top	264
Left	207
Height	171
Width	*User-defined*
Background color	Window

4   Click **OK**.

Add the CardAddress Control

The CardAddress control is a TextBox control that reflects the values that the user types in the address boxes in the upper portion of the Business Card Request form. When the user changes a value in one of the address fields, the value is automatically updated in the CardAddress control. To accomplish this, you create a formula for the CardAddress control that automatically changes the value in the label when a value in one of the address fields changes.

▶ To add the CardAddress control

1 Drag a TextBox control on top of the BusinessCardImage control.

2 Right-click the TextBox control, and then click **Properties** on the shortcut menu.

3 On the **Value** page, click **New**.

4 In the **Name** text box, type **CardAddress**, and then click **OK**.

5 On the **Value** page, click the **Edit** button, and then in the **Formula** text box, type the formula, as shown in Figure 10.11, and then click **OK**.

6 Click **Calculate this formula automatically**.

Figure 10.11 Formula for the CardAddress field

7 On the **Display** page, set the following properties for the control.

Property	Setting
Name	CardAddress
Top	271
Left	215
Height	79
Width	*User-defined*

Property	Setting
Font	9 pt. Times New Roman
Foreground color	Window Text
Background color	Window
Read-only	Selected
Sunken	Cleared
Multi-line	Selected

8 Click **OK**.

Add the CardName Control

The CardName control is a Label control that reflects the values that the user types in the **Name** text box in the upper portion of the Business Card Request form. When the user types in the **Name** text box, the CardName field is automatically updated. To accomplish this, you create a formula for the CardName field that automatically changes the value in the field when a value in text **Name** box changes.

▶ **To add the CardName control**

1 Drag a Label control on top of the BusinessCardImage control.

2 Right-click the Label control, and then click **Properties** on the shortcut menu.

3 On the **Value** page, click **New**.

4 In the **Name** text box, type **CardName**, and then click **OK**.

5 In the **Initial Value** text box, type: **[BusinessCardName]**.

6 Click **Calculate this formula automatically**.

7 On the **Display** page, set the following properties.

Property	Setting
Name	CardName
Caption	Remove caption name from text box
Top	394
Left	217
Height	15
Width	*User-defined*
Font	9 pt. Times New Roman Bold
Foreground color	Window Text
Background color	Window

8 Click **OK**.

Add the CardTitle Control

The CardTitle control is a Label control that shows the value on the business card that the user types in the **Title** text box. When the user makes changes to the **Title** text box, the changes are automatically reflected in the CardTitle control. The CardTitle control is bound to the Title field that you created earlier in this chapter. In addition, you create an expression for the CardTitle field so that the value of the field is automatically updated when the user changes the value in the Title control.

▶ **To add the CardTitle control**

1 Drag a Label control on top of the BusinessCardImage control.

2 Right-click the Label control, and then click **Properties** on the shortcut menu.

3 On the **Value** page, click **New**.

4 In the **Name** text box, type **CardTitle**, and then click **OK**.

5 In the **Initial Value** text box, type: **[BusinessCardTitle]**.

6 Click **Calculate this formula automatically**.

7 On the **Display** page, set the following properties.

Property	Setting
Name	CardTitle
Caption	Remove caption name
Font	9 pt. Times New Roman
Top	414
Left	217
Height	15
Width	*User-defined*
Foreground color	Window Text
Background color	Window

8 Click **OK**.

Add the CompanyLogo Control

The CompanyLogo control is a Label control that shows the company name. The CompanyLogo control is not bound to a field.

▶ **To add the CompanyLogo control**

1 Drag a Label control on top of the CardImage control, as shown in Figure 10.12.

2 Right-click the Label control, and then click **Properties** on the shortcut menu.

3 On the **Display** page, set the following properties.

Property	Setting
Name	CompanyLogo
Caption	Northwind Traders
Top	356
Left	329
Height	31
Width	203
Font	18 pt. Times New Roman Bold
Foreground color	Window Text
Background color	Window

4 Click **OK**.

Figure 10.12   The CardAddress, CardName, CardTitle, and CompanyLogo controls are added to the form.

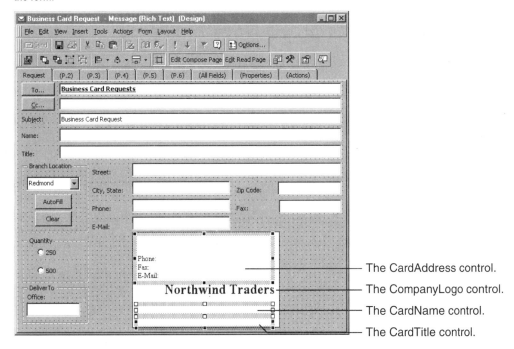

The CardAddress control.

The CompanyLogo control.

The CardName control.

The CardTitle control.

Set the Tab Order for the Compose Page

There are a few nuances to setting the tab order that are worth noting. Label controls can be tabbed to at design time, but are skipped over at run time. So you don't need to worry about Label controls in the **Tab Order** dialog box. Also, Frame controls have their own tab order for controls in the frame.

▶ **To set the tab order**

1 On the **Layout** menu, click **Tab Order**.

2 In the **Tab Order** dialog box, make sure that the controls are listed in the following relative order. If Label controls are located between the controls below, that's OK. Outlook does not tab to Label controls at run time.

   BusinessCardName, BusinessCardTitle, BusinessCardStreet, BusinessCardCityState, BusinessCardZipCode, BusinessCardPhone, BusinessCardFax, BusinessCardEMail, BusinessCardBranchLocation, Quantity, DeliverTo

Test the Compose Page Layout

Before you design the **Read** page of the form, it's a good idea to view the layout of the **Compose** page in Run mode.

▶ **To test the layout**

• On the **Form** menu, click **Run This Form**.

Edit the Read Page

Now you will edit the **Read** page.

• Close the form in Run mode to return to Design mode.

To design the **Read** page, you delete the Message control on the **Read** page, and then copy the controls from the **Compose** page.

▶ **To switch to the Read page and delete the Message control**

1 On the **Form Design** toolbar, click the **Edit Read Page** button.

2 Click the Message control, and then press DELETE.

Copy Controls from the Compose Page

Now you switch back to the **Compose** page.

▶ **To copy controls from the Compose page**

1 On the **Form Design** toolbar, click the **Edit Compose Page** button.

2 On the **Edit** menu, click **Select All**.

3 Hold down the CTRL key, and click the following controls in the header area so that they are not selected: To, cc, and Subject. See Figure 10.13.

4 On the **Standard** toolbar, click the **Copy** button.

5 On the **Form Design** toolbar, click the **Edit Read Page** button.

6 On the **Standard** toolbar, click the **Paste** button.

7 Reposition the controls so they fit correctly on the page. The fit is a little tight. However, at run time, there will be ample room on the form because the **Form Design** toolbar is not shown.

Figure 10.13   The header fields are not selected.

Add the Status Page to the Form

Now you add the **Status** page to the form. The **Status** page is used by the Business Card Request administrator to indicate that the order has been processed and to send a notification to the requester that their business cards will arrive in two weeks.

Note Each form page has its own **Read** and **Compose** pages which are activated when **Separate Read Layout** is selected from the **Form** menu while on that page. Click the desired page first, for example **(P.2)**. Next, select **Separate Read Layout**, and then choose **Compose** or **Read** page.

▶ **To name the Status page**

1 Click the **(P.2)** page.

2 On the **Form** menu, click **Separate Read Layout**. You are now on the **Compose** page.

3 On the **Form** menu, click **Rename Page**.

4 Type **Status** in the **Page name** text box, and then click **OK**.

5 On the **Form Design** toolbar, click the **Edit Read Page** button.

Add the BusinessCardRequestStatus Control

The BusinessCardRequestStatus control is a ComboBox control. With this control, the administrator can select a Request Pending or Request Processed value to indicate the status of the request.

▶ **To add the BusinessCardRequestStatus control**

1 Drag a ComboBox control to the form.

2 Right-click the control, and then click **Properties** on the shortcut menu.

3 On the **Value** page, click **New**.

4 In the **Name** text box, type **BusinessCardRequestStatus**, and then click **OK**.

5 In the **List Type** drop-down list box, click **Droplist**.

6 In the **Possible values** text box, type **Request Pending; Request Processed**.

7 In the **Initial Value** text box, type **Request Pending**.

8 On the **Display** page, set the following properties.

Property	Setting
Name	BusinessCardRequestStatus
Top	16
Left	132
Height	24
Width	*User-defined*

9 Click **OK**.

10 Drag a Label control from the **Control Toolbox** to the form.

11 Click the Label control, and then type **Request Status:**.

12 Resize and position the label as shown in Figure 10.14.

Add the BusinessCardDateProcessed Control

At run time, when the administrator clicks **Request Processed** in the BusinessCardRequestStatus control, the current date is shown in the BusinessCardDateProcessed control.

▶ **To add the BusinessCardDateProcessed control**

1 Add a TextBox control to the form.

2 Right-click the control, and then click **Properties** on the shortcut menu.

3 On the **Value** page, click **New**.

4 In the **Name** text box, type **BusinessCardDateProcessed**, and then click **Date/Time** in the **Type** drop-down list box.

5 Click **OK**.

6 On the **Display** page, set the following properties.

Property	Setting
Name	BusinessCardDateProcessed1
Top	47
Left	132
Height	24
Width	196

7 Click **OK**.

8 Drag a Label control from the **Control Toolbox** to the form.

9 Click the Label control, and then type: **Date Processed:**.

10 Resize and position the label as needed.

Add the BusinessCardRequestAdministrator Control

At run time, when the administrator clicks **Request Processed** in the
BusinessCardRequestStatus control, the administrator's name shows in
BusinessCardRequest Administrator control.

▶ **To add the BusinessCardRequestAdministrator control**

1 Add a TextBox control to the form.

2 Right-click the control, and then click **Properties** on the shortcut menu.

3 On the **Value** page, click **New**.

4 In the **Name** text box, type **BusinessCardRequestAdministrator**, and then click
   OK.

5 On the **Display** page, set the following properties.

Property	Setting
Name	BusinessCardRequestAdministrator
Top	78
Left	132
Height	24
Width	235

6 Click **OK**.

7 Drag a Label control from the **Control Toolbox** to the form.

8 Click the Label control, and then type **Request Administrator:**.

9 Resize and position the label as needed.

Add the SendDeliveryMessage Control

The SendDeliveryMessage control is a CommandButton control that you will create a
Click procedure for later in this chapter.

▶ **To add the SendDeliveryMessage control**

1 Drag a CommandButton control to the form.

2 Right-click the control, and then click **Properties** on the shortcut menu.

3 On the **Display** page, set the following properties.

Property	Setting
Name	SendDeliveryMessage
Caption	Send date of delivery message
Top	72
Left	384
Height	32
Width	*User-defined*

4   Click **OK**.

Add the BusinessCardComments Control

With the BusinessCardComments control, the administrator can enter comments about the request if necessary.

▶ **To add the BusinessCardComments control**

1   Add a TextBox control to the form.

2   Right-click the control, and then click **Properties** on the shortcut menu.

3   On the **Value** page, click **New**.

4   In the **Name** text box, type **BusinessCardComments**, and then click **OK**.

5   On the **Display** page, set the following properties.

Property	Setting
Name	BusinessCardComments
Top	112
Left	132
Height	125
Width	*User-defined*
Resize with form	Selected
Multi-line	Selected

6   Click **OK**.

7   Drag a Label control from the **Control Toolbox** to the form.

8   Click the Label control, and then type **Comments:**.

9   Resize and position the label as shown in Figure 10.14.

10   When you're finished, the **Status** page should look like the illustration in Figure 10.14.

Figure 10.14 The finished layout of the Status page

The BusinessCardRequestStatus control.

The BusinessCardDateProcessed control.

Tip To view the layout of the **Read** page, you must publish the form, create a Business Card Request, send it, and then open it in the Business Card Requests folder. If you click **Run This Form** on the **Form** menu at this time, the **Compose** page is shown. You can view the **Read** page later in the chapter when you test the application.

Make a Backup Copy of the Form Before Proceeding

Before you go any further, it's a good idea to make a backup copy of the form.

▶ **To make a backup copy of a form**

1 With the form open, click **Save As** on the **File** menu.

2 In the **Save In** drop-down list box, select the default Outlook template folder, such as C:\ Program Files\Microsoft Office\Templates.

3 In the **File name** text box, type a name for the form.

4 In the **Save as type** drop-down list box, select **Outlook Template (.oft)**.

5 Click **Save**.

▶ **To open your backup copy of a form**

1   Select **New** on the **File** menu, and then click **Choose Form**.

2   Click **Templates in File System** in the **Look In** drop-down list box, and then click on the form you'd like to open.

Create Procedures for the Form By Using the Script Editor

With the Outlook Script Editor, you create procedures for the form by using Visual Basic Scripting Edition.

Create a Procedure for the AutoFill Command Button

To help users complete the Business Card Request form and to ensure consistency in business card requests, you create an AutoFill_Click procedure that automatically fills in the values in the address boxes on the form when the user clicks the AutoFill button. Before loading the values into the address fields on the form, the AutoFill procedure finds the value of the BusinessCardBranch field, and then loads the set of address values based on that BusinessCardBranchLocationList field value.

▶ **To create the AutoFill_Click procedure**

1   On the **Form Design** toolbar, click the **View Code** button.

2   Add the following procedure to the Script Editor window (You can copy this sample code from the Business Card Request form on the companion CD). Feel free to substitute your own address value in the procedure.

```
'loads the values in the address boxes based on the value in the
Branch Location box.
Sub AutoFill_Click
    Select Case Item.UserProperties.Find("BusinessCardBranch").Value
        Case "Redmond"
            Item.UserProperties.Find("BusinessCardStreet").Value = _
                "One Valley Way"
            Item.UserProperties.Find("BusinessCardCityState").Value = _
                "Redmond, WA"
            Item.UserProperties.Find("BusinessCardZipCode").Value = _
                "98052"
            Item.UserProperties.Find("BusinessCardFax").Value = _
                "(555) 555-5534"
        Case "Bellevue"
            Item.UserProperties.Find("BusinessCardStreet").Value = _
                "10 State St."
            Item.UserProperties.Find("BusinessCardCityState").Value = _
                "Bellevue, WA"
            Item.UserProperties.Find("BusinessCardZipCode").Value = _
                "98115"
            Item.UserProperties.Find("BusinessCardFax").Value = _
                "(555) 555-5535"
```

```
      Case "Seattle"
        Item.UserProperties.Find("BusinessCardStreet").Value = _
          "1 Beach Dr."
        Item.UserProperties.Find("BusinessCardCityState").Value = _
          "Seattle, WA"
        Item.UserProperties.Find("BusinessCardZipCode").Value = _
          "98116"
          Item.UserProperties.Find("BusinessCardFax").Value = _
          "(555) 555-5536"
      End select
  End Sub
```

▶ **To test the AutoFill procedure**

1 On the **Form** menu, click **Run This Form**.

2 In the **Branch Location** drop-down list box, click a value, and then click **AutoFill**.

3 Repeat for each value in the **Branch Location** drop-down list box.

4 When you're finished testing, close the window in Run mode to switch to Design mode. In the **Do you want to save changes?** message box, click **Yes** only if you want to save a backup copy into the Drafts folder.

Create a Procedure for the Clear Command Button

The Clear_Click procedure clears the values from the address fields. With the **Clear** button, users can automatically remove values if they make a mistake with the **AutoFill** button.

▶ **To create the Clear_Click procedure**

1 On the **Form Design** toolbar, click the **View Code** button.

2 Add the following procedure to the Script Editor window.

```
'clears the values in the address boxes.
Sub Clear_Click
    Item.UserProperties.Find("BusinessCardStreet").Value = ""
    Item.UserProperties.Find("BusinessCardCityState").Value = ""
    Item.UserProperties.Find("BusinessCardZipCode").Value = ""
    Item.UserProperties.Find("BusinessCardFax").Value = ""
End Sub
```

▶ **To test the Clear procedure**

1   On the **Form,** menu, click **Run This Form**.

2   In the **Branch Location** drop-down list box, click a value, and then click **AutoFill**.

3   Click **Clear**.

4   Repeat steps 1–3 for each value in the **Branch Location** drop-down list box.

5   When you're finished testing, close the window in Run mode to return to Design mode.

Create a Procedure for the SendDeliveryMessage Command Button

When clicked, the **SendDeliveryMessage** button on the **Status** page opens a Message form that is addressed to the requester. The text in the **Subject** box of the message informs the user that the business cards will arrive in two weeks.

▶ **To create the SendDeliveryMessage procedure**

1   On the **Form Design** toolbar, click the **View Code** button.

2   Add the following procedure to the Script Editor window.

```
'creates a message item that tells the user their cards will be ready
'in about two weeks.
Sub SendDeliveryMessage_Click
    AdminName = Application.GetNameSpace("MAPI").CurrentUser
    Set MyItem = Application.CreateItem(0)
    MyItem.To = Item.SenderName
    MyItem.Subject = "Your business card request has been processed. " _
        & "Your cards will be delivered in about two weeks."
    MyItem.Body = "If you have questions, feel free to contact me."
    MyItem.Display
End Sub
```

Because the SendDeliveryMessage control is located on the **Read** page, you must submit a Business Card Request item to the Business Card Requests folder, and then open the item to test the procedure. You will test this procedure later in this chapter.

:

Add Code to the CustomPropertyChange Event

The **CustomPropertyChange** event is an Outlook event that occurs when the user changes a value on the Business Card Request form. In this case, you add code to the **CustomPropertyChange** event to determine the field value that has changed. If the field is the Request Status field and the value of the field is Request Processed, then the Request Administrator and Date Processed fields are automatically filled in.

▶ **To add code to the CustomPropertyChange event**

1 On the **Script** menu of the **Script Editor**, click **Event Handler**.

2 In the **Insert Event Handler** list box, click **CustomPropertyChange**, and then click the **Add** button.

3 Change the **Name** value in parentheses to **myFieldName** as shown in the first line of code in the following sample. Then add the following code.

```
'if Request Processed is selected in the Request Status box, the Date
'Processed and Request Administrator boxes are automatically filled in
Sub Item_CustomPropertyChange(ByVal myFieldName)
    If myFieldName = "BusinessCardRequestStatus" and _
            Item.UserProperties.Find("BusinessCardRequestStatus") = _
            "Request Processed" then
        Item.UserProperties.Find("BusinessCardDateProcessed") = Now
        AdminName = Application.GetNameSpace("MAPI").CurrentUser
        Item.UserProperties.Find("BusinessCardRequestAdministrator").Value = AdminName
    Else
        Item.UserProperties.Find("BusinessCardDateProcessed").Value = "1/1/4501"
        Item.Userproperties.Find("BusinessCardRequestAdministrator").Value = ""
    End If
End Sub
```

Because the controls involved in this procedure are located on the **Read** page, you must submit a Business Card Request item to the Business Card Requests folder, and then open the item to test the procedure. You will test this procedure later in this chapter.

Add Code to the Open Event

The **Open** event is an Outlook event that occurs when users open the Business Card Request form to compose or read an item. In this case, you add code to the **Open** event to hide the **Status** page if the user opens the form to compose a business card request. When a submitted Business Card Request item is opened, the **Status** page is displayed.

▶ To add code to the Open event

1 On the **Script** menu of the **Script Editor**, click **Event Handler**.

2 In the **Insert Event Handler** list box, click **Open** and then click the **Add** button.

3 Add the following code.

```
'hides the Status page when the user opens the form to compose an
'item.
Function Item_Open()
    Set MyInspector = Item.GetInspector
        If Item.SenderName = "" then
            MyInspector.HideFormPage("Status")
        Else
            MyInspector.ShowFormPage("Status")
        End if
End Function
```

Set Form Properties

Now you set the Form Properties for the Business Card Request form.

▶ To set Form Properties

• Click the form **(Properties)** page, and then set the following properties.

Property	Setting
Contact	*Your name*
Description	Use this form to send a business card request to the Business Card Requests folder.
Version	1.0
Form Number	1-1

Make a Backup Copy of the Form

It's always a good idea to make a backup copy of the form before you publish it.

▶ To save the Business Card Request form

1 With the form open, click **Save As** on the **File** menu.

2 In the **Save In** list box, select the default Outlook template folder, such as C:\Program Files\Microsoft Office\Templates.

3 In the **File name** text box, type a name for the form.

4 In the **Save as type** drop-down list box, select **Outlook Template (.oft)**.

5 Click **Save**.

Publish the Form

It's quite likely that you will not be able to publish the form to the Organizational Forms Library because you don't have administrator permissions. Instead, you can publish it to your Personal Forms Library. You can then open the form and send a business card request to the Business Card Requests folder to test the forms. In addition to the Personal Forms Library, you also publish the form in the Business Card Requests Folder Forms Library. This provides a convenient way for an administrator to create a Business Card Request item because a New Business Card Request command is added to the **Actions** menu of the folder.

Note For more information regarding the circumstances in which you would use Organizational Forms Library, Personal Forms Library, or a folder's forms library, see Chapter 13, "Distribute and Maintain Applications."

▶ **To publish the form to your Personal Forms Library**

1   On the **Form Design** toolbar, click the **Publish Form As** button.

2   Choose **Personal Forms Library** in the **Look In** drop-down list box.

3   In the **Display name** text box and the **Form name** text box, type **Business Card Request**, and then click **Publish**.

▶ **To publish the form to the Business Card Requests folder forms library**

1   On the **Tools** menu, select **Forms** and then click **Publish Form As**.

2   Click the **Look in** drop-down list box, and then click the Business Card Requests folder.

3   In the **Display name** text box and the **Form name** text box, type **Business Card Request**.

4   Click **Publish**.

Tip In the Business Card Requests folder, click the **Actions** menu. Note that the **New Business Card Request** command is added to the menu. Outlook automatically adds the menu command when you publish the form in the Business Card Requests folder forms library.

Create Views

The Request Status view groups items by the Request Pending or Request Processed value in the Request Status field. Items in each group are then sorted by the date they were received. When an administrator opens an item and completes the order, he selects **Request Processed** in the **Request Status** box. The item is then moved to the Request Processed group.

Create the Request Status View

The Request Status view, as shown in Figure 10.15, groups items by the Request Pending or Request Processed value in the BusinessCardRequestStatus field. Items in each group are then sorted by date processed. If there is not a date in the DateProcessed field, items are sorted by date received.

Figure 10.15   The Request Status view in the Business Card Requests folder

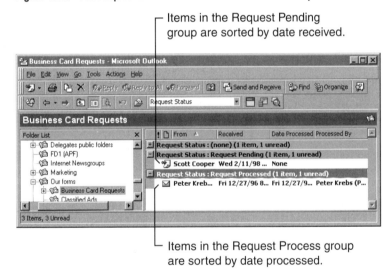

⌐ Items in the Request Pending
  group are sorted by date received.

└ Items in the Request Process group
  are sorted by date processed.

▶ **To create the Request Status view**

1 In the Folder List, click the Business Card Requests folder.

2 On the **View** menu, select **Current View**, and then click **Define Views**.

3 Click **New**.

4 In the **Name of new view** text box, type **Request Status**.

5 Click **OK** twice, and then click **Apply View**.

Remove Columns

Now you remove the fields that aren't necessary for the Request Status view.

▶ **To remove fields**

- Drag the **Flag Status**, **Attachments**, and **Subject** column headings, as shown in Figure 10.16, away from the column heading row until an X appears through the column heading; then release the mouse button.

Figure 10.16   Drag the Flag Status, Attachments, and Subject column headings from the column heading row.

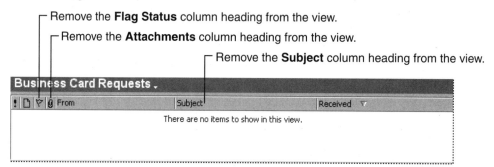

Remove the **Flag Status** column heading from the view.

Remove the **Attachments** column heading from the view.

Remove the **Subject** column heading from the view.

Add Columns

Now you add columns to the Request Status view.

▶ **To add a column to a view**

1 On the **Advanced** toolbar, click the **Field Chooser** icon.

2 In the top drop-down list box in the **Field Chooser**, click the **Business Card Request** field set.

3 Drag the BusinessCardDateProcessed field from the **Field Chooser** to the column heading row and drop it to the right of the **Received** column heading.

4 Right-click the BusinessCardDateProcessed column heading, and then click **Format Columns** on the shortcut menu.

5 In the **Label** text box, type **Date Processed**, and then click **OK**.

6 Drag the BusinessCardRequestAdministrator field from the **Field Chooser** to column heading row and drop it to the right of the DateProcessed column heading.

7 Right-click the BusinessCardRequestAdministrator column heading, and then click **Format Columns** on the shortcut menu.

8 In the **Label** text box, type **Processed By**, and then click **OK**.

The column heading should now look similar to the column heading in Figure 10.17. If you want to set the exact width of the columns, right-click the column heading, and then click **Format Columns** on the shortcut menu. Then type the column width in the **Specific width** text box.

Figure 10.17   The column heading row for the Request Status view

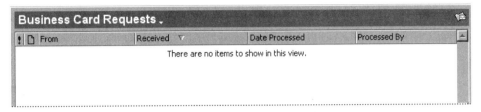

Group By

Now you group by the BusinessCardRequestStatus field. However, before you group items, you add the BusinessCardRequestStatus field as a column. Next, you format the column to change the label to Request Processed, then you remove the column. You cannot directly format a group label, so this method provides a handy alternative.

▶ **To format the BusinessCardRequestStatus field**

1   From the **Field Chooser**, drag the BusinessCardRequestStatus field to the column heading row. It really doesn't matter where you put the column heading at this time.

2   Right-click the BusinessCardRequestStatus column heading, and then click **Format Columns** on the shortcut menu.

3   In the **Label** field, type **Request Status**.

4   Click **OK**.

▶ **To group by BusinessCardRequestStatus**

1   On the **Advanced** toolbar, click the **Group By Box** icon.

An area with the text **Drag a column header here to group by that column** appears above the column heading row.

2   Drag the **Request Status** column heading into the **Drag a column header here to group by that column** area.

3   On the **Advanced** toolbar, click the **Group By Box** icon.

Sort By

- Click the **Date Processed** column heading, so items in each group are listed in order according to date processed.

Create the By Requester Name View

The By Requester Name view, as shown in Figure 10.18, shows request items sorted in ascending order by the requester's name, so a user's request is easy to find in the folder.

Figure 10.18 The By Requester Name view

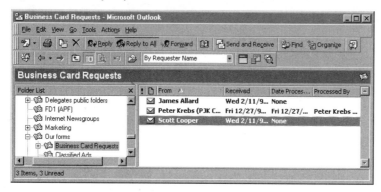

▶ To create the By Requester Name view

1 On the **View** menu, select **Current View**, and then click **Define Views**.

2 Click **Request Status**, and then click **Copy**.

3 In the **Name of new view** text box, type **By Requester Name**, and then click **OK**.

4 Click **Group By** in the **View Summary** dialog box

5 In the **Group items by** drop-down list box, click **From**, click **OK** twice, and then click **Apply View**.

6 Click the **From** column heading so the arrow points up, as shown in the preceding illustration in Figure 10.18.

Set Permissions

For the Business Card Requests folder, you give the general public, represented by the **Default** name in the **Permissions** dialog box, a Contributor role so users can send items to the folder. However, after an item is submitted in the folder, users cannot change items. You then give those people who are responsible for processing business card requests an Editor role so they can edit and save items in the folder. In addition, you give those people who are responsible for designing and maintaining the folder Owner permissions, so they can make any necessary changes to the folder.

▶ **To set permissions for the Business Card Requests folder**

1   In the Folder List, right-click the Business Card Requests folder, and then click **Properties** on the shortcut menu.

2   Click the **Permissions** tab.

3   Set the following permissions for the folder.

Name	Role	Assign To
Default	Contributor	General users who will submit business card requests
Business Card Request administrators	Editor	Administrators who are responsible for processing business card request orders
Application designers or system administrators	Owner	People responsible for maintaining and designing applications

See Also   For more information about setting permissions, see "Set Permissions" in Chapter 8, "Folders."

Test the Application

Now it's a good idea to test the application to make sure it's working as expected.

▶ **To test the application**

1   On the **File** menu, select **New**, and then click **Choose Form**.

2   Click **Personal Forms Library**, and then double-click **Business Card Request**.

3   Fill in the form, and then click **Send**.

4   In the Folder List, click the Business Card Requests folder.

5   Double-click the Business Card Request item you just sent to the folder.

6   Click **Enable Macros**.

7   Click the **Status** page.

8   In the **Request Status** drop-down list box, click **Request Processed**.

9   Click **Send date of delivery message**, and then click the **Send** button to send the form.

10   Close the Business Card Request form. When asked if you want to save the changes, click **Yes**.

11   In the **Current View** drop-down list box, click **By Requester Name**.

12   Repeat Steps 1–10 several times to make sure the application is working correctly.

Send the Form to the Administrator

When you are sure the application is working as expected, you create a message and attach the form as a file attachment in the message. The administrator is responsible for checking the form for harmful macros and viruses. If the form is clean, the administrator clears the **Send form definition with item** option on the **Properties** page of the form, and then publishes the form to the Organizational Forms Library where it can be opened by all users on the Microsoft Exchange Server system.

▶ **To send the attached form**

1   On the **Actions** menu, click **New Mail Message**.

2   Fill in the To field with the name of the administrator.

3   In the **Message** text box, type the following:

Please check this form for viruses and harmful macros. If none are found, clear the Send form definition with item option on the Properties page of the form, and then publish the form to the Organization Forms Library.

4   On the **Insert** menu, click **File**, and then open the folder in which you saved the Business Card Request.oft file earlier in the chapter.

5   Double-click the Business Card Request.oft file.

6   Click **Send**.

Check the Form for Viruses and Harmful Code

If you are the administrator, you open the form, and then save the file attachment. You then check the form for viruses and harmful macros. If none exist, you clear the **Send form definition with item** option, and then publish the form to the Organization Forms Library.

▶ **To check a form that has been sent to you**

1   Save the form file to a folder, and then run a virus-checking tool on the form.

2   When you are certain the form is virus-free, hold down the SHIFT key and then double-click the form .oft file.

Important When you hold down the SHIFT key when opening a form, you prevent any code from executing when the form opens.

3   Click **New Business Card Request** on the **Actions** menu.

4   On the **Tools** menu, select **Forms**, and then click **Design This Form**.

5   Click the **Properties** page.

6   Clear the **Send form definition with item** check box.

▶ **To publish the form**

1   On the **Tools** menu, select **Forms**, and then click the **Publish Form As** button.

2   In the **Look In** drop-down list box, click **Organizational Forms Library.**.

3   In the **Display name** text box and **Form name** text box, type **Business Card Request**.

4   Click **Publish**.

5   On the **Tools** menu, select **Forms** and then click **Publish Form As**.

6   In the **Look In** drop-down list box, click **Public Folders**, and then locate and click the Business Card Requests folder.

7   In the **Display name** text box and the **Form name** text box, type **Business Card Request**.

8   Click **Publish**.

Release the Application

Before you release the application, it's a good idea to test the folder one more time. When you're sure the application is working as expected, you set the **Initial View on Folder** property to Request Status and you make the folder available by clicking the **All users with access permission** option.

▶ **To set administration properties**

1   In the Folder List, right-click the Business Card Requests folder, and then click **Properties**.

2   Click the **Administration** tab.

3   In the **Initial View on folder** drop-down list box, click **Request Status**.

4   Click the **All users with access permission** option button.

Now that the folder is ready to use, send a message to your co-workers to notify them that the application is available. You might want to include a shortcut to the folder in your message to make it easy for your co-workers to find the folder.

The Help Desk Application

In This Chapter

Overview of the Help Desk Application   389

Set Up the Application   395

The Help Request Form   401

The Assigned Help Task Form   410

One of the best ways to learn how to design Microsoft Outlook applications is to take a look at the sample applications in the Outlook companion CD-ROM. In this chapter, we'll take a look at the sample Help Desk application. There are several reasons for examining the Help Desk application. It showcases most of the design techniques that you use when creating applications. It shows you how to create an application that consists of multiple forms and folders. And, it shows you how to create an application that creates and stores a variety of item types, including custom tasks, posts, and messages.

To introduce the Help Desk application and its components, we'll walk through the Help Request process to demonstrate how Outlook can be used to automate a process in your organization. Then we'll take a look at how to set up the Help Desk application in your organization. After you set up the application, we'll explore some of the design techniques that are implemented in this application.

Overview of the Help Desk Application

The Help Desk application provides users with an easy way to submit a request for technical assistance to your organization's Help Desk group. In addition, the application makes it possible for Help Desk personnel to assign, organize, track, collaborate on, and resolve Help Desk requests. Perhaps the easiest way to explain how the Help Desk application works is to walk you through the entire Help Request process from beginning to end.

The user opens the Help Request form.   The Help Request form is a Message form published in the forms library of the Help Desk folder. It can also be published in the Organizational Forms Library, by following the instructions in Chapter 13, "Distribute and Maintain Applications." To open the Help Request form, click the Help Desk folder, and then click **New Help Request** on the **Actions** menu. The form is preaddressed to the Help Request folder, so the user does not need to specify the folder address to submit the request. The user simply fills in the request and clicks the **Send** button.

Figure 11.1   The Compose page of the Help Request form

The user clicks the **Send** button to send the request.
The hidden To field is preaddressed to the Help Desk folder.

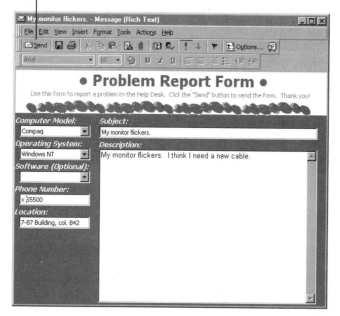

The Help Request form arrives in the Help Desk folder, as shown in Figure 11.2.

Figure 11.2   The Help Desk folder

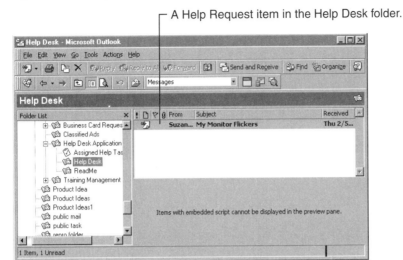

A Help Request item in the Help Desk folder.

A Help Desk administrator opens the Help Request form in the Help Desk folder, as shown in Figure 11.3.

Figure 11.3   The Read page—page 2—of the Help Request form

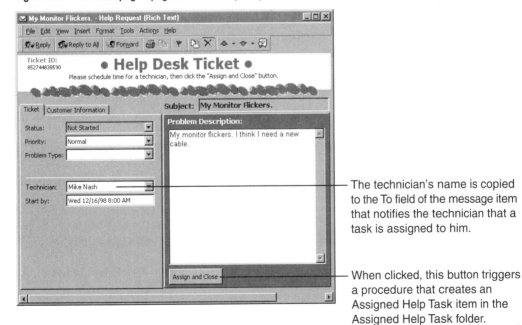

The technician's name is copied to the To field of the message item that notifies the technician that a task is assigned to him.

When clicked, this button triggers a procedure that creates an Assigned Help Task item in the Assigned Help Task folder.

The administrator clicks the Assign and Close button.   When the Help Desk administrator clicks the **Assign and Close** button on the Help Request form, three things happen:

- Information in the item is written from the Help Request form to the newly created Assigned Help Task item. This new item is created and saved in the Assigned Help Tasks folder, as shown in Figure 11.4.

Figure 11.4   The Assigned Help Tasks folder

The Assigned Help Task item is created and saved in the Assigned Help Tasks folder.

- The original item is deleted from the Help Desk folder.
- A message is created and sent to the Inbox of the technician assigned to the request. When the message is created, the Assigned Help Task item just created and saved in the Assigned Help Tasks folder is inserted as an attachment in the message, as shown in Figure 11.5.

Figure 11.5   The Read page—page 1—of the Help Request form

The message is addressed to the assigned technician.

An attachment is inserted in the message box of the form.

The assigned technician double-clicks the attachment in the message.   When the technician double-clicks the attachment in the message, the Assigned Help Task item opens, as shown in Figure 11.6.

Figure 11.6   The Assigned Help Task form

└ The technician can click the **Send Mail to User** button to open the Correspondence Mail form.

The technician can send correspondence mail to the user to get more information.   In many cases, the technician requires additional information to resolve the request. To send mail to the user, the technician clicks the **Send Mail to User** button to show the Correspondence Mail form, shown in Figure 11.7.

Figure 11.7   The Compose page of the Correspondence Mail form

┌ The item is automatically addressed to the user.

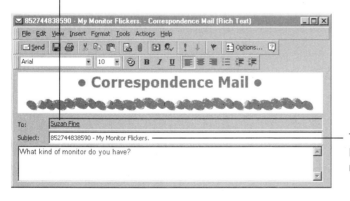

The Subject field shows the Ticket ID and the subject of the original request item.

The technician can click the Start Discussion button to start an online conversation about the request.   If the technician experiences problems resolving the request, she clicks the **Start Discussion** button to open the Task Discussion form, as shown in Figure 11.8. The technician can then post a Discussion item (or post) to the folder. Other technicians can review the post and post their own suggestions or solutions to the problem.

Figure 11.8 The Compose page of the Task Discussion form. The Discussion item is posted in the Assigned Help Tasks folder.

The technician clicks the **Post Reply** button to post the Task Discussion item to the Assigned Help Tasks folder.

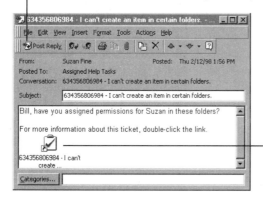

An attachment to the Assigned Help Task item is included in the message box.

When the problem is solved, the technician clicks the Resolve Problem button   on the Assigned Help Task form to send a message to the user saying that the Help Request is resolved. The task is then shown as completed in the Assigned Help Tasks folder, as shown in Figure 11.9.

Figure 11.9 The resolved task in the Assigned Help Tasks folder

When the Assigned Help Task item is resolved, a strikethrough line appears through the item in the view.

Set Up the Application

Before you can run the Help Desk application, you must customize the application so it works in your environment. For example, you must copy the Help Desk Application folder to Public Folders and then publish the folder address. In addition, you must set the address in the To field of the Help Request form to the Help Requests folder. You also add the names of your organization's Help Desk technicians to the form.

Copy the Help Desk Folder to Public Folders

To make the Help Desk application available to users in your organization, you copy the Help Desk Application folder from the Building Microsoft Outlook 98 Applications folder to Public Folders. Before you copy the folder, however, make sure you have owner permission in the folder to which you would like to copy.

▶ **To check your permission for a folder**

1 In the Folder List, right-click the folder you want to check, and then click **Properties** on the shortcut menu.

2 Click the **Permissions** tab.

3 If you have owner permission for the folder, you should see your name in the list with the owner role assigned.

4 If you do not have owner permission for the folder you want to copy to, see your administrator.

▶ **To copy the Help Desk Application folder to Public Folders**

1 In the Folder List, expand the Building Microsoft Outlook 98 Applications folder, and then expand the Beyond the Basics folder.

2 Right-click the Help Desk Application folder, and then click **Copy "Help Desk Application"** on the shortcut menu.

3 Double-click the folder you want to copy the Help Desk Application folder to.

Publish the Folder Address and Restrict Folder Access

For the Help Desk application to operate properly, you must preaddress the Help Request form with the address of the Help Desk Application folder. Before you can do this, however, you must publish the folder address to your Personal Address Book. You can also ask your administrator to publish the folder in the Global Address Book. It's much easier and faster, however, to publish the folder address to your Personal Address Book for use during development and testing.

Note If you have not yet done so, you can add your Personal Address Book by selecting **Services** on the Outlook **Tools** menu. Click **Add**, and then click **Personal Address Book**.

▶ **To publish the Help Desk folder address to your Personal Address Book**

1   In the Folder List, right-click the Help Desk folder copied to Public Folders, and then click **Properties** on the shortcut menu.

2   Click the **Administration** tab, and then click **Personal Address Book**.

The Help Desk folder address is now available in your Personal Address Book. This enables you to set the To field of the Help Request form to this address. First, however, you restrict user access to the folder while you work on it.

▶ **To prevent users from opening the folder**

•   On the **Administration** page, click **Owners Only** under **This folder is available to**, and then click **OK**.

Set Permissions

With Outlook, you can define flexible permissions for folders. For example, for the Help Desk folder, you give general users contributor permission so they can submit items to the folder but cannot change items after they are submitted. You give the Help Desk administrator and technicians editor permission so they can edit and create items in the folder. And you give the Help Desk manager and application designers owner permission so they can maintain the folder.

Set Permissions for the Help Desk Folder

▶ **To set permissions for the Help Desk folder**

1   In the Folder List, right-click the Help Desk folder in the Help Desk Application folder, and then click **Properties** on the shortcut menu.

2   Click the **Permissions** tab, and then set the permissions as shown in the following table. When you are done, click **OK**.

Name	Role	Description	Assign to
Default	Contributor	Can submit items to the folder, but cannot open or edit items in the folder	General users who submit Help Request items.
Help Desk technicians	Editor	Can create, read, and edit all items	Help Desk technicians or administrators responsible for assigning the Help Request task
Help Desk manager	Owner	All permissions	Managers who supervise Help Desk technicians
Application designers or system administrators	Owner	All permissions	People responsible for maintaining and designing applications

Set Permissions for the Assigned Help Tasks Folder

For the Assigned Help Tasks folder, you restrict access to Help Desk administrators, technicians, and managers only.

▶ **To set permissions for the Assigned Help Tasks folder**

1   In the Folder List, right-click the Assigned Help Tasks folder in public folders, and then click **Properties** on the shortcut menu.

2   Click the **Permissions** tab, and then set the permissions as shown in the following table. When you are done, click **OK**.

Name	Role	Description	Assign to
Default	None	General users cannot access the folder.	
Help Desk technicians	Editor	Can create, read, and edit all items	Help Desk technicians or administrators responsible for assigning the Help Request task.
Help Desk manager	Owner	All permissions	Managers who supervise Help Desk technicians.
Application designers or system administrators	Owner	All permissions	People responsible for maintaining and designing applications.

Customize the Help Request Form for Your Organization

Now that the folders are set up, you customize the Help Request form to your environment. First, you preaddress the To field of the form to the Help Desk folder address you published to your Personal Address Book. Then you add the names of the technicians to the AssignedTo field. When you are done, you publish the form to the Personal Forms Library and the Help Desk forms library. After you thoroughly test the application, you can submit the Help Request form to your administrator who can then publish the Help Request form in the Organizational Forms Library. Be sure the address values are available in Global Address Book. You can then delete the temporary form you published in your Personal Forms Library.

Preaddress the Help Request Form

Now you set the initial value of the To field in the Help Request form to the Help Requests folder. In this way, when users open the form, they can submit a Help Request to the public folder without worrying about or knowing the folder address. To preaddress the form, you must go back and forth between Run and Design mode.

▶ **To preaddress the Help Request form**

1 In the Folder List, click the Help Desk folder in public folders.

2 On the **Actions** menu, click **New Help Request**.

3 On the form **Tools** menu, select **Forms**, and then click **Design This Form** to switch to Design mode.

4 Click the **Message** tab on the **Compose** page.

5 Right-click on the **To** text box, and then click **Properties**.

6 On the **Value** page, type **Help Desk** in the **Set the initial value of this field to text** box.
For this to be valid, **Help Desk** must be a valid entry in the Personal Address Book, (set earlier in this chapter) or in the Global Address book (set by your system administrator).

Specify the Technician Names in the AssignedTo Field

Next, you set the names that appear in the **Technician** drop-down list box on the **Read** page of the Help Request form. This control, as shown in Figure 11.10, is actually named AssignedTo and is bound to the AssignedTo field.

Figure 11.10   The AssignedTo control on the Read page of the Help Request form

Specify technician names for the AssignedTo field bound to the AssignedTo control.

▶ **To specify the names in the AssignedTo field**

1 In Design mode, click the **Edit Read Page** button on the **Form Design** toolbar.

2 Click the **Ticket** tab.

3 Right-click the AssignedTo control—shown as the **Technician** drop-down list box on the form—and then click **Properties** on the shortcut menu.

4 Click the **Value** tab.

5 In the **Possible values** text box, type the full names of the technicians whose names you want available in the **Technician** drop-down list box at run time.

The names you type in the **Possible values** text box, as shown in Figure 11.11, are the names used to address messages sent to technicians to notify them that tasks are assigned to them. Make sure the names you enter in the **Possible values** text box are names that resolve when copied to the To field of a message and have permissions for this folder.

Figure 11.11   The names of the technicians are possible values in the AssignedTo field.

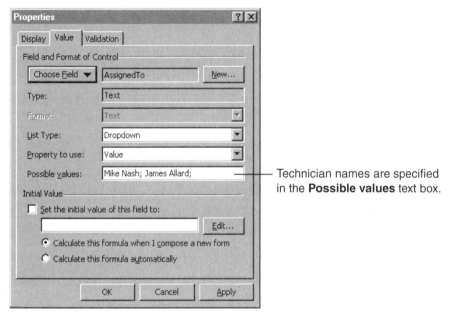

Technician names are specified in the **Possible values** text box.

▶ **To make a backup copy of the Help Request form**

1 With the form open, click **Save As** on the **File** menu.

2 In the **Save In** list box, select the default Outlook template folder, such as C:\Program Files\Microsoft Office\Templates.

3 In the **File name** text box, type a name for the form.

4 In the **Save as type** drop-down list box, select **Outlook Template (.oft)**.

5 Click **Save**.

Later, you will use this form to send to the administrator.

▶ **To publish the form in the Personal Forms Library**

1   On the **Tools** menu, select **Forms**, and then click **Publish Form As**.

2   In the **Look in** drop-down list box, select **Personal Forms Library**.

3   In the **Display name** text box and **Form name** text box, type **Help Request**.

4   Click **Publish**.

5   Select **No** in the **Save form definition with item** message box.

▶ **To publish the form in the Help Desk folder forms library**

1   On the **Tools** menu, select **Forms**, and then click **Publish Form As**.

2   Select **Outlook Folders** in the **Look in** drop-down list box.

3   Click **Browse** and select the **Help Desk** folder in the public folders. Be sure not to select **Help Desk** from the **Look in** drop-down list box, because you will overwrite the form in the personal folder (.pst) file generated by the CD-ROM.

4   Double-click the **Help Desk** form to publish and overwrite the existing form in the public folders.

5   Click the **Close** button, and select **No** in the message box. Changes do not need to be saved in draft form, since the form is already published.

If you don't publish the customized form to the Help Desk folder forms library, the names of the technicians do not appear in the **Technician** drop-down list box. Instead, the old Help Request form in the Help Desk folder forms library opens when you double-click a submitted item in the Help Desk folder.

Test the Application

Now that the application is set up, you test it to make sure the application works as planned.

▶ **To test the Help Desk application**

1   On the **File** menu, select **New**, click **Choose Form**, and then double-click the **Help Request** form in the Personal Forms Library

2   Fill in the Help Request form, and then click **Send**.

3   In the Folder List, open the Help Desk folder, and then double-click the item you just sent to open it.

4   In the **Technician** drop-down list box, make sure the names you added to the list are available. Type your name in the box, select a choice from the **Problem Type** drop-down list box, and then click the **Assign and Close** button.

5   Open your Inbox and double-click the Assigned Help Task item that just arrived.

6   In the message box, double-click the attachment.

7 Click the **Send Mail to User** button, type a message in the message box, and then click **Send**.

8 Click the **Start Discussion** button, type a message in the message box, and then click **Post**.

9 Click the **Resolve Problem** button, and then click **Yes**.

10 Close the forms.

You should now have a good idea of how this application works. Let's move on to take an in-depth look at some of the design techniques used in the Help Desk application.

The Help Request Form

The Help Desk application provides a common Outlook groupware scenario. In the Help Desk application, Assigned Help Task items are saved in the Assigned Help Tasks folder. However, unless a Help Desk technician opens the Assigned Help Tasks folder, he has no idea that a new task has been assigned to him. To solve this problem, the Submit_Click procedure is added to the Help Request form. The Submit_Click procedure is triggered when the Help Desk administrator clicks the **Assign and Close** button. The Submit_Click procedure automatically creates and saves an Assigned Help Task item in the Assigned Help Tasks folder. The procedure then sends a message to the assigned technician's Inbox to notify her that she has an Assigned Help Task item. A shortcut to the Assigned Help Task item is included in the message, so when the message arrives in the technician's Inbox, she can click the shortcut to view the item.

In addition to the technique just described, we'll explore several other useful techniques in this section, including how to:

- Assign script-level variables.

- Determine the Compose mode or Read mode of an item.

- Create a unique Ticket ID.

- Automatically create a custom Assigned Help Task item and post it in the Assigned Help Tasks folder.

- Automatically send a message to the technician who is assigned an item and include a shortcut to the Assigned Help Task item in the message.

▶ **To view the code in the Help Request form**

1 Open the Help Desk folder.

2 On the **Actions** menu, click **New Help Request**.

3 On the **Tools** menu, select **Forms,** and then click **Design This Form**, as shown in Figure 11.12.

4 On the **Form Design** toolbar, click the **View Code** icon.

Figure 11.12   The Help Request Form Compose and Read Pages

The preaddressed Message page is hidden.

Assign Script-Level Variables

In the Help Request code, as shown in this example, several script-level variables are declared at the top of the Script Editor window. These variables are used among procedures that create the Ticket ID value for the Help Request item.

```
'**************************************************************************
'* Help Request code
'* Functions/Procedures:
'* Standard Events:
'* Item_Open()
'* Item_CustomPropertyChange(ByVal String)
'*
'* Helpers:
'*    ChangeProblemType()
'*    TrimUserName()
'*    CreateDateAsNumber()
'**************************************************************************
```

```
Dim UserName            ' Script level variables used for the Ticket ID.
Dim Trimmed
Dim Munged
Dim TicketID
```

Determine If the Help Request Form Is in Compose Mode or Read Mode

In many of the applications you create, you need to determine if the form is in Compose mode or Read mode. To determine if a Message form is in Compose mode or Read mode, you can add a statement to the Item_Open event to get the **SenderName** property of an item. As shown in the following example, if the **SenderName** property is equal to "", then the form is in Compose mode and the code to create the TicketID value is executed.

```
'************************************************************
'* Procedure: Item_Open()
'* Description: Upon open, create a unique ID if the
'*      item has not been sent (by checking the SenderName
'*      property).
'************************************************************
Sub Item_Open()
   Dim MyDate
   Dim NowID

   If (Item.SenderName = "") Then      ' If item is in Compose mode, create the ID.
      UserName = Application.GetNameSpace("MAPI").CurrentUser

      ' Trim the user name of spaces.
      Trimmed = TrimUserName(UserName)

      NowID = Now
      ' Get date as numbers only.
      MyDate = CreateDateAsNumber(NowID)

      ' Set the Ticket ID for this item.
      TicketID = MyDate & Trimmed

      Item.UserProperties.Find("TicketID").Value = TicketID

      Item.BillingInformation = TicketID
   End If
End Sub
```

Create a Unique Ticket ID for Each Item

To create a unique Ticket ID for each item, as shown in Figure 11.13, the Item_Open event calls two functions: the **TrimUserName** function and the **CreateDateAsNumber** function.

Figure 11.13   A unique Ticket ID is created for each Help Request.

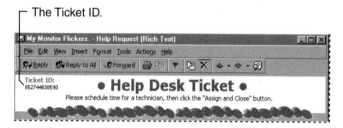

The Ticket ID.

The TrimUserName Function

When a Help Request item is opened in Compose mode, the code in the Item_Open event gets the **CurrentUser** property and passes it to the TrimUserName function. The TrimUserName function converts the name into a numeric value and returns it to the Trimmed variable, as shown in this example.

```
'******************************************************************
'* Procedure:  TrimUserName(ByVal UserName)
'* Description:  Trims the user name so that it can be used in the
'*        Ticket ID.
'******************************************************************
Function TrimUserName(ByVal UserName)
    Dim Counter          ' Declare variables.
    Dim AscName
    Dim KeepChar
    Dim KeepName
    Dim DiscardChar
    Dim RightName
    Temp = ""
    KeepName = ""

    For li = 0 To 2    ' For first three letters of user name.
       CharName = Mid(UCase(UserName), li + 1, 1)

       AscName = Asc(CharName)

       If ((AscName >= 48) and (AscName <= 57)) or ((AscName >= 65) _
            and (AscName <=90)) Then
          KeepName = KeepName + CStr(AscName)
       End If
    Next

    RightName = Right(KeepName, 6)
    TrimUserName = RightName
End Function
```

The CreateDateAsNumber Function

The code in the Item_Open event also gets the **Now** property. This property returns
the current date and passes it to the CreateDateAsNumber function. The
CreateDateAsNumber function converts the date to a numeric value and returns the
value to the MyDate variable. The values of Trimmed and MyDate are then combined
in the Item_Open event code to form the Ticket ID value. The BillingInformation field
of the item is then set to the value of the Ticket ID.

```
'*********************************************************************
'* Procedure:  CreateDateAsNumber(ByVal NowID)
'* Description:  Manipulates the date so that it can be used in the
'*       Ticket ID.
'*********************************************************************
Function CreateDateAsNumber(ByVal NowID)
For li = 0 To 16     ' For all 17 characters of the date stamp.
CharName = Mid(UCase(NowID), li + 1, 1)
AscName = Asc(CharName)
If ((AscName >= 48) and (AscName <= 57)) Then
KeepName = KeepName + CStr(CharName)
End If
Next
RightID = Right(KeepName, 6)
CreateDateAsNumber = RightID
End Function
```

Automatically Create and Save an Assigned Help Task Item

On the **Read** page of the Help Request form, you see an **Assign and Close** button, as
shown in Figure 11.14. When this button is clicked, it triggers the Submit_Click
procedure. This procedure performs several tasks that follow.

Figure 11.14   The Assign and Close button triggers the Submit_Click procedure that creates and saves an Assigned Help Task item in the Assigned Help Tasks folder.

The **Assign and Close** button triggers the Submit_Click procedure.

- Sets the active folder as the Assigned Help Tasks folder, and then creates an Assigned Help Task item.

- Copies the necessary values from the Help Request item to the Assigned Help Task item.

- Sets the value of the item Importance field to **!** if the value of the Task Priority field is not "Normal."

- Saves the Assigned Help Task item in the Assigned Help Tasks folder.

- Creates a message, inserts a shortcut to the Assigned Help Task item in the message box of the message, and then sends the message to the assigned Help Desk technician.

In this section, we'll take a look at the Submit_Click procedure and discuss the techniques used in this procedure. Many of these techniques, once mastered, can be used in a variety of other applications.

Set the Active Folder as the Assigned Help Tasks Folder

One of the problems you face in creating Outlook applications with multiple folders is setting the active folder. For example, with the Help Desk application, you open the Help Request item in the Help Desk folder, and then create an Assigned Help Task item and save it in the Assigned Help Tasks folder. To do this, you must set the Assigned Help Tasks folder as the active folder. The fastest and easiest way to do this is to use the **Parent** property of the Help Request item to return the active folder, which, in this case, is the Help Desk folder. You then use the **Parent** property of the Help Desk folder to return the Help Desk Application folder. As shown in this example, you can then set the active folder as the Assigned Help Tasks folder.

Important   To create a custom item such as **IPM.Task.Assigned Help Task**, you must use the items collection from the folder that contains the form. In addition, the form associated with the item you want to create must be contained in the forms library for that folder. You then use the **Add** method of the **Items Collection** object to create the item.

```
'*********************************************************************
'* Procedure:  Submit_Click
'* Description:  When the Submit button is clicked, copy all fields
'*        into the Task item, and finally delete this item.
'*********************************************************************
Sub Submit_Click
If Item.UserProperties.Find("AssignedTo").Value = "" Then
Temp = MsgBox("Please enter a technician before trying to " _
& "assign a task.",0,"Create Task")
Else
      Assign = MsgBox("This will create a task in the Assigned Tasks folder, " _
           & "delete this item, and send mail to the technician indicating that " _
           & "they have a task to complete.",1,"Create Task")
If Assign = 1 Then
Set HelpDeskFolder = Item.Parent
Set HelpDeskAppFolder = HelpDeskFolder.Parent
Set TaskFolder = HelpDeskAppFolder.Folders("Assigned Help Tasks")
Set AssignedItem = TaskFolder.Items.Add("IPM.Task.Assigned Help Task")
```

Copy Values from the Help Desk Item to the Assigned Help Task Item

After the Submit_Click procedure creates the Assigned Help Task item, it copies the necessary values from the Help Desk item to the Assigned Help Task item. Notice that, in some cases, the field from the original item is actually different from the field in the new item. For example, in the first line of code in this example, the value of the Computer Model field of the current item (the Help Request item) is copied to the Computer Brand and Model field of the Assigned Help Task item. To get or set the value of a custom field, you must use the **Find** method of the **UserProperties** object.

```
Submit_Click    (continued)
        ' Populate the Assigned Help Task form with all the corresponding
        ' fields in this item.
        AssignedItem.UserProperties.Find("Computer Brand and Model").Value = _
            Item.UserProperties.Find("Computer Model").Value
        AssignedItem.UserProperties.Find("Problem Type").Value = _
            Item.UserProperties.Find("Problem Type").Value
        AssignedItem.UserProperties.Find("Phone").Value = _
            Item.UserProperties.Find("Phone Number").Value
        AssignedItem.UserProperties.Find("Computer OS").Value = _
            Item.UserProperties.Find("Operating System").Value
        AssignedItem.UserProperties.Find("Ticket ID").Value = _
            Item.UserProperties.Find("TicketID").Value
        AssignedItem.Subject = _
            Item.UserProperties.Find("TicketID").Value & " - " & Item.Subject
        AssignedItem.UserProperties.Find("Description").Value = Item.Body
        AssignedItem.UserProperties.Find("Technician Name").Value = _
            Item.UserProperties.Find("AssignedTo").Value
        AssignedItem.UserProperties.Find("Received Date").Value = Item.SentOn
        AssignedItem.UserProperties.Find("Computer Software").Value = _
            Item.UserProperties.Find("Software").Value
        AssignedItem.UserProperties.Find("From User").Value = Item.SenderName
        AssignedItem.UserProperties.Find("User Location").Value = _
            Item.UserProperties.Find("Request Location").Value
        AssignedItem.UserProperties.Find("Task Priority").Value = _
            Item.UserProperties.Find("Task Priority").Value
        AssignedItem.UserProperties.Find("AssignedOn").Value = _
            Item.UserProperties.Find("Start by").Value
```

Set the Importance Property of the Assigned Task Item

The following code provides an example of how you set standard property values and custom property values in an item. In this example, the **Find** method and the **Value** property are used in the **Select Case** statement to get the value of the user-defined Task Priority field. When the property is a standard property of the item, as is the case in this example where **Importance** is a standard property of the **TaskItem** object, you can set the value without using the **Find** method or the **Value** property.

```
Submit_Click    (continued)
   ' If Task Priority is something other than Normal, set the
   ' Importance icon to !.
   Select Case Item.UserProperties.Find("Task Priority").Value

   Case "Normal"
      AssignedItem.Importance = 1
   Case Else
      AssignedItem.Importance = 2
   End Select
```

Save the Assigned Help Task Item

After the Submit_Click procedure copies information from the Help Request item to the Assigned Help Task item and then sets the **Importance** property of the Assigned Help Task item, it saves the item in the Assigned Help Tasks folder.

```
Submit_Click    (continued)
     AssignedItem.Save
```

Create a Message, Insert a Shortcut to the Assigned Help Task Item in the Message, and Send

After the Assigned Help Task item is saved, the Submit_Click procedure creates a message. In this case, the message is a standard **MailItem** object, so there is no need to worry about setting the active folder. However, remember that when creating standard items, you must use the numeric value of the item rather than the constant. In this example, the Application.CreateItem(0) statement creates a standard message item. After the item is created, the Subject and Body text are set for the item. The To field of the item is then set to the technician's name specified in the AssignedTo field of the Help Desk item. Finally, the saved Assigned Help Task item is inserted as a shortcut in the message box of the message. The item is then sent to the technician's Inbox, and the Help Desk administrator is given the option to save or delete the submitted Help Request in the Help Request folder.

```
Submit_Click    (continued)
     Set myItem = Application.CreateItem(0)
     MyItem.Subject = "Assigned Help Task at " & Now()
     MyItem.Body = "There is a Help Desk task for you at " & chr(13)
     On Error Resume Next
     MyItem.To = Item.UserProperties.Find("AssignedTo").Value
     Set MyAttachments = MyItem.Attachments
     MyAttachments.Add AssignedItem, 4
     MyItem.Send
     If err Then
        MsgBox("The Mail did not send because the technician was not recognized")
     End If
     Item.Delete    ' After everything was submitted, delete this item.
     End If
   End If
End Sub
```

The Assigned Help Task Form

The Assigned Help Task form is a custom form based on the standard Task form. When creating forms for tracking applications, the Task form often serves as a good starting point, as you'll see in this chapter and in Chapter 12, "The Document Tracking Application." The Task form, and the Task items created with it, have built-in fields and functionality for tracking the progress of a task. For example, the Task form has a Status field and a % Complete field. In addition, when a task is complete, a line is drawn through the item in the folder indicating the task is complete.

Perhaps most important, however, the Task form makes it easy to update and save Task items because the Task form has a **Save and Close** button, which is used to submit new items, and to update existing items. As a result, the user is never confused about whether he should save or post an item.

The Assigned Help Task form appears when you double-click an Assigned Help Task item in the Assigned Help Tasks folder. With the **Read** page of this form, as shown in Figure 11.15, a Help Desk technician can send mail to a user, post a Discussion item to the Assigned Help Tasks folder, or indicate that the Help Task is resolved.

Figure 11.15   The Read page of the Assigned Help Task form

The technician clicks to resolve the Assigned Help Task item.

The technician clicks to create a Task Discussion item.

The technician clicks to create a Correspondence Mail item.

▶ **To view the code in the Assigned Help Task form**

1 Open the Assigned Help Tasks folder.

2 Double-click an Assigned Help Task item.

3 If an Assigned Help Task item does not exist in the folder, follow the instructions in "Test the Application" earlier in this chapter.

4 On the form **Tools** menu, select **Forms**, and then click **Design This Form**.

5 On the **Form Design** toolbar, click the **View Code** icon.

The Open Event of the Assigned Help Task Item

For the Item_Open event, we'll look at several techniques, including how to:

- Write the initial Help Request information into the History Log.

- Lock controls on the form if the item is resolved.

- Set script-level variables to the original values of the fields. In other procedures, the values of these variables are compared to the current value of the field to determine if the field value has changed.

Write the Initial Help Request Item into the History Log

At the bottom of the **Read** page of the Assigned Help Task form, there is a TextBox control that is bound to the Flag field, as shown in Figure 11.16. The Flag field is used to determine if the form is being opened for the first time.

Figure 11.16   The TextBox control is bound to the Flag field.

 └ This control is bound to the Flag field.

The initial value of the Flag field is set to Opened, as shown in Figure 11.17.

Figure 11.17   The Value properties for the Flag field

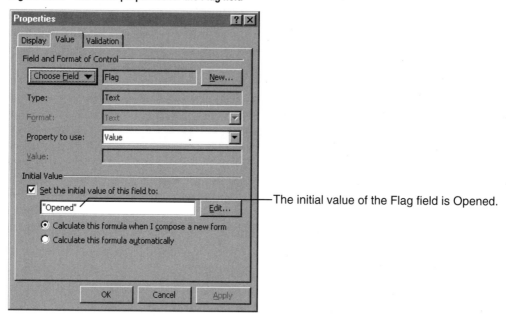

—The initial value of the Flag field is Opened.

The code in the Item_Open event checks the value of the Flag field. If the field value is Opened, then the user description of the problem and the date the item is received is written to the History Text field of the item. The value of the Flag field is then set to Done.

```
'*************************************************************************
'* Procedure:  Item_Open
'* Arguments:
'* Description:  Upon opening, set the History Log to list opening
'*          information. Store the initial values of certain fields
'*          for use in later functions.
'*************************************************************************
Sub Item_Open()
Dim MyPage
Dim Resolved

Ticket_Resolved = False
If (Item.UserProperties.Find("Flag").Value = "Opened") Then
    Item.UserProperties.Find("History Text").Value = Chr(164) & _
        " Ticket Received on " & Item.UserProperties.Find("Received Date").Value
```

```
        If (Item.UserProperties.Find("Description").Value <> "") Then
            Item.UserProperties.Find("History Text").Value = Chr(164) & _
                " User Description of Problem - " & _
                Item.UserProperties.Find("Description").Value & Chr(10) & _
                Item.UserProperties.Find("History Text").Value
Else
            Item.UserProperties.Find("History Text").Value = Chr(164) & _
                " No User Description of Problem" & Chr(10) & _
                Item.UserProperties.Find("History Text").Value
End If
Item.UserProperties.Find("Flag").Value = "Done"
Item.Status = 0
End If
```

If the Item Is Resolved, Lock the Controls on the Form

When the Help Desk technician clicks the **Resolve Problem** button on the Assigned
Help Task form, the status of the item is set to 2, meaning the request is resolved. If
the item is resolved, many of the controls on the Assigned Help Task form are locked
so they cannot be changed. Notice in the following code example that the **Ticket** page
must first be referenced with the
`Item.GetInspector.ModifiedFormPages.Add("Ticket")` statement before
controls on the page can be referenced.

```
Item_Open    (continued)
    Resolved = Item.Status

    ' Comment this code out if you don't want to lock all values for the
    ' fields when the task is "Resolved".
    If (Resolved = 2) Then              ' 2 = Closed.
        Set MyPage = Item.GetInspector.ModifiedFormPages.Add("Ticket")
        MyPage.Controls("Status").Locked = True
        MyPage.Controls("Priority").Locked = True
        MyPage.Controls("CompletePercent").Locked = True
        MyPage.Controls("NewLogEntry").Locked = True
        MyPage.Controls("TechnicianName").Locked = True
    End If
```

Set Variables to Store the Initial Information

The Item_Open event stores the original values of the Task Priority, PercentComplete,
and Status fields. If these values change, a log entry is made in the History Text field
of the form when the user clicks the **Save and Close** button on the Assigned Help
Task form. The process of making a log entry in the History Text field is covered in
more detail in "The Item_Write Event" later in this chapter.

```
Item_Open    (continued)
' Sets variables to store the initial information.
    Orig_Priority = Item.UserProperties.Find("Task Priority").Value
    Orig_Complete = Item.PercentComplete
    Orig_Status = Item.Status
End Sub
```

The PropertyChange Event

The PropertyChange event occurs when a change is made to a standard property of an item. For example, the **Status** and **PercentComplete** properties are standard properties of a task. The PropertyChange event for the Assigned Help Task form, as shown in the following example, checks to see whether the PercentComplete or Status fields have been changed. If they have been changed, the Property_Changed field value is set to **True**. Then if the PercentComplete field value is changed, the Set_Complete_Changed procedure is called. If the Status field value is changed, the Set_Status_Changed procedure is called.

When the value of a standard field is changed, the name of the changed field is passed to the PropertyChange event. As shown in this example, you can then use the **Select Case** statement to determine the field that has been changed and to call procedures based on the field that is passed to the event.

```
'***********************************************************************
'* Function:  Item_PropertyChange
'* Arguments:
'* Description:  Checks whether any non-user defined task fields
'*        have changed.
'***********************************************************************
Sub Item_PropertyChange(ByVal MyProperty)      ' Checks if Status or
                                               ' % complete changed.

    Property_Changed = True

    Select Case MyProperty
       Case "PercentComplete"
          Call Set_Complete_Changed()
       Case "Status"
          Call Set_Status_Changed()
       Case Else
          Property_Changed = False      ' If it wasn't changed, set
    End Select                          ' flag to False.
End Sub
```

The Set_Status_Changed Procedure

As shown in the following code example, the Set_Status_Changed procedure compares the value of the original Status field value against the current Status field value. If the values are different, the Status_Changed variable is set to **True**. In addition, if the Status field value is 2, then the PercentComplete field value is automatically set to 100 when the status is changed to complete.

```
Sub Set_Status_Changed()
    Dim x        ' Temp variable.
    Dim y        ' Temp variable.

x = Orig_Status
y = Item.Status

Status_Changed = (x <> y)
If (y = 2) Then
Item.PercentComplete = "100"
End If
End Sub
```

The CustomPropertyChange Event

The CustomPropertyChange event is used to check whether custom field values have changed. As shown in the following example, if the values of the Task Priority or Complete Percent fields are changed, the Item_Change flag is set to **True** and the respective procedures are called based on the field that is passed as an argument to the CustomPropertyChange event.

```
'*****************************************************************
'* Function:  Item_CustomPropertyChange()
'* Arguments:  MyProperty - String
'* Description:  Checks whether any user-defined fields have changed.
'*        Only Task Priority and Complete Percent are affected.
'*****************************************************************
Sub Item_CustomPropertyChange(ByVal MyProperty)
' This is just the event handler, all code should be elsewhere.
Item_Changed=True      ' Initially sets the Changed flag.
Select Case MyProperty
Case "Complete Percent"
Call Set_Complete_Changed()
Case "Task Priority"
Call Set_Priority_Changed()
Case Else
        Item_Changed=False          ' If nothing changes, set flag
    End Select                      ' as False.
End Sub
```

The Set_Priority_Changed Procedure

The Set_Priority_Changed procedure is called from the Item_CustomPropertyChange procedure. The Set_Priority_Changed procedure compares the original value of the field against the new value and sets the value of the Priority_Changed flag based on the results. The Priority_Changed flag is then used in the Write event to determine if the field value is written to the History Log of the Assigned Help Task item.

```
Sub Set_Priority_Changed()
' If the user changes the value of priority,
' flag it as dirty and to be logged.
Dim x          ' Temp variable.
Dim y          ' Temp variable.

x = Orig_Priority
y = Item.UserProperties.Find("Task Priority").Value
' The following statement...
Priority_Changed = (x <> y)

' ...is equivalent to the next five lines of code:
' If x <> y Then
'     Priority_Changed = True
' Else
'     Priority_Changed = False
' End If
End Sub
```

The Item_Write Event

The Item_Write event is triggered when the technician clicks the **Save and Close** button on the Assigned Help Task form. The Item_Write event checks the values of the Item_Changed and Property_Changed flags. Based on the values that changed in the item, it then writes the values to the History Text field of the Assigned Help Task item. The code in the Item_Write event also converts the Status field value into a text version for the History Text field.

```
'****************************************************************************
'* Function:  Item_Write()
'* Arguments:
'* Description:  Writes all changed fields into the History Log.
'****************************************************************************
Sub Item_Write()
Dim Priority_Conversion

    ' If the status, priority, %complete, or severity changed,
    ' enter these into the log.
    If (Item_Changed or Property_Changed) Then
       LogEntry = ""                    ' Clear the initial LogEntry.
```

```
If (Priority_Changed) Then
   If LogEntry <> "" Then
      LogEntry = LogEntry & ", "    ' Commas in LogEntry after each entry.
   End If

   ' Assign the Task Priority value.
   Select Case Item.UserProperties.Find("Task Priority").Value
      Case "Normal"   ' To display the default Importance icon upon save.
         Item.Importance = 1
      Case Else
         Item.Importance = 2
   End Select

   LogEntry = LogEntry & "Priority Changed to " & _
      Item.UserProperties.Find("Task Priority").Value
   Orig_Priority = Item.UserProperties.Find("Task Priority"").Value
   Priority_Changed = False
End If

If (Complete_Changed) Then      ' Check %Complete.
   If LogEntry <> "" Then
      LogEntry = LogEntry & ", "
   End If
   LogEntry = LogEntry & "%Complete changed to " & _
      (Item.PercentComplete) & "%"
   Orig_Complete = Item.PercentComplete
   Complete_Changed = False
End If

If (Status_Changed) Then
   If LogEntry <> "" Then
      LogEntry = LogEntry & ", "
   End If

   If (Orig_Status = 2) Then
      Item.UserProperties.Find("Close Date").Value = "None"
   End If

' Convert the enumerated value of Status into a text
' representation (for the History Log).
Select Case Item.Status
   Case 0
      Status_Conversion = "Not Started"
   Case 1
      Status_Conversion = "In Progress"
   Case 2
      Status_Conversion = "Completed"
   Case 3
      Status_Conversion = "Waiting on Someone Else"
   Case 4
      Status_Conversion = "Deferred"
End Select
```

```
            LogEntry = LogEntry & "Status Changed to " & Status_Conversion

            Orig_Status = Item.Status
            Status_Changed = False
        End If


        MailEntryLog = ""

        If (SentMail_Flag) Then    ' If resolution mail was sent, report in log.
            MailEntryLog = "Resolution mail sent to user on " & Now() & _
                Chr(13) & Chr(10)
            SentMail_Flag = False
        End If

        ' Write History Log.
        HistoryLog = Item.UserProperties.Find("History Text").Value
        NewHistoryLog = Now() & ": " & _
            Application.GetNameSpace("MAPI").CurrentUser & " - " & LogEntry
        NewHistoryLog = Chr(164) & " " & NewHistoryLog & Chr(10)
        Item.UserProperties.Find("History Text").Value = _
            MailEntryLog & NewHistoryLog & HistoryLog

        If (Ticket_Resolved) Then        ' When ticket is resolved.
            Item.UserProperties.Find("History Text").Value = Chr(164) & _
                " Ticket closed on " & Now() & Chr(10) & _
                Item.UserProperties.Find("History Text").Value
            Ticket_Resolved = False
        End If

        Item_Changed = False
    End If
End Sub
```

Create a Correspondence Mail Item

If a technician wants to send mail to the user, he can click the **Send Mail to User** button to open the Correspondence Mail form, as shown in Figure 11.18. The Correspondence Mail form is a hidden Message form that is published in the Assigned Help Tasks folder forms library.

Figure 11.18   The Correspondence Mail form

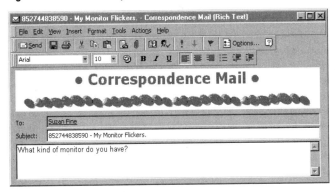

Important   You can publish different types of forms—such as Message, Post, Task, or Appointment—in the same folder forms library. For example, the Assigned Help Tasks folder forms library contains a Message form, a Post form, and a Task form.

When the technician clicks the **Send Mail to User** button, he triggers the SendCorrespondence_Click procedure. This procedure demonstrates several very important techniques that are well worth adding to your bag of tricks. For example, this procedure demonstrates how to:

- Use the `Item.Parent` statement to set the parent folder of the item as the active folder.
- Use the **EntryID** and **StoreID** properties to identify the Assigned Help Task item.
- Use the **GetItemFromID** method to write information from the Correspondence Mail item to the Assigned Help Task item.

Use the Item.Parent Statement to Identify the Assigned Help Tasks Folder

The SendButton_Click procedure of the Assigned Help Task form shows that the **Parent** property of the item is used to return the name of the parent folder of the active folder. Using the `Item.Parent` statement often provides a handy way to set the folder associated with the item as the active folder.

```
'************************************************************************
'* Procedure:  SendButton_Click
'* Arguments:
'* Description:  Sends mail to end user. Calls the Correspondence
'*       Mail item and populates with the necessary fields,
'*       then displays the form. EntryID and StoreID contain
'*       address of the Assigned Help Task item.
'************************************************************************
Sub SendButton_Click
    ' Stick the Ticket ID into a native field so that it can be "Found"
    ' by the mail form.
    Item.Save
    Set AssignedFolder = Item.Parent
```

Use the EntryID and StoreID Properties to Identify the Assigned Help Task Item

After the Assigned Help Task folder is set as the active folder, a Correspondence Mail item is created and several of the field values from the Assigned Help Task item are copied to the Correspondence Mail item, as shown in the following example.

The SendButton_Click procedure demonstrates how the **EntryID** and **StoreID** properties provide a way to write values between forms in a non-response situation. For example, after the technician opens the Correspondence Mail form and sends a Correspondence Mail item, information from the Correspondence Mail item is written into the History Text field of the Assigned Help Task item. To identify the Assigned Help Task item that the Correspondence Mail form was opened from, the **EntryID** and **StoreID** property values of the Assigned Help Task item are copied to the Correspondence Mail item. After the necessary values are copied from the Assigned Help Task item to the Correspondence Mail item, the item is displayed.

```
Sub SendButton_Click     (continued)
    Set CorrespondenceItem = AssignedFolder.Items.Add("IPM.Note.Correspondence Mail")
    CorrespondenceItem.To = Item.UserProperties.Find("From User").Value
    CorrespondenceItem.Subject = Item.Subject
    Item.Role = Item.UserProperties.Find("Ticket ID").Value
    CorrespondenceItem.UserProperties.Find("AssignedEntryID").Value = _
        Item.EntryID
```

```
        CorrespondenceItem.UserProperties.Find("AssignedStoreID").Value = _
            Item.Parent.StoreID
        CorrespondenceItem.UserProperties.Find("Ticket ID").Value = _
            Item.UserProperties.Find("Ticket ID").Value
        CorrespondenceItem.Display
End Sub
```

Use the GetItemFromID Method to Write Information from the Correspondence Item to the Assigned Help Task Item

When a Correspondence Mail item is sent, a log entry is written to the History Text field in the Assigned Help Task form. To make this happen, code is added to the Item_Send procedure of the Correspondence Mail form. Remember that the Send_Correspondence_Click procedure copied the **EntryID** and the **StoreID** property values to the Correspondence Mail item. The Item_Send procedure, as shown in the following example, uses the values as arguments in the following statement to return a pointer to the Assigned Help Task item.

```
Set MyItem = MyNameSpace.GetItemFromID(TaskItemID,TaskStoreID)


'*********************************************************************
'* Procedure:  Item_Send()
'* Description:  On Send, find the task that called it and place the body
'*        of the message into the History Log.
'*********************************************************************
Function Item_Send()
        TaskItemID = Item.UserProperties.Find("AssignedEntryID").Value
        TaskStoreID = Item.UserProperties.Find("AssignedStoreID").Value
        Set MyNameSpace = Application.GetNameSpace("MAPI")
        Set MyItem = MyNameSpace.GetItemFromID(TaskItemID,TaskStoreID)
        ' Store message and write it into the log.
        History = MyItem.UserProperties.Find("History Text").Value
        If (Item.Body <> "") Then
            MyItem.UserProperties.Find("History Text").Value = _
                Chr(164) & " " & Now() & ": " & _
                Application.GetNameSpace("MAPI").CurrentUser & _
                " - Correspondence Mail sent to User - " & Item.Body & _
                Chr(13) & Chr(10) & History
            MyItem.Save
            MyItem.Display
        End If
End Function
```

Create a Task Discussion Item

The Discussion item portion of the Help Desk application provides a good example of how you can use the **Form Action Properties** dialog box in conjunction with Microsoft Visual Basic Scripting Edition to create a customized response item. In the Assigned Help Task form, the Discussion response action is defined on the **Form Action Properties** dialog box. However, the action is started by the **Start Discussion** button, as shown in Figure 11.19, that triggers a procedure that executes the action.

Figure 11.19   The Start Discussion button triggers the Discussion action.

└ The technician clicks to create a Task Discussion item.

In this section, we'll cover three techniques for creating custom responses. We'll cover how to:

- Attach an action defined in the **Form Action Properties** dialog box of the form to a CommandButton control.

- Use the Item_CustomAction event to set properties for a response item.

- Combine posts and tasks in a folder view. In the Assigned Help Tasks folder, Assigned Help Task items (tasks) and Task Discussion items (posts) are combined in a view in this folder.

Attach a Defined Action to a Command Button

One way to create custom actions for a form is to define the action in the **Form Action Properties** dialog box. Using the **Form Actions Properties** dialog box minimizes the amount of code you need to add to the form to create the Task Discussion response item and provides a quick way to create a custom response. The properties for the Discussion action are set in the **Form Action Properties** dialog box, as shown in Figure 11.20.

▶ **To view the properties for the Discussion action**

1   While the Assigned Help Task form is in Design mode, click the **Actions** tab.

2   Double-click the **Discussion** cell.

Figure 11.20   The Form Action Properties dialog box for the Discussion action

The **Show action on** check box is cleared.

Specifies an attachment to the Assigned Help Task item to appear in the message box of the Task Discussion item.

Notice two things about the properties set for the Discussion action. First, the properties specify that an attachment to the original message is included. This means that a shortcut to the Assigned Help Task item appears in the message box of the Task Discussion form. Second, the **Show action on** check box is cleared, so no action button appears on the form. Instead, the **Start Discussion** button is used to initiate the response.

Add a Command Button to the Form and Create a Procedure to Trigger the Action Defined in the Form Action Properties Dialog Box

To trigger the Discussion action, the **Start Discussion** button is added to the form. As shown in this example, a procedure is created for the Discussion_Click procedure that executes the Discussion action defined in the **Form Action Properties** dialog box for the Assigned Help Task form.

```
'*******************************************************************
'* Procedure:  Discussion_Click
'* Arguments:
'* Description:  Starts a discussion on the problem or request in
'*       the Assigned Help Tasks folder.
'*******************************************************************
Sub Discussion_Click
   Item.Save
   Item.Actions("Discussion").Execute
End Sub
```

Set Properties on the Response Item

Defining a response action in the **Form Action Properties** dialog box is fast and easy, but there are many properties, such as the message text of the response item, that you must set using a different method. To do this, you use the Item_CustomAction event procedure. The Item_CustomAction event occurs any time a custom action is triggered for the form. One important feature of the Item_CustomAction event is that the newly created response item object is passed to the Item_CustomAction event. As a result, you can use this object to set properties on the response item.

As shown in this example, the Task Discussion object, **MyResponse**, is passed to the Item_CustomAction procedure. The **Body** property of the item is then set and the item appears, as shown in Figure 11.21.

```
'*****************************************************************
'* Procedure:   Item_CustomAction
'* Arguments:
'* Description:  Executes when a custom action is executed.
'*****************************************************************
Function Item_CustomAction(ByVal MyAction, ByVal MyResponse)
    Select Case MyAction.Name
      Case "Discussion"
        MyResponse.Body = "For more information about this ticket, " _
          & "double-click the shortcut." & Chr(10)
        MyResponse.Display
    End Select
End Function
```

Figure 11.21   The Task Discussion item created by the Discussion action

The technician clicks **Post** to post the item to the Assigned Help Tasks folder.

The attachment to the Assigned Help Task item.

Combine Different Item Types in a View

With Outlook, you can combine a variety of item types in a folder, and then creatively organize them in a view. As shown in Figure 11.22, tasks and posts are combined in the By Discussion Topic view.

▶ **To switch to the By Discussion Topic view**

- In the Folder List, open the Assigned Help Tasks folder, and then click **By Discussion Topic** in the **Current View** drop-down list box.

Figure 11.22   The Discussion item (post) is posted as a response to the Assigned Help Task item (task).

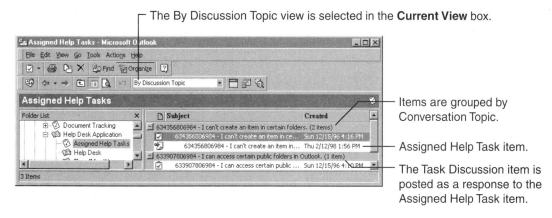

The By Discussion Topic view is selected in the **Current View** box.

Items are grouped by Conversation Topic.

Assigned Help Task item.

The Task Discussion item is posted as a response to the Assigned Help Task item.

The By Discussion Topic view groups items by Conversation Topic, and then sorts them by Conversation Index, resulting in a conversation thread, as shown earlier.

▶ **To view the properties for the By Discussion Topic view**

1 On the **View** menu, select **Current View**, and then click **Define Views**.

2 Click the **By Discussion Topic** view, click **Modify**, and then click **Sort**.

3 Close the dialog box.

Create the Resolve Item

The Resolve process in the Help Desk application serves several purposes. It enables the Help Desk technician to send a Resolved confirmation message to the user. It also automatically marks the task complete and draws a strikethrough line through the task in the Assigned Help Tasks folder.

In this section, we'll cover two techniques for creating custom responses, including how to:

- Automatically create a **MailItem** object.
- Set the standard properties of a task.

The Resolve_Click Procedure

When the technician clicks the **Resolve Problem** button, the Resolve_Click procedure in the Assigned Help Task form is triggered. This procedure opens a message box that tells the technician that a message will be sent to the user to indicate the problem is resolved. If the technician clicks **Yes**, the status of the Assigned Help Task item is set to 2 to indicate that the task is complete. In this case, the **Status** property is a standard property of the task. Rather than using the constants as defined in the Outlook Visual Basic Reference Help file, you must use the literal value as shown in the code example. Also notice that the Resolve_Click procedure calls the **Now** function to return the current date and time. This value is then written into the Close Date field. After the Resolve_Click procedure sets values for the Status, Percent Complete, and Close Date fields, it calls the SendMailToUser procedure.

```
'*******************************************************************
'* Procedure:  Resolve_Click
'* Arguments:
'* Description:  When the technician decides to mark the task
'*        as resolved, "Status" and "%Complete" are set to
'*        Closed and 100, respectively, the form is saved,
'*        and mail is sent to the user.
'*******************************************************************
Sub Resolve_Click
    Dim User_Item

    User_Item = MsgBox("This will send a mail message to the user indicating _
        that the problem is resolved." & Chr(13) & Chr(10) & Chr(13) & Chr(10) & _
        " Would you like to save and close this form?",4,"Completed")

    On Error Resume Next

    If User_Item = 6 Then    ' Item 6 is answer "Yes" to above message box question.
        Item.Status = 2
        Item.PercentComplete = "100"
        Item.UserProperties.Find("Close Date").Value = Now()
        Ticket_Resolved = True
        Call SendMailToUser()
        Item.Save
        Item.Close(0)
    End If
End Sub
```

The SendMailToUser Procedure

The SendMailToUser procedure creates a standard message. As such, you do not need to set a folder address. The procedure copies the value of the From User field of the Assigned Help Task item to the To field of the message. Then, the procedure sets the Subject and Message text of the item and sends the item to the user.

```
'*********************************************************************
'* Procedure:  SendMailToUser()
'* Arguments:
'* Description:  Upon exiting when resolved, this automatically sends
'*        a mail message to the end user, stating the problem is now
'*        resolved.
'*********************************************************************
Sub SendMailToUser()
   Set MyItem = Application.CreateItem(0)    ' Creates native Mail form.
   ' Populate the native fields.
   MyItem.To = Item.UserProperties.Find("From User").Value
   MyItem.Subject = "Problem - resolved"
   MyItem.Body = Item.Subject & " -- Your request was resolved by the _
      Help Desk at " & Now() & "."
   MyItem.Send
   SentMail_Flag = True
End Sub
```

The AddToHistory_Click Procedure

When the **Add to History** button is clicked, the AddToHistory_Click procedure adds the contents in the New History Log field to the History Text field, as shown in Figure 11.23.

Figure 11.23   The Add to History button on the Assigned Help Task form

This control is bound to the New Log Entry field.

The technician clicks to add the text in the New Log Entry field to the History Text field.

This control is bound to the History Text field.

As shown in this example, the AddToHistory_Click procedure adds the text in the New Log Entry field to the History Text field. The procedure then clears the contents of the New Log Entry field.

```
'*********************************************************************
'* Procedure:  AddToHistory_Click
'* Arguments:
'* Description:  Each time the "Add to History" button is clicked,
'*        the contents of the New Log Entry field is copied into
'*        the History Log and the New Log Entry field is cleared.
'*********************************************************************
Sub AddToHistory_Click
    Dim HistoryLog              ' Temp for the old History Log.
    Dim NewHistoryLog           ' Temp for the new History Log.
    Dim LogEntry                ' Temp for the new History Log entry line.

    ' If the New Log Entry field is not empty, we need to record the description
    ' in the log and clear out the description.
    If Len(Item.UserProperties.Find("New Log Entry").Value) > 0 Then
        HistoryLog = Item.UserProperties.Find("History Text").Value
        NewHistoryLog = Now() & ": " & _
            Application.GetNameSpace("MAPI").CurrentUser & " - " & _
            Item.UserProperties.Find("New Log Entry").Value
        NewHistoryLog = NewHistoryLog & Chr(13) & Chr(10)
        Item.UserProperties.Find("History Text").Value = _
            Chr(164) & " " & NewHistoryLog & HistoryLog
        Item.UserProperties.Find("New Log Entry").Value = ""
    End If
End Sub
```

A Suggested Enhancement

Although not covered in this chapter, a logical enhancement to this application is to create an Appointment folder in the Help Desk Application folder to make it possible for the Help Desk administrator, technicians, and managers to schedule, organize, and track Help Desk appointments. To create this enhancement, you can implement many of the techniques covered in this chapter.

The Document Tracking Application

In This Chapter

Overview of the Document Tracking Application   430

Setting Up the Document Tracking Application   436

Testing the Document Tracking Application   443

The Document Tracking Form   445

The Document Tracking Database   471

Document Tracking Folder Views   472

Releasing the Document Tracking Application   474

The Document Tracking application provides a good example of how you can build Microsoft Outlook applications to streamline a process, enhance group collaboration, and facilitate tracking of information. In most organizations, the process of writing, editing, and releasing marketing materials is a group activity that involves many different phases. For example, in some organizations, including Microsoft, after a writer finishes a document, he or she submits it to a production manager. The production manager is then responsible for assigning tasks such as editing, copy editing, legal approval, part number assignment, Hypertext Markup Language (HTML) conversion, virus checking, and final posting of the document.

The Document Tracking application described in this chapter is used not only to automate the assignment of tasks, but also to track the progress of a document as it moves through the approval and production process. In addition, the Document Tracking application provides a user-friendly and mail-enabled front end to a Microsoft Access 97 database. When a Document Tracking item is saved in the Document Tracking folder, the information in the item is written to a Microsoft Access database. The database can then be used for generating queries and monthly reports.

This chapter covers how to:

- Modify a standard Task form.
- Create Help for a control.
- Build a small-scale application that can be used by a specific workgroup.
- Use Microsoft Visual Basic Scripting Edition (VBScript) to create messages and provide a shortcut to the Document Tracking item in the message.
- Create a Microsoft Access database record when an item is saved in a folder.
- Find the record of an item in a Microsoft Access database and automatically update the record for the user.

Overview of the Document Tracking Application

The Document Tracking application provides an easy way to submit a document for editing, legal approval, virus checking, and posting. In addition, the Document Tracking application streamlines the process of assigning tasks for the production manager. For example, after a Document Approval item is submitted to the Document Tracking folder, the production manager can click the **Send Edit Request** button on the Document Tracking form to send a task request to an editor. The editor can then use the Document Tracking form to open the submitted document and to indicate he or she has finished the edit. Along the way, the production manager can easily scan the Document Tracking folder to get an overview of the document's progress. Perhaps equally important, each time a change is made to a Document Tracking item, the information in the item is automatically updated in the Microsoft Access Document Tracking database. In this way, production managers can always produce up-to-date status reports from the database.

To demonstrate how the Document Tracking application works, the rest of this section goes through the process of using the Document Tracking application to submit, edit, approve, and post a document.

A user opens the Marketing Handoff form, which then opens the Document Tracking form.   In this chapter, you can assume that the Document Tracking application is used by a specific group in an organization, rather than an entire organization, so the Marketing Handoff form is installed in the Personal Forms Library. To open the form, the user selects **New** on the **File** menu, then clicks **Choose Form**, and then clicks the Marketing Handoff form in the Personal Forms Library.

The Marketing Handoff form is never visible to the user, however. In fact, the sole purpose of the Marketing Handoff form is to set the Document Tracking folder as the active folder, and then create and show a Document Tracking item. The Marketing Handoff form is then closed. The invisible Marketing Handoff form is necessary because if you were to open a Document Tracking form from the Personal Forms Library, and then attempt to save the Document Tracking item, the item would be saved in the active folder, which quite often is the Inbox. As a workaround to this problem, code is added to the Item_Open procedure of the Marketing Handoff form to accomplish the task of setting the Document Tracking folder as the active folder, and then creating and showing a Document Tracking item, as shown in Figure 12.1.

Figure 12.1   The Document Tracking form

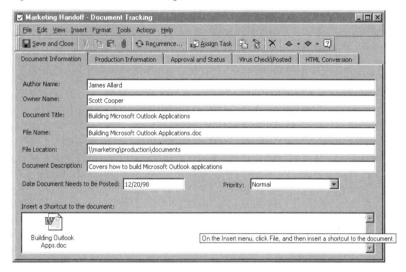

The user clicks the Save and Close button on the Document Tracking form.   After the user fills in the Document Tracking form, he or she clicks the **Save and Close** button on the form. This causes three things to happen:

* A record is created for the item in the Document Tracking database, as shown in Figure 12.2.

Figure 12.2   The Tracking Information table contains records of Document Tracking items.

┌ The information in the item is written to a database record.

- The Document Tracking item is saved in the Document Tracking folder, as shown in Figure 12.3.

Figure 12.3   The Document Tracking item is saved in the Document Tracking folder.

⌐ The item is saved in the Document Tracking folder.

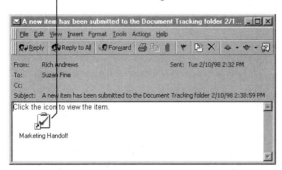

- A procedure in the Document Tracking form creates a notification message and sends it to the production manager. A shortcut to the Document Tracking item is included in the notification message, as shown in Figure 12.4.

Figure 12.4   The notification message that is sent when an item is submitted in the Document Tracking folder

⌐ The production manager double-clicks the icon to open the
  Document Tracking item in the Document Tracking folder.

The production manager opens the item.   He or she starts the production and approval process by assigning tasks to various people in the organization. To assign tasks, the production manager clicks one of the Send Request buttons on the **Approval and Status** page of the Document Tracking form, as shown in Figure 12.5.

Figure 12.5   The Approval and Status page of the Document Tracking form

└─ The production manager clicks one of the Sent Request buttons to create and send a task request.

For example, when the **Send Edit Request** button is clicked, a message is automatically created that includes a shortcut to the Document Tracking item, as shown in Figure 12.6.

Figure 12.6   The Edit Request item that is automatically created when the Send Edit Request button is clicked

A shortcut to the Document Tracking item is inserted in the message box of the Edit Request item.

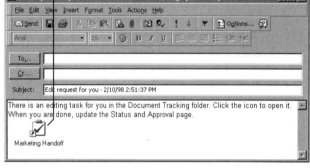

When the message arrives in the editor's Inbox, he or she double-clicks the Task icon in the message box to open the item in the Document Tracking folder. The editor can then double-click the linked document to open and edit it. When the editor finishes editing the document, he or she can update the **Edited** options on the **Approval and Status** page, as shown in Figure 12.7.

Figure 12.7   Edited options are updated on the Approval and Status page of the Document Tracking form.

The editor updates the **Edited** options and enters his e-mail name in the **Edit Completed By** text box.

When the editor saves the item, the record is automatically updated in the Document Tracking database.

When all the necessary tasks are completed and the item is posted on the server, the production manager clicks **Completed** in the **Production Status** box on the Document Tracking form. He or she then saves the item in the Document Tracking folder. The item is updated in the database and a line appears through the item in the Document Tracking folder to indicate that the task is complete.

Setting Up the Document Tracking Application

Before you can run the Document Tracking application, there are a few tasks you must perform to customize the application for your environment. This section explains these tasks.

Copying the Document Tracking Folder

These instructions assume that you have added the Building Microsoft Outlook 98 Applications personal folder (.pst) file to your Microsoft Exchange Server system. If you haven't, see "Add the Personal Folder (.pst) File to Outlook" in the Introduction at the beginning of this book.

To make it possible for a variety of people to easily submit, collaborate upon, and track the progress of Document Tracking items, you must make the Document Tracking folder publicly available. To do this, you copy it from the Building Microsoft Outlook 98 Applications personal folder (.pst) to Public Folders.

Note   If you don't have permission to copy the folder to Public Folders, see your administrator.

First, create your destination folder. Next, copy the Document Tracking folder to your destination folder.

▶ **Create the Marketing folder**

1   In the Folder List, right-click on **All Public Folders** in the Public Folders directory.

2   Select **New Folder**.

3   In the **Name** text box, type **Marketing**, and then click **OK**.

▶ **To copy the Document Tracking folder**

1   In the Folder List, open the **Building Microsoft Outlook 98 Applications** folder.

2   Open the **Beyond the Basics** folder.

3   Right-click the **Document Tracking** folder, and then click **Copy "Document Tracking"** on the shortcut menu.

4   In the **Copy the selected folder to the folder** box, open the **Public Folders** folder, and then double-click the folder you want to copy the Document Tracking folder to.

Restricting Access to the Folder

To prevent users from opening the folder while you test or modify it, you need to restrict access to it.

▶ To restrict access to the Document Tracking folder

1   In the Folder List, right-click the **Document Tracking** folder you just added to Public Folders, and then click **Properties** on the shortcut menu.

2   Click the **Administration** page.

3   Click **Owners only**, and then click **OK**.

Opening and Modifying the Marketing Handoff Form

The Marketing Handoff form is the form that you publish in the Personal Forms Library of those people who use the application. The Marketing Handoff form does not appear when opened from the Personal Forms Library. Instead, its purpose is to set the Document Tracking folder as the active folder, and then to create a Document Tracking item from that folder.

To modify the Marketing Handoff form, you modify its Open_Click procedure so that the specified Document Tracking folder address matches the folder address of the Document Tracking folder you just added to Public Folders.

▶ To open the Marketing Handoff form

1   In the Folder List, right-click the **Document Tracking** folder you just created, and then click **Properties** on the shortcut menu.

2   Click the **Forms** page.

3   Click **Manage**.

4   In the **Forms** list box on the right, click **Marketing Handoff**, and then click **Properties**.

5   Clear the **Hidden** check box, and then close all the dialog boxes.

6   Hold down the SHIFT key, and then click **New Marketing Handoff** on the **Actions** menu.

   When you hold down SHIFT while opening a form, Visual Basic Scripting Edition code in the form is prevented from executing.

Changing the Folder Address in the Item_Open Procedure

Now you can switch to Design mode and change the address that is specified for the Document Tracking folder in the Item_Open procedure of the Marketing Handoff form.

▶ **To modify the Item_Open procedure**

1 On the **Tools** menu of the Marketing Handoff form, select **Forms**, and then click **Design Outlook Form**.

2 On the **Form Design** toolbar, click **View Code**.

3 Change the code in the Item_Open procedure to set the active folder to the Document Tracking folder address.

For example, assume you copied the Document Tracking folder to the Public Folders\All Public Folders\Marketing folder. You would then modify the Item_Open procedure as shown in this example.

```
Function Item_Open()
    Set MyNameSpace = Application.GetNameSpace("MAPI")
    Set PublicFolders = MyNameSpace.Folders("Public Folders")
    Set AllPublicFolders = PublicFolders.Folders("All Public Folders")
    Set MarketingFolder = AllPublicFolders.Folders("Marketing")    Set
DocumentTrackingFolder = _
        AllPublicFolders.Folders("Document Tracking")
    Set MyItem = _
        DocumentTrackingFolder.Items.Add("IPM.Task.Document Tracking")
    MyItem.Display
    Item.Close 1
End Function
```

4 After you change the code in the Item_Open procedure, click **Run This Form** on the **Form** menu to make sure that you have no syntax errors.

5 Close Run mode. Click **No** in the **Do you want to save changes?** message box.

Making a Backup Copy of the Marketing Handoff Form

At this point, you make a backup copy of the Marketing Handoff form. When you're ready to release the application, you can send a copy of this form to users so they can install it in their Personal Forms Library.

▶ **To make a backup copy of the Marketing Handoff form**

1 With the form open, click **Save As** on the **File** menu.

2 In the **Save In** box, select the default Outlook template folder, such as C:\Program Files\Microsoft Office\Templates.

3 In the **File name** text box, type **Marketing Handoff**.

4 In the **Save as type** text box, select **Outlook Template (.oft)**.

5 Click **Save**.

▶ **To open your backup copy of a form**

1 Select **New** on the **File** menu, and then click **Choose Form**.

2 Click **Templates in File System** in the **Look In** drop-down list box, and then click on the form you'd like to open.

Publishing the Marketing Handoff Form

Now you can publish the Marketing Handoff form to your Personal Forms Library so that you can test the application in your environment.

▶ **To publish the Marketing Handoff form in the Personal Forms Library**

1 On the **Tools** menu, select **Forms**, and then click **Publish Form As**.

2 Select **Personal Forms Library** from the **Look In** drop-down list box.

3 Type **Marketing Handoff** in the **Display name** text box and the **Form name** text box.

4 Click **Publish** to publish the form to the Personal Forms Library.

5 Close the Marketing Handoff form.

Hiding the Marketing Handoff Form

Now you need to reset the **Hidden** property for the Marketing Handoff form in the forms library of the Document Tracking folder.

▶ **To hide the Marketing Handoff form**

1 In the Folder List, right-click the **Document Tracking** folder, and then click **Properties** on the shortcut menu.

2 Click the **Forms** page.

3 Click **Manage**.

4 In the **Forms** list box on the right, click **Marketing Handoff**, and then click **Properties**.

5 Select the **Hidden** check box, and then close all the dialog boxes.

Copying the Document Tracking Database

Next, you need to copy the Document Tracking database to a new location. The Document Tracking database is attached in an item in the ReadMe and .mdb subfolder in the Document Tracking folder.

The code in the Document Tracking form is currently set up to write to a database called Document Tracking in C:\My Documents. If you want to test the application without modifying the code in the Document Tracking form, save the database to C:\My Documents.

Important   The Document Tracking application only works if a user has Microsoft Office 97 (not stand-alone Outlook) installed. In addition, the user must install the "Data Access Objects for Visual Basic" during Setup. To install the "Data Access Objects for Visual Basic," run Office 97 Setup, select the **Data Access** option, and then click **Change Option**. Under **Options**, select **Data Access Objects for Visual Basic**, and then click **OK**.

▶ To copy the Document Tracking database

1   In the Folder List, go to the **Marketing** folder in **All Public Folders**, and then open the **ReadMe** and **.mdb** folders in the **Document Tracking** folder.

2   Double-click the **ReadMe** item.

3   Right-click the **Document Tracking.mdb** icon, and then click **Save As** on the shortcut menu.

4   From the **Save in** drop-down list box, click the folder to which you would like to save the Document Tracking database.

   If you don't want to modify the code while you test the application, save the Document Tracking item in C:\My Documents. Later, when you're sure the application is working as expected, you can move the database to a server and then modify the code in the Document Tracking item so that it points to the database on the server.

5   Click **Save**.

6   Close the ReadMe window.

Opening and Modifying the Document Tracking Form

The Document Tracking form has three procedures that you must modify. These are the SendNotification procedure, the AddNewDatabaseRecord procedure, and the UpdateDatabaseRecord procedure. For the SendNotification procedure, you specify your name as the person who is notified. For the AddNewDatabaseRecord and the UpdateDatabaseRecord procedures, you specify the path of the Document Tracking database that you just copied.

▶ To open the Document Tracking form

1   Select the **Document Tracking** folder from the **Marketing** folder in **All Public Folders**.

2   Hold down the SHIFT key, and then click **New Document Tracking** on the **Actions** menu. It's essential that you hold down the SHIFT key to prevent the VBScript code from executing.

3 On the Document Tracking form **Tools** menu, select **Forms**, and then click **Design This Form**.

4 On the **Form Design** toolbar, click **View Code**.

5 In the Script Editor window, locate the SendNotification procedure. It's the last procedure in the Script Editor.

Customizing the SendNotification Procedure

If you want to use this feature in the Document Tracking application, uncomment the code. Then replace "Your Name" in the RequestItem.To statement with your e-mail name. Later, when you're ready to release the application for general use, you can change the names to the names of production managers in your organization. For now, however, it's best to use just your name.

```
RequestItem.To = "Your Name"
```

The SendNotification procedure, as shown in the following code example, creates a message item, addresses it to the specified people, attaches a link to the Document Tracking item, and then sends the message. The SendNotification procedure is called from the Item_Closed event if the value of NewItemCreated is **True**.

```
'*******************************************************************
' Procedure: SendNotification
' Description: Called by Item_Close when the Document Tracking item is first
' submitted, this procedure sends a message to the production manager to
' notify him or her that a new item has been submitted in the folder.
'*******************************************************************

Sub SendNotification
    Set DocTrackItem = Application.ActiveInspector.CurrentItem
    DocTrackItem.Save
    Set RequestItem = Application.CreateItem(0)
    RequestItem.Subject = _
        "A new item has been submitted to the Document Tracking folder " & Now()
    RequestItem.Body = "Click the icon to view the item. " & Chr(13)
    RequestItem.To = "Jon Grande; Don Funk"
    Set MyAttachments = RequestItem.Attachments
    MyAttachments.Add DocTrackItem, 4
    RequestItem.Send
End Sub
```

After you change the code in the SendNotification procedure, click **Run This Form** on the **Form** menu to make sure you have no syntax errors.

Customizing the AddNewDatabaseRecord and the UpdateDatabaseRecord Procedures

The AddNewDatabaseRecord and UpdateDatabaseRecord procedures point to C:\My Documents\Document Tracking.mdb by default, as shown in this example:

```
Set MyDB = Dbe.Workspaces(0).OpenDatabase("C:\My Documents\Document Tracking.mdb")
```

If you saved the Document Tracking database somewhere other than C:\My Documents, you must change the path in the AddNewDatabaseRecord and UpdateDatabaseRecord procedures.

▶ **To modify the code in the Document Tracking form**

1 In the Script Editor window, find the AddNewDatabaseRecord procedure.

2 In the AddNewDatabaseRecord procedure, locate the following line of code, and then change it to point to the new database location.

```
Set MyDB = Dbe.Workspaces(0).OpenDatabase("C:\My Documents\" _
    & "Document Tracking.mdb")
```

For example, if the database is located in \\Marketing\Production, you modify the code as follows:

```
Set MyDB = Dbe.Workspaces(0).OpenDatabase("\\Marketing\Production\" _
    & "Document Tracking.mdb")
```

3 In the Script Editor window, locate the UpdateDatabaseRecord procedure, and then repeat Step 2 in the UpdateDatabaseRecord procedure.

4 In Design mode, click **RunThis Form** on the **Form** menu, to make sure there are no syntax errors.

5 Close the **Script Editor**.

Publishing the Document Tracking Form

Now you can publish the Document Tracking form to the forms library of the Document Tracking folder.

▶ **To publish the Document Tracking form**

1 On the **Tools** menu, select **Forms**, and then click **Publish Form As**.

2 Select **Outlook Folders** in the **Look In** drop-down list box, and then select the **Document Tracking** folder from **Marketing** folder in **All Public Folders**.

3 Click on **Document Tracking** in the list box, and then click **Publish**.

4 Close the Document Tracking form.

Testing the Document Tracking Application

You're now ready to test the Document Tracking application to make sure your changes work. To start, you open the Marketing Handoff form in the Personal Forms Library.

Creating a Document Tracking Item

To test the application, you open the Marketing Handoff form in the Personal Forms Library. You fill in the Document Tracking form that is opened by the Marketing Handoff form, and then click the **Save and Close** button. When you save the item, a record is automatically created in the Document Tracking database.

▶ **To create a Document Tracking item and database record**

1 In the Folder List, click **Inbox**. This is most often the active folder when a user opens the Marketing Handoff form.

2 On the **File** menu, select **New**, and then click **Choose Form**.

3 In the Personal Forms Library, double-click **Marketing Handoff**.

4 Fill in the options on the **Document Information** page.

5 In the **Insert a Shortcut to the document** message box, insert a shortcut by clicking **File** on the **Insert** menu.

6 Fill in the options on the **Production Information** page of the form.

7 On the toolbar, click **Save and Close**.

8 From the Windows taskbar, click **Start** and select **Programs**. Then click **Windows Explorer**.

9 Select the folder where the Document Tracking database is located, such as C:\My Documents.

10 In the list of items, double-click the **Document Tracking.mdb** icon to open the database.

11 On the **Tables** page, double-click the **Tracking Information** icon.

Notice that a record is created for the item you just saved in the Document Tracking folder. If it is not saved, because the database is read-only, then clear the **Read only** button in the **Properties** box of the **Document Tracking.mdb** file.

12 Close the Tracking Information table.

Updating a Document Tracking Item and Sending Requests

After a Document Tracking item is submitted, the production and approval process begins. To help understand how this works, you can open the notification message in your Inbox, double-click the Document Tracking icon in the message box of the notification message, and then send an Edit Request item. Then, update the **Production Status** option and save the item.

Note   If you didn't change the name in the SendNotification procedure to your e-mail name, a notification message will not appear in your Inbox. If you don't want to modify this procedure, you can simply open the saved Document Tracking item in the Document Tracking folder.

▶ To update the Document Tracking item and send task requests

1   In the Outlook Folder List, click **Inbox**.

2   Double-click the notification message in your Inbox, and then double-click the icon in the message box of the form. Click **Yes** in the message box.

3   On the Document Tracking form, click the **Approval and Status** page.

4   Click **Send Edit Request** at the bottom.

5   When the Message form appears, address it to yourself, and then click **Send**.

6   Click **In Progress** on the **Approval and Status** page.

7   On the toolbar, click **Save and Close**.

Testing the Edit Task Request

Now you can play the role of the editor in this production and approval process. You open the Edit Task Request item in your Inbox, and then double-click the linked Document Tracking item. You can then open the document in the Document Tracking item and update the **Approval and Status** page of the Document Tracking form.

▶ To test the Edit Task Request item

1   Click **Inbox** in the Outlook Folder List.

2   Double-click the Edit Request item you just sent.

3   Double-click the icon in the message box of the item. Click **Yes** in the message box.

4   When the Document Tracking item opens, double-click the shortcut to the document in the message box. If you are the editor, you can edit the document.

5   Close the document, and then click the **Approval and Status** page.

6   Under **Edited**, click **Yes, it has been edited**, and then type your name in the **Edit Completed By (e-mail name)** box.

7   On the toolbar, click **Save and Close**.

Checking the Database Record

When you make changes to a Document Tracking item and then save the item, the record for the Document Tracking item is automatically updated in the Document Tracking database. To make sure the record is properly updating, you can reopen the Tracking Information table and make sure your new changes are reflected in the database record.

▶ **To open the Tracking Information table**

1 From the Windows taskbar, click **Start** and select **Programs**. Then click **Windows Explorer**.

2 Click the folder where the Document Tracking database is located.

3 In the list of items, double-click the **Document Tracking** icon to open the database.

4 On the **Tables** page, double-click the **Tracking Information** icon.

5 Look at the **Edited** column heading.

   You can see that the changes you made to the Document Tracking item are reflected in the database record.

The Document Tracking Form

The Document Tracking form is based on the standard Task form. The Task form works well in the Document Tracking application because it makes it possible for users to easily submit and update an item in the folder by clicking the **Save and Close** button on the Document Tracking form. For example, with a Post form, when users open a submitted item, a **Post Reply** button appears on the form. Users can be confused about whether to click the **Post Reply** button on the form or click **Save** on the **File** menu. With the Task form, the **Save and Close** button appears when the form is in Compose mode and Read mode, so this confusion is eliminated.

Also, the Task form that the Document Tracking form is based on does not require a separate layout for composing and reading items, so there is less design work involved in creating the form. Finally, the Task form provides built-in task management features such as the **Status** property. For example, when **Completed** (which is bound to the Status field) is selected in the **Production Status** box on the Document Tracking item, and the item is saved, Outlook draws a line through the task to show it is complete.

This section discusses some of the design techniques and implementations of the Document Tracking form, including how to:

- Hide the standard **Task** page.
- Write values from the Document Tracking form to a Microsoft Access 97 or above database.
- Update values in the database when field values are changed in the Document Tracking item.
- Check if values exist in the fields. This is important because if you try to write a field value from a field that is empty, the procedure stops execution.

▶ **To open the Document Tracking form**

1   In the Folder List, click the **Document Tracking** folder in the **Marketing** folder in **All Public Folders**.

2   On the **Actions** menu, click **New Document Tracking**.

3   On the Document Tracking **Tools** menu, select **Forms,** and then click **Design This Form**.

The Task Page

For the Document Tracking form, the standard **Task** and **Detail** pages are hidden at run time. This is done because these standard pages cannot be sufficiently modified to suit the purposes of this application. For example, you can't add or remove controls from standard **Task** pages. As shown in Figure 12.8, the **Task** page label is in parentheses, indicating that it is not visible at run time.

▶ **To hide a page**

- Click the page, and then clear the **Display This Page** option on the **Form** menu.

Figure 12.8 The Task page is hidden at run time.

The **Task** page is hidden at run time.

Marketing Handoff is specified in the Subject field.
It also appears in the title bar of the form.

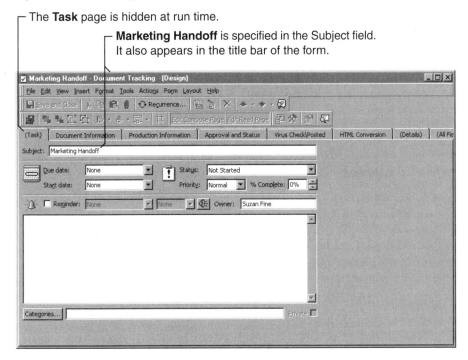

The Subject Field

Although the **Task** page is hidden at run time, the value of the Subject field, as shown in Figure 12.8, determines the text that appears in the title bar of the form. So the Subject field is set to "Marketing Handoff" to reflect the name the user clicks when opening the form in the **New Form** dialog box. The remainder of the text in the title bar of the form is determined by the text specified for the **Form Name** property of the form, when the form is published.

In addition, when a shortcut to a Document Tracking item is attached in an Edit Request item, the text under the shortcut is the **Subject** property value of the item. To set the value of the Subject field, "Document Tracking" is entered into the **Subject** text box on the **Task** page of the Document Tracking form.

The Document Information Page

The **Document Information** page, as shown in Figure 12.9, is the page that's filled in by the author of the document. This section doesn't cover how to add each field. Rather, it discusses how to add several different types of fields and controls, and then explains the properties for them.

Figure 12.9 The Document Information page

This section discusses the following techniques for the **Document Information** page:

- Using the **Field Chooser**
- Setting display properties
- Setting validation properties
- Working with Date data type fields
- Working with the Priority field
- Using the Message control
- Adding control TipText
- Setting tab order

Using the Field Chooser to Add Controls and Fields

For creating Text fields, you can save time by using the **Field Chooser** to create controls and fields. When you use the **Field Chooser** to create a field, Outlook automatically creates a control and label for the field. When you add the control to the form by dragging the field from the **Field Chooser**, the field is already bound to the control.

Setting Display Properties

In most cases, you want TextBox controls to resize when the form is resized. As a general rule, if the right border of the control is next to the right border of the form, you turn on the **Resize with form** option for the control. For the **Document Information** page, the **Resize with form** option is turned on for all controls on the **Document Information** page, with the exception of the DateDocumentNeedsToBe Posted control and the Label controls.

▶ **To set the Resize with form option**

1 Right-click the control you want to set display properties for, and then click **Properties** on the shortcut menu.

2 On the **Display** page, select the **Resize with form** check box.

Setting Validation Properties

For the **Document Information** page, the **A value is required for this field** option is turned on for the Author Name, Owner Name, Document Title, File Name, File Location, and Document Description fields. At run time, if a value is not entered in one of these fields, the user sees a message indicating that a field that requires a value is empty.

▶ **To set the A value is required for this field option**

1 Right-click the control you want to set validation properties for, and then click **Properties** on the shortcut menu.

2 On the **Validation** page, select the **A value is required for this field** check box.

Note The "None" value is automatically supplied as the initial value for fields with the Date/Time data type, so the **A value is required for this field** option is not available. For this form, no validation property is required for the Date Document Needs to Be Posted field.

Working with Date Data Type Fields

On the **Document Information** page, the controls are bound to Text fields, with the exception of the Message control, the Label controls, and the DateDocumentNeedsToBePosted control. The field type for the Date Document Needs to Be Posted field is a Date/Time data type. The format is mm/dd/yy.

Working with the Priority Field

The Priority field is a standard field of a Task item. By default, the Priority field is located on the **Task** page. However, for the Document Tracking form, the **Task** page is hidden at run time. So a standard Priority field is dragged from the **Field Chooser** to the **Document Information** page.

Using the Message Control

With Outlook Forms, shortcuts to files can only be inserted in the Message control. In addition, only one Message control can be used per **Compose** or **Read** page. For the Document Tracking form, the Message control on the **Task** page of the form is not used. Instead, a Message control is added to the **Document Information** page. At run time, the user inserts a shortcut to the document into the Message control on the **Document Information** page.

Adding TipText for Controls

For some controls, such as the Message control, you may want to provide TipText Help for controls, as shown in Figure 12.10. With control TipText, the TipText appears when the pointer is positioned over the control at run time. If you click **Run This Form** on the **Form** menu to switch to Run mode, you can see that TipText Help is provided for the AuthorName, OwnerName, and Message controls.

Figure 12.10   TipText for the Message control

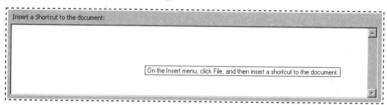

▶ **To create TipText Help**

1 Right-click the control, and then click **Advanced Properties** on the shortcut menu.

2 Click the **ControlTipText** cell to select it, and then type the text you want for the control TipText in the text box at the top of the window.

3 Close the **Advanced Properties** dialog box.

Setting Tab Order

When designing forms, it's usually best to set the tab order of a page before you move on to the next page by selecting **Tab Order** from the **Layout** menu. At design time, you can tab through all controls on the page. However, at run time, the user cannot tab to Label controls. Figure 12.11 shows the tab order for the controls on the **Document Information** page.

Figure 12.11   The tab order for the Document Information page

The Production Information Page

For the **Production Information** page, as shown in Figure 12.12, this section discusses several techniques, including how to:

- Make multi-line text boxes, such as **Document Summary**.

- Specify keywords.

- Create combo boxes, like the Type of Tool field.

- Create a unique Document ID.

- Enable or disable a control when a particular field, such as Database Record Created, is changed

- Automatically create a message when the **Send General Correspondence** command button is clicked.

Figure 12.12   The Production Information page

Locates the database record for the item.

Indicates if a database record exists for the item.

Document Summary

There are two things worth noting about the **Document Summary** text box. The **Multi-line** option is selected for this control, which allows users to type multiple lines of text in the control. In addition, the **Resize with form** option is selected, so the control automatically resizes when the user resizes the form.

▶ **To set the Multi-line and Resize with form options**

1   Right-click the control, and then click **Properties** on the shortcut menu.

2   On the **Display** page, select the **Resize with form** and **Multi-line** check boxes.

Keywords

In the **Keywords** box, users can type keywords that can be used in filters, searches, and queries to locate an item. For example, an administrator may want to filter all items in the Document Tracking folder that have the keyword "Outlook" in the Keywords field.

The Product, Platform, Type of Tool, and Target Audience Fields

The Product, Platform, Type of Tool, and Target Audience fields all share a common trait. Each is bound to a ComboBox control. As a result, you create these fields by first adding the ComboBox control from the **Control Toolbox**, and then binding the field to the control. This example explains how the Type of Tool ComboBox control is created and bound.

▶ **To add a ComboBox control and bind it to a field**

1   Drag a ComboBox control from the **Control Toolbox** to the form.

2   Right-click the ComboBox control, and then click **Properties** on the shortcut menu.

3   On the **Display** page, type **TypeofTool** in the **Name** field.

4   On the **Value** page, click **New**.

5   In the **Name** text box, type **Type of Tool**, and then click **OK**.

6   In the **Possible values** text box, type the values you want to appear in the **Type of Tool** list at run time. Separate the values with a semicolon, as shown in Figure 12.13.

Figure 12.13   The Value properties for the Type of Tool field

The Document ID Field

When a Document Tracking item is submitted, a unique Document ID is created for the Document Tracking item. The Document ID uniquely identifies the Document Tracking item, most specifically in the Document Tracking database. When an item is changed and when updates are made to the Document Tracking database, the Document ID is used to find the document record in the Document Tracking database. Updates can then be made to the record. Note that the Document ID field is bound to the DocumentID control. The **Read only** option is selected for the DocumentID control.

Creating the Unique Document ID

To create a unique Document ID for a Document Tracking item, much of the code is borrowed from the Help Desk application covered in Chapter 11, and then modified for the Document Tracking application. When the form is opened, the value of the Database Record Created field is evaluated. If the field value is "No," a unique Document ID is created for the Document Tracking item.

The following script-level variables are declared at the top of the Script Editor window for the procedures involved in creating the Document ID.

```
'****************************************************************
Dim UserName        ' Script-level variables used for the Document ID.
Dim Trimmed


'****************************************************************
'* Procedure: Item_Open()
'* Description: Check the value of the Database Record Created field.
'* If the value is "No", create a unique ID.
'****************************************************************
Sub Item_Open()
    Dim MyDate
    Dim NowID
    RequestButton = "False"
    If Item.UserProperties.Find("Database Record Created") = "No" Then

        ' If document is new.
        UserName = Application.GetNameSpace("MAPI").CurrentUser

        ' Trim the user name of spaces.
        Trimmed = TrimUserName(UserName)
```

```
    NowID = Now
    ' Get date as numbers only.
    MyDate = CreateDateAsNumber(NowID)

    ' Set the ticket ID for this item.
    DocumentID = MyDate & Trimmed

    Item.UserProperties.Find("Document ID").Value = DocumentID

  End If
End Sub
```

See Also   For more information about the TrimUserName or CreateDateAsNumber functions, see "Create a Unique Ticket ID for Each Item" in Chapter 11, "The Help Desk Application."

The Database Record Created Field

The value of the Database Record Created field is set to "Yes" when a database record is created for the Document Tracking item. The value of this field is evaluated during the Item_Write event. The Item_Write event is triggered when a user clicks the **Save and Close** button on the form. In addition, the Item_Write procedure is triggered when a user clicks a command button on the form to send a General Correspondence item or a Request item. In this case, the Item_Write event is triggered because the item must be saved before a shortcut to the item can be included in a message.

If the value of the Database Record Created field is "No," then the AddDatabaseRecord procedure is called, a new record is created, and the Database Record Created field is set to "Yes." Note that the initial value of the Database Record Created field is "No."

In the Item_Write procedure, if the value of the Database Record Created field is "Yes" and the ItemChanged variable is **True**, then the UpdateDatabaseRecord procedure is called. Note also that the DatabaseRecordCreated control, bound to the Database Record Created field, is read-only.

The Send General Correspondence Command Button

The **Send General Correspondence** command button makes it possible for anyone who is working with a Document Tracking item to a send a message to another user. For example, the production manager may want to send a message to a user to request a more realistic Date Document Needs to Be Posted date. Or an editor may want to send a message to the production manager to notify him or her of a change in the schedule. When the **Send General Correspondence** button is clicked, the item is created and displayed, as shown in Figure 12.14.

Figure 12.14   The message created when the Send General Correspondence button is clicked

A shortcut to the Document Tracking item is included
in the General Correspondence item.

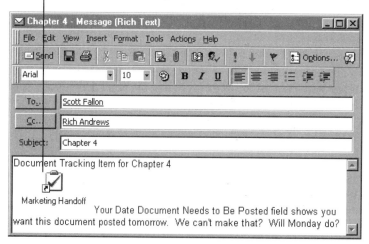

The SendGeneralCorrespondence_Click Procedure

To add a Click event for a command button, you type **Sub** in the Script Editor window, and then type the name of the CommandButton control followed by **_Click**. As shown in this example, the SendGeneralCorrespondence_Click procedure shows a message box that asks the user if they want to save the item. If the user clicks "Yes" in the message box, then the CorrespondenceMessageLink procedure is called. If the user clicks "No," the CorrespondenceMessage procedure is called.

```
'**********************************************************************
'* Procedure: SendGeneralCorrespondence
'* Description: Ask the user if they want to save the item. If Yes, the
'* item is saved, a database record is created, and a message with a shortcut
'* to the item is created. If No, a message is created.
'**********************************************************************
Sub SendGeneralCorrespondence_Click
    If Item.UserProperties.Find("Database Record Created") = "No" Then
        SaveItem = MsgBox("Do you want to save this item in the folder " _
            & "at this time?",3,"Save item")
        If SaveItem = 2 Then
            Exit Sub
        ElseIf SaveItem = 7 Then                ' If No, create message without shortcut.
            Call CorrespondenceMessage
        ElseIf SaveItem = 6 Then                ' If Yes, create message with shortcut.
            Call CorrespondenceMessageLink
        End If
    Else
        Call CorrespondenceMessageLink
    End If
End Sub
```

The CorrespondenceMessageLink Procedure

The CorrespondenceMessageLink procedure, as shown in this example, sets the
DocTrackItem object to the active item and then saves the item. It then creates a
shortcut to the Document Tracking item in the message box.

```
'**********************************************************************
'* Procedure: CorrespondenceMessageLink
'* Description: Creates a general message item with a shortcut to the
'* Document Tracking item.
'**********************************************************************
Sub CorrespondenceMessageLink
    Set DocTrackItem = Application.ActiveInspector.CurrentItem
    DocTrackItem.Save
    Set CorrespondenceItem = Application.CreateItem(0)
    DocTitle = Item.UserProperties.Find("Document Title").Value
    CorrespondenceItem.Subject = DocTitle
    CorrespondenceItem.Body = "Document Tracking Item for " & DocTitle & Chr(13)
    Set MyAttachments = CorrespondenceItem.Attachments
    MyAttachments.Add DocTrackItem, 4
    CorrespondenceItem.Display
End Sub
```

The Approval and Status Page

The **Approval and Status** page, as shown in Figure 12.15, is used by various members of the production team. For example, the production manager can click the Send Request buttons at the bottom of this page to send edit, copy edit, part number, or legal approval requests. When the requests are complete, the person who completes the request uses this page to update the status of the request and to enter his or her e-mail name. In addition, after the production manager sends out the various request items, he or she changes the **Production Status** option to **In Progress**. When the Document Tracking item is saved, the record is updated in the Document Tracking database.

Figure 12.15   The Approval and Status page of the Document Tracking form

Send Request buttons.

The Edited, Copy Edited, Part Number, and Approved By Legal Group Boxes

Setting properties for OptionButton controls can be tricky. First, you must add the OptionButton control to the form by dragging it from the **Control Toolbox**. You then bind the option buttons in the group to a common field. For example, each OptionButton control in the **Edited** group is bound to the Edited field. Remember, after you bind the OptionButton control to the field, you must change the **Value** property for the field. As shown in Figure 12.16, the **Value** property of the **Yes, it has been edited** option button is changed to **Yes, it has been edited**.

Figure 12.16   The Value properties set for the Yes, it has been edited option button

┌ The **Yes, it has been edited** option button is bound to the Edited field.

This text appears in views in the Document Tracking folder when the **Yes, it has been edited** option button is clicked.

Production Status

The **Production Status** box is actually the standard Status field. To add the Status field, you click the **All Tasks fields** field set in the **Field Chooser**, and then drag the Status field to the form. You can then change the label for the control, such as the Production Status label on the **Approval and Status** page.

The Send Request Command Buttons

At the bottom of the **Approval and Status** page, you can see a series of command buttons. With each of these buttons, the production manager can send a request to another person in the organization. When clicked, each of these buttons creates a message that includes a shortcut to the original Document Tracking item, as shown in Figure 12.17.

Each of the procedures for the Send Request buttons on the **Approval and Status** page are very similar, so this section only covers the SendEditRequest and the SendCopyEditRequest procedures.

Figure 12.17   The message created when the Send Edit Request button is clicked.

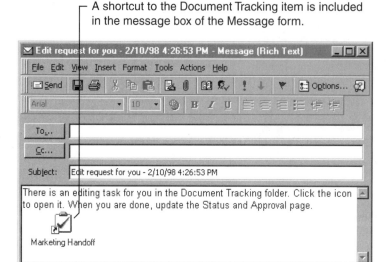

A shortcut to the Document Tracking item is included in the message box of the Message form.

The SendEditRequest_Click Procedure

When the **Send Edit Request** button is clicked, the SendEditRequest_Click procedure sets the **DocTrackItem** object to the active Document Tracking item. The Document Tracking item is saved, and the **CreateItem** method is used to create a message. The Document Tracking item is then added as a shortcut in the message box of the message.

```
'**********************************************************************
' Procedure: SendEditRequest
' Description: Creates a message request for an editor with a shortcut to the
' Document Tracking item in the message box.
'**********************************************************************
Sub SendEditRequest_Click
    Set DocTrackItem = Application.ActiveInspector.CurrentItem
    DocTrackItem.Save
    Set RequestItem = Application.CreateItem(0)
    RequestItem.Subject = "Edit request for you - " & Now()
    RequestItem.Body = "There is an editing task for you in the Document Tracking " _
        & "folder. Double-click the icon to open it. When you are done, update " _
        & "the Approval and Status page." & Chr(13)
    Set MyAttachments = RequestItem.Attachments
    MyAttachments.Add DocTrackItem, 4
    RequestItem.Display
End Sub
```

The SendCopyEditRequest_Click Procedure

The SendCopyEditRequest_Click procedure is almost identical to the
SendEditRequest_Click procedure. However, notice that the text for the **Subject** and
Body properties is changed to reflect the nature of the task request.

```
'*************************************************************************
' Procedure: SendCopyEditRequest
' Description: Creates a message request for a copy editor with a shortcut
' to the Document Tracking item in the message box.
'*************************************************************************
Sub SendCopyEditRequest_Click
    Set DocTrackItem = Application.ActiveInspector.CurrentItem
    DocTrackItem.Save
    Set RequestItem = Application.CreateItem(0)
    RequestItem.Subject = "Copy edit request for you - " & Now()
    RequestItem.Body = "There is a copyediting task for you in the " _
        & "Document Tracking folder. Double-click the icon to open it. " _
        & "When you are done, update the Approval and Status page." & Chr(13)
    Set MyAttachments = RequestItem.Attachments
    MyAttachments.Add DocTrackItem, 4
    RequestItem.Display
End Sub
```

The Virus Check\Posted Page

The **Virus Check\Posted** page, as shown in Figure 12.18, is very similar to the **Approval and Status** page. It is used by the production manager to send a Virus Check Request for print and HTML versions of the document. It is used by people who perform virus checks to update the Virus Check status and to enter their e-mail names. It is also used by the production manager to enter posted information for each version of the form.

Figure 12.18 The Virus Check\Posted page

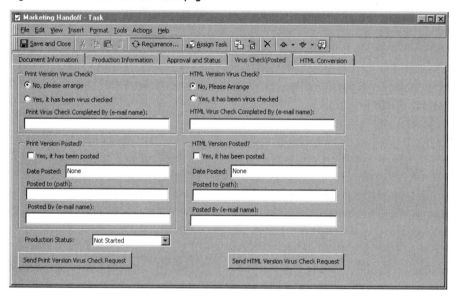

The HTML Conversion Page

The **HTML Conversion** page, as shown in Figure 12.19, makes it possible for the writer, editor, or production manager to include comments or instructions about converting the document to HTML. Note that the **Resize with form** and **Multi-line** check boxes are selected for this control.

Figure 12.19   The HTML Conversion page

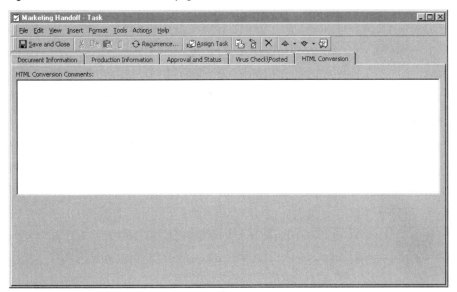

Script-Level Variables

For the Document Tracking form, the following script-level variables are declared at the top of the Script Editor window. The UserName and Trimmed variables are used in the Item_Open procedure and in the TrimUserName and CreateDateAsNumber functions, as discussed earlier in this chapter.

The ItemChanged variable is used to determine if field values on the form have changed. The ItemChanged variable is used in the Item_Write, Item_PropertyChange, and Item_CustomPropertyChange procedures.

The NewItemCreated variable is set in the Item_Write procedure when a new item is first saved in the Document Tracking folder. When the item is closed, the Item_Close event calls the SendNotificationProcedure if NewItemCreated is **True**.

The script-level database variables are used in the AddNewDatabaseRecord and UpdateDatabaseRecord procedures.

```
' Script-level variables used for the document ID.
Dim UserName
Dim Trimmed

' Script-level variable, set in Item_Write event.
' Item_Close calls SendNotification if True.
Dim NewItemCreated

' Script-level variable, set if field values change.
Dim ItemChanged

' Script-level database variables.
Dim Dbe
Dim MyDB
Dim Rs
Dim DbOpenTable
```

The Item_PropertyChange Event Procedure

The Item_PropertyChange event procedure, as shown in this example, is triggered any time a standard property is changed on the Document Tracking form. On the Document Tracking form, there are two standard fields that are visible and can be changed: the Priority field and the Status field. If a user makes a change to one of these fields after opening the Document Tracking form, then the ItemChanged variable is set to **True**.

```
'**********************************************************************
' Procedure: Item_PropertyChange
' Description: Checks to see if standard field values have changed.
'**********************************************************************
Sub Item_PropertyChange(ByVal Name)
    ItemChanged = True
End Sub
```

The Item_CustomPropertyChange Event Procedure

The Item_CustomPropertyChange event procedure, as shown in this example, is triggered when a value is changed in a user-defined field on the Document Tracking form. If a user-defined field is changed, the ItemChanged variable is set to **True**.

When the Item_CustomPropertyChange event is triggered, the name of the changed field is passed to the Item_CustomPropertyChange event procedure. As shown in the following code example, the **Select Case** statement is used to determine the field that has changed. In this procedure, if the changed field is the Format Other field and the value of the field is **True**, then the Other Comments control is enabled. If the Format Other field is **False**, the Other Comments control is not enabled.

```
'*************************************************************************
' Procedure: Item_CustomPropertyChange
' Description: Checks to see if field values have changed. If the Format
' Other check box is selected, the Other Comments box is enabled.
'*************************************************************************
Sub Item_CustomPropertyChange(ByVal FieldName)
    ItemChanged = True
    Select Case FieldName
        Case "Format Other"
            Set MyPage = Item.GetInspector.ModifiedFormPages("Production Information")
            Set MyOtherComments = MyPage.Controls("Other Comments")
            If Item.UserProperties.Find("Format Other").Value = True Then
                MyOtherComments.Enabled = True
            Else
                MyOtherComments.Enabled = False
                Item.UserProperties.Find("Other Comments").Value = ""
            End If
    End Select
End Sub
```

The Item_Write Event Procedure

The Item_Write event procedure is triggered when a user clicks the **Save and Close** button on the Document Tracking form. It's also triggered when a user clicks one of the Send Request command buttons or the **Send General Correspondence** command button. The Item_Write procedure evaluates the Database Record Created field to see if a database record has been created. If the value is "No," the AddNewDatabaseRecord procedure is called. In addition, the NewItemCreated variable is set to **True**. This variable is evaluated during the Item_Close event procedure, as described in the following section.

If the value of the Database Record Created field is "Yes," and the ItemChanged variable is set to **True** (a value has changed in the item), the UpdateDatabaseRecord procedure is called and the record is updated in the database.

```
'*************************************************************************
' Procedure: Item_Write
' Description: If the item is new, then the AddNewDatabaseRecord procedure
' is called. If the item record is in the database, the UpdateDatabaseRecord
' procedure is called if field values have changed (ItemChanged = True).
'*************************************************************************
Function Item_Write()
    If Item.UserProperties.Find("Database Record Created") = "No" Then
        Call AddNewDatabaseRecord
        NewItemCreated = True
        Item.UserProperties.Find("Database Record Created") = "Yes"
    Else
        If ItemChanged = True Then
            Call UpdateDataBaseRecord
        End If
    End If
End Function
```

The Item_Close Event Procedure

If NewItemCreated is **True**, then the SendNotification procedure is called. As discussed earlier in this chapter, the SendNotification procedure notifies a production manager that a new item is posted in the Document Tracking folder.

```
'****************************************************************************
'* Procedure: Item_Close
'* Description: Calls SendNotification if the value of NewItemCreated
'* is True.
'****************************************************************************
Function Item_Close()
    If NewItemCreated = True Then
        Call SendNotification
        NewItemCreated = False
    End If
End Function
```

The AddNewDatabaseRecord Procedure

The AddNewDatabaseRecord procedure is called from the Item_Write procedure if the value of the Database Record Created field is "No." The AddNewDatabaseRecord procedure opens the Document Tracking database, and then writes the value of the Status field that is in the item to the Status field in the database record. Status is handled in this way because it's a field that always has a value selected. Other fields, however, such as Audience Restrictions, may be empty, so the FieldValues procedure is called to handle additional processing of the fields.

Note The AddNewDatabase Record procedure requires that the user has installed Microsoft Office 97 or above (not stand-alone Outlook). In addition, the user must install the "Data Access Objects for Visual Basic" during Office 97 Setup. To install the "Data Access Objects for Visual Basic," run Office 97 Setup, select the **Data Access** option, and then click **Change Option**. Under **Options**, select **Data Access Objects for Visual Basic**, and then click **OK**.

```
'****************************************************************************
' Procedure: AddNewDatabaseRecord
' Description: Adds a new record to the Document Tracking database
' for the Document Tracking item.
'****************************************************************************

Sub AddNewDatabaseRecord
    DbOpenTable = 1
    On Error Resume Next
    Set Dbe = Application.CreateObject("DAO.DBEngine.35")
    If Err.Number <> 0 Then
        Msgbox Err.Description & " -- Some functions may not work correctly" _
            & Chr(13) & "Please make sure that DAO 3.5 is installed on this machine"
        Exit Sub
    End If
```

```
        Set MyDB = Dbe.Workspaces(0).OpenDatabase("C:\My Documents\Document Tracking.mdb")
        Set Rs = MyDB.OpenRecordset("Tracking Information", DbOpenTable)
        Rs.AddNew
        Rs("Status") = Item.Status
        Call FieldValues
        Rs.Update
        Rs.MoveLast
        Rs.Close
        MyDB.Close
    End Sub
```

The UpdateDatabaseRecord Procedure

The UpdateDatabaseRecord procedure is called from the Item_Write procedure if the value of the Database Record Created field is **True** and the value of the ItemChanged variable is **True**. The UpdateDatabaseRecord procedure uses the **Seek** method to find the record by the value of the Document ID field in the database.

```
'*************************************************************************
' Procedure: UpdateDatabaseRecord
' Description: Adds a new record to the Document Tracking database
' for the Document Tracking item.
'*************************************************************************

Sub UpdateDatabaseRecord

DbOpenTable = 1
On Error Resume Next
Set Dbe = Item.Application.CreateObject("DAO.DBEngine.35")
    If Err.Number <> 0 Then
        Msgbox Err.Description & " -- Some functions may not work correctly" & Chr(13) _
            & "Please make sure that DAO 3.5 is installed on this machine"
        Exit Sub
    End If

    Set MyDB = Dbe.Workspaces(0).OpenDatabase("C:\My Documents\Document Tracking.mdb")
    Set Rs = MyDB.OpenRecordset("Tracking Information", DbOpenTable)

    Rs.Index = "Document ID"              ' Define current index.
    Rs.Seek "=", Item.UserProperties.Find("Document ID").Value
    Rs.Edit
    Rs("Status") = Item.Status
    Call FieldValues
    Rs.Update
    Rs.MoveLast
    Rs.Close
    MyDB.Close
End Sub
```

The FieldValues Procedure

Not every field value in the Document Tracking item is written to the Document Tracking database, but most of them are. The FieldValues procedure calls the CheckValue procedure for each field whose value is potentially written to the database and passes the CheckValue procedure the name of the form field and the database field.

The FieldValues procedure is called by both the AddNewDatabaseRecord procedure and the UpdateDatabaseRecord procedure.

```
'*************************************************************************
' Procedure: FieldValues
' Description: Calls the CheckValue function and passes it the name of the
' form field and the database field.
'*************************************************************************

Sub FieldValues
    On Error Resume Next
    CheckValue "Author Name", "Author Name"
    CheckValue "Owner Name", "Owner Name"
    CheckValue "Document ID", "Document ID"
    CheckValue "Document Title", "Document Title"
    CheckValue "Date Document Needs to Be Posted","Posting Date"
    CheckValue "Document Title", "Document Title"
    CheckValue "File Name", "File Name"
    CheckValue "File Location", "File Location"
    CheckValue "Doc Description", "Document Description"
    CheckValue "Doc Summary", "Document Summary"
    CheckValue "Doc Keywords", "Document Keywords"
    CheckValue "Product", "Product"
    CheckValue "Version Number", "Version Number"
    CheckValue "Platform", "Platform"
    CheckValue "Customer Ready", "Customer Ready"
    CheckValue "Type of Tool", "Type of Tool"
    CheckValue "Target Audience", "Target Audience"
    CheckValue "Audience Restrictions", "Audience Restrictions"
    CheckValue "Format Print", "Format Print"
    CheckValue "Format HTML", "Format HTML"
    CheckValue "Format Other", "Format Other"
    CheckValue "Other Comments", "Other Comments"
    CheckValue "Production Manager", "Production Manager"
    CheckValue "Edited", "Edited"
    CheckValue "Edit Completed By", "Edit Completed By"
    CheckValue "Copy Edit","Copy Edit"
    CheckValue "Copy Edit Completed By","Copy Edit Completed By"
    CheckValue "Part Number Status", "Part Number Status"
    CheckValue "Part Number", "Part Number"
    CheckValue "Part Number Assigned By", "Part Number Assigned By"
    CheckValue "Approved By Legal", "Approved By Legal"
    CheckValue "Approved By Legal Name", "Approved By"
    CheckValue "Print Version Virus Check", "Print Version Virus Check"
    CheckValue "Print Virus Checked By", "Print Virus Checked By"
```

```
        CheckValue "HTML Version Virus Check","HTML Version Virus Check"
        CheckValue "HTML Virus Checked By","HTML Virus Checked By"
        CheckValue "Print Version Posted","Print Version Posted"
        CheckValue "Print Version Date Posted", "Print Version Date Posted"
        CheckValue "Print Version Posted To Path", "Print Version Posted To Path"
        CheckValue "Print Version Posted By", "Print Version Posted By"
        CheckValue "HTML Version Posted","HTML Version Posted"
        CheckValue "HTML Version Date Posted","HTML Version Date Posted"
        CheckValue "HTML Version Posted To Path","HTML Version Posted To Path"
        CheckValue "HTML Version Posted By", "HTML Version Posted By"
End Sub
```

The CheckValue Procedure

The CheckValue procedure runs a series of checks on the fields whose values are
potentially written to the database. If the field does not contain valid data, the field
value is not written to the database.

The CheckValue procedure first checks if the field exists on the form, and then checks
to see if the field is empty. It then checks if the field is a Date/Time field. If it's not,
the value is written to the database. If it is, the CheckValue procedure checks whether
the value of the field is "1/1/4501." In an Outlook Date/Time field, this value
represents "None." If the value is not "None," the value is written to the database.

```
'**********************************************************************
' Procedure: CheckValue
' Description: Checks the field for valid data. If valid data exists, write
' the field value to the database.
'**********************************************************************

Sub CheckValue (ByVal FormField, ByVal DbField)
    If Not UserProperties.Find(FormField) Is Nothing Then
        If UserProperties.Find(FormField).Value <> "" Then
            If IsDate(UserProperties.Find(FormField).Value) Then
                If UserProperties.Find(FormField).Value <> "1/1/4501" Then
                    Rs(DbField) = UserProperties.Find(FormField).Value
                Else
                    Rs(DbField) = Null
                End If
            Else
                Rs(DbField) = UserProperties.Find(FormField).Value
            End If
        End If
    End If
End Sub
```

The SendNotification Procedure

The SendNotification procedure, as shown in the following code example, automatically notifies the specified people when a Document Tracking item is submitted in the Document Tracking folder. This procedure is called by the Item_Write procedure and creates a message, addresses it to the specified people, attaches a shortcut to the Document Tracking item, and then sends the message.

```
'*******************************************************************
'* Procedure: SendNotification
'* Description: Called by Item_Close when the NewItemCreated variable is
'* True. Sends a message to the production manager to notify her or him
'* that a new item has been submitted in the folder.
'*******************************************************************

Sub SendNotification
    Set DocTrackItem = Application.ActiveInspector.CurrentItem
    DocTrackItem.Save
    Set RequestItem = Application.CreateItem(0)
    RequestItem.Subject = _
        "A new item has been submitted to the Document Tracking folder " & Now()
    RequestItem.Body = "Click the icon to view the item. " & Chr(13)
    RequestItem.To = "Peter Krebs"
    Set MyAttachments = RequestItem.Attachments
    MyAttachments.Add DocTrackItem, 4
    RequestItem.Send
End Sub
```

The Document Tracking Database

The Document Tracking database is a Microsoft Access 97 database that consists of a Tracking Information table. When you release this application for general use, make sure the Document Tracking database is located on a server to which all users have access.

The Document Tracking database is relatively simple and consists of the Tracking Information table, as shown in Figure 12.20. The ID field serves as the primary key and an index is specified for the Document ID field. In the UpdateDatabaseRecord procedure in the Document Tracking form, the Document ID field is defined as the active index and the **Seek** method is used to find the recordset in the database.

Figure 12.20   The Tracking Information table

The ID field is the primary key.

The Document ID field is indexed.

ID	Document ID	Author Name	Owner Name	Posting Date	Document Title
1	625944806984	James Allard	Scott Cooper	12/22/98	Building Microsoft Outlook Applications
2	103432838590	Rich Andrews	Suzan Fine	12/20/98	Chapter 12
3	104635838590	Dave Goodhand	Suzan Fine	12/23/98	Chapter 13
4	105004838590	David Goodhand	Suzan Fine	12/19/98	Chapter 14
6	811642838590	Scott Fallon	Suzan Fine	12/16/98	Chapter 5

Record: 1 of 7

Datasheet View

Document Tracking Folder Views

The Document Tracking folder consists of two custom views that organize the Document Tracking items: the By Document Status view and the By Production Manager view. For the Document Tracking folder, the **Only show views created for this folder** option is selected, as shown in Figure 12.21, so that the standard list of views for a Tasks folder are not available.

▶ **To define views for the Document Tracking folder**

1   On the Folder list, select **Document Tracking**.

2   Select **Current View** on the **View** menu, and then click **Define Views**.

Figure 12.21   The Define Views dialog box

When selected, only the By Document Status and By Production Manager views are available in the **Current View** box.

The By Document Status View

The By Document Status view groups Document Tracking items by the value in the Status field, as shown in Figure 12.22. The By Document Status view makes it possible for production managers to quickly view the tasks that have been accomplished in the document approval and production process. When an item is first saved in the Document Tracking folder, its status is **Not Started**. After a production manager opens the item and sends the various Edit and Part Number requests to others in the organization, he or she changes the status of the Document Tracking item to **In Progress** and then saves the item. As shown in Figure 12.22, completed items have a line through them.

Figure 12.22   The By Document Status view

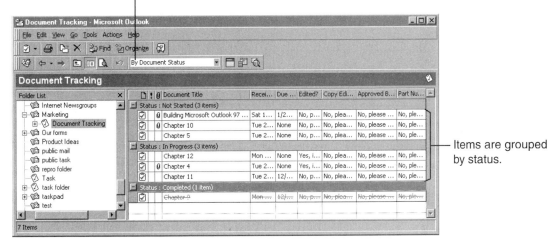

The By Document Status view is selected in the **Current View** box, on the **Advanced** toolbar.

Items are grouped by status.

The By Production Manager View

With the By Production Manager view, production managers can quickly view the progress of documents they are responsible for. As shown in Figure 12.23, items in the By Production Manager view are grouped by the value in the Production Manager field.

Figure 12.23   The By Production Manager view

Items are grouped by production manager.

Releasing the Document Tracking Application

Before you release the Document Tracking application for public use, you must set permissions for the Document Tracking folder, so that those people who use the folder can submit and update items in the folder. You must also distribute the Marketing Handoff form to those users who will participate in the document production process. Those users must then publish the Marketing Handoff form to their Personal Forms Library.

Setting Permissions

You use the **Properties** dialog box to set permissions for the Document Tracking folder.

▶ **To set permissions for the Document Tracking folder**

1   In the Folder List, right-click the **Document Tracking** folder, from the **Marketing** folder in **All Public Folders**.

2   Click **Properties** on the shortcut menu.

3   Click the **Permissions** page.

4   Set the following permissions for the folder.

Name	Role	Assign to
Default	None	
All participants in the document production process	Editor	People responsible for submitting documents or updating document tracking items
Application designers or system administrators	Owner	People responsible for maintaining and designing applications

See Also   For more information about setting permissions, see "Set Permissions" in Chapter 8, "Folders."

Setting Administration Properties

You can then set the Administration properties on the folder so it's available to all users with access permissions.

▶ **To set administration properties**

•   On the **Administration** page of the **Properties** dialog box, click **All users with access permission**, and then click **OK**.

Distributing a Form for Publishing in a Personal Forms Library

Now you can distribute the Marketing Handoff form to those people who will participate in the document production process.

Inserting the .oft Attachment in a Message

To make a form accessible to a specific workgroup, the form must be published in the Personal Forms Library of each person who needs to use the form. The easiest way to send an .oft file is in the message box of a message.

▶ **To insert an .oft attachment in a message**

1 After selecting the Inbox, or another folder containing mail items, click **Actions** on the Outlook menu.

2 Click **New Mail Message**.

3 On the **Insert** menu, click **File**.

4 In the **Look in** drop-down list box, select the folder where you saved the Marketing Handoff .oft file.

5 Under **Insert as**, click **Attachment**, and then click **OK**.

6 In the **To** text box, type the names of the people you want to receive the attached .oft file, or click the **To** button and then select the names from the list.

7 In the message box under the attachment, include the instructions listed in the following procedure "To publish the attached form in your Personal Forms Library."

8 Click **Send**.

Including Instructions About How to Publish the Form

Along with the .oft file, you can include the following instructions that explain to users how to publish the attached form in their Personal Forms Library.

▶ **To publish the attached form in your Personal Forms Library**

1 Double-click the attachment.

2 On the form **Tools** menu, select **Forms**, and then click **Publish Form As**.

3 In the **Look In** drop-down list box, click **Personal Forms Library**.

4 Type **Marketing Handoff** in the **Display name** text box and **Form name** text box.

5 Click **Publish**.

CHAPTER 13

Distribute and Maintain Applications

In This Chapter

Distribute Forms   477

Manage Forms   485

The Forms Cache   488

Form Activation   489

Distribute Folders   489

The process of distributing and maintaining Microsoft Outlook applications varies with each organization. In some organizations, the application designer develops the application and then submits it to an administrator who is responsible for its distribution, maintenance, and security. In other organizations, the application designer both develops the application and serves as its administrator.

This chapter covers basic concepts and procedures the administrator can use for distributing and maintaining Outlook applications within an organization.

Distribute Forms

This section provides information, strategies, and instructions for distributing forms in your organization. It covers how to:

- Make forms available in the Organizational Forms Library, the Personal Forms Library, or a folder forms library.
- Send a form to an administrator or to another user.
- Distribute forms in a personal folder (.pst) file.
- Make forms available for offline use.

Make Forms Available in the Organizational Forms Library

Most often, the types of forms contained in the Organizational Forms Library are general purpose Message forms that you want to make available to the entire organization. The Organizational Forms Library is located on Microsoft Exchange Server, so access to the forms in this library is determined by the structure and configuration of your Microsoft Exchange Server system.

Usually, there are two types of Message forms that you publish in the Organizational Forms Library:

- General purpose Message forms, such as the While You Were Out form and Vacation Request form, that are used to send messages from one user to another.

- Message forms that make it possible for users to submit information in a public folder. For example, the Business Card Request form covered in Chapter 10 and the Help Request form covered in Chapter 11 are used to send items to a public folder. In other cases, the Message form in the Organizational Forms Library is used to set a public folder as the active folder and then create an item in that public folder.

Note Non-Message forms such as Post, Contact, and Task forms are contained in the forms library within the folder. So if the folder is located in a public folder, the forms contained in the folder's forms library are made available to all users who have access to the folder.

Submit the Form to an Administrator

In most organizations, only administrators have permission to publish forms in the Organizational Forms Library. As such, application designers who want forms published in the Organizational Forms Library must submit the forms to the administrator.

When a form is published in a forms library, such as the Organizational Forms Library, the form definition (and ability to view the file) can be shared by everyone with access to the library. Thus, when the form is published, you do not also need to send the form definition with the item. The **Send form definition with item** check box on the form's **Properties** page should be cleared.

▶ **To submit a form to an administrator**

1 With the form in Design mode, click **Save As** on the **File** menu.

2 In the **Save in** drop-down list box, click the Outlook default template folder, such as C:\Program Files\Microsoft Office\Templates\Outlook.

3 In the **File name** text box, type the form name.

4 In the **Save as type** drop-down list box, select **Outlook Template (.oft)**.

5 Click **Save**.

6 On the form's **Actions** menu, click **New Mail Message**.

7 On the **Insert** menu, click **File**.

8 In the **Look in** drop-down list box, click the folder you saved the .oft file in.

9 On the right side of the dialog box, select the **Attachment** option button under **Insert as,** and then click **OK**.

10 In the **To** text box, type the administrator's name, or click the **To** button and then select the administrator's name from the list.

11 Click **Send**.

Check the Form for Viruses and Harmful Code

The administrator is responsible for making sure the form is free of viruses and harmful code.

Publish the Form

If the administrator finds the form is free of viruses and harmful code, he clears the **Send form definition with item** check box on the **Properties** page of the form and publishes the form in the Organizational Forms Library.

▶ **To clear the Send form definition with item check box**

1 With the form in Design mode, click the **Properties** tab.

2 Clear the **Send form definition with item** check box.

See Also For more information about the **Send form definition with item** option, see "About the Send Form Definition with Item Check Box" later in this chapter.

▶ **To publish the form in the Organizational Forms Library**

1 With the form in Design mode, select **Forms** from the **Tools** menu, and then click **Publish Form As**.

2 In the **Look In** drop-down list box, click **Organizational Forms Library**.

3 Type the form name in the **Display name** text box and the **Form name** text box.

4 Click **Publish**.

Note You must have owner permissions to publish in the Organizational Forms Library. See your system administrator.

Make Forms Available in the Personal Forms Library

There are three good reasons to publish a form in the Personal Forms Library:

- In many cases, you want to limit the number of people who have access to a form. For example, with the Document Tracking application covered in Chapter 12, you want to limit access to the Document Tracking folder to only those people responsible for submitting and tracking marketing documents. To do this, you publish the Marketing Handoff form in the Personal Forms Library of only the people who use the application.

- In some cases, you may want to publish a form in your Personal Forms Library so you are the only person who can use the form. For example, you may want to create a customized announcement form for communicating with a specific group of customers.

- You want to test a form that will later be published in the Organizational Forms Library. In this case, you can test the form in the Personal Forms Library before you submit it to an administrator for publishing in the Organizational Forms Library.

About the Send Form Definition with Item Check Box

If you are distributing forms to users who will install the form in their Personal Forms Libraries or you are publishing a form to your own Personal Forms Library, you should clear the **Send form definition with item** check box.

▶ **To clear the Send form definition with item check box**

1 With the form in Design mode, click the **Properties** tab.

2 Clear the **Send form definition with item** check box.

By default, the **Send form definition with item** check box is cleared. However, when the form is published, the user is prompted to either select the check box or leave it cleared. When users have access to the forms library, you do not need to send the form definition along with the item. In this case, select **No** to keep the **Send form definition with item** check box clear, and to keep the file size small.

Distribute a Form for Publishing in a Personal Forms Library

Quite often, you want to distribute a form to a specific group of users and give them instructions about how to publish the form in their Personal Forms Library. The following instructions describe how to do this.

Save the Form as an .oft File

First, you save the form as an .oft file so you can distribute it to other users.

▶ **To submit a form to an administrator**

1   With the form in Design mode, select **Save As** on the **File** menu.

2   In the **Save in** drop-down list box, select the default Outlook template folder, such as C:\Program Files\Microsoft Office\Templates.

3   In the **File name** text box, type the form name.

4   In the **Save as type** drop-down list box, select **Outlook Template (.oft)**.

5   Click **Save**.

Insert a Form (.oft) File as an Attachment in a Message

To make a form accessible to a specific workgroup, the form must be published in the Personal Forms Library of each person who needs to use the form. The easiest way to do this is to save the form as an .oft file and then insert the .oft file into a message box of a message.

▶ **To insert a form (.oft) file as an attachment in a message**

1   On the form's **Actions** menu, click **New Mail Message**.

2   On the **Insert** menu, click **File**.

3   In the **Look in** drop-down list box, click the folder you saved the .oft file in.

4   In the **Insert as** box on the right side of the dialog box, select the **Attachment** option button, and then click **OK**.

5   In the **To** text box, type the names of the people you want to receive the attached .oft file, or click the **To** button and then select the names from the list. Click **OK**.

6   In the message box, include the instructions listed in the following section to publish the attached form in the users' Personal Forms Libraries.

7   Click **Send**.

Include Instructions About How to Publish the Form

Along with the form (.oft) file, include these instructions that explain to users how to publish the attached form in their Personal Forms Libraries.

▶ **To publish the attached form in a Personal Forms Library**

1 Double-click the attachment.

2 If a prompt appears, click **Disable Macros**.

3 On the **Tools** menu, select **Forms**, and then click **Publish Form As**.

4 In the **Look In** drop-down list box, click **Personal Forms Library**, and then click **OK**.

5 Type the form name into the **Display name** text box and the **Form name** text box.

6 Click **Publish**.

7 Click **No** to keep the **Send form definition with item** check box clear. (When items are published, and then run from the place where they are published, they do not need embedded form definitions. This will only slow down form loading time.)

Publish a Form in Your Personal Forms Library

In some cases, you may want to create a form and then publish it in your Personal Forms Library. If the form will be sent to people who do not have the form, you may want to leave the **Send form definition with item** check box selected.

▶ **To publish a form in your Personal Forms Library**

1 On the form's **Tools** menu, select **Forms,** and then click **Publish Form As**.

2 In the **Look In** drop-down list box, click **Personal Forms Library**, and then click **OK**.

3 Type the form name in the **Display name** text box and the **Form name** text box.

4 Click **Publish**.

5 Click **No** to keep the **Send form definition with item** box clear. (When items are published, and then run from the place where they are published, they do not need embedded form definitions. This will only slow down form loading time.)

Make Forms Available in a Folder Forms Library

Forms libraries for folders are containers for forms. Each folder contains a unique forms library. As such, a forms library can exist on the server or on the user's hard disk, depending on the location of the folder. There are two good reasons for publishing forms to the forms library of a folder:

- Most often, the forms stored in the library of a folder are used to post or save information in a folder. Such forms may include a standard or custom Post, Contact, or Task form. However, in some cases, Message forms are installed in the forms library of the folder so that users can send items from the folder. For example, in the Help Desk application covered in Chapter 11, the Correspondence Mail form is located in the forms library of the Assigned Help Tasks folder, so users can send messages while working in the folder.

- Another reason to publish forms in the folder's forms library is to transport the forms in a personal folder (.pst) file. You can use the personal folder (.pst) file for storing and distributing forms. Making forms available in a personal folder (.pst) file is described in "Distribute Forms in a Personal Folder (.pst) File" later in this chapter.

▶ **To publish a form in a folder forms library**

1 On the form **Tools** menu, select **Forms**, and then click **Publish Form As**.

2 In the **Look In** drop-down list box, click the folder forms library that you want to publish the form to.

3 Type the form name in the **Display name** text box and the **Form name** text box.

4 Click **Publish**.

5 Select **No** to keep the **Send form definition with item** check box cleared on the **Properties** page of the form. Select **Yes** to enable the reader of your item to have a complete and self-contained form with definition, which enables the form to be viewed without publishing.

Use the Send Form Definition with Item Check Box to Send a Form to Another User

In some cases, you need to send items using a Message form to users who do not have access to the form associated with the item. For example, you may want to send a Product Announcement form to a customer. To ensure that the item appears in the form it was created with, you select the **Send form definition with item** check box on the **Properties** page of the form when the form is in Design mode. You then publish the form in a forms library, as described earlier in this chapter. At publishing, select **Yes** when you are prompted to **Send form definition with item.**

This results in a larger file size, but the form is self-contained and can be viewed, whether the user has access to the forms library or not.

Distribute Forms in a Personal Folder (.pst) File

If you want to distribute one or more forms using a floppy disk, a CD-ROM, or a network drive, publish the form to the forms library of a folder that is located in a personal folder (.pst) file. You can then make a copy of the .pst file and use it for distribution. For more information about distributing a .pst file, see "Distribute a Folder in a Personal Folder (.pst) File" later in this chapter.

Make Forms Available for Offline Use

Users can set up Outlook so they can work offline with forms and folders.

▶ To set up Outlook for offline use

- See offline folder (.ost) file topics, such as "Set Outlook to Start Offline," in Outlook Help.

When the user sets up her computer for offline use, Outlook creates an .ost file on the user's hard disk. The .ost file contains the following items:

- The default folders in the user's Mailbox.
- Any other folders in the user's Mailbox that are designated as offline folders.
- Folders in the user's Favorites folder that are designated as offline folders.
- Forms that are used to compose and read items in the offline folders.

How Forms Are Made Available for Offline Use

Any form associated with an item in the user's offline folder file is automatically made available for offline use when the user selects **Synchronize** on the **Tools** menu and then clicks a choice. When the user selects **Synchronize**, and then clicks a choice, Outlook searches the items in each offline folder and copies any forms associated with the items to the offline folder (.ost) file (if the forms are not already in the .ost).

For example, suppose a Weekly Schedule item is sent to a user's Inbox, and the user has set up her computer for offline use. When the user synchronizes her offline folders, the Weekly Schedule form, which is the form associated with the Weekly Schedule item, is copied to the user's offline folder file and is available for offline use.

How Form Conflicts Are Resolved

Changes made to forms while the user is working offline are not transferred back to Microsoft Exchange Server. Any changes made to forms on Microsoft Exchange Server, however, are automatically reflected in the user's .ost file when the user synchronizes folders.

Make Forms Available for Remote Use

Users in remote locations with dial-up connections to Microsoft Exchange Server can use forms just as if they were connected directly to the server. Before users can work with a dial-up connection, however, they must prepare their computers for dial-up work. The recommended way to work with a dial-up connection is to use offline folders. Users can then work with items in offline folders exactly as they work with items in folders on the server.

Manage Forms

This section describes how to copy and delete forms and change form properties using the **Forms Manager**. It also provides some strategies and tricks for making changes to forms.

The Forms Manager

With the **Forms Manager**, as shown in Figure 13.1, you can copy and delete forms and change form properties.

▶ **To open the Forms Manager**

1 Select **Options** on the **Tools** menu, and then click the **Other** tab.

2 Click **Advanced Options** under **General**, and then click **Custom Forms**.

3 Click **Manage Forms**.

This allows you to manage forms in the Personal and Organizational Forms Libraries simultaneously with the forms libraries of folders.

Figure 13.1   The Forms Manager dialog box

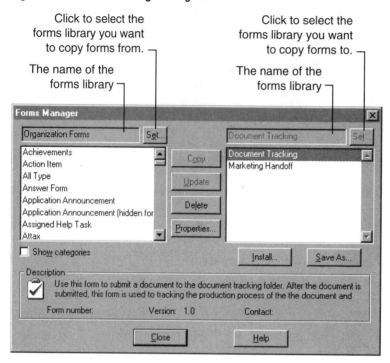

Click to select the forms library you want to copy forms from.

The name of the forms library

Click to select the forms library you want to copy forms to.

The name of the forms library

▶ **To copy a form**

1   Click the left **Set** button to choose the forms library you want to copy forms from.

2   In the lower-left list box, select the forms you want to copy.

3   Click the right **Set** button to choose the forms library you want to copy forms to.

4   Click **Copy**.

▶ **To set form properties**

1   In the lower-right list box, select the form you want to set properties for.

2   Click **Properties**.

3   Select the options you want.

▶ To delete a form

1   In the lower-right list box, click the forms you want to delete.

2   Click **Delete**.

To synchronize one form with an updated version, select the one you wish to update. For the update process to work, the form must be visible in both forms libraries (in both the right and left list boxes.)

▶ To update forms published in different forms libraries

In the right list box, click the form, and then click **Update**. Although you won't see an action, the forms will now be updated.

Note   The **Install** and **Save As** buttons are used to install and save forms developed for Microsoft Exchange Client.

Modify Forms

Quite often, changing a form can impact another form or folder. When modifying a form, here are some things to consider:

- If a view or rule is based on a particular field, and you remove or modify a field name, the view or rule must be updated to reflect the change.

- If fields are renamed on an existing form, their associated field values in items created using a previous version of the form do not appear on the new form.

- If the form contains Microsoft Visual Basic Scripting Edition, any changes you make to the form components, such as the controls or fields, must also be changed in the Script Editor if the components are referenced in script.

- If you add new fields to an existing form, then publish the modified form in a forms library, and then open old items with the new form, the new fields on the form will be blank or show the initial value for the field if there is one.

- Forms with the same name, but different contents, may cause unpredictable results. It is recommended to use unique names or update the form in all the forms libraries in which it is published. For more information, see the preceding section, "Forms Manager," or "How Folders are Synchronized" later in this chapter.

Manage Changes to Forms

Let's assume you make changes to a form in an application that's been in use for several months. Rather than remove the old form, you can keep the old form in the forms library and set its **Hidden** property. This way, users can't create new items with the form, but they can view existing items with the form that the items were created with.

▶ **To set the Hidden property of a form**

1   In the Folder List, right-click the folder that contains the form you want to change.

    For the Organizational and Personal Forms Library, you can right-click Inbox.

2   On the shortcut menu, click **Properties**.

3   Click the **Forms** tab, and then click **Manage**.

    The **Forms Manager** shows the forms in the active folder forms library in the lower-right list box, as shown earlier in Figure 13.1.

4   Click the right **Set** button to choose the forms library that contains the forms you want to set the **Hidden** property for.

5   In the lower-right list box, click the form you want to set the **Hidden** property for, and then click **Properties**.

6   Select the **Hidden** check box, and then click **OK**.

Note Another way to set the **Hidden** property for a form is to select the **Use form only for responses** check box on the **Properties** page of a form.

The Forms Cache

The forms cache is a folder located in C:\Windows\Forms that serves as a storage location for forms. The forms cache improves the load time of a form because commonly used forms are loaded from the hard disk rather than downloaded from the server. When a form is activated for the first time, the form definition file is copied from its forms library to the user's C:\Windows\Forms folder. The forms cache keeps a temporary copy of the form definition in a subfolder whose name roughly matches the name of the form.

The form table, Frmcache.dat, also located in C:\Windows\Forms, is used to locate a form and also to prevent multiple instances of the same form from being loaded in the cache. When a form is activated, Outlook checks to see if a form with the same message class is already in the cache. If not, it copies the form definition to the cache. In addition, if a change has been made to a form, Outlook copies the new form definition to the cache.

The size of the forms cache can be determined by the user.

▶ **To specify the amount of disk space allocated for forms**

1 Click **Options** on the **Tools** menu.

2 Click the **Other** Tab, and then click **Advanced Options**.

3 In the **Advanced Options** dialog box, click the **Custom Forms** button.

4 Specify the disk space under **Temporary storage for forms**.

Form Activation

A form is activated when the user selects a form to compose an item, or when the user performs an operation on a existing item. For example, the user double-clicks an existing item in a folder to open it. Outlook uses the following form caching scheme to activate forms:

- Application Forms Library—Checks for standard forms, such as Note, Post, Standard Default, Contact, and Appointment.

- Cached Forms—Checks for a form in the forms cache.

- Active Folder Library—Checks for a form in the forms library of the active folder.

- Personal Forms Library—Checks for the form definition in the Personal Forms Library. If found, Outlook opens the form.

- Organizational Forms Library—Checks the form definition in the Organizational Forms Library. If found, Outlook opens the form.

Distribute Folders

After a folder is designed, you can copy it to a Mailbox folder, Personal Folders, or Public Folders.

This section discusses the different methods for making a folder available for use. It also discusses offline folder issues and offers references for archiving and aging folders.

Important Do not attempt to distribute folders using the Outlook Import and Export Wizard. The Import and Export Wizard is designed for importing and exporting data, not distributing folders.

Make a Folder Available to All Users in Your Organization

You can make a folder available to all users in your organization by creating the folder in or copying the folder to Public Folders. Then it is up to the administrator to determine if the folder is replicated throughout the organization. You or the administrator can set permissions for who can access the folder and to what extent those users can work in the folder.

Note   To copy a folder to Public Folders, you are required to have permission to create subfolders for that part of the Microsoft Exchange Server folder hierarchy.

Based on the policies of your organization, you may not have permission to copy a folder to Public Folders. You may be required to hand off the folder to your administrator who then copies the folder and completes the design tasks according to your specifications. Or you may be given permission to copy your folder to a specific public folder and then complete the task yourself. See your administrator for specific instructions.

▶ To create a folder in Public Folders

1   In Public Folders, right-click the folder you want to create the subfolder in, and then click **New Folder** on the shortcut menu.

2   In the **Name** text box, type a name for the folder.

3   Select the options you want.

4   If prompted, select a choice about creating a shortcut on the Outlook Bar, and then click **OK**.

▶ To copy a folder to Public Folders

1   In the Folder List, right-click the folder you want to copy, and then click **Copy "*folder name*"** on the shortcut menu.

2   Click the public folder you want to copy the folder to, and then click **OK**.

Set Permissions for the Folder

When you set permissions on the folder, you determine who can access the folder and the functions they can perform in the folder.

▶ To set permissions for the folder

1   In the Folder List, right-click the folder you copied to Public Folders, and then click **Properties** on the shortcut menu.

2   Click the **Permissions** page.

3   Set permissions for the folder.

See Also For more information about setting permissions, see "Set Permissions" in Chapter 8, "Folders."

If the folder is replicated to other servers, make sure you set the permissions so that all users who need access to the folder have the appropriate permissions.

Make a Folder Available for Personal Use

Private folders are stored in the user's Mailbox folder or in a personal folder (.pst) file. There are three good reasons for storing a folder in a personal folder file:

- The user has exclusive rights to the folder. For example, many users keep a list of personal contacts in their Contacts folder in their Mailbox.
- The user can access information in the folder even when not logged on to Microsoft Exchange Server. This can be especially useful for people who travel, because they can access information in a personal folder on their laptop without a live connection to the server.
- The user can easily distribute the folder in a personal folder file. For example, many of the applications in this book were tested in Public Folders. After they were tested in Public Folders, they were copied to the Building Microsoft Outlook 98 Applications folder so they could be distributed in a .pst file.

See Also If you have not yet created a Personal Folder file, see "Create a Personal Folder (.pst) File" later in this chapter.

▶ To create a folder in your Mailbox or in a personal folder (.pst) file

1 In the Folder List, right-click the Mailbox folder or personal folder you want to create the subfolder in, and then click **New Folder** on the shortcut menu.

2 In the **Name** text box, type a name for the folder.

3 Select the options you want.

▶ To copy a folder to your Mailbox or personal folder (.pst) file

1 In the Folder List, right-click the folder you want to copy, and then click **Copy** "*folder name*" on the shortcut menu.

2 Click the Mailbox folder or personal folder you want to copy the folder to, and then click **OK**.

Distribute a Folder in a Personal Folder (.pst) File

A personal folder (.pst) file provides a convenient way to distribute applications using a floppy disk, a CD-ROM, or a network drive. For example, you can create folders on your Microsoft Exchange Server system either in public folders or personal folders. When you are ready to distribute the folders, you can create a personal folder file, and then copy the folders to the file.

Create a Personal Folder File

▶ **To create a personal folder (.pst) file**

1 On the **File** menu, click **New**, and then click **Personal Folders File (.pst)**.

2 On the **Save in** drop-down list box, specify the location for your personal folder (.pst) file.

3 In the **File name** text box, enter a name for the personal folder (.pst) file.

4 Click **Create**.

5 In the **Create Microsoft Personal Folders** dialog box, select the options you want, and then click **OK**.

Copy Folders to a Personal Folder File

▶ **To copy a folder to a personal folder (.pst) file**

1 In the Folder List, right-click the folder you want to copy, and then click **Copy "*folder name*"** on the shortcut menu.

2 Click the personal folder you want to copy the folder to, and then click **OK**.

Distribute the Personal Folder File

To distribute the personal folder (.pst) file, open Windows Explorer and copy the .pst file to a floppy disk, a network drive, or a CD-ROM.

Make an Existing Personal Folder File Available on Your Microsoft Exchange System

▶ **To make an existing personal folder (.pst) file available on your Microsoft Exchange System**

1 On the **File** menu, select **Open**, and then click **Personal Folders File (.pst)**.

2 Specify the location you want, and then double-click the personal folder (.pst) file you want.

The file appears in your Folder List.

Making Changes to a Folder

If you are responsible for maintaining an application, you are often asked to make modifications to the forms or folder that make up the application. For example, users may ask for enhancements to a form, for additional folder views, or for permission.

If the changes to the folder are substantial, you should copy the design of the folder to another folder, make the necessary changes to the folder, and then copy the design back to the original folder. If the changes are minor, such as adding a permission or a view, you can modify the folder directly. To make changes to a folder, you must have owner permission for the folder.

See Also   For more information about how to modify a folder, see Chapter 8, "Folders."

Make Folders Available for Offline Use

To work offline or with a dial-up connection, the user should prepare his computer for offline and dial-up work. Once the computer is set up, the task of setting up folders for offline use is simple.

See Also   For more information about setting up a computer and Outlook with a dial-up connection or for setting up offline folders, see Outlook Help or Windows Help.

To make a folder available for offline use, the user designates the folder as an offline folder. The following folders can be designated as offline folders:

- Inbox, Outbox, Sent Items, Calendar, Tasks and Deleted Items are default Outlook folders in the user's Mailbox that can be made available for offline use.

- Any folder in the user's Mailbox that the user created.

- Any folder in the user's Favorites folder.

How Folders Are Made Available for Offline Use

When the user sets up his computer for offline use, an offline folder (.ost) file is created on his hard disk. The offline folder file contains a replica of folders he works with offline.

Once the folders are set up for offline use, they must be synchronized by the user so the offline folders contain the same information as the folders on the server. To synchronize folders, the user selects **Synchronize** on the **Tools** menu and then clicks the desired choice.

For specific procedures, see "Set Outlook to start offline" and "Synchronize offline folders" in Outlook Help.

How Folders Are Synchronized

While working offline, the contents of both the offline folder and the folder on the server can change. For example, the user may post items in a Contacts folder while offline. At the same time, users connected to the server may also post items to the Contacts folder.

To make sure the contents of offline folders are identical to the contents of folders on the server, the user selects the **Synchronize** command on the **Tools** menu and then clicks the desired choice. Offline folders can be synchronized individually or all at once. When the user synchronizes folders, the changes made in the server folder are reflected in the offline folder, and the changes made in the offline folder are reflected in the server folder.

When a user of offline folders reconnects to Microsoft Exchange Server, changes made in the offline folders are reflected in the folders on the server. However, changes made in the folder on Microsoft Exchange Server while the user was offline are not reflected in the offline folders until the user synchronizes the folders.

Folder Replication Issues

Replication is the process by which Microsoft Exchange Server keeps folders synchronized that are in different locations. Generally, folder replication is handled by Microsoft Exchange Server administrators and involves careful planning and coordination between site administrators.

If you are an application designer, here are a few issues you should be aware of regarding folder replication:

- If a folder contains critical data that must be refreshed immediately in all locations when new data is received, the folder should not be replicated.

- Replicate applications from a central location. It often makes sense to store all applications on one server and perform all replication and updates to the application from this central location.

- Make sure each site that needs to replicate the application has appropriate permission to support replication.

Age and Archive a Folder

You can have Outlook automatically remove items of a specified age and transfer them to an archive file. To do this, you must first turn on AutoArchive and then set the AutoArchive properties for each folder you want automatically stored.

To	See
Age and archive a personal folder	Outlook Help
Age and archive a public folder	Microsoft Exchange Server documentation

Index

A

actions
  Approve Vacation 197
  Course Catalog Entry form 211
  Course Offering 213
  Create Offering, properties 213
  defined, attaching to Command buttons 422
  forms, basic characteristics 110
  new, creating for the Product Idea form 83
  Post to Folder, new 212
  Product Idea form, setting 81
  Product Idea Response form, setting 85
  properties, setting for forms 132
  Reply to Folder, making unavailable 211
  Reply, new 195
  specifying for rules 263
  Task Discussion, viewing properties 422
  Vacation Request form 194
  Voting buttons, setting automatically 190
AddNewDatabaseRecord procedure, Document
  Tracking form 442
AddressEntry object,
  defined 291
Address form like a option
  Course Offering form 215
  Message forms 199
  Post forms 215
Address property 294
AddressEntries collection object
  290
AddressEntry object
  deleting an item 293
  displaying details of an item 292
  getting free/busy information 293
  methods 292
  properties 294
addresses
  Business Card Requests folder, publishing 345
  folder, adding to Personal Address Book 162, 256

addresses *(continued)*
  Help Desk, publishing to Personal Address
    Book 396
  reply, specifying for Art Approval form 188
AddressList object,
  defined 290
AddressLists collection object 289
aligning controls 128
Application objects
  Automation objects, creating 285
  defined 284
  Help 274
  methods 284
  standard Outlook items, creating 285
AppointmentItem object
  defined 306
  deleted appointment, determining 310
  exception to original date, determining 310
  recurring appointment, creating 307
  recurring pattern, changing 307
  single appointment in a series 308
Approval and Status page
  defined 458
  illustrated 458
  Production Status box 459
  Send Request command buttons 459
  Value properties, setting 458
Art Approval form
  actions, automatically setting for Voting
    buttons 190
  Art Approval folder 186
  creating 186
  options, setting 187
  overview 186
  publishing to the Personal Forms Library 189
  Read page, illustrated 184
  reply address, specifying 188
  reviewing replies 191
  sending procedure 191
  Subject field, setting initial values 187
  testing 191
  To field, preaddressing 187

Art Approval form (*continued*)
    Tracking item, specifying storage 188
    Tracking page, illustrated 185
Assign and Close button, Help Request form 406
Assigned Help Task
    code, viewing 411
    CustomPropertyChange event 415
    folder, resolved tasks 394
    folders 392
    form
        illustrated 393
        Item_Write event 416
        PropertyChange events 414
        Read page 410
        Resolve Click procedure 426
        Resolve Problem option 394
        resolved items 413
        SendButton Click procedure 420
        SendMailToUser procedure 427
        Set_Priority_Changed procedure 416
        Set_Status_Changed procedure 415
        Text Box control 411
    items
        identifying using EntryID and StoreID 420
        Importance property 408
        Item_Open event 411
        linking from Message items 409
        receiving information from the Correspondence
          item 421
        saving 409
        values copied from Help Desk item 408
AutoArchive properties 494
AutoFill Click procedure, creating for Business Card
  Request form 375
Automation, using
    VBScript 340

B

Best Fit feature
    resizing columns 39
    selecting 24
Beta Contacts Application
    releasing 59
    setting administration properties 59
    testing 57
Beta Contacts folder
    copying to Public Folders 57
    creating 35

Beta Contacts folder (*continued*)
    illustrated 31
    items
        creating 42
        deleting 57
    permissions, setting 58
    publishing the Contacts form 55
    specifying Beta Contacts form as the default
      form 56
Beta Participants view
    columns, adjusting to Best Fit width 41
    creating 40
    filters, creating 42
Beta Participants views
    Beta Agreement Sent fields, entering dates 45
    fields, adding and removing 41
    illustrated 42
Body property 305
Building Microsoft Outlook 98 Applications
    CD-ROM, installing xi
    file, adding to Outlook xi
built-in forms
    applications based on, possible 30
    basic characteristics 104
Business Card Request application
    releasing to other users 387
    sending to the administrator for virus checking 386
    testing 385
    virus checking 386
Business Card Request forms
    administration properties, setting 387
    AutoFill command button, creating 375
    backing up 379
    BusinessCardBranch control, adding 357
    BusinessCardBranchLocation control, adding 356
    BusinessCardCityState control, adding 352
    BusinessCardComments control, adding 373
    BusinessCardDateProcessed control, adding 371
    BusinessCardEMail control, adding 355
    BusinessCardFax control, adding 354
    BusinessCardImage control, adding 363
    BusinessCardName controls, adding 349
    BusinessCardOffice control, adding 362
    BusinessCardPhone control, adding 354
    BusinessCardRequestAdministrator, adding 372
    BusinessCardRequestStatus control, adding 370
    BusinessCardStreet control, adding 352
    BusinessCardTitle control, adding 350
    BusinessCardZipCode control, adding 353

Business Card Request forms *(continued)*
  CardAddress control, adding 364
  CardName control, adding 365
  CardQuantity1 control, adding 360
  CardQuantity2 control, adding 360
  CardTitle control, adding 366
  Clear command, creating 376
  Clear control, adding 358
  CompanyLogo control, adding 366
  Compose page
    copying controls to the Read page 369
    editing 346
    illustrated example 343
    tab order 368
    testing the layout 368
  CustomPropertyChange events, adding code 378
  DeliverTo control, adding 361
  Display properties, BusinessCardName controls 349
  Item_Open events, adding code 378
  Message controls, removing 348
  properties, setting 379
  publishing 380
  Quality control, adding 359
  Read page
    editing 368
    illustrated example 344
  renaming Message page 347
  SendDeliveryMessage command, creating 377
  SendDeliveryMessage control, adding 372
  Status page 370
  Subject field, setting the initial value 348
  virus checking 386
Business Card Requests folder
  addresses, publishing to Personal Address Book 345
  creating 345
  design mode, activating 346
  illustrated 342
  Message forms, using in form design process 346
  overview 342
  preaddressing forms 346
buttons
  Assign and Close, Help Request form 406
  AutoFill command, creating 375
  Clear command, creating 376
  command, defined actions 422
  Create Offering, Course Catalog Entry form 212
  custom command 195
  Save and Close, Document Tracking form 431
  Send General Correspondence 456

buttons *(continued)*
  Send Mail to User 393
  Send Request, Approval and Status page 459
  SendDeliveryMessage command, creating 377
  Task Discussion form 394
  Vacation Request form 196
  Voting *See* Voting buttons

C

Calendar forms, procedure for creating 118
captions, specifying for OptionButton controls 171
ChangeBookNameValues procedure,
  Library Order application 338
CheckBox controls
  binding to fields 172
  Contacts form, adding 53
  defined 172
  initial values, setting 173
  properties, setting for Contacts form 53
Click events 330
Close events 330
code,
  testing samples 280
collection objects, Microsoft Outlook 283
colors, changing foreground and background for
  controls 141
columns
  adding to views 233
  Beta Participants view, resizing to Best Fit 41
  changing format properties 235
  combination
    changing labels or formulas 237
    creating 235, 237
    showing only value for first non-empty field 238
  creating 233
  formulas, creating 239
  heading order
    arranging for Product Category view 90
    rearranging 37
  Potential Beta Participants view, resizing to Best
    Fit 39
  Product Category view, removing 382
  removing from views 234
  Request Status view, adding 382
Combination fields
  adding for views 237
  changing labels or formulas 237
  creating 149

ComboBox controls
   Contacts form, adding 48
   defined 173
   initial values, setting 174
   labels, Contacts form 50
   list types 174
   properties, setting for Contacts form 49
   values, adding 174
CommandButton controls
   adding 177
   Click procedure, testing 178
   defined 177
   procedures, creating 178
Compose pages
   Business Card Request form
      editing 346
      illustrated example 343
      copying controls from Read page 369
      testing the layout 368
   Correspondence Mail form, illustrated 393
   Course Offering form 210
   editing for Product Ideas form 67–73
   Help Request form
      determining 403
      opening 390
   illustrated 119
   Product Ideas form
      copying controls to the Read page 75
      illustrated example 64
      tab order 73
   Product Ideas Response form
      editing 78
      illustrated example 65
   tab order
      setting for the Business Card Request form 368
      setting the sequence 129
   Task Discussion form 394
   Vacation Approved form 196
Contacts form
   CheckBox controls, adding 53
   ComboBox controls, adding 48
   customizing overview 46
   Label control 50
   opening in Design mode 47
   pages, renaming and displaying 48
   procedure for creating 118
   properties, setting 54
   publishing to the Beta Contacts folder 55
   testing at design time 55

Contacts form *(continued)*
   TextBox controls, adding 51
Contacts module
   Beta Contacts form 33
   overview 31
Control object
   adjusting controls horizontally and vertically 324
   binding a control to a field 325
   defined 323
   methods 323
   setting enabled property 323
   setting possible values property 324
Control Toolbox
   showing and customizing 123
controls
   adding to Frame 170
   adding to the Document Information page with Field
      Chooser 449
   Advanced Properties window 123, 143
   aligning 128
   AssignedTo, Help Request form 398
   AutoFill, adding 358
   background colors, changing 141
   BackStyle properties 143
   binding to existing fields 125, 144
   BusinessCardBranch, Business Card Request
      form 357
   BusinessCardBranchLocation, Business Card
      Request form 356
   BusinessCardCityState, Business Card Request
      form 352
   BusinessCardComments, Business Card Request
      form 373
   BusinessCardDateProcessed, Business Card Request
      form 371
   BusinessCardEMail, Business Card Request
      form 355
   BusinessCardFax, Business Card Request form 354
   BusinessCardImage, Business Card Request
      form 363
   BusinessCardName, Business Card Request
      forms 349
   BusinessCardOffice, Business Card Request
      form 362
   BusinessCardPhone, Business Card Request
      form 354
   BusinessCardRequestAdministrator, Business Card
      Request form 372

controls *(continued)*

BusinessCardRequestStatus, Business Card Request form 370

BusinessCardStreet, Business Card Request form 352

BusinessCardTitle, Business Card Request form 350

BusinessCardZipCode, Business Card Request form 353

CardAddress, Business Card Request form 364

CardName, Business Card Request form 365

CardQuantity1, Business Card Request form 360

CardQuantity2, Business Card Request form 360

CardTitle, Business Card Request form 366

Categories, removing when creating Product Ideas form 67

CheckBox 172

Clear, Business Card Request form 358

Combination fields 149

ComboBox

adding and binding to the Product Information page 453

adding to Contacts form 48

CommandButton 177

CompanyLogo, Business Card Request form 366

Control Toolbox

customizing 123

showing 123

copying from Compose page to Read Page 75, 369

DeliverTo, Business Card Request form 361

display properties, viewing 140

editing on forms 128

foreground colors, changing 141

form, basic characteristics 107

formula fields, creating 151–155

Frame 169–170

Image 180

Label

binding 167

setting initial values 168

layering 143

ListBox 175

Message

adding labels 72

adjusting when creating Product Ideas form 67

Document Information page 450

restrictions for usage 165

MultiPage 178

OptionButton 170

controls *(continued)*

Product Category

adding 68

aligning 71

labeling 71

properties, displaying 123

Quality, Business Card Request form 359

read-only status 130

removing 348

removing from Frame 170

requiring VBScript 181

selecting on forms 128

SendDeliveryMessage, Business Card Request form 372

sending to front and back layers 143

setting display properties 140

spacing 129

SpinButton 181

Subject, aligning 71

tab order, setting 129

TabStrip, differences from MultiPage controls 179

TextBox

Assigned Help Task form 411

specifying initial value 169

TipText

creating 129

Document Information page 450

Controls collection object

methods 321

properties 322

Controls collection object, methods and properties 321

Conversation Index property 246

Conversation property 245

conversation threads 244

Correspondence Mail form

Compose page 393

defined 419

opening by using the Send Mail to User button 419

Count property 291

Course Catalog Entry form

Actions page, illustrated 211

overview 208

Read page, illustrated 209

Course Offering form

Create Offering action 213

This action will option 215

Course Offering form

Action Name option 213

Address form like a option 215

Course Offering form *(continued)*
  Compose page 210
  defined 209
  naming 214
  Post to Folder actions 212
  Reply to Folder action 211
  Show Action On option 215
  Subject prefix option 215
  When responding option 214
CurrentFolder property 289
CurrentUser property 288
CustomAction events 331
Customize Current View feature, grouping items 242
CustomPropertyChange event
  defined 332
  Library Order Application 338
CustomPropertyChange event, Assigned Help Task
  form 415

D

databases, Document Tracking 439
dates, calculating totals for formulas 155
Design Environment Personal folders, creating 34
Design mode
  Advanced Properties dialog box 19
  components 98–100
  Properties dialog box 19
  switching to Run mode 131
  viewing forms in 17
distribution lists 258
Document Information page
  A value is required for this field option, setting 449
  controls, adding with Field Chooser 449
  Date Document Needs to Be Posted field 449
  defined 448
  Display properties 449
  fields, adding with Field Chooser 449
  illustrated 448
  Message controls 450
  Priority field 450
  Resize with form option 449
  tab order, setting 451
  TipText for controls 450
  TipText Help, creating 450
  Validation properties 449

Document Tracking
  application
    Administration properties, setting 475
    overview 430
    releasing 474
    setting up 436–442
    testing 443
  Approval and Status page 458
  database record
    checking 445
    creating 443
  database, defined 471
  databases, copying 439
  Document Information page 448
  Edit Task Request, testing 444
  folder views 472
  folders, restricting access 437
  form code, modifying 442
  form
    AddNewDatabaseRecord procedure 442
    Approval and Status page 433
    illustrated 431
    opening 440, 446
    overview 445
    procedures that must be modified 440
    publishing 442
    Save and Close button 431
    script-level variables 463
    SendNotification procedure 441
    Task page 446
    UpdateDatabaseRecord procedure 442
  HTML Conversion page 463
  items
    creating for Document Tracking testing 443
    Send Edit Request button 434
    sending task requests 444
    Tracking Information table 431
    updating 444
  Notification message 432
  Product Information page 451
  Tracking Information table, opening 445
  Virus Check\Posted page 462
Document Tracking form
  By Document Status view 473
  By Production Manager view 474

E

EntryID properties, Assigned Help Task items 420
events
    adding 328
    Click 330
    Close 330
    CustomAction 331
    CustomPropertyChange
        adding code 378
        Assigned Help Task form 415
        defined 332
        Library Order application 338
    defined 280
    firing sequence 328
    firing, preventing 329
    Forward 332
    Item_Open
        adding code 378
        Assigned Help Task item 411
        defined 333
        Library Order application 336
    Item_Write, Assigned Help Task form 416
    modifying 328
    PropertyChange
        Assigned Help Task form 414
        defined 333
        Outlook Script Editor 269
    Read 334
    Reply 334
    ReplyAll 335
    Send 335
    testing code example 328
    Write 335
Explorer object
    methods 289
    Outlook Window 288
    properties 289

F

Field Chooser
    adding controls and fields to the Document
        Information page 449
    adding or removing columns 23
    availability for different forms 145
    when to use 126
fields
    adding from form to Field List procedure 125
    adding from the Field Chooser 127

fields *(continued)*
    adding new, Potential Beta Participants view 37
    adding to the Document Information page with Field
        Chooser 449
    adding to view 41
    AssignedTo, Help Request form 398
    automatic calculation of formulas 152
    Beta Agreement Sent, entering dates 45
    binding controls 125, 144
    BusinessCardName, creating 349
    BusinessCardRequestStatus, formatting 383
    BusinessCardTitle, creating 351
    calculating date differences 155
    calculating totals for formulas 153
    Combination
        adding to views 235
        building expressions 150
        creating procedure 149
    custom, specifying conditions 262
    Database Record Created, Product Information
        page 454
    Date Document Needs To Be Posted 449
    deleting from the Field Chooser 128
    Document ID, Product Information page 454
    dragging to column heading row 38
    Field Chooser
        availability for different forms 145
        when to use 126
    Flag 411
    form, basic characteristics 108
    Format drop-down list box, illustrated 147
    formats, specifying 148
    formula, creating 151–155
    initial values, setting 156
    Message, overview of task capabilities 164
    Priority, Document Information page 450
    Product Category, removing 89
    removing from Request Status view 382
    removing from view 40
    shared between Vacation Request and Vacation
        Approved forms 201
    shared, capabilities 115
    specifying a value is required 157
    strings, combining 150
    Subject, setting initial values 163
    To, setting initial values 161
    types, specifying 148
    user-defined, procedure for creating 125, 146
    using to create columns 233

fields *(continued)*
    validating amounts by using formulas 159
    validation formulas, creating 158
    value strings, combining with text fragments 150
    values
        combining 151
        comparing with values of other fields 160
        copying to the Reply form 201
        copying to the Response form 215
        filtering 250
    Visual Basic Expression Service 20
filters
    Beta Participants views, creating 42
    By Ad Type view example 248
    conditions, advanced and simple 248
    creating 42
    defined 247
    message properties 249
    using field values 250
    using message class 249
folder forms libraries
    advantages of publishing forms 482
    form publishing procedure 226, 483
    Help Request forms, publishing 400
    Reply forms, publishing 204
folders
    active, setting to Assigned Help Tasks folder 407
    addresses, adding to Personal Address Book 162, 256
    advantages of personal use 491
    applications 11
    Art Approval, creating 186
    Assigned Help Tasks 392, 397
    attributes of different types 223
    automatic archiving 494
    based on built-in modules 11
    Beta Contacts
        creating 35
        illustrated 31
    Business Card Requests
        creating 345
        overview 342
        preventing users from opening 345
        setting permissions 385
    choosing where to locate 223
    Classified Ads, opening 222
    Contacts module 31
    copying designs, procedure 225
    copying in Mailbox or personal folder file 491

folders *(continued)*
    copying to new locations 254
    copying to Public Folders for distribution to other users 490
    creating in Mailbox or personal folder file 491
    custom views, showing 232
    default permissions 258
    Design Environment personal, creating 34
    design recommendations 223
    Discussion 12
    distributing to other users from Public Folders 490
    distribution strategies 489–494
    Document Tracking 436
    Document Tracking, securing 437
    drag/drop posting 256
    Folder Assistant 256
    Folders collection methods 295
    Folders collection object 295
    forms and views, testing 253
    forms cache storage location 488
    General properties, setting 253
    grouping items 24, 241
    Help and Web Sites 16
    Help Desk
        checking permissions 395
        copying to Public Folders 395
        illustrated 391
        setting permissions 396
    in-cell editing option, selecting 24
    initial view, specifying 255
    Internet newsgroup, identify 254
    items, specifying 227
    Library Orders 339
    making available for personal use 491
    making available to all users 490
    making available to users with access permissions 264
    making unavailable 256
    Marketing, creating 436
    materials that can be stored in 14
    methods, designing 223
    Microsoft Exchange views, automatically generating 253
    moderated folder 257
    modifying directly 224
    name list permissions 258
    names, adding to the name list 258
    new, creating 34, 116, 224
    offline use, make available 493

folders *(continued)*
  offline, using 484
  permissions
    assigning 257
    setting 490
  personal
    distributing 492
    making available on Microsoft Exchange
      system 492
    procedure for creating 116
  pilot testing 264
  planning before creating 222
  Potential Beta Participants view, illustrated 32
  preaddresssed forms 161
  Product Ideas
  copying to Public Folders 92
  Product Ideas
    creating 65
    Product Ideas
    permissions 93
    Product Ideas
    specifying default Product Ideas form for 90
  Properties dialog box 24
  protecting 254
  publishing addresses, Business Card Requests
    folder 345
  publishing forms 226
  reference applications 14
  replication issues 494
  restricting access 254–256
  rules, designing 260
  shortcuts, inserting in Message controls 165
  subfolder, creating 35
  Synchronize command for establishing offline
    use 494
  Tracking 13
  Training Management, opening 207
  Vacation Request, opening 193
  VBScript, opening 274
  views, defined 230
  Volunteer Registration, illustrated 236
Folders collection object 295
  adding a folder to Outlook Folder List 295
  iterating through collection of folders 295
  methods 295
Folders property 288, 297
Form (Inspector) Object 318–320

forms
  action properties, setting 131
  actions, basic characteristics 110
  activating 489
  advantages of publishing in a folder forms
    library 482
  advantages of publishing in the Personal Forms
    Library 480
  Art Approval, overview 186
  Assigned Help Task, illustrated 393
  attached to message, publication instructions 482
  backup copies, saving 217
  basic types 101
  Beta Contacts
    illustrated 33
    specifying as default form 56
    testing 57
  built-in modules 9, 30
  built-in, basic characteristics 104
  cache, storage location 488
  Calendar, procedure for creating 118
  checking for viruses and harmful code 479
  components 105–112
  Compose page
    basic characteristics 105
    illustrated 119
  conflicts, resolving 485
  Contacts
    customizing 46
    procedure for creating 118
  controls
    adding 123
    basic characteristics 107
    selecting and editing 128
  copying to folders 229
  Correspondence Mail, Compose page 393
  Course Catalog Entry, Training Management
    application 208
  Course Evaluation, Training Management
    application 210
  Course Offering, Training Management
    application 209
  creating from Outlook templates 118
  definitions, saving with items 113
  deleting 229
  Design mode 5, 100
  disk space, specifying 488
  distributing for publication in the Personal Forms
    Library 475, 480–482

forms *(continued)*

distributing in personal folder file 484

distribution strategies 477–485

Document Tracking

illustrated 431

opening 440

overview 445

Field Chooser availability for specific types 145

fields, basic characteristics 108

Forms Manager

changing the libraries in 229

opening 228

Help Request

overview 390

preaddressing 397

hiding Message pages 122

inserting .oft file as attachment in a message 481

Journal, procedure for creating 118

Library Materials Post 337

locating and loading using the Frmcache.dat
table 488

making available for remote use 485

managing changes 487–488

Marketing Handoff

defined 430

opening and modifying 437

saving a backup copy 438

message class box 198

message class, changing 135

Message

basic characteristics 101

examples 6

procedure for creating 117

testing 138

Microsoft Outlook Web site reference 14

modifying rules 487

names

procedure for specifying 135

specifying for Course Offering 214

New Post in This Folder option 253

Notes, procedure for creating 118

Office Document

basic characteristics 103

description 8

procedure for creating 117

offline, using 484

opening process 114

opening, containing VBScript 273

page, viewing 226

forms *(continued)*

pages, basic characteristics 106

Post

basic characteristics 102

procedure for creating 117

testing 138

preaddressing Message forms 161, 346

Product Ideas

creating 66

testing at design time 76

properties

basic characteristics 109

setting for Contacts form 54

setting procedure 132

viewing 229

publishing in an Outlook folder 226

publishing procedure 137

publishing tips 136

publishing to Organizational Forms Library 479

publishing to Personal Forms Library, Business Card
Request form 380

publishing to Personal Forms Library,
description 482

publishing

purpose of 135

to a folder forms library 217

Read page

basic characteristics 105

illustrated 120

Reply

characteristics 199

overview 203

Response, creating 217

saving a backup copy 134

saving as an .oft file 481

saving backup copy, Business Card Request 374

script editing, basic characteristics 111

Send form definition with item option

basic characteristics 112–113

clearing 480

sending to other users with Send form definition
with item option 483

Separate Read Layout option 120

setting action properties 132

setting the Hidden property 229, 488

Signup, Training Management application 210

submitting to an administrator for publication 478

Synchronize command for establishing offline
use 484

forms *(continued)*
Task Discussion 394
Tasks, procedure for creating 118
testing, Art Approval 191
text strings, building 154
types published in the Organizational Forms
Library 478
updating 229, 487
Vacation Approved 196
Vacation Request application 193
viewing in Design mode 17
viewing in Run mode 129
Volunteer Registration, illustrated 236
While You Were Out 154
Forms Manager
changing the libraries in 229
copying forms 486
defined 485
deleting 487
opening 485
setting properties 486
formulas
amount validation 159
column labels, changing 240
columns, creating 239
combination columns, changing 237
comparing field values 160
date calculation 155
field
automatic calculation 152
calculating totals 153
creating 151
validation, creating 158
Visual Basic Expression Service 21
Forward events 332
Frame controls 169–170
Frmcache.dat, using to locate and load forms 488

G

General properties, setting for folders 253
GetInspector property 304
Group By box, displaying 242

H

help
Application object 274
Assigned Help Task folders 392

help *(continued)*
control TipText, creating 129
Help and Web Sites folder 16
Help Desk folders 391
Microsoft Forms 2.0, viewing 279
Microsoft Outlook object model, viewing 279
Microsoft Outlook Visual Basic Reference 275
Microsoft Outlook Visual Basic, overview 273
Microsoft Outlook Web site 273
Microsoft Outlook, overview 15
Microsoft Visual Basic Scripting Edition Web
site 273
Outlook, offline folder file topics 484
programming tasks in Outlook 270
TipText, creating for the Document Information
page 450
tutorial, Library Order Application 336
viewing numeric values for Outlook constants 275
Help Desk
address, publishing to Personal Address Book 396
application
copying to Public Folders 395
making available to other users 395
overview 389
Assigned Help Task form, illustrated 393
Assigned Help Tasks folder, permissions 397
Correspondence Mail form, illustrated 393
folder forms library, publishing Help Request
forms 400
folder
copying to Public Folders 395
illustrated 391
security 396
Help Request form
preaddressing 397
technician names 398
items, copying values to Assigned Help Task
item 408
permissions
checking 395
setting 396
resolved tasks 394
Task Discussion form 394
testing the application 400
Help Request form
Assign and Close button 406
Assigned Help Tasks folder 392
AssignedTo controls 398
backing up 399

Help Request form *(continued)*
    code, example 401
    Compose mode, determining 403
    Compose pages 390
    CreateDateAsNumber function 405
    overview 390
    preaddressing 397
    publishing in Help Desk folder forms library 400
    publishing in Personal Forms Library 400
    Read mode, determining 403
    Read page 391–392
    Ticket IDs, creating 404
    TrimUserName function 404
    variables, script-level 402
Help Request items
    initial, writing to the History Log 411
    setting active folders to Assigned Help Task
      folders 407
    Ticket ID value 402
    TrimUserName function 404
Hidden property
    Marketing Handoff form 439
    Product Idea Response form, setting 91
    Response forms 218
    setting for forms
      overview 229
      procedure 488
HTML Conversion page 463
HTMLBody property 305
hyperlinks, Message controls 166

I

Image controls 180
Importance property, Assigned Help Task item 408
in-cell editing option, selecting 24
initial values
    CheckBox controls, setting 173
    ComboBox controls, setting 174
    fields, overview 156
    Label controls, setting 168
    ListBox controls, setting 176
    OptionButton controls, setting 172
    Product Category field, clearing 79
    Subject field, Business Card Request form 348
    Subject fields, setting 163
    To field, setting 161
Inspector object *See* Form (Inspector) object

installation
    Microsoft Outlook Development Tools 270
    Microsoft Outlook Visual Basic Help 16
    Outlook Forms Help folder 16
Internet newsgroup,
    identify folder as 254
Item objects
    AppointmentItem object 306
    defined 275
    MailItem object 303
    MeetingItem object 311
    PostItem object 301
    TaskItem object 315
    TaskRequestItem object 316
Item_Open event,
    Library Materials Order form 336
items
    Beta Contacts folder, deleting 57
    Beta Contacts, creating 43
    Correspondence Mail, creating 419
    defined 112
    Discussion, creating 422
    folders
      drag/drop posting 256
      Folder Assistant 256
      grouping 241
      Moderated Folder 257
      rule conditions 260
      sorting 243
    inserting in Message controls 165
    objects, implied 275
    Product Category view, grouping and sorting 89
    Resolve, creating 425–428
    saving with form definitions 113
    sorting, in folders 243
    standard Outlook, creating 285
    types, combining in a view 425
Items collection
    methods 299–301
Items collection
    creating custom items 299
    object properties 301
    object, defined 298
Items property 297

J

Journal forms, procedure for creating 118

L

Label controls 167
labels
    BusinessCardName control, adding 350
    BusinessCardTitle control, adding 351
    column, changing for formulas 240
    combination columns, changing 237
    ComboBox control, Contacts form 50
    Message control, adding 72
    Product Category control, adding 71
    Product Idea, changing 79
    TextBox control, Contacts form 52
layer controls 143
libraries, Organizational Forms, example of opening
    forms 115
Library Order application
    ChangeBookNameValues procedure 338
    CustomPropertyChange event 338
    Item, Open event 336
    Library Materials post form 337
    Library Orders folder 339
    SubmitBookOrder_Click procedure 338
    tutorials, overview 336
ListBox controls 175–176

M

MailItem object
    closing an item 304
    defined 303
    methods 303
    properties 304
    replying to a message 303
    sending a message 303
MAPIFolder object
    defined 296
    EntryID properties 298
    methods 296
    properties 297
    StoreID properties 298
Marketing folder, creating 436
Marketing Handoff form
    defined 430
    hiding 439
    Item_Open procedure, modifying 438

Marketing Handoff form (continued)
    opening 437
    publishing 439
    saving a backup copy 438
MeetingItem object
    defining 311
    determining recipients response to meeting
        request 314
    responding to a meeting request 312
    retrieving associated appointment 312
Members property 294
Message class box
    Course Offering form, naming 214
    Vacation Request form, naming 198
Message controls
    file attachments, inserting 165
    folder shortcuts, inserting 165
    guidelines 165
    hyperlinks, inserting 166
    items, inserting 165
    objects, inserting 167
    shortcuts, inserting 165
Message forms
    Address form like a option 199
    Art Approval form, overview 186
    basic characteristics 101
    opening when creating Art Approval forms 187
    preaddressing to a distribution list or a person 161
    preaddressing to Business Card Requests folder 346
    procedure for creating 117
    Separate Read Layout option 120
    testing in Personal or Organization Forms
        Library 138
    Voting buttons 184–192
    When responding option 199
methods
    AddressEntries collection object 290
    AddressEntry object 292
    AddressLists collection object 290
    Application objects 284
    Control object 323
    Controls Collection object 321
    Explorer object 289
    Folders collection object 295
    Form (Inspector) object 318
    GetItemFromID 421
    Items collection 299
    MailItem object 303
    MAPIFolder object 296

methods *(continued)*
  NameSpace objects 287
  object library, defined 280
  PostItem objects 301
  Recipients collection object 326
  TaskItem object 315
  UserProperties collection object 326
Microsoft Excel 97
  object browser
    defined 277
    illustrated 278
  referencing Outlook Object Library 277
Microsoft Exchange
  folder replication issues 494
  making personal folder files available 492
  Organizational Forms Library 478
  views, automatically generating 253
Microsoft Forms 2.0
  Object Library, defined 277
  viewing 279
Microsoft Outlook
  Application object 284
  application tasks that can be accomplished 4
  applications that can be created vii, 5
  collection objects 283
  column heading order, arranging for views 90
  constants, viewing numeric values 275
  design capabilities 18
  Design mode for forms 5, 17
  design tools 15–25
  events 328–336
  folder applications 11
  Folders collection object 295
  Form (Inspector) object 318
  form caching scheme for activating forms 489
  Help
    offline folder file topics 484
    overview 15
  implied Item object 275
  Items collection object 298
  items, automatically archiving 494
  Library Order application tutorial 336
  MAPIFolder object 296
  Microsoft Excel 97 object browser 277
  NameSpace objects 287
  Object Model 277
  object models, viewing 279
  offline, using 484
  Page object 321

Microsoft Outlook *(continued)*
  Pages collection object 320
  PostItem objects 301
  Recipients collection object 326
  referencing the object library from Microsoft Excel 97 277
  Script Editor 21, 268
  templates, using to create forms 118
  UserProperties Collection Object 325
  VBScript folder, opening 274
  view features 230
  Visual Basic Reference Help 273
  web sites, overview 15, 273
  Window (Explorer object) 288
Microsoft Visual Basic Scripting Edition Web site 273
ModifiedFormPages property 319
modules
  built-in 9
  Contacts 31
MultiPage controls
  defined 178
  differences from TabStrip controls 179

N

Name property 294
NameSpace object 287–288
New Post in This Folder option, specifying for forms 253
Notes forms, procedure for creating 118

O

object browser
  Microsoft Excel 97, using in Outlook 277
  moving around in 278
  selecting an object library 278
object library
  defined 276
  Folders collection 295
  methods, defined 280
  Microsoft Excel 97 object browser 277
  Microsoft Forms 2.0 277
  Microsoft Outlook 277
  object models 279
  Outlook, referencing from Microsoft Excel 97 277
  properties, defined 280
  selecting in the object browser 278

object models
defined 279
Outlook, viewing 279
objects
AddressEntries collection 290
AddressEntry 291
AddressList 290
AddressLists collection 289
Application 284
AppointmentItem 306
Automation 285
Control 323
Explorer 288
Folders collection 295
Form (Inspector) 318
Item 275
Items collection 298
MailItem 303
MAPI NameSpace 286
MAPIFolder 296
MeetingItem 311
NameSpace 287
Page 321
Pages collection 320
PostItem 301
Recipients collection 326
TaskItem 315
TaskRequestItem 316
UserProperties collection 325
Office Document forms
basic characteristics 103
examples 8
procedure for creating 117
oft attachment, inserting in a message box 475
Open events 333
OptionButton controls
captions 171
defined 170
initial values, setting 172
value properties, setting 171
Organizational Forms Library
checking forms for viruses and harmful code 479
form publishing, procedure 479
opening forms, example 114
Reply forms, publishing 204
submitting forms to an administrator for
publication 478
types of forms published 478
Outlook Object Browser 277

Outlook Script Debugger
Call Stack window, viewing 272
Command Window 272
Debug toolbar, using 272
defined 270
opening 271
script commands, entering 272
Outlook Script Editor
Clear_Click procedure, creating 376
creating procedures, Business Card Request
form 375
CustomPropertyChange event, adding code 378
event templates 22
Help 270
Item PropertyChange event 269
jumping to lines of code 270
Object Browser 277
object library 276
Open event, adding code 379
overview 268
reference materials 270
SendDeliveryMessage procedure, creating 377
variables 281
viewing 22, 269
Window, basic characteristics 111
Owners only option 256

P

Page object, defined 321
pages
Approval and Status, Document Tracking form 433,
458
Contacts form, renaming and displaying 48
Document Information 448
form, basic characteristics 106
HTML Conversion, Document Tracking form 463
Message
hiding 122
renaming for Business Card Request form 347
Product Information 451
renaming procedure 122
Separate Read Layout option 121
Task, Document Tracking form 446
Virus Check\Posted, Document Tracking form 462
Pages collection object 320
permissions
Assigned Help Tasks folder, setting 397
Beta Contacts folder 58

permissions *(continued)*
    Business Card Requests folder, setting 385
    custom roles, assigning 259
    default 258
    defined 257
    distribution lists 258
    Document Tracking application, setting 475
    Help Desk folder
        checking 395
        setting 396
    name list 258
    page, opening 258
    predefined roles, assigning 258
    Product Ideas folder 93
    roles, assigning 258
    setting for folders 490
Permissions page, opening 258
Personal Address Book
    Business Card Requests folder address,
        publishing 345
    folder addresses, adding 162, 256
    Help Desk folder address 396
personal folders
    copying 492
    creating 116
Personal Forms Library
    advantages of publishing forms 480
    distributing forms for publication 475
    form publishing procedure 482
    publication instructions for attached forms 482
    publishing Art Approval forms 189
    publishing Help Request forms 400
    publishing Reply forms 204
    publishing the Marketing Handoff form 439
Post forms
    Action Name option 213
    basic characteristics 7, 102
    ideas for using with Outlook in Design mode 7
    procedure for creating 117
    Product Ideas folder, opening in Design mode 67
    Reply to Folder actions 207
    Separate Read Layout option 120
    testing in Personal or Organization Forms
        Library 138
PostItem object
    properties 304
PostItem objects
    copying and moving an item 301
    creating or displaying a post item 302

PostItem objects *(continued)*
    defined 301
    methods 301
    posting an item 302
Potential Beta Participants view
    columns
        headings 37
        resizing to Best Fit 39
    creating 36
    fields
        adding new 37
        dragging to column heading row 38
        removing 36
    illustrated 32
    Product Category view 90
procedure-level variables 281
procedures
    AddNewDatabaseRecord 466
    AutoFill Click, creating for Business Card Request
        forms 375
    CheckValue 469
    Clear_Click, creating for Business Card Request
        forms 376
    FieldValue 468
    Item_Close event 466
    Item_CustomPropertyChange 464
    Item_PropertyChange event 464
    Item_Write Event 465
    SendDeliveryMessage, creating for Business Card
        Request forms 377
    SendNotification 470
    UpdateDatabaseRecord 467
Product Category controls
    adding procedure 68
    aligning 71
    defined 68
    labels 71
    properties, setting 69
    read-only status, applying 78, 79
Product Category view
    column heading order, arranging 90
    creating procedure 88
    defined 87
    fields, removing 89
    items
        grouping by product category, then by
            conversation 89
        sorting by the Conversation Index field 90
    Potential Beta Participants view 90

Product Ideas
  administration properties, setting 93
  application
    overview 62
    releasing to other users 93
    setting Initial View on Folder property 93
    testing 92
  folder
    copying to Public Folders 92
    creating 65
    illustrated 63
    Product Category view 63
  form
    actions 81
    aligning controls 71
    backing up 84
    creating new actions 83
    editing the Compose page 67–73
    editing the Read page 74–76
    illustrated example 64
    making Reply to Folder action unavailable 82
    opening in Design mode 81
    properties 76
    publishing 84
    specifying as default for Product Ideas folder 90
    testing at design time 76
  forms
    creating 66
    publishing 77
    saving a backup copy 76
  Response form
    actions 85
    backing up 86
    creating 78–81
    editing the Compose page 78
    editing the Read page 79
    Hidden property 91
    illustrated 65
    making Reply to Folder action unavailable 86
    opening in Design mode 85
    properties 80
    publishing 80, 87
    saving backup copy 80
Product Information page
  ComboBox controls, adding and binding 453
  CorrespondenceMessageLink procedure 457
  Database Record Created field 454
  defined 451
  Document ID fields 454

Product Information page *(continued)*
  Document Summary text box 452
  illustrated 452
  keywords 452
  Multi-line option, setting 452
  Resize with form option, setting 452
  SendGeneralCorrespondence_Click procedure 456
properties
  Action name, Vacation Request form 198
  Address 294
  AddressEntries collection object 291
  AddressEntry object 294
  Administration
    Document Tracking application 475
    setting 254
  advanced control, setting 143
  Advanced dialog box
    forms in Design mode 19
    viewing 20
  Advanced, setting for controls 123
  AutoArchive, setting for folders 494
  BackStyle 143
  Body 305
  Business Card Request, setting 379
  By Discussion Topic view 425
  CheckBox control, Contacts form 53
  ComboBox control, Contacts form 49
  Contacts form, setting 54
  Control objects 323
  control, displaying 123
  Controls collection object 322
  Conversation 244
  Conversation Index 246
  Count 291
  Create Offering action 213
  creating conditions by using 262
  CurrentFolder 289
  CurrentUser 288
  dialog box
    folders 24
    forms in Design mode 19
    viewing 19
  Display
    BusinessCardName controls 349
    Document Information page 449
  EntryID
    identifying a folder 298
    identifying Assigned Help Task items 420

properties *(continued)*
  Explorer object 289
  Folders 288, 297
  Form (Inspector) object 319
  form
    basic characteristics 109
    setting procedure 132
  Forms page, viewing 226
  General, setting 253
  GetInspector 304
  Hidden
    Marketing Handoff form 439
    setting for the Training Management Response
      forms 218
  HTMLBody 305
  Importance, Assigned Task item 408
  initial value, clearing for the Product Category
    field 79
  Items 297
  Items collection object 301
  MailItem object 304
  MAPIFolder object 297
  Members 294
  message, filtering 249
  ModifiedFormPages 319
  Multi-line, setting for Product Information page 452
  Name 294
  NameSpace objects 288
  object library, defined 280
  object
    getting 281
    setting example 281
  PostItem object 304
  Product Category, setting 69
  Product Ideas form, setting 76
  Product Ideas Response form, setting 80
  Resize with form
    Document Information page 449
    Product Information page 452
  SenderName 306
  setting display, for controls 140
  setting on the Response item 424
  StoreID
    identifying a folder 298
    identifying Assigned Help Task items 420
  Task Discussion,viewing 422
  TextBox control, Contacts form 52
  To 305
  user-defined fields, creating 146

properties *(continued)*
  Validation
    BusinessCardName fields 350
    Document Information page 449
  value, OptionButton control 171
PropertyChange event 269, 333, 414
protocols supported for hyperlinks in Message
  controls 166

R

Read events 334
Read pages
  Art Approval form example 184
  Assigned Help Task form
    illustrated 393
    viewing code 410
  Business Card Request form
    editing the Read page 368
    illustrated 344
  Course Catalog Entry form, illustrated 209
  editing for Product Ideas form 74–76
  Help Request form
    defined 392
    determining 403
    illustrated 391
    Technician names 398
  illustrated 120
  Product Ideas form, illustrated 74
  Product Ideas Response form, editing 79
  setting properties for controls 130
  tab order, setting 131
  Vacation Request form 194
  viewing in Run mode 131
read-only, control property 131
Recipients collection objects 326
Reply events 334
Reply forms
  backup copies, creating 204
  characteristics 199
  custom for non-Microsoft Exchange users 206
  defined 203
  publishing to forms libraries 204
  Show Action On option 200
  Subject prefix option 201
  This action will option 200
  values copied from original forms 201
ReplyAll events 335

Response forms
    copying values to 215
    creating 217
    Hidden property, setting 218
roles, assigning 258–259
rules
    actions, specifying 263
    advanced conditions, specifying 261
    applying to items not matching conditions 262
    conditions, specifying 260
    creating 260
    folders, overview 260
    simple conditions, specifying 261
    syntax 261

S

saving a backup copy of a form 135
saving a form as an .oft file 481
Script Debugger *See* Outlook Script Debugger
Script Editor *See* Outlook Script Editor
script-level variables
    Help Request form 402
    overview 281
security
    Business Card Requests folders 345
    controls 130
    Document Tracking folders 437
    folders 254
    Help Desk folders 396
    Product Category controls 78, 79
Send events 335
Send form definition with item
    basic characteristics 112–113
Send form definition with item option
    form security with 133
Send form definition with item option, clearing 480
SenderName property 306
SendNotification procedure, Document Tracking
    application 441
Separate Read Layout
    defined 120
    specifying for pages 121
Set_Priority_Changed Procedure
    Assigned Help Task form 416
Set_Status_Changed procedure 415
shared fields 115

shortcuts
    folder, inserting 165
    URL, inserting in Message controls 165
Show Action On option
    Course Offering form 215
    Reply forms 200
Show only custom views option,
    selecting 24
SpinButton controls 181
StoreID properties, Assigned Help Task items 420
Subject fields
    initial values
        setting 163
        setting for Art Approval form 187
    Task page 447
Subject prefix option
    Course Offering form 215
    Reply forms 201
SubmitBookOrder_Click procedure,
    Library Order application 338
Synchronize command for establishing offline use 484

T

tab order
    Compose page
        Business Card Request form 368
        Product Ideas form 73
    Document Information page 451
    Read page, Product Ideas form 75
    setting for form controls 129
tables, Tracking Information 431
TabStrip controls 179
Task Discussion form 394
Task page 446
TaskItem object 315
TaskRequestItem object 316
Tasks forms, procedure for creating 118
templates, using to create forms in Outlook 118
testing code samples 280
TextBox controls
    Assigned Help Task form Flag field 411
    Contacts form, adding 51
    defined 169
    initial values, setting 169
    labels, Contacts form 52
    multi-line options 169
    properties, setting for Contacts form 52

This action will option
   Course Offering form 215
   Reply forms 200
threaded conversations, Discussion folders 12
Ticket IDs
   creating 404
   value, Help Request form 402
TipText, Document Information page 450
To field
   preaddressing for Art Approval form 187
   setting values 161
To property 305
TOTAL field 152
Tracking Information table
   defined 431
   opening 445
Tracking page, Art Approval form 185
Training Management
   application, overview 207
   folder, illustrated 208
   folders, opening 207
   forms 208
   forms, testing 218
   Response forms, setting the Hidden property 218
tutorial, Library Order application 336

U

UpdateDatabaseRecord procedure, Document Tracking form 442
updating forms 487
UserProperties collection object
   defined 325
   methods 326

V

Vacation Approved form 196
Vacation Request
   Address form like a option, Message form 199
   application, overview 193
   folders, opening 193
   forms
      Actions page 194
      described 193
      naming 198
      Read page 194
      testing 205
   When responding option, Message form 199

validation formulas, creating 158
values
   Approval and Status page, setting 458
   Help Desk item, copying to Assigned Help Task item 408
variables
   lifetime 282
   limitations in VBScript 281
   MyDate 405
   names 281
   object, assigning and setting 282
   procedure-level, overview 281
   scopes 282
   script-level
      Document Tracking form 463
      Help Request form 402
      overview 281
   setting to store initial information for Item_Open events 413
   Status_Changed 415
   Ticket ID value 402
   Trimmed variables 404
   Visual Basic Scripting Edition 281
Variant data type 282
VBScript
   Automation 340
   code, preventing from executing when opening forms 273
   folders, opening 274
   opening forms that contain 273
   programming forms using Script Editor 21
   variables 281
   Variant data type in Outlook 282
views
   Beta Participants, creating procedure 40
   By Discussion Topic, Help Desk application 425
   By Document Status, Document Tracking form 473
   By Production Manager, Document Tracking form 474
   By Requester Name, Business Card Request application 384
   columns
      adding 233
      defined 230
      removing 234
   Combination fields 235
   conversation threads 244
   custom, showing for folders 232
   customizing 23

views *(continued)*
    defined 230
    different item types 425
    Document Tracking folder 472
    Filter, defined 230
    folder, design tools 23
    Format, defined 230
    formatting 252
    Groups, defined 230
    Microsoft Exchange, automatically generating 253
    new, creating 231
    Outlook 230
    Potential Beta Participants
       creating 36
       Product Category view 90
    Product Category
       creating 87–90
       overview 63
    Request Status, creating in Business Card Requests
       folder 381
    Show only custom views option 24
    Sort, defined 230
    specifying initial, folders 255
    testing 253
Virus Check\Posted page, Document Tracking
  form 462
Visual Basic
    Expression Service, Microsoft Outlook 20
    Outlook, Help overview 273–274
    Scripting Edition
       form scripts 111
       variables 281
Voting buttons
    actions, automatically setting 190
    described 184
    options, setting 188
    responding to Art Approval items 191

W

Web sites
    Help and Web Sites folder 16
    Microsoft Outlook 273
    Microsoft Outlook, overview 15
    Microsoft Visual Basic Scripting Edition 273
    shortcuts 16

When responding option
    Course Offering form 214
    Message forms 199
While You Were Out forms 154
Write events 335

COM
without the
complexity.

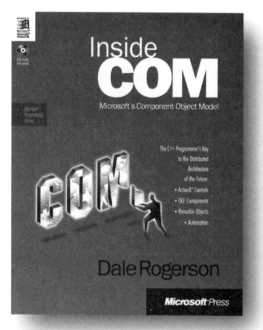

U.S.A. **$34.99**
U.K.   £32.99 [V.A.T. included]
Canada $46.99
ISBN 1-57231-349-8

The Component Object Model (COM) isn't just another standard. It's the basis of Microsoft's approach to distributed computing. It's also the method for customizing Microsoft® applications, present and future. And it's the foundation of OLE and ActiveX™. In short, COM is a major key to the future of development. And this is the book that unlocks COM. In it, you'll discover:

- A clear and simple, practical guide to building elegant, robust, portable COM components
- An eye-opening presentation of how accessible COM can be—especially for those already familiar with C++
- An insightful, progressive view of COM design
- Plenty of illustrations in the form of code samples

INSIDE COM is for intermediate to advanced C++ programmers; beginning to advanced COM, ActiveX, and OLE programmers; academics with an interest in component design; and even programmers who want to use COM when it's ported to UNIX, MVS, and other environments. To put it simply, if you work with COM, then INSIDE COM was written for you.

Microsoft ®*Press*

Build it
faster *and better*
with the richest
Java building
blocks!

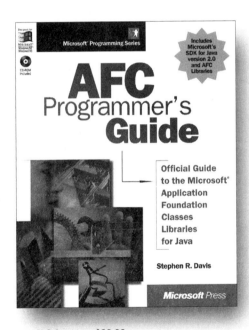

Microsoft Programming Series

Includes Microsoft's SDK for Java version 2.0 and AFC Libraries

AFC
Programmer's
Guide

Official Guide
to the Microsoft
Application
Foundation
Classes
Libraries
for Java

Stephen R. Davis

Microsoft Press

U.S.A.	**$39.99**
U.K.	£37.49 [V.A.T. included]
Canada	$55.99
ISBN 1-57231-732-9	

You can kick Internet application development into high gear by using the advanced building blocks in the Application Foundation Classes (AFC)—Java class libraries from Microsoft. If you're an intermediate-level Java programmer, this book shows you how. You'll discover how to mix, match, and customize a wide variety of prebuilt elements—buttons, toolbars, listview controls, and far more—to create full-featured interfaces. And extensive sample code makes everything perfectly clear. This book is a must-have for Java programmers (especially those using Microsoft® Visual J++™), Internet content developers, and developers who intend to write or rewrite their applications in Java. In fact, AFC PROGRAMMER'S GUIDE is the practical programming assistance you've been looking for.

Microsoft ®*Press*

In-depth reference and *inside tips* *from the* software experts.

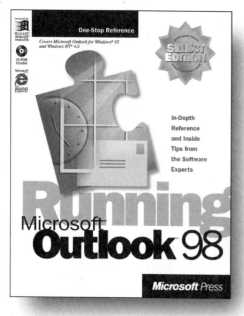

It's packed with everything from quick, clear instructions for new users to comprehensive answers for power users. And it's complete in one volume. In short, RUNNING MICROSOFT® OUTLOOK™ 98 is the authoritative handbook you'll keep by your computer and use every day.

CD loaded with must-have extras:
- Get fast on-screen answers from a searchable version of the book
- Cruise the Web using Microsoft® Internet Explorer 4

U.S.A.	**$34.99**
U.K.	£32.99 [V.A.T. included]
Canada	$50.99
ISBN 1-57231-840-6	

Microsoft®*Press*

IMPORTANT—READ CAREFULLY BEFORE OPENING SOFTWARE PACKET(S). By opening the sealed packet(s) containing the software, you indicate your acceptance of the following Microsoft License Agreement.

MICROSOFT LICENSE AGREEMENT

Building Applications with Microsoft Outlook 98

(Book Companion CD)

IMPORTANT—READ CAREFULLY: This Microsoft End-User License Agreement ("EULA") is a legal agreement between you (either an individual or an entity) and Microsoft Corporation for the Microsoft product identified above, which includes computer software and may include associated media, printed materials, and "online" or electronic documentation ("SOFTWARE PRODUCT"). Any component included within the SOFTWARE PRODUCT that is accompanied by a separate End-User License Agreement shall be governed by such agreement and not the terms set forth below. By installing, copying or otherwise using the SOFTWARE PRODUCT, you agree to be bound by the terms of this EULA. If you do not agree to the terms of this EULA, you are not authorized to install, copy or otherwise use the SOFTWARE PRODUCT; you may, however, return the SOFTWARE PRODUCT, along with all printed materials and other items that form a part of the Microsoft product that includes the SOFTWARE PRODUCT, to the place you obtained them for a full refund.

SOFTWARE PRODUCT LICENSE

The SOFTWARE PRODUCT is protected by United States copyright laws and international copyright treaties, as well as other intellectual property laws and treaties. The SOFTWARE PRODUCT is licensed, not sold.

1. **GRANT OF LICENSE.** This EULA grants you the following rights:

   a. **Software Product.** You may install and use one copy of the SOFTWARE PRODUCT on a single computer. The primary user of the computer on which the SOFTWARE PRODUCT is installed may make a second copy for his or her exclusive use on a portable computer.

   b. **Storage/Network Use.** You may also store or install a copy of the SOFTWARE PRODUCT on a storage device, such as a network server, used only to install or run the SOFTWARE PRODUCT on your other computers over an internal network; however, you must acquire and dedicate a license for each separate computer on which the SOFTWARE PRODUCT is installed or run from the storage device. A license for the SOFTWARE PRODUCT may not be shared or used concurrently on different computers.

   c. **License Pak.** If you have acquired this EULA in a Microsoft License Pak, you may make the number of additional copies of the computer software portion of the SOFTWARE PRODUCT authorized on the printed copy of this EULA, and you may use each copy in the manner specified above. You are also entitled to make a corresponding number of secondary copies for portable computer use as specified above.

   d. **Sample Code.** Solely with respect to portions, if any, of the SOFTWARE PRODUCT that are identified within the SOFTWARE PRODUCT as sample code (the "SAMPLE CODE"):

      i. **Use and Modification.** Microsoft grants you the right to use and modify the source code version of the SAMPLE CODE, *provided* you comply with subsection (d)(iii) below. You may not distribute the SAMPLE CODE, or any modified version of the SAMPLE CODE, in source code form.

      ii. **Redistributable Files.** Provided you comply with subsection (d)(iii) below, Microsoft grants you a nonexclusive, royalty-free right to reproduce and distribute the object code version of the SAMPLE CODE and any modified version of the SAMPLE CODE.

      iii. **Redistribution Requirements.** If you redistribute the SAMPLE CODE, you agree to: (i) distribute the SAMPLE CODE in object code form only in conjunction with and as a part of your software application product; (ii) not use Microsoft's name, logo, or trademarks to market your software application product; (iii) include a valid copyright notice on your software application product; (iv) indemnify, hold harmless, and defend Microsoft from and against any claims or lawsuits, including attorney's fees, that arise or result from the use or distribution of your software application product; and (v) not permit further distribution of the SAMPLE CODE by your end user. Contact Microsoft for the applicable royalties due and other licensing terms for all other uses and/or distribution of the SAMPLE CODE.

2. **DESCRIPTION OF OTHER RIGHTS AND LIMITATIONS.**

   - **Not For Resale Software.** If the SOFTWARE PRODUCT is labeled "Not For Resale" or "NFR," then, notwithstanding other sections of this EULA, you may not resell, or otherwise transfer for value, the SOFTWARE PRODUCT.

   - **Limitations on Reverse Engineering, Decompilation, and Disassembly.** You may not reverse engineer, decompile, or disassemble the SOFTWARE PRODUCT, except and only to the extent that such activity is expressly permitted by applicable law notwithstanding this limitation.

- **Separation of Components.** The SOFTWARE PRODUCT is licensed as a single product. Its component parts may not be separated for use on more than one computer.

- **Rental.** You may not rent, lease or lend the SOFTWARE PRODUCT.

- **Support Services.** Microsoft may, but is not obligated to, provide you with support services related to the SOFTWARE PRODUCT ("Support Services"). Use of Support Services is governed by the Microsoft policies and programs described in the user manual, in "online" documentation and/or other Microsoft-provided materials. Any supplemental software code provided to you as part of the Support Services shall be considered part of the SOFTWARE PRODUCT and subject to the terms and conditions of this EULA. With respect to technical information you provide to Microsoft as part of the Support Services, Microsoft may use such information for its business purposes, including for product support and development. Microsoft will not utilize such technical information in a form that personally identifies you.

- **Software Transfer.** You may permanently transfer all of your rights under this EULA, provided you retain no copies, you transfer all of the SOFTWARE PRODUCT (including all component parts, the media and printed materials, any upgrades, this EULA, and, if applicable, the Certificate of Authenticity), **and** the recipient agrees to the terms of this EULA.

- **Termination.** Without prejudice to any other rights, Microsoft may terminate this EULA if you fail to comply with the terms and conditions of this EULA. In such event, you must destroy all copies of the SOFTWARE PRODUCT and all of its component parts.

3. **COPYRIGHT.** All title and copyrights in and to the SOFTWARE PRODUCT (including but not limited to any images, photographs, animations, video, audio, music, text, SAMPLE CODE, REDISTRIBUTABLES, and "applets" incorporated into the SOFTWARE PRODUCT), the accompanying printed materials, and any copies of the SOFTWARE PRODUCT are owned by Microsoft or its suppliers. The SOFTWARE PRODUCT is protected by copyright laws and international treaty provisions. Therefore, you must treat the SOFTWARE PRODUCT like any other copyrighted material **except** that you may install the SOFTWARE PRODUCT on a single computer provided you keep the original solely for backup or archival purposes. You may not copy the printed materials accompanying the SOFTWARE PRODUCT.

4. **U.S. GOVERNMENT RESTRICTED RIGHTS.** The SOFTWARE PRODUCT and documentation are provided with RE-STRICTED RIGHTS. Use, duplication, or disclosure by the Government is subject to restrictions as set forth in subparagraph (c)(1)(ii) of the Rights in Technical Data and Computer Software clause at DFARS 252.227-7013 or subparagraphs (c)(1) and (2) of the Commercial Computer Software—Restricted Rights at 48 CFR 52.227-19, as applicable. Manufacturer is Microsoft Corporation/One Microsoft Way/Redmond, WA 98052-6399.

5. **EXPORT RESTRICTIONS.** You agree that you will not export or re-export the SOFTWARE PRODUCT, any part thereof, or any process or service that is the direct product of the SOFTWARE PRODUCT (the foregoing collectively referred to as the "Restricted Components"), to any country, person, entity or end user subject to U.S. export restrictions. You specifically agree not to export or re-export any of the Restricted Components (i) to any country to which the U.S. has embargoed or restricted the export of goods or services, which currently include, but are not necessarily limited to Cuba, Iran, Iraq, Libya, North Korea, Sudan and Syria, or to any national of any such country, wherever located, who intends to transmit or transport the Restricted Components back to such country; (ii) to any end-user who you know or have reason to know will utilize the Restricted Components in the design, development or production of nuclear, chemical or biological weapons; or (iii) to any end-user who has been prohibited from participating in U.S. export transactions by any federal agency of the U.S. government. You warrant and represent that neither the BXA nor any other U.S. federal agency has suspended, revoked or denied your export privileges.

DISCLAIMER OF WARRANTY

NO WARRANTIES OR CONDITIONS. MICROSOFT EXPRESSLY DISCLAIMS ANY WARRANTY OR CONDITION FOR THE SOFTWARE PRODUCT. THE SOFTWARE PRODUCT AND ANY RELATED DOCUMENTATION IS PROVIDED "AS IS" WITHOUT WARRANTY OR CONDITION OF ANY KIND, EITHER EXPRESS OR IMPLIED, INCLUDING, WITHOUT LIMITATION, THE IMPLIED WARRANTIES OR MERCHANTABILITY, FITNESS FOR A PARTICULAR PURPOSE, OR NONINFRINGEMENT. THE ENTIRE RISK ARISING OUT OF USE OR PERFORMANCE OF THE SOFTWARE PRODUCT REMAINS WITH YOU.

LIMITATION OF LIABILITY. TO THE MAXIMUM EXTENT PERMITTED BY APPLICABLE LAW, IN NO EVENT SHALL MICROSOFT OR ITS SUPPLIERS BE LIABLE FOR ANY SPECIAL, INCIDENTAL, INDIRECT, OR CONSEQUENTIAL DAMAGES WHATSOEVER (INCLUDING, WITHOUT LIMITATION, DAMAGES FOR LOSS OF BUSINESS PROFITS, BUSINESS INTERRUPTION, LOSS OF BUSINESS INFORMATION, OR ANY OTHER PECUNIARY LOSS) ARISING OUT OF THE USE OF OR INABILITY TO USE THE SOFTWARE PRODUCT OR THE PROVISION OF OR FAILURE TO PROVIDE SUPPORT SERVICES, EVEN IF MICROSOFT HAS BEEN ADVISED OF THE POSSIBILITY OF SUCH DAMAGES. IN ANY CASE, MICROSOFT'S ENTIRE LIABILITY UNDER ANY PROVISION OF THIS EULA SHALL BE LIMITED TO THE GREATER OF THE AMOUNT ACTUALLY PAID BY YOU FOR THE SOFTWARE PRODUCT OR US$5.00; PROVIDED HOWEVER, IF YOU HAVE ENTERED INTO A MICROSOFT SUPPORT SERVICES AGREEMENT, MICROSOFT'S ENTIRE LIABILITY REGARDING SUPPORT SERVICES SHALL BE GOVERNED BY THE TERMS OF THAT AGREEMENT. BECAUSE SOME STATES AND JURISDICTIONS DO NOT ALLOW THE EXCLUSION OR LIMITATION OF LIABILITY, THE ABOVE LIMITATION MAY NOT APPLY TO YOU.

MISCELLANEOUS

This EULA is governed by the laws of the State of Washington USA, except and only to the extent that applicable law mandates governing law of a different jurisdiction.

Should you have any questions concerning this EULA, or if you desire to contact Microsoft for any reason, please contact the Microsoft subsidiary serving your country, or write: Microsoft Sales Information Center/One Microsoft Way/Redmond, WA 98052-6399.